Education £12.99

BBCA

375.006

CURRICULUM EVALUATION IN SCHOOLS
(Second edition)

CURRICULUM EVALUATION IN SCHOOLS

Robert McCormick and Mary James

ROUTLEDGE

First published 1983 by Croom Helm Ltd
Reprinted 1989 by Routledge
11 New Fetter Lane, London EC4P 4EE
29 West 35th Street, New York, NY 10001

© 1983 Robert McCormick and Mary James

Printed and bound in Great Britain by
Mackays of Chatham PLC, Chatham, Kent

British Library Cataloguing in Publication Data

McCormick, Robert
  Curriculum evaluation in schools.
  1. Schools. Curriculum. Assessment
  I. Title. II. James, Mary
  375'.006

  ISBN 0-415-04038-8

Contents

Acknowledgements

As any reader of this book will be fully aware, we owe an enormous debt to our colleagues on the E364 course team at the Open University. In large measure, the idea for a book on school-level evaluation grew out of the work that went into preparing the course material. We are also indebted to a number of individuals who discussed certain ideas with us and who commented on drafts of various chapters. In particular, we would like to thank Desmond Nuttall, John Bynner, Tim Horton, David Zeldin, Dave Ebbutt and John Elliott. Despite their best efforts to help us understand the issues we suspect that a number of errors and misconceptions remain. For these we accent total responsibility.

We would also like to convey our thanks to Pat Chalk who managed to find time among her many other commitments to type most of the manuscript, and to Gwen Green who typeset the first edition.

Finally, and most importantly, our love and gratitude to Di-An and Dave who were unfailing in their support and tolerated our worst excesses in terms of late nights at desks, a tendency to be preoccupied, and a certain dereliction of domestic duties.

Preface to the Second Edition

At the time when the first edition of this book was published events in education were developing apace. Four years later the rate of change has increased and its direction has been maintained. In the United Kingdom the Conservative Government has embarked on its third term, with a substantial majority, and looks set to implement its programme of radical change in the legislative framework of education. A major thrust of this will be to consolidate recent moves by both Labour and Conservative governments to establish a greater degree of central control over the curriculum, whilst at the same time strengthening the hand of consumers.

In view of this we were forced to reconsider whether the central thesis of the first edition of our book still holds good. In essence this was that the evaluation of the curriculum in schools will only be effective if teachers are given the major responsibility, because improvements in the curriculum depend upon their efforts. The provision of appropriate resources and organisational structures is a necessary but not sufficient condition for change; a commitment on the part of teachers to use these for the benefit of pupils is equally vital. Our argument was that teachers will not have this commitment if they are excluded from the evaluation of curriculum and teaching. In other words, if evaluations identify curricular changes as necessary these will only come about, in any genuine way, if the sympathies and energies of teachers are engaged. This is only likely to happen if teachers are involved in the conduct of evaluation processes.

On balance we still feel that this thesis is justified. The centralist tendencies in the current educational scene may appear to be diminishing the power of teachers but there are signs that teachers are actually gaining more control over the curriculum, albeit in different ways. For example, teacher-based assessment in the GCSE (General Certificate of Secondary Education), teacher-pupil dialogue and recording in Records of Achievement, and even the move towards giving schools more control over budgets, are extending the teacher's role in new directions (and perhaps increasing their accountability). Central initiatives, such as TVEI (Technical and Vocational Education Jnitiative), ironically, have been accompanied by a growth in local evaluations which often involve teachers in self-evaluation. All these developments require teachers to develop skills they have not hitherto possessed, but which could increase their professional regard.

Undoubtedly, groups outside of schools are being given more influence in relation to the curriculum. We believe that this will be welcomed if it is exercised in a spirit of partnership with schools. But if teachers encounter confrontation, instead of collaboration, then it is unlikely that they will have much enthusiasm for self-evaluation. We dedicate this book to teachers in the hope that their efforts will indeed be encouraged.

Robert McCormick and Mary James

PUZZLE a Day!

What seasonal message is this?

ABCDEFGHIJKMNOPQ
RSTUVWXYZ

SOLUTION:
Noel,
(There is no 'L').

DAY 151

Introduction

What is curriculum evaluation?

It is common, particularly in the USA, to use the terms 'evaluation' and 'assessment" synonymously. We distinguish them, however, by referring to the *evaluation of the curriculum* and the *assessment of pupils*. But this presupposes some understanding of the term 'curriculum', and this presents us with something of an enigma. There is, first of all, a wide variation in both teachers' use of the word and definitions found in the literature on the subject; these variations range from reference to subjects on the timetable, to everything that happens in the school. In addition there is the problem of giving a definition at the outset and then finding that it excludes something that appears to be important later on. Despite these difficulties we feel able to state that our concern is with *all* of the following:

1. the intended curriculum as formally stated by the timetable, in syllabuses and schemes of work, in aims, or as it exists in the general but unstated intentions of teachers;
2. the actual curriculum as experienced by pupils when they are involved in learning activities;
3. the hidden curriculum where pupils experience and 'learn' through such activities as lining up to enter school, wearing school uniform, standing up when a teacher enters the classroom, or being locked out of the school at break and lunch-times;
4. the outcome of learning in terms of the understandings, attitudes etc. that pupils develop.
   (This view of the curriculum implies that curriculum evaluation is concerned with questions about what should be taught as well as with finding out what happens in the classroom.)

The classroom is not our only concern, as the list of activities related to the hidden curriculum indicates. Nor do the activities outside the classroom, which are the focus of evaluation, have to involve pupils;

the decision-making procedures in the school are likely to affect, in some indirect way, the 'actual' or 'hidden' curriculum. Thus we are committed to looking at evaluation not just as the evaluation of classrooms and what goes on in them, but as the evaluation of school-wide curricular issues. There are differing views on this, however, and we explore them in *Chapter 2*.

Why evaluate?

The professional response to this question stresses the improvement of pupil learning or, more generally, the improvement in the quality of education. This approach sees evaluation as an element of professional development. Those working in the curriculum projects of the 1960s and early 1970s, and to whom we owe a great debt in developing evaluative thinking and methods, would give two reasons. One would point to the need to improve the materials and teaching techniques being developed; the other would make reference to the demands of project sponsors — the Schools Council, Nuffield Foundation, and more recently the Department of Education and Science (DES) and the Manpower Services Commission (MSC). Such sponsors not only wanted to know if their money was well spent but whether the approaches adopted should be developed or discarded. Evaluation in this setting is political as well as technical.

In schools, too, evaluation must be seen as more than a technical problem of choosing the correct method for the subject of evaluation. In the 1970s and 1980s schools and local education authorities (LEAs) have been subjected to increasing pressure from outside to give more information on what they are doing and to reassure the public about the quality of education in schools (though often the definition of 'quality' was a chimera). The watch-word became 'accountability', which to some meant that schools were to evaluate themselves or, better still, be evaluated by others. As we shall show, some have disputed this view of accountability and reiterated the professional response, but even here evaluation is not a technical exercise for it takes place in a human organisation which engages peoples' sensitivities, frailties and motivations. As if in defiance of such human concerns some advocates of accountability, initially fired with the desire to cut resources and consequently to shed teachers, are concerned about *teacher* evaluation. While many of the issues are common to curriculum evaluation, a proper treatment of teacher evaluation would require a different kind of book (which might be depressing to write!). However, we consider it briefly in Chapter 1.

What is the purpose and scope of the book?

Quite simply we wish to help and inform those teachers in schools, and those outside who support and work with them, who are faced with the the task of evaluation, whether they are responding to outside pressures or to internal needs, or both. Such a statement implies a commitment to the involvement of teachers in evaluation. Although we look in some detail at a variety of approaches, our basic stance is one of encouraging teachers, with outside support and help, to participate actively in the evaluation of the schools in which they work. The programme and project evaluation tradition does of course provide some guidance for schools, but the context and problems that schools face are considerably different.

First, the pressures of accountability and the trend towards school-based and school-focused in-service education and training (INSET) offer different, sometimes conflicting, paths for schools to tread. In *Part One: Directions* we explore these paths and the implications for evaluation. We explore these in some depth because we feel it is important to understand these issues and because it is crucial that those involved with curriculum evaluation in schools establish a rationale for their approach.

Secondly, schools are faced with decisions about how to evaluate, which, unlike the decisions of programme evaluators, are strategic rather than methodological. This is not to say that programme and project evaluators did not have to face strategic decisions, but that they tended to discuss these in the literature through considerations of methodology, and in particular through discussions of evaluation models. Schools, on the other hand, are faced with questions such as: should outsiders or insiders carry out the evaluation and how should it be organised? We explore questions such as this in *Part Two: Strategies*, and we do so by examining practice, both established and developing, and by examining principles. These strategic decisions may not always be in the hands of schools themselves, but it is no less important that they be aware of them. Of course for those outside, in local authorities, universities, colleges etc., strategic considerations may be central.

Thirdly, evaluation methods do have to be selected. The range available includes not only measurement instruments, but methods that make use of the teacher as a data source or resource. In this area the experience of programme evaluation (and other forms of 'outside' evaluation), as well as that available from educational and social science research, can be drawn upon. There is, however, relatively little experience of evaluation in schools which involves teachers as evaluators. A discussion of evaluation methods could occupy a whole book; however, we have avoided this because we feel there are other equally important things to say. Also we feel that teachers would be better advised to begin by exploring the potential of various methods and trying out those that seem most useful. For this reason *Part Three: Techniques* consists mainly of a *review* which provides an account of the basic techniques with reference to the literature, and where possible gives examples of their use in schools. In addition we consider the practical and theoretical issues faced specifically by teachers carrying out evaluations.

Finally, the effort of evaluation should clearly result in something. Sadly there is still much to learn about the way evaluation is used. Many evaluations culminate in a report, but little is known about their impact, particularly the impact on teachers. We have to admit to being puzzled by this area and in *Part Four: Using Evaluation* we offer only an exploration of the issues along with some practical guidance. However this exploration is extended to cover the ultimate use of evaluation in terms of *action,* and we look both at the idea of combining research activity with action, and at the need for various kinds of support structures.

In writing a book covering a wide range of issues, and for a variety of people both inside and outside schools, we have been faced with the task of presenting the main ideas and arguments, while still feeling able to justify them and explore related issues. This is particularly important in the review of techniques in *Chapter 8.* We have therefore made extensive use of notes at the ends of chapters. Our intention has been to enable readers to follow the flow of the text, consulting the notes only when they doubt us or want to see how (or where) a point is developed. *Chapter 8,* apart from being by far the largest chapter, also presents a contrast in style. Once the main argument has been appreciated, we hope it will be treated as a kind of reference section.

Our purpose, to reiterate, is two-fold. First, we offer an account of the theoretical issues, because we believe that teachers, and those who work with teachers in a pre- and in-service capacity, need to appreciate them in order to provide a rationale for action. Secondly, we provide a number of ideas and pointers regarding ways in which evaluations can be implemented.

Part One

Directions

1 Accountability and Evaluation

Introduction

It has now become commonplace to observe that the 1960s witnessed a rapid increase in educational investment on both sides of the Atlantic. However, in relation to the theme of this chapter, this development was significant because it created an urgent need to justify the massive input of resources. Taxpayers, ratepayers, policy makers and administrators all demanded information about the way in which the money they provided was being spent. Thus, by the 1970s, the age of accountability had arrived and the concept of educational evaluation had acquired a new meaning.

By the early 1980s, the concept of educational evaluation was often so interwoven with the concept of accountability that the two were difficult to distinguish; indeed Nuttall (Open University, 1982, Block 1) suggests that the distinction may be untenable. However, Elliott (1981b), following Becher (1979), argues that whilst evaluation and accountability are closely inter-related, the relationship is not symmetrical. Accountability usually presupposes evaluation, but evaluation does not necessarily imply accountability. This latter view is the one we subscribe to in this book, for although we consider evaluation as a response to, or the process of, accountability, we also consider evaluation in two other contexts, which, unlike Nuttall, we have chosen to distinguish from accountability. (See chapters 2 and 3.)

Accountability Pressures

We have already mentioned one of the factors that gave rise to the emergence of accountability as a central issue in education: the need to justify increased spending in the 1960s. This was, however, only the most obvious of a number of complex social, economic and political pressures, which contributed to a gradual change in the climate that

7

surrounds most public institutions in the western world. Equally important, although in many ways distinct, was a perceptible decline in public confidence. According to Halsey (1979) the 1970s witnessed a widespread 'rotting of public confidence in public institutions'. As a consequence we seem to have entered a strongly conservative phase with an unmistakeable emphasis on consumer rights.

Before focusing on the way in which educational accountability has manifested itself in evaluation procedures we want to spend a little time exploring this more general picture. Our thesis is this: educational accountability is not a localised phenomenon, therefore, what appear to be local responses may have a wider significance than was imagined at their inception. After all, policy makers rarely start from first principles but borrow and adapt structures and procedures which they see operating effectively elsewhere. For this reason the American experience has relevance to the United Kingdom, and perhaps vice versa; and developments in law, medicine, the police force and the social services are worthy of the attention of those within education. It should perhaps come as no surprise that the Assessment of Performance Unit (APU) in England and Wales has some of the characteristics of the National Assessment of Educational Progress (NAEP) in the US; or that new moves in the UK to establish procedures to make incompetent teachers liable to sanctions (reported in the *Times Educational Supplement.* 27 Nov. 1981) coincided with the publication (on 25 Nov. 1981) of the Scarman Report which recommended the introduction of an independent element in the police complaints procedure.

In two papers outlining some of the causes of public discontent and their impact on education in the United States, Atkin (1979, 1980) provides a useful framework for comparing the situation in the UK (especially England and Wales) with that in the USA. Educational accountability emerged in the United States earlier than the United Kingdom, where the term did not appear in an official document until the publication of the 'Green Paper' (DES, 1977b). Despite this qualification, the trend on this side of the Atlantic now seems established and many of the features of North American accountability have counterparts here. In the rest of this section, therefore, we have used Atkin's framework to draw out some of these similarities.

Economic decline and the failure of education to improve industrial performance.

After the economic boom years of the 1960s, industrial expansion has been arrested, on both sides of the Atlantic. In large measure this is attributable to the world recession which developed after the oil crisis in 1974, although another contributory factor is associated with the failure of western societies to respond sufficiently quickly to the development of new technologies. In particular, the lack of investment planning has hindered the shift in the industrial base of western economies. Anxieties aroused by the economic crisis have rebounded on the education service which, fairly or otherwise, stands accused of not meeting the needs of advanced industrial society. Although the USA has always tended to look to education to solve its national problems, education in the UK has traditionally been viewed more as a benefit to the individual (Taylor, W., 1978). The advent of accountability in the UK has therefore had the effect of bringing closer together the values ascribed to education by both UK and US governments. Offering an American view of British accountability House (1978) describes a shift from individualist to societal values in the following way:

> The major shift in values is from individualist values, the traditional emphasis, to society goals and values, from the individual to the government. The longstanding consensus on traditional aims has been broken and the pattern of educational governance is at issue. Education is being pushed more towards being an instrument of national policy, or so it would appear to an outsider. (p.207)

House is perhaps mistaken in believing that individualist values have always held sway in the UK. In earlier periods pressures to provide an education service fitted to the needs of the society have been observed. For instance the Taunton Commission Report, 1868, and the Hadow Report, 1926, were both much influenced by the contemporary view of the needs of the economy (see Musgrave, 1968). It is nevertheless true that the creation of the single subject GCE examinations in the 1950s, and the subsequent development of the CSE (Mode III), allowed considerable power to swing to the teachers. They now had the means to tailor curricula to suit what they perceived to be the abilities and interests of individual children (Lawton, 1980). The advent of the accountability movement in the UK represents, therefore, something in the nature of another swing of the pendulum: back to a reconsideration of societal needs. The current UK trend found an early official expression in the Ruskin College Speech of the Labour Prime Minister, James Callaghan. In this he initiated the Great Debate by exhorting teachers to 'satisfy parents and industry that what you are doing meets their requirements and the needs of their children' (Callaghan, 1976). Subsequent government documents, emanating from both the Department of Education and Science (i.e. Secretaries of State and HMI) and the Department of Industry, have pursued the same theme and in 1985 *Better Schools* (DES, 1985a) contained the following statement:

> It is vital that schools should always remember that preparation for working life is one of their principal functions. The economic stresses of our time and the pressures of international competition make it more necessary than ever before that Britain's work-force should possess the skills and attitudes, and display the understanding, the enterprise and adaptability that the pervasive impact of technological advance will increasingly demand. This applies to those who will be employed by others and to the many who may expect, for part or all of their working lives, to be self-employed. The balance within the curriculum and the emphasis in teaching it now need to alter accordingly. (DES, 1985a, para. 46, p. 15)

One manifestation of this statement in terms of policy has been the Technical and Vocational Education Initiative (TVEI) funded by the MSC.

Falling standards, falling roles and higher costs.

Criticism of the education service for failing to meet the needs of an advanced industrial economy is undoubtedly linked with a widely held belief that educational standards, generally, are in decline. In the United States a sharp drop in Scholastic Aptitude Test (SAT) scores (an examination used widely to select students for college admission) has been evinced as 'proof' of falling standards. The ensuing public alarm encouraged the setting up of a national commission (chaired by the former Secretary of Labour, Willard Wirtz) to investigate the reasons for such a sharp decline. The commission identified a variety of factors including lack of parental support, the influence of television, the increased proportion of eighteen-year-olds taking the SAT, and a decrease in the importance of formal education in determining life-time earnings. Significantly this list does not include any indication that the quality of educational provision had, itself, declined. Nevertheless the indictment of schooling remains strong in the public mind and an apparent increase in violence in schools serves only to compound this belief.

In England and Wales there is no convenient, popularly accepted, indicator of the effectiveness of schooling to compare with the SAT. No single attainment test is administered to all schools, and GCE and CSE examinations were always dogged by problems of comparability (Schools Council, 1979; Nuttall, Backhouse, and Willmott, 1974). Notwithstanding that, from 1969 onwards, the authors of a series of Black Papers saw fit to castigate schools for falling standards[1]. Unfortunately they tended to use polemical fervour as a substitute for evidence. Indeed what evidence there was at that time, for instance from a number of reading surveys, suggested the maintenance or improvement of attainment, although the single exception provoked more media interest (Start and Wells, 1972).

With the publication of the Green Paper (DES, 1977b), the 'standards' issue became an official concern. Once more the suggestion was that educational standards had fallen and that this decline was in some way connected with the introduction of progressive forms of education. Again the accusation was presented without evidence. The fact that two years later the HMI Secondary Survey (DES, 1979a) showed that popular fears about falling standards were largely unfounded did conspicuously little to change the prevailing attitude.[2]

According to MacDonald (1978) the standards debate in England was as much stimulated by an idealised 'distillation from the past' as any so called 'objective' measures. He writes: 'It may be that when we "invent" the past, especially the lived past, we serve our self esteem by creating an idealized image of our experience, holding it in our heads until it yields measures of virtue' (p 30). Certainly, a large section of the British public came to *believe* that standards had declined, and, as Thomas (1928) observed, 'if men define situations as real, they are real in their consequences'. Moreover, as in America, a growing youth movement was attracting media attention and added to the impression that 'kids can't read, don't know how to behave, and aren't willing to work'. (Taylor, W., 1978).

The finger pointed at education could not easily be pushed aside, particularly at a time when the period of education had been extended and the school population, on both sides of the Atlantic, was beginning to diminish — factors which should have favoured significant improvement. Furthermore the public expected increased 'productivity' in return for the substantial increases in salaries achieved in the 1970s by unionised teachers in both the UK and the USA. To the layman it seemed that a decreasing service was being provided at increasing expense. As a consequence the recent decline in public spending on services, such as education, has gone virtually unchecked.

The failure of education as an instrument of social reform.

Commenting on the US federal government's increasing involvement in education, Atkin (1980) observed a shift in national priorities during the Kennedy years, which influenced the nature of that involvement. An earlier preoccupation with the space race and national defence had focused attention on improving the state of science education, in the USA. In the 1960s this preoccupation gave way to an urgent need to consider domestic problems such as racial disharmony and poverty. In 1965, Lyndon Johnson, who, according to Atkin, wanted to be remembered as the 'Education President', devoted much of his energies to the passage of the Elementary and Secondary Education Act, which appropriated large sums of money for a compensatory education programme. 'It was a period of considerable optimism in some quarters that the nation's ills could be ameliorated by wise policy, diligent effort, and lots of money' (Atkin, 1979, p.18).

The emphasis on individualism that House (1978) observed prevented education in the UK ever being regarded as an agent of social reform to the extent that it was in the United States. Nevertheless a similar concern was evident in the discussions of 'positive discrimin-ation' and the establishment of educational priority areas (EPAs) sub-sequent to the publication of the Plowden Report in 1967. Moreover, in the secondary sector, it was hoped that comprehensivisation would be effective in equalising opportunities among different social groups.

Faith in this doctrine of meliorism (that progress is inevitable if sufficient money and resources are provided) soon began to fade. In the UK it became increasingly apparent that organisational change in schools was not sufficient to guarantee change in established social attitudes. For instance, some observers suggest that there are few genuine comprehensive schools in this country i.e. schools fully com-mitted to physical, social and curricular integration (see Reynolds *et al*, 1987, for a recent analysis). Indeed comprehensivisation is now likely to be reversed by government policy to allow schools to opt out of LEA control. In the USA disillusionment was even more obvious, especially after Vietnam and Watergate had turned the national mood from optimism to self-criticism. Furthermore, disagreement over racial desegregation and the policy of bussing revealed a lack of consensus over the social goals that schools were supposed to advance.

Distrust of authority and scepticism concerning competence

According to Atkin (1979) lack of agreement about social purposes is related to an increasing lack of confidence in those in positions of authority or those who claim specialist knowledge. Nisbet (1979) has pointed out the irony that this new distrust may itself be a product of modern education, since a number of new approaches to teaching and learning encourage children to 'think for themselves'. Certainly 'professionalism' is beginning to be viewed sceptically (Hoyle, 1980) and competence is no longer assumed. On both sides of the Atlantic the decisions of architects, civil engineers, environmental planners, doctors etc. attract public scrutiny and the numbers of government regulating agencies increase.

In the UK the established professions (law and medicine) and some of the semi-professions, such as the police, have traditionally been self-monitoring. Now, however, they are finding this position increasingly difficult to maintain. In the 1980 series of Reith Lectures on BBC radio, Ian Kennedy, a Reader in Law, argued that the disciplinary procedures of the medical profession are more concerned with etiquette than competence. Supporting a notion of consumerism he proposed litigation as a more satisfactory procedure than the existing forms of self-regulation provided by the General Medical Council. In October 1981, a court case, concerning the death of a Down's Syndrome baby, was brought against a paediatrician by the association 'Life'. Although in this instance, the doctor's action was vindicated, the case was illustrative of a greater public willingness to take legal action in circumstances such as these.

In the US this trend has been evident for some time. In the educational sphere, the minimum competencies legislation passed by at least 38 states has provided a possible vehicle (litigation) for ordinary laymen to demand that certain tasks are fulfilled by the professionals. In this context, 'minimum competencies' legislation refers to the State's requirement that pupils should attain an agreed level of mastery of basic skills and satisfactory performance of functional literacy in order to graduate from high school. As a way of ascertaining whether minimum levels had been achieved state-wide testing programmes were initiated. [3] Given that the minimum levels of pupil competence were set by each school district in cognisance of local circumstances, a question was raised concerning whether students who failed to reach the agreed standards could recover damages for their failure to learn, if they were able to demonstrate teacher negligence. In one famous Californian court case a school leaver sued the State Department of

Education for precisely this reason. In this instance the case was dismissed but the fact that such action was taken at all was profoundly significant.[4]

Minimum competencies testing has not been a feature of the UK experience, although the government's announcement in 1987 that a national curriculum was to be established, with benchmarks for achievement at ages 7, 11 and 14, appeared at first to have similar implications. At the time of writing, it seems that the intention is not to assess progress in relation to benchmarks through a blanket testing programme but through assessment by teachers akin to that in GCSE and Records of Achievement. In other words, rather than representing minimum competencies, benchmarks are intended to raise expectations. What happens in practice remains to be seen!

In some measure, these examples of lack of public confidence in professional skill, expertise and judgement, provide evidence of what Habermas (1974, 1975) has called the 'legitimation crisis of late capitalism'. According to his analysis distrust of authority and scepticism concerning the competence of specialists is a function of the breakdown of value consensus. Thus a 'working' or 'practical' agreement can only be achieved through a process of dialogue. If recent events are anything to go by, one forum for this 'dialogue' will be the courts of law.

The application of economic management systems to public services

The final two factors that we wish to consider here seem to have more influence in the USA, although there are signs that they are becoming increasingly important in the UK. Americans may have little more trust in businessmen than other specialists, but they do believe they have the ability to 'deliver the goods' (Atkin, 1979, p.17). For this reason the adoption of economic management systems, such as 'management by objectives' and 'cost-benefit analysis', by the public services rapidly found favour. It was generally believed that this would increase their efficiency in line with private industry. In the early 1960s this new attitude was clearly demonstrated in the appointment of Robert McNamara, the director of the Ford Motor Company, to the post of Secretary of the Department of Defence. In Britain this trend has been less marked although the more recent appointment of Sir Derek Rayner, the managing director of Marks and Spencer, as the Conservative government's economic 'watchdog', is significant for similar reasons. The Jarratt Report, based on efficiency studies in a number of universities, and the Green Paper, *The Development of Higher Education into the*

1990s (DES, 1985b), provide evidence of a similar trend in higher education. The latter advocated the establishment of objectives and the monitoring of their achievement through the development of measures of performance (DES, 1985b, pp. 30-1).

The growth of single interest groups

If there is any truth in the observation that, in many things, Britain tends to follow one step behind the United States, then we might expect the single interest group to have a real impact in this country in the future. The beginnings of such a growth are already being recognised in the vastly increased membership of CND, conservation groups, the Women's Movement, and the emergence of professional lobbyists. In America the increased activity of the single interest group has led to a reduction in the strength of the political party. The internal wrangles, sometimes over single issues, which are coming to characterise British party politics in the 1980s, may well foreshadow a similar process.

Summary

In his analysis Atkin (1979) points to the 'fragmentation of community' as the single most important factor feeding accountability pressures in the USA[5]. The growth of single interest groups, the loss of confidence in specialists, and anxiety over the apparent failure of education to deliver a variety of 'goods', may all be regarded as manifestations of the weakening of common purpose. Where there is agreement about goals the public assumes that professionals share in that consensus but 'if consensus is in doubt, there is an accompanying uncertainty about the values and practices that guide professional activity' (Atkin, 1980, p. 15). Clearly this phenomenon is not confined to the United States; value pluralism has created something of an educational Tower of Babel in Britain also (Taylor, W., 1978).

Paradoxically however, the breakdown in value consensus that generated the accountability movement might seem to require a new form of consensus if accountability demands are to be satisfied. Unless there is some agreement about purposes how can schools and teachers be expected to render account? How will they know what they are being held accountable for? These questions, among others, exercised a group of educationists who met at a seminar on accountability sponsored by the SSRC and held at Cambridge (England) in 1977[6]. While most participants perceived the problem they differed somewhat over the matter of its resolution. MacDonald (1978) argued that no genuine consensus is possible; anything so called would represent only the views of the most powerful and reinforce their hegemony. Becher (1978) denied that a general ideological consensus about educational ends is 'necessary in theory'; in practice he believed that teachers can, and do, negotiate a working consensus, usually framed in terms of basic minima. Nisbet (1978) and Kogan (1978) responded to the problem by turning their attention to the procedures which might be employed to meet accountability demands. Both, in rather different ways, advanced pluralist or multiple solutions which acknowledge multiple values and purposes, although Nisbet admitted that some methods (viz. testing) were likely to pre-empt the field and destroy the balance. The question of whether it is possible to establish a normative consensus, based on rational discussion undistorted by values, has also been addressed by Habermas (1975, 1979). He has argued that such a thing is indeed possible and offers a potential solution to the 'legitimation crisis'.

Responses

While the intention of the 1977 Cambridge Accountability Seminar was to clarify the conceptual background to the accountability movement, the participants were swift to recognise its inevitability and admissibility, in one form or another. Thus they spent much of their time debating the validity of various evaluation procedures as potential responses. Details of some of these strategies, and others, are discussed fully in *Part Two* (chapters 4 to 6) but since not all are considered there *from an accountability perspective*, they need some introduction here.

It is in the development of specific accounting procedures that the US and UK experience has most obviously diverged. Although any generalisation should be regarded with caution, the dominance of economic input-output models in the United States has encouraged a dependence on the evaluation, or, more accurately, the assessment of outcomes or products of schooling. Hence the ubiquity of testing, and evaluation schemes which involve the assessment of teacher or student performances. Atkin (1979) lists the following as employed in some areas of the USA, at some time in the recent past:

1. *Performance contracting* – the commissioning of private firms to work with teachers in schools to raise achievement levels of children;
2. *Competency-based teacher education* — the requiring of teacher education institutions to specify and demonstrate

what each *teacher* is expected to be able to do as a result of his/her training;

3. *Programme evaluation* — the routine assessment of the effectiveness of costly new educational programmes. (This created an 'evaluation industry' which sometimes consumed one-fifth to one-third of the total costs associated with particular programmes.[7])

4. *Zero-based budgeting, cost-benefit analysis, management by objectives* — the application of management techniques which demand the assessment of highly operationalised programme goals as a guide to financial allocations;

5. *Educational vouchers* — a system of enhancing school competitiveness by issuing vouchers to parents to be 'cashed' at the school of their choice;

6. *The National Assessment of Educational Progress* — an attempt to establish the condition of the nation's overall educational well-being by administering selected tests to carefully chosen 'light' samples of the school population. (Latterly some states, e.g. Florida, have instituted their own 'blanket' testing programmes.)

7. *Minimal-competency testing* — as mentioned earlier, some 38 states have now introduced laws which require that *students* should be able to demonstrate that they possess certain basic skills after attendance at public school.

It is significant that all these schemes, with the exception of educational vouchers, involve some form of testing. In the United Kingdom the attitude to testing has been more ambivalent, although examinations and tests have played an important part in British education for well over a century. In 1862, Robert Lowe's notorious Revised Code introduced 'payment by results' which relied upon a form of minimum competencies testing. Public examination statistics have regularly been collected although difficulties of establishing comparability over time, and across different examination boards and subjects, have reduced their usefulness for assessing the performance of the education system as a whole. In the 1970s the Department of Education and Science pinned its hopes on the APU to provide a general measure of the achievement of children at schools and, implicitly, changes in standards over time.[8] Ten years after the establishment of the APU, hopes for the kind of information it was intended to provide had faded. Fierce criticism of the mathematical model (the Rasch model) on which the testing programme was founded (Goldstein, 1979a, 1981b, Nuttall,

1979) encouraged the DES to begin looking elsewhere for a thermo-meter to take the temperature of the education system; the bench-marks mentioned earlier may be the new thermometer (Chapter 4 considers these criticisms of the APU).

Other schemes of American origin are not without their advocates on this side of the Atlantic. Recent Secretaries of State for Education have been known to favour educational vouchers as a way of increasing parental choice and allowing the quality of schools to be judged by market forces[9] though they have been unable to find a workable system. Instead the traditional role of the national and local inspectorate was enhanced; there was more systematic utilisation of public examina-tion results as an indicator of educational well-being[10]; and newer strategies (such as local authority school evaluation and teacher appraisal schemes) are being devised, adapted or extended.

Nisbet (1978) identifies five broadly defined strategies that might be employed as accountability procedures, namely: testing, monitoring of standards by conventional examination, inspection, the development of standardised pupil record systems, and various forms of school self-evaluation (which he calls self-assessment). Nisbet maintains that these five strategies represent the range of possibilities and that they can each be located on a spectrum, the poles of which can be described as 'hard' and 'soft'. Testing stands as the 'hard' pole because procedures tend to be external, formal, judgemental, product-orientated, and analytic in their method of assessment. In contrast, forms of self-evaluation can be located towards the 'soft' pole because they tend to be internal, informal, descriptive, process-orientated and holistic in their mode of assessment. Although, as we shall illustrate in *Part Two*, it is an over-simplification to assign certain categories of evaluation strategies to specific locations on a hard/soft spectrum, Nisbet's analysis serves to map the field of actual and possible accountability procedures.

The Concept of Accountability

At this point we think it worth using a little space to examine the concept of accountability. The diversity of responses to accountability pressures suggests that the concept is interpreted differently by differ-ent groups according to their different interests. In other words, it is a social construct. The East Sussex Accountability Project, which (like the Cambridge Accountability Project and a Scottish study conducted by researchers at Stirling) was funded subsequent to the 1977 SSRC Seminar at Cambridge, attempted a conceptual analysis. Three facets of accountability were distinguished:

(1) *answerability* to one's clients i.e. pupils and parents (moral accountability).
(2) *responsibility* to oneself and one's colleagues (professional accountability).
(3) *accountability* in the strict sense to one's employers or political masters ('contractual' accountability).
(East Sussex Accountability Project, 1979, p. 97).

From this analysis it appears that the term 'accountability' is only strictly correct when reference is made to contractual relations with employers. The sense in which the term is used is formal-legalistic, and implies that accountability is largely one way (i.e. of teachers to employers) and that accountability procedures involve sanctions (e.g. withdrawal of resources and other forms of support). Much of the public debate has, indeed, been about contractual (strict) accountability. It is interesting, therefore, that the evidence of the UK accountability projects suggests that teachers operate with a very different model: one that is grounded in concepts of answerability or responsibility (see Becher, Eraut and Knight, 1981; East Sussex Accountability Project, 1979; Cambridge Accountability Project, 1981; Elliott, 1980a; Elliott, Bridges, Ebbutt, Gibson and Nias, 1981).

In this context Elliott (1980a) has pointed out that the association of answerability, responsibility and accountability with specific audiences (i.e. clients, colleagues and employers, respectively) is problematic. Thus in describing the perspectives of various groups on school accountability, the East Sussex Accountability Project's alternative classification (moral, professional and contractual accountability) is probably more useful. Certainly, Elliott finds less conceptual difficulty with this classification, and it has been used extensively elsewhere (OU, 1982), in the analysis of various approaches to evaluation. In *Part Two*, it will be referred to in a similar way; for instance, insider approaches to evaluation will be discussed as a mode of professional accountability, and inspections and local authority schemes will be examined as responses to contractual accountability demands.

Levels of Accountability

Another problem, and one that was intimated in the previous paragraph, is the question of *who* is to be considered accountable *to whom*. It is usually assumed that teachers and heads are held to account but whether they are accountable to resource providers (ratepayers, taxpayers, policy makers, administrators), customers (pupils, parents, employers), or their professional colleagues, is ill-defined (Nisbet, 1978). In the UK this issue was thrown into bold relief by the Tyndale Affair, which some observers have, mistakenly, assumed to be a cause rather than a symptom of the accountability debate. The public inquiry, conducted by Robin Auld QC, into the teaching, organisation and management of the William Tyndale Junior School in Islington, North London (ILEA, 1976) revealed considerable confusion regarding the various levels of accountability. Three are commonly identified i.e. national, local and school, and in an attempt to clarify them the following paragraphs examine each in turn.

According to the 1944 Education Act the Secretary of State has a duty to 'promote the education of the people of England and Wales and the progressive development of institutions devoted to that purpose ...', although effective control was, at the time of the Tyndale dispute, devolved to the LEAs. Similarly, after a report of the 1968 Parliamentary Select Committee, a greater share of inspection was also left to LEAs: the 'duty' of the Minister to cause inspections was officially interpreted as a 'right'. Thus during the Tyndale affair the DES tended to keep its collective head below the parapet (Gretton and Jackson, 1976).

LEAs have a statutory obligation to provide an 'efficient' and 'suitable' education, as far as possible 'in accord with parental wishes'. Through its Rules of Management, however, the Inner London Education Authority (ILEA) had, at that time, effectively divested itself of the exercise of its control. When things went wrong the early warning system was supposed to be the authority's inspectorate. However this body was experiencing some role ambiguity and since it possessed no formal power to ensure that its professional judgement was heeded, it tended to define its function as advisory rather than inspectorial[11].

Rule 2(a) of the authority's Rules of Management gave the schools' Managers (now, since the 1980 Education Act, called 'governors') responsibility for the 'oversight of the conduct of the curriculum of the school, in consultation with the headteacher'. What precisely was entailed in oversight was not made clear and in practice the control of the school, its aims, policies and methods of teaching was left to the headteacher. It was not until a junior school staff, which regarded its professional status as inviolable, was confronted by its Managers that the whole taken-for-granted structure of accountability was thrown into question.

The main target for the Auld Report's (ILEA, 1976) criticisms was the LEA because it had interpreted its responsibilities in terms largely confined to the provision of resources. Clearly Auld was of the opinion that the Tyndale incident could have been avoided if the authority had taken a wider view of its role. In other words, he held the local authority as partly accountable for the situation that developed at the school . In so doing he emphasised the need for accountability at all levels of the system. It is always difficult to establish the precise nature of the relationship between events, but it seems significant that the ILEA published its booklet *Keeping the School Under Review* in the year following the conclusion of the Tyndale inquiry (See also Chapter 6.)

Undoubtedly LEAs have reassessed their stance on accountability issues as a result of the Auld Report, but at school level the impact of the national debate seems to have been erratic. The Cambridge Accountability Project, after two years of investigations in six schools, reported that teachers rarely saw their accountability extending beyond their colleagues and clients (children and parents) to governors and local government officials (Elliott, 1981c). Neither did governing bodies regard their role as primarily concerned with monitoring the curriculum (Ebbutt, 1981). The schools chosen for investigation by the Cambridge project team considered themselves to be 'responsive' to the interest and concerns of local audiences. In the generation and communication of information, they also believed themselves to be 'self-accounting'. Their concept of accountability however, appears rather different from that of Robin Auld, QC – more 'moral' or 'professional' than 'contractual'.

At the end of the end of the 1980s the pattern of accountability is changing. DES proposals for a national curriculum, the growth of categorical funding by the DES and MSC in priority areas specified by central government (Harland, 1985), the dismantling of the Burnham Committee on teachers' pay, and changes in the control of polytechnics and colleges of higher education are all moves designed to reduce the power of the LEAs and increase central control. At the same time schools are being placed in the front line of accountability by the proposal to give headteachers and governors direct control of budgets and the opportunity to opt out of LEA control. The Conservative government's principal objective is to allow market forces to operate and enable popular schools to expand to their full capacity i.e. to the numbers they were built to accommodate before falling rolls. Correspondingly, unpopular schools might expect to contract to a point at which they lose their viability. In this sense the policy represents the essence of consumerism. At the time of writing, the required changes in legislation are promised in a major new Education Act scheduled for 1988.

Criteria for Accounting Procedures

Few people today would deny the need for some form of accountability in education. However the seemingly irreconcilable interests (eg. professional versus lay) that are brought into the forum for debate, require that criteria be established for judging the adequacy of accounting procedures in given contexts. This need for criteria was recognised at the Cambridge seminar in 1977 and three papers specified criteria that schemes would need to satisfy (Nisbet, 1978; Eraut, 1978; Becher and Maclure, 1978b). For the purposes of comparison these have been summarised in Figure 1.1.

Although Nisbet states a greater number of methodological criteria, the lists in Figure 1.1 show many similarities. Drawing these together for the purpose of an Open University course (OU, 1982), Nuttall compiled a list that was intended to embody 'the best and clearest features of them all and that is reasonably comprehensive'. Thus he proposed that an accountability scheme should:

(a)   be fair and perceived as fair by all the parties involved;
(b)   be capable of suggesting appropriate remedies;
(c)   yield an account that is intelligible to its intended
        audience(s);
(d)   be methodologically sound;
(e)   be economical in its use of resources;
(f)   be an acceptable blend of centralised and delegated control.

(OU, 1982, p. 30)

There is a problem with all these formulations of criteria, however. They tend to be regarded as lists against which particular accountability schemes need only to be checked off. We would argue that

Figure 1.1: Criteria for Satisfactory Accountability Procedures.

NISBET, 1978, p100	ERAUT, 1978, p172	BECHER & MACLURE, 1978b, p224
1. They must be FAIR.	1. They do not DISTORT the curriculum or unduly interfere with teaching.	1. They should be calculated to maintain CONFIDENCE in the schools.
2. They should be VALID.	2. They do not direct too much TIME and EFFORT away from teaching.	2. They must therefore be INTELLIGIBLE to a lay audience.
3. They should provide FEEDBACK for decision making.	3. They INVOLVE TEACHERS and provide FEEDBACK for decision making, in such a way that there is a reasonable chance that pupils will ultimately benefit.	3. They must be FAIR.
4. They should either be OBJECTIVE or make their SUBJECTIVITY EXPLICIT.	4. They provide information of sufficient VALIDITY to be acted upon with reasonable confidence, or else indicate where further investigation is needed.	4. They must be combined with REMEDIES.
5. They should be VERIFIABLE.	5. They gain the TRUST and support of external audiences.	
6. They should not DAMAGE or DISTORT the processes of learning and teaching.		
7. They should be UNDERSTAND-ABLE and COMMUNICABLE.		
8. They should be COMPREHENSIVE.		

depending on the concept of accountability (moral, professional, contractual) that the procedure seeks to satisfy, and the features of the particular context (sector of education, local pressures etc.), the individual criteria will assume relatively greater or lesser importance. In some cases they may appear to be in conflict. For instance we have argued elsewhere (OU, 1982, Block 2 Part 2) that if accountability is interpreted in a professional sense then the question of intelligibility to lay audiences is rarely an issue because the primary audience is teachers' professional colleagues. Furthermore to insist that a procedure must include a significant element of external control could hinder the implementation of remedies: a criticism which is often regarded as the most important (Simons, 1981). (This theme will be returned to in Chapter 5.)

The implication of the above discussion is that the adequacy of any accountability scheme will depend on (1) the particular interpretation being employed in a particular context, and (2) a holistic, or overall, judgement of the extent to which the procedures meet the criteria. Clearly there is no simple formula for resolving the problems of educational accountability. Although one group can be encouraged to understand and respond to the interests of another, we need to acknowledge that true consensus is unlikely. A 'working' agreement is the best we can hope for, though probably sufficient none the less. For this reason then, the criterion of FAIRNESS seems superordinate. We will draw upon these criteria in Part Two in judging the various strategies of evaluation.

As a final comment it is worth attempting to put the accountability debate in some perspective. Currently the question of educational accountability appears to be less of an issue than was predicted in the 1970s. As mentioned earlier the current government (1987) is set to increase consumerism in education by allowing popular schools to take in as many pupils as possible without the requirement on the part of LEAs to balance intake among schools. It also intends to set up city technical colleges funded by industry in an effort to increase parental choice, and this is seen as a way of reducing the power of the LEAs. Indeed, their proposals to give budget control to headteachers is explicitly seen as a way of making a direct link to schools not mediated by LEAs. However, the government has not been so preoccupied with accountability procedures as appeared to be the case in the early 1980s. It appeared then to favour teacher appraisal, the publication of examination results, and to a lesser extent the evaluation and review of schools (especially through curriculum review). Now the publication of examination results has become routine, and has not apparently delivered the goods (we look at this in Chapter 4). Teacher appraisal did appear to be part of the accountability process, but, as we shall see, this has changed to some extent.

Some kind of assessment of the competence of teachers was seen as a way of weeding out those who were incompetent: a reaction to severe cuts in education (along with the effects of falling rolls), and the need to thin out the teaching force. (HMI did not find this an important objective of existing appraisal schemes in the mid-1980s – DES, 1985c.) Thus it was taken up as part of a larger review of education in general, and teachers' conditions of service in particular. *Better Schools* (DES, 1985a), which made the definitive statement on this general review, discussed teacher appraisal in the context of the management of the teaching force. This White Paper saw appraisal as providing 'reliable, comprehensive and up-to-date information necessary for the systematic and effective provision of professional support and development and the deployment of staff to best advantage' (DES, 1985a, p.55). This approach became part of the negotiations with the teachers' unions, who did not in principle object to appraisal, but wanted to ensure that they obtained good conditions of service and an adequate pay increase before agreeing to it. The implementation of an appraisal scheme, and pilot studies to develop the details, have been held up by the drawn out teachers' dispute.

Despite the government's interest in appraisal as being both developmental (for the teacher) and directly related to salary and career advancement, early experience of schools in developing schemes was almost entirely based on teacher development (Turner and Clift, 1985). Both ends can be achieved, but it is more usual for a school to start with a developmental aim, if for no other reason than that it is less threatening. In fact some appraisal schemes developed from an interest in, and experience of, school self-evaluation (e.g. Clift, Nuttall and McCormick, 1987 Chapter 7). King (*TES*, 8 August, 1986, p. 15) rightly points out that a scheme which is intended to weed out poor teachers is not necessarily the best to engender the trust and confidence required to develop the work of teachers. In addition such a scheme focuses on individuals and not groups of teachers, which, we will argue in Chapter 2, is an important focus for evaluation. Group development might also encourage peer assessment which a contractual appraisal scheme is not likely to include. King also wonders whether the impact of teacher appraisal on school improvement will be commensurate with the cost of such schemes. (See also Suffolk Education Department,

1985, and Wilcox 1986.)

Until the 'official' pilot schemes are instituted we only have the experience of the formative approaches in the UK to guide us on how appraisal is to be conducted. The existing schemes in the early and mid-1980s were usually based upon an annual interview by a member of the Senior Management Team of a school, or perhaps a head of department. Occasionally classroom observation of the teacher under review would also be carried out by the senior teacher, and sometimes an observation schedule was used. In the USA teacher competency tests are also included; these test teacher knowledge. As we will show in subsequent chapters observation is an important tool in evaluation in general (i.e. outside of the context of teacher appraisal), but it is likely that given the context of contractual obligations and salary enhancement, teacher appraisal will not form part of school evaluation.

The accountability debate was, however, important in that it highlighted a need for systematic evaluation in education. Teacher interest was aroused and LEAs began to devise various schemes to encourage school self-evaluation, although current changes, and those expected in the Education Act 1988, make the future of these uncertain.

Notes

1. Three Black Papers were published in 1969 and 1970: 'Fight for Education', 'The Crisis in Education', and 'Goodbye, Mr. Short'. All were edited by C.B. Cox and A.R. Dyson.
2. The discussion of the 'standards' issue is developed further by Lawton (1980) and Reid (1978). Reid demonstrates the similarities between the contemporary debate and earlier debates in British education. For instance, he compares the content of the Yellow Book (the confidential brief for Callaghan's Ruskin College speech) with the proceedings of the Taunton Commission in 1868.
3. Conflicting views concerning state government initiatives in minimum competencies testing are presented in Brandt (1978), Stenhouse (undated), and Murphy and Cohen (1974). The first two concern Florida, and the last relates to Michigan.
4. An account of the California case can be found in Abel and Conner (1978).
5. We have made no attempt to explain why there should be a fragmentation of community and value consensus. This question, whilst of the utmost importance, is beyond the scope of this book. However, in this connection the work of Habermas (1974, 1975) would repay further study.
6. This is fully reported in Becher and Maclure (1978b).

7. On a smaller scale this development also took place in the UK. For instance, subsequent to 1968 (and the Humanities Curriculum Project) Schools Council curriculum development projects had evaluation built into their design.
8. This body was set up soon after Brian Kay, the APU's first director, had visited the USA and investigated the NAEP.
9. It is interesting that Sallis (1979), a member of the Taylor Commission appointed because of her experience as a parent-governor, remains sceptical of consumerism as a way of maintaining and improving standards in education.
10. In the UK the 1980 Education Act required that from 1982 all schools should publish their pupils' results in public examinations.
11. This is borne out in a comprehensive study of the work of LEA advisers carried out by Bolam, Smith and Canter (1978). An important finding was that many advisers did not see inspection as part of their job. However the researchers noted a change in climate during the period of their research (1973-75) which favoured more inspection. This trend has continued and a number of LEAs have changed the titles of their advisers to inspectors.

2 Professional Development and Educational Improvement

Introduction

In this book we have chosen to distinguish three contexts in which evaluation procedures operate. These provide the titles for our first three chapters. The discussion of concepts of accountability in Chapter 1 suggests, however, that such a separation may not be justified. If we accept that accountability can be interpreted in a moral and professional, as well as a contractual, sense then it is possible to *assume* a concept of professional development. If teachers regard themselves as professionally accountable to themselves and their colleagues then they have accepted a commitment to the maintenance and improvement of their practice. Thus professional development becomes a *condition* of professional accountability. According to this interpretation, at least two of the contexts for evaluation that we have identified become aspects of the same thing.

If a narrower interpretation of accountability is adopted, one more closely associated with contractual accountability, then the case for considering the relationship between evaluation and professional development, *as a separate issue,* is strengthened. There seems to be some justification for this since most of the contemporary debate has been concerned with accountability in a 'strict' or contractual sense. Nevertheless it is worth considering whether some *implicit* model of accountability underlies all forms of evaluation whatever their *stated* purposes (an issue that was raised at the very beginning of Chapter 1).

In similar vein, it is also possible to argue that some view of how improvement in practice takes place is a necessary prerequisite of any accountability procedure. After all there is little point in an evaluation revealing educational provision to be unsatisfactory (by anybody's standards) if the question of how the situation may be remedied has not been considered. One British observer (Stones, 1979) has pointed out how curious it is that *assessment* of performance procedures has been developed (by the APU) without any reference to procedures for

28

the *improvement of* performance.

However, perhaps the strongest support for the concept of *professional accountability* derives from the argument that this has the best chance of promoting positive change in the practices of individuals and institutions[1]. This stance is premised on the view that effective change depends on the genuine commitment of those required to implement it, and that commitment can only be achieved if those involved feel that they have control of the process. In other words teachers and schools will readily seek to improve their practice if they regard it as part of their professional responsibility, whereas they are likely to resist change that is forced on them.

This argument has a psychological (and ideological!) appeal although the empirical evidence to support it is rather thin. The work of Bennis, Benne and Chin (1969), and other strategy theorists, is relevant here, although in collating the evidence of various strategies of change little attempt has been made to judge their relative effectiveness. For instance, the major contribution of the research of Bennis *et al* was to *identify* and *describe* three broad categories of strategies for change in social systems:

1. *power-coercive strategies* - based on the intervention of those with legal authority to alter conditions (e.g. the government);
2. *empirical-rational strategies* - based on the assumption that people are rational beings who will change their ideas or behaviour if the effectiveness of a concept or practice is clearly demonstrated by research;
3. *normative-re-educative strategies* - based on the assumption that patterns of action are maintained by the commitment of individuals to socio-cultural norms (the *status quo*). Thus change only occurs when individuals are encouraged to change their normative orientations in attitudes, beliefs, values, knowledge, skills, roles and relationships. In order for this to happen it is necessary to 'activate forces within the system to alter the system'.

In relation to curriculum evaluation, this analysis is important because it can assist the identification of assumptions about change which are implicit in various accountability procedures and evaluation strategies. We shall return to this issue later in this chapter, but before we do we need to take a brief look at the way in which ideas of change have influenced other aspects of education, in particular curriculum development and innovation. Our assumption is that if evaluation is directed towards problem solving (Becher *et al*, 1981, p.22-26) then it presupposes a need for change, and most of the obstacles associated with other forms of educational innovation are likely to be encountered in the implementation of proposed 'remedies'.

Ideas Concerning Educational Development and Change.

When considering those things that prevent the successful implementation of curriculum project materials and strategies, Bolam (1975) located most barriers within the 'user system'. Thus a school's organisational structure, the role of its head, and the values and attitudes of its teachers come to be regarded as crucial to the survival of any curriculum project. According to Hoyle (1975) the root of the innovation problem lies in a dilemma: 'Curriculum innovation requires change in the internal *organisation* of the school. Change in the internal organisation of the school is a major innovation' (p.342). Since social systems, in this instance like physical systems, tend towards inertia, the challenge to innovation is bound up with reversing the usual trend. Hoyle's solution to the problem lies in his concept of the 'creative school': a school whose organisational character is sufficiently 'open' and flexible to enable changes to its authority structures, its decision-making procedures, its professional relationships, and its pedagogical 'code' (eg. from 'traditional' to 'progressive').

Hoyle's major assumption is that the school as *a social system* can be creative. It is an assumption which is open to the charge of *reification* since many people would argue that only individuals can be creative. The OECD Centre for Educational Research and Innovation, for whom Hoyle first wrote his paper, comes to his defence and expounds the relationship between school and the individual in the following way:

> It has been argued that it is the individual not the institution who is creative and that the schools can only adopt the ideas of individuals. Initially new ideas and practices must stem from the imagination and initiatives of individuals and, similarly, innovations developed outside the school will only 'take' if they have the commitment and practical support of the individual teacher. Nevertheless, in practice, innovation must be seen as a function of the quality of the school. There are two reasons for this. Firstly, many

innovations are school-wide in their application and cannot be implemented at all unless a number of teachers, perhaps even the entire staff of a school, both agree to, and become committed to, their implementation. Secondly, because of the integration between different components of the social system of the school, an innovation introduced by a single teacher will often have repercussions in other parts of the system - perhaps because there is a need for additional resources, or for more time, or because it is predicted [sic] upon new pupil roles, or involves a greater degree of integration. This is not to deny the significance of the creative individual, but his or her efforts at innovation can only be really sustained when they take root in and pervade the school as a whole. (OECD, 1978, pp. 15 and 16)

It needs to be acknowledged that Hoyle takes a very wide view of what constitutes a school's 'organisational character' or 'deep structure'. At one point he rephrases the central dilemma of innovation (Hoyle, 1975, p. 341) and in so doing he implies that the most important characteristic of a school's internal organisation is a 'collaborative professional relationship' among teachers. He then argues the case that teacher professionality is both an input *and* output of the school. In other words teacher professionality contributes to the creativity of the school, but the school itself can also be an agent of professional development in teachers. In this context he formulates his now familiar, if still empirically untested, distinction between 'restricted' and 'extended' professionality. The following is a recent formulation of this distinction:

By *restricted* professionality I mean a professionality which is intuitive, classroom-focused, and based on experience rather than theory. The good restricted professional is sensitive to the development of individual pupils, an inventive teacher and a skilful classmanager. He is unencumbered with theory, is not given to comparing his work with that of others, tends not to perceive his classroom activities in a broader context, and values his classroom autonomy. The *extended professional*, on the other hand, is concerned with locating his classroom teaching in a broader educational context, comparing his work with that of other teachers, evaluating his own work systematically, and collaborating with other teachers. Unlike the restricted professional, he is interested in theory and current educational developments. Hence he reads educational books and journals, becomes involved in various professional activities and is concerned to further his own professional development through in-service work. He sees teaching as a rational activity amenable to improvement on the basis of research and development.   (Hoyle, 1980, p. 49)

This description of the extended professional takes some account of Stenhouse's criticism of Hoyle's earlier formulation (Hoyle, 1975, pp. 341 and 342) which seemed to emphasise an uncritical acceptance of theory and consequently reduced teacher autonomy. Some of this criticism still applies but what is perhaps more important is the alternative formulation that Stenhouse offered. For him the critical characteristic of the extended professional is: 'a capacity for autonomous professional self-development through systematic self-study, through the study of the work of other teachers and through the testing of ideas by classroom research procedures' (Stenhouse, 1975, p. 144). This proposition forms the basis of Stenhouse's concept of the 'teacher-as-researcher': an idea which he developed in the context of the Humanities Curriculum Project (HCP), and which has since influenced approaches to curriculum development and curriculum evaluation (especially teacher self-evaluation). According to MacDonald and Walker (1976), HCP offered the teacher a dream-image of himself that, far from undermining his existing professional identity, gave him the opportunity to acquire an additional identity. 'The promise was a future in which through a process of redefinition of the relationship between teacher, taught and knowledge, schools would be transformed into democratic institutions, teachers into research-based master craftsmen of a new professional tradition, and pupils [invariably called "students" by HCP] into reflective scholars' (p. 81). MacDonald and Walker point to the fact that HCP acquired the characteristics of an exclusive club in speculating that, 'Stenhouse invited the teachers to create an alliance with him against the forces of institutional and attitudinal inertia in the school system' (p. 84). What Stenhouse was proposing was a humanistic solution to the dilemma posed by Hoyle. Whereas the problem, as Hoyle saw it, was only amenable at the level of the social system (the creative school), Stenhouse was here proposing systematic change based essentially on individual action. Stenhouse's proposal was in marked contrast, not only to Hoyle's, but, for different reasons, to the tradition of curriculum development that had developed in the 1960s, both in the UK and the USA. As was noted in Chapter 1, the 1960s were characterised by educational expansion on both sides of the Atlantic. It was a time of large scale educational programmes in the United States and the genesis of centralised curriculum development projects in the United Kingdom.

Like the National Science Foundation in the USA, the Nuffield Foundation sponsored a number of ambitious science education projects in
Britain. Although born mainly out of an attempt by the British government to gain control of the curriculum (Lawton, 1980), the 1960s also
saw the establishment of the Schools Council, a quango whose role was
to advise the government on curriculum and examinations. Immediately
dominated by the teacher unions, who were committed to the maintenance of teacher autonomy, the Council soon came to view its tasks as
increasing the range of choice available to teachers but in no way
prescribing what and how they taught. For this reason it initiated a
substantial number of research and development projects from which
teachers and schools could make their choice (a cafeteria system).

Most of these early curriculum development projects approximated
to the Research Development and Diffusion (R, D & D) model of
innovation, which was already familiar in industry and agriculture.
Accordingly the process of curriculum development involved a team of
'experts' at the 'centre' providing the knowledge base for an innovation,
then producing an appropriate content and strategy, and finally
communicating it effectively to potential users at the periphery. The
criteria for judging the success of an innovation became the extent to
which a curriculum package (materials, and/or strategy) was 'adopted'
by the user group. 'Users' were generally regarded as 'passive' but open
to persuasion by rational and empirically supported argument (an
'empirical-rational' strategy in terms of Bennis, Benne and Chin's
categories). Unfortunately practical reality fell somewhat short of the
theoretical ideal. The strategy which had proved so successful in the
sphere of science and technology encountered serious problems when
applied to complex social systems.

Stenhouse's notion of the 'teacher-as-researcher' grew out of his (and
others') disillusionment with the R, D & D model, which began to
appear mechanistic and technocratic (House, 1981) and unlikely to
enjoy the kind of teacher commitment that he saw as necessary for
effective change. In this respect Hoyle shared some of Stenhouse's view
(if only implicitly) since his concept of the 'creative school' and his
concept of the 'extended professional' imply that innovations are
unlikely to be effective unless they take account of the need for
organisational support within the school, or teacher commitment to
professional development.

Whether one takes the view that the whole school (c.f. Hoyle) or
the individual teacher (c.f. Stenhouse) holds the key to successful
curriculum development, the argument for suggesting that the

'periphery' (the schools and teachers), rather than the 'centre' (government bodies or centralised curriculum development agencies), is the prime focus of change is very persuasive[2]. The implication is that the R, D and D or centre-periphery model had been wrongly conceived in its application to education, because it was premised on the possibly mistaken view that people are rational beings who will implement ideas that have been demonstrated to be effective. The experience of the early curriculum projects seemed to demonstrate that it was not sufficient to change knowledge, but necessary also to change the attitudes, values and the taken-for-granted ways of doing things that govern professional activity. Thus 'normative-re-educative' strategies for change came to be regarded as important. The influence of social networks was also acknowledged, as was the need to solve specific problems in specific contexts[3]. For all these reasons an alternative to the centralised curriculum development project was sought, and the ideas of Stenhouse, and those like him, came to have considerable influence. Our response was the growth of school-based curriculum development (SBCD) grounded in 'situational analysis' (Skilbeck, 1975) of the unique patterns of internal and external constraints, influences, needs and resources of individual schools. In the late 1970s this model of curriculum development found favour in the UK. It also underpinned some of the Schools Council's programmes of work in the period 1980 to 1983, which were more concerned with supporting and developing existing initiatives, taken at the 'periphery', than devising new ones from the 'centre'.

The evolution of theory and practice in curriculum development and innovation has, to a large extent, been paralleled in the area of in-service education and training (INSET). The reasons for such a development are much the same. Early forms of INSET were based on courses located outside schools and dealing with generalised INSET issues. Like centralised curriculum development, 'courses have come to be increasingly criticised for their failure to deal with needs in a way which offers ready transfer of practice to the individual teacher's classroom or beyond that to the whole school' (Henderson, 1979, p.19). This loss of faith in course-based INSET to influence practice gave rise to growth of *school-based INSET*: the INSET equivalent of school-based curriculum development. However INSET which is located entirely within the school and drawing exclusively on its own resources can be criticised for parochialism. According to Henderson (1979), 'no school can reasonably be so bold as to suggest tht it has nothing to learn from other schools, from professional teacher-trainers or from educational scholarship and research' (p. 19). Thus a third alternative has emerged: *school-focused INSET.* This attempts to synthesise the course-based and school-based models but 'emphasises the direction of INSET towards the immediate and specific needs of one school and its teachers' (p. 21). Although there is still little empirical evidence of its effectiveness, Bolam (1980) indicates that this approach is gathering considerable support. Indeed this trend has been maintained and further developed under Grant Related In-Service Training (GRIST).

The same may also be true of a similar approach to curriculum development, because a number of recent curriculum development projects have attempted to combine the resource advantages of the centralised project with the relevance of school-based development. The Schools Council Industry Project, now called the School Curriculum and Industry Partnership, could be described as school-focused curriculum development. Assuming that schools-industry liaison is a good thing and that schools should do more of it, the project team has set out to support the development of 'local solutions to local problems', rather than prescribe a particular kind of development. Similarly, the Teacher - Pupil Interaction and the Quality of Learning (TIQL) Project, directed by John Elliott for Schools Council Programme 2, aimed to encourage the development of teachers as researchers by allowing teachers to define their own problems (within a general framework), to carry out their own research, propose subsequent action, and monitor the consequences of its implementation. Likewise the Secondary Science Curriculum Review adopted a periphery-centre strategy whereby the products of local or school-based teachers' working groups were evaluated and published by the central project team. Thus the role of the central team is one of facilitation: the provision of resources, consultancy, practical assistance and co-ordination.

One of the most interesting things about the recent history of curriculum development and in-service education and training is that most strategies owe more to argument than empirical evidence. It is significant that having conducted a review of the 'state of the art' in these areas, and drawn up a list of generalisations about the change process in education, Bolam (1982a) cautions that generalisations 'should be regarded as working hypotheses and pointers for future study since their basis in research is weak' (p. 5). He also makes the point that what evidence there is may be culture-bound, since most of it comes from the USA and possesses a dominant technological perspective[4].

In the UK one of the few recent studies of the impact of educational innovation was undertaken by the Schools' Council's Impact and Take-Up Project (see Steadman, Parsons and Salter, 1980). In order to assess the extent to which the Council's curriculum development had impinged on schools, the researchers chose to investigate the degree of 'contact', 'some use' and 'extensive use' of project materials. Unfortunately these criteria are more problematic than they first appear; among other things they give no indication of what might be a reasonable expectation of success against which percentage 'contact' etc. might be judged.

As early as 1974, Shipman suggested that professional development is possibly the only legitimate indicator of the success of an innovation, although it is considerably more difficult to measure than take-up of project materials. Recent support for Shipman's view comes from Bolam (1982a) who, on the basis of his review of innovation research, emphasises that educational change is a process, not an event, and that the individuals and social systems involved interact with each other over time and are changed by the change process itself. At a common-sense level, therefore, the professional development of teachers, individually or collectively as part of the social system of the school, appears crucially important to the improvement of educational provision. If this is so, it is worth looking at professional development a little more closely.

The Nature of Professional Development

The proposition that professional development assumes a concept of professionalism appears tautological. However, 'professionalism' can be interpreted in a variety of ways, some of which are now regarded as pejorative. Some writers (Hoyle, 1980; OU, 1981c) have pointed out that the notion of professionalism is occasionally used to improve the image, prestige and rewards of teachers with little or no reference to any commitment to improve educational practice. Without the latter, the former is indefensible. It is significant, therefore, that Hoyle (1975, 1980) employs the term 'professionality' in preference to 'professionalism'. He thereby differentiates procedures designed to improve professional *practice* from those concerned with enhancing status. If professional development is understood in terms of increased professionality then clearly it can be associated with the goal of increasing teacher *effectiveness*. No one would deny the value of this.

There is another problem however. This time the difficulty lies not in the term 'professional' but in the term 'development'. 'Professional development' seems to imply that we have some developmental theory concerning the professional growth of teachers, and that it is a 'natural' process. This is the assumption that underpins a comparison between teacher development and child development made by Eraut (1977), an extract from which follows:

1. A teacher doesn't develop a child, but seeks to understand, promote and foster the development which is already taking place. So we cannot have a strategy for teacher development any more than a teacher can have a strategy for child development. We can only have strategies for promoting or fostering teacher development.
2. Teacher development is natural, just as child development is natural. So perhaps we need to be more concerned with providing the right environment and with removing constraints than with creating 'master plans'.
3. Our expectations of teachers have as significant an effect on them as their expectations have on pupils. The best way to promote teacher development may be to expect it, or at least to be careful that one's actions do not implicitly suggest that one does not expect it.
4. The child often learns best when an appropriate variety of concrete experiences are reflected upon, talked about and assimilated or accommodated into his growing mind. Perhaps the reflection upon and discussion of concrete personal experience should play a role of similar importance in teacher development, especially when our language for communicating about educational problems is so obviously deficient. Surely the fact that teachers are at the 'formal operational' stage does not mean that they prefer to discuss at an abstract level! Might it also be that the common phenomenon of token adoption of an innovation is an example of assimilation without accommodation?
5. According to Piaget [1929] the child organises his experience through 'schema'; and according to Kelly [1955] people organise their experience through 'personal constructs'. Even though Piaget was concerned with development and Kelly with personality the comparison increases our understanding of both. It also explains why experience in the classroom is so difficult to communicate. Teacher development has to build on those constructs which exist, and cannot easily be promoted in any other way.
6. The child is best motivated when following his own interests. These are often a combination of personal and peer-group interests; and pursuing them can lead to the development

of a wide range of knowledge and skills. Likewise, the teacher is most motivated to study educational problems when pursuing his own problem defined in his own language. This can also lead to the development of a wide range of knowledge and skills, as nearly all educational problems are multi-faceted and one problem inevitably leads on to another.

(Eraut, 1977, pp. 10-11)

Eraut's argument is appealing particularly in the light of recent experience of curriculum development, outlined in the previous section. However Piaget's theory of child development is an empirically grounded *description* of the *structure* of cognitive learning. We would suggest that there is no comparable description of teacher development as such. (We assume all teachers have reached the stage of 'formal operations'!) Elsewhere, Eraut (1978) admits this himself. In fact, he identifies two theoretical questions to which he seemed to have assumed answers in his earlier paper: (1) Why do teachers change, or fail to change? (2) How do teachers learn? Here, he also contends that 'we have no theory of professional learning on the job which seeks to explain how teachers learn from classroom experience, how they learn from colleagues, or how they learn from people and publications outside the school' (Eraut, 1978, p. 190).

In the absence of a theory (description and explanation) of teacher development, we are left with a number of statements which are essentially normative or prescriptive. In other words they give an account of what a professional *ought* to be like, or *advocate* a particular process for increasing professionality. It should be stressed that this is also true of other so-called developmental theories. For instance, Kohlberg's (1964) theory of the development of moral reasoning has been criticised for proposing a *hierarchy* of stages, supported more by wishful thinking than empirical evidence:

Furthermore, the empirical base of the theory rests on the Kohlberg moral judgement scale. The status of this scale is curious. After more than 23 years of use, the reliability of the measure is still undefined, the validity of the measure unknown, and the scoring system still under development. (See *Psychology Today*, February 1979.) Finally, and most important, Kohlberg's Stage 5 corresponds to traditional conservative legal philosophy, whereas Stage 6 reflects traditional liberal and radical political reasoning. The implication is clear: liberals are more advanced

morally than conservatives. Liberals may appreciate that conclusion, but it has little basis in empirical fact. Thus Kohlberg's
theory seems more a political manifesto than a scientific statement.   (Hogan and Schroeder, 1981)

Could it be that statements about the professional development of
teachers are mostly rhetoric, or at least moral rather than empirical
argument? It seems so. If, however, we accept the moral argument we
still need to find adequate reasons for our belief that professional
development is a good thing *per se*.

Eraut (1977) avoids specifying the *content* or *outcomes* of teacher
development, having rejected the assumption that a teacher who has
developed has necessarily become a better teacher. Other writers are
less hesitant about attempting to describe what a fully developed
professional is like. Hoyle's description of the extended professional is
one such formulation. As we shall see later, a number of school and
teacher self-evaluation schemes are prescriptive in that they are premised on a particular view of the competent professional (and/or
institution). This is perhaps particularly true of LEA schemes (Chapter
6) which are heavily dependent on checklists. *Questions* relating to the
way teachers perform their tasks can readily be translated into *statements* about what teachers *ought* to be doing!

Any prescription of the content or outcomes of teacher development is likely to be controversial because it is formulated from a value-
position, but is a specification of *process* any less contentious? Eraut
(1977) adopts a process viewpoint when he argues that: 'A teacher who
is not developing to any noticeable extent is becoming a worse teacher,
because development is natural and to avoid it is to deteriorate' (p.10).
Stenhouse's concept of 'the teacher as researcher' could be described as
a prescription for the process of teacher development, although the
process, as he conceives it, is not natural but learned.

Whether natural or learned, we would concur with the importance
Eraut attaches to understanding the process of change and the factors
that facilitate or constrain it. As he points out there has been surprisingly little research in this area and what there is derives mostly from the
sociology of education under the heading of teacher socialisation. As
the term 'socialisation' suggests this research has tended to concentrate
on the macro-level, emphasising the influence of the social structure on
the individual. (It has also been more concerned with attitudes and
values than teacher knowledge and skills.) Studies by Dan Lortie
(1975), in the United States, and Colin Lacey (1977), in the UK, have

been less determinist than most. Lacey, for instance, develops a model of socialisation based on a modification of Becker's concept of social strategy. The idea that teachers can have a *strategy* emphasises the power of individuals to act in social situations. This concept of strategy, and the attempt to relate the macro and micro factors that have a bearing on teacher action, constitute the current research interest of a number of educational sociologists (Woods, 1980a; Pollard, 1982a; Riseborough, 1981). One major thrust of this recent research trend is towards greater recognition of what Lortie calls a 'biographical orientation', which investigates the interaction of personal and structural influences in an individual's career.

In general, sociologists are more interested in advancing 'knowledge' than developing strategies to influence 'practice'. However some organisational sociologists and humanistic psychologists working in applied fields have long acknowledged the important influence of personal styles and predispositions on professional and organisational effectiveness. For instance, in the United States, Argyris and Schon (1974) have investigated professional effectiveness at managerial level across a number of professions. Observing that people's perceptions of reality are often determined by their expectations (they see what they want to see) and that this can contribute to a serious disjunction between 'espoused theory' and 'theory in use', they proposed strategies for increasing professional effectiveness based on encouraging receptivity to critical feedback. In the United Kingdom, the Tavistock Institute of Human Relations offers managerial courses on organisational effectiveness and professional development which pay considerable attention to the individual's need for a sense of personal competence.

In the specific context of developing strategies for increasing teacher effectiveness, the importance of this personal dimension has often been neglected, at least in the U.K. Thus teacher education has tended to focus on the needs of children or the needs of the institution, rather than the individual needs and motivations (including career motivations) of teachers. This is not to deny that the purpose of teaching is the education of children, but to stress the crucial relationship between a teacher's professional development and his or her personal growth. During his involvement with the Ford Teaching Project, Elliott (1976) observed a link between a teacher's capacity to develop self-monitoring ability and his tolerance of losses in self-esteem. The source of his personal identity and the nature of financial and status rewards also seemed to affect a teacher's ability to change his classroom practice.

In a recent article, William Taylor (1980) argues that professional development and personal development are not distinguishable processes but one and the same thing. For this reason, programmes of teacher education need to recognise and respect individual teachers' responsibility for their own growth. If they fail in this they are likely to be ineffective and encourage forms of organisation and control that are essentially unprofessional in their character and consequences. Taylor concludes:

> ... one of the essential purposes of every kind of organisational provision must be to establish, maintain and enhance the teacher's own commitment to his own education. Every teacher who makes excessive sacrifices in the time and attention needed for his own personal growth to the demands of the organisation within which he works or to its students is ultimately denying to that organisation and those students the very knowledge, understanding and skill which it is his professional responsibility to offer. It is easier and less contentious to talk about professional development in terms of structures, frameworks, resources and methods, rather than in relation to desirable forms of personal knowledge and understanding. Thus the new interest in professional development ... runs the risk of stressing form at the expense of substance.   (Taylor, 1980, p. 338)

With this the argument comes full circle and we need to ask again: what is more important, the content/outcomes or process of teacher development? (The importance of the personal factor will be taken up again in Chapter 11.)

Professional Development and Institutional Development.

If, as Taylor argues, professional development is closely bound up with personal growth we must question whether it is feasible to talk of institutional development. Quite apart from the earlier argument about reification, is it legitimate to assume that the development of the whole school will be achieved by the collective professional development of its teachers? Or is the organisation more than the sum of its parts? Some people would argue that it is. For instance, in the following extract Alun Jones (1980) argues for an in-school approach to in-service training based on his experience in the Industrial Training Service:

> .. .in-service training is often much less effective than it could be because it is based on an 'educational model' i.e. is focussed largely on the individual. A number of organisations have benefitted from basing their in-service training on an 'organisational learning model' i.e. focussing on a more effective balance between organisational needs and individual needs. At best this achieves virtual elimination of the transfer problem ('I learned a lot of good stuff but we could never apply it here!') as it demands a clear 'contract' being made between any individual and his/her organisation (his 'managers' or superiors) *before* any training takes place. The contract includes agreement not only about *what* new skills and knowledge need to be learned but also about *why* they are needed, *how* they will be applied and *what is expected* to result from them within the school or office.
>
> (Jones, 1980, p.6).

The reference here to 'managers' or 'superiors' as representing the organisation is an interesting one because professional development in this context could be interpreted as merely serving the interest of the dominant hegemony. The model is essentially a conservative one, permitting little radical change of the organisation as a whole (including managers).

The issue, concerning personal versus institutional development, set out in these two very different statements of Taylor and Jones is a fundamental one. Positions taken in relation to it will usually reflect markedly different perspectives regarding the position of people in organisations. On the one hand it will be argued that organisations possess characteristics and pose problems that go beyond those of their individual members; on the other hand, some people will take the view that only people, not systems, are capable of change. In essence this is the same issue as that outlined earlier concerning the creativity of the school. Of course few people possess sufficient evidence to argue strongly for the extreme poles of the personal/institutional development issue, and it is unlikely that even Stenhouse or Hoyle would have denied that there is a middle ground which acknowledges the interaction of the system and the individual. Certainly Bolam (1982a) stresses the dynamic relationship between the two in the process of change. Whatever the relative merits of encouraging teacher development or the development of the whole school, the ultimate goal remains the same: the improvement of opportunities for learning among pupils. In this respect dissatisfied teachers, and schools lacking a sense of common purpose, are unlikely to be able to provide educational experiences of an appropriate quality. The task of management, therefore, is to provide the kind of structures for career development, in-service education, and curriculum development and review that are likely to enhance the quality of educational provision. And it is likely these will incorporate a blend of individual and institutional concerns.

Professional Development and Evaluation.

In much the way that curriculum development and in-service education relinquished their dependence on centralised projects and courses and came to be focused on the particular contexts of schools, so also the preoccupation of project evaluation with theoretical models and procedures gave way to a practical need to solve concrete problems of educational practice in schools. (It is this shift which, as we noted in the Introduction, supplies the chief rationale for this book.) It is interesting therefore that many leading advocates of school-based evaluation have themselves been involved with large-scale project evaluations at some point in their careers (e.g. Elliott, MacDonald, Shipman and Simons). Some of these now strongly argue that evaluation which is initiated and conducted by teachers in response to their own perceived needs and interests has a greater capacity to promote professional development, because the role of teachers is extended but their autonomy is preserved. It becomes the teachers' responsibility to identify and investigate problems connected with their own and their school's practice; to evaluate existing provision in relation to context; and to propose, implement and evaluate remedies that are within their resources.

This view of the potential of evaluation to contribute to change in practice implies support for normative-re-educative strategies of change. As stated earlier these strategies are defined as 'activating forces within the system to alter the system', and they involve either improving the problem-solving capabilities of the system, or releasing and fostering growth in the persons who make up the system to be changed. The promise is that evaluation, particularly self-evaluation, can accomplish these tasks.

According to a number of writers, the crucial condition, governing the effectiveness of evaluation in promoting development, is that *control* of the process should rest entirely with those whose practice is to be evaluated. Simons (1981), for instance, argues that evaluation which is forced on schools by outsiders (a power-coercive strategy) is likely to be half-hearted, distort reality, engender defensiveness and hostility in teachers, and is unlikely to be sustained. For these reasons it is also unlikely to bring about genuine professional development and change. (The concept of *self*-evaluation will be developed further in Chapter 5.)

Simons's argument appeals to common sense but we need to bear in mind an alternative point of view. Compulsion cannot be dismissed as incapable of bringing about change, after all we compel children to attend school between the ages of five and sixteen and it would be foolish to suggest that no genuine change takes place as a result. It is surely true that occasionally interest is awakened only after individuals have been coerced into doing something. Indeed a number of recent centralised initiatives, such as TVEI, seem to be based on this premise, although, as Harland (1985) points out, compliance cannot simply be bought with the allocation of resources. Teachers, schools and LEAs are quite adept at subverting or transforming the aims of central government. Nevertheless, in a liberal democracy, normative-re-educative or empirical-rational strategies for change are generally more acceptable than those that are power-coercive.

In summary then, evaluation in the context of professional development and educational improvement refers to the monitoring of practice in order to diagnose problems and develop, implement and evaluate remedies, or to assure oneself that all is well. It is assumed that the evaluation of particular practices in particular contexts is more relevant to the educational and professional needs of teachers and schools and therefore more likely to result in improvement. Some strategies for evaluation are built on practical theories concerning the way individual professional development takes place; others relate more closely to a concept of institutional development. In *Part Two* we shall examine these in more detail and consider some of the mundane influences which have a bearing on their execution.

Notes

1. Advocates of this view include Elliott (1979), Simons (1981) and MacDonald (1978).
2. Schon (1971) delineated three models of diffusion of innovation: the centre-periphery model, the proliferation of centre model, and the shifting-centres model (the Movement). The centre-periphery model of diffusion is characteristic of the Research Development and Diffusion model of innovation.

3. Havelock (1973) distinguished three principal models of educational change, and added another as a proposal of his own. The three were the R, D and D model, the Social-Interaction model (involving personal contact at diffusion), and the Problem-Solving model (which starts with user needs). His own was a combination of problem-solving and an empirical-rational (R, D and D) approach. He called this his Linkage Model.
4. See also Bolam (1981, 1982b).

3 Curriculum Review

Introduction

Traditionally all schools are involved in routine reviewing of the curriculum, but this may not involve either questioning basic assumptions or considering the whole curriculum of the school. The timetabling operation, a routine review of the curriculum in secondary schools, does not usually question the weighting and nature of subjects offered, or the pupil grouping. New courses may be introduced by subject departments and merely 'fitted into' the timetable. Discussions on core and option schemes covering the final two years of compulsory schooling do of course question some curricular assumptions and consider the curriculum as a whole. Nevertheless the HMI secondary survey (DES, 1979a) expressed some disquiet at the complexity of option schemes and the resulting individual curricula so generated, in addition to their general concern about the extent of the 'core' (too many pupils were discontinuing study of important subjects well before the end of their schooling). In a case study of a school's discussions of an option scheme Hurman (1978, p. 263-4) noted that they were really about the status of various subject departments, and that discussions on the core curriculum ignored what lay beneath the subject label. For pupils of below average ability it is not so unusual to find discussions of the whole curriculum taking place, perhaps because of their perceived 'low' status or because there are no public examination constraints.

Primary schools, while considering the whole curriculum for a single class, assume that 'the primary school curriculum that a particular child encounters [is] ... the sum of his experiences in a number of classes' (Garland, 1981, p.68). Various commentators, therefore, have expressed concern about the lack of attention to the whole curriculum across the primary school[1]; and the Inspectorate in its primary survey (DES, 1978a) was unhappy with the extent of discussion that took place between schools to establish curriculum continuity. It would therefore not be too unfair to conclude that many teachers, whether in primary

46

or secondary schools, are, by tradition, unfamiliar with discussions that involve the whole curriculum of a school[2].

Naturally there are exceptions, and the opening of new schools and the reorganisation under comprehensivisation schemes or falling rolls, provide the ideal opportunity for whole curriculum discussions. Although there is never a clean slate on which to start planning, the new start provides the necessity for such planning. However the examples of planning exercises that come to light are usually the 'exotic' ones that so often feature in Open University case studies: Stantonbury Campus; Countesthorpe College; North Westminster Community School! The general lack of attention to whole curriculum issues has resulted in what Becher and Maclure (1987a) call fragmentation[3]. This occurs at the transition between sectors, at the barriers put up by subject boundaries in secondary schools, and at the ability barriers erected by streaming and banding. Becher and Maclure also lament the reinforcing of subject fragmentation encouraged by the Schools Council, which paid little attention to the whole curriculum; their few attempts giving 'predictably marshmallow results' (p. 63). The House of Commons Committee on Education, Science and Arts (Education, Science and Arts Committee, 1981) was also concerned about the way subject traditions defend their own patch, with the result that pupils receive an offering of a series of unrelated specialisms (paragraph 4.16), and it was anxious to encourage a more holistic consideration of the curriculum. The concentration on parts rather than the whole, Becher and Maclure (1978a) claimed, is the result of decentralisation of curriculum responsibility (p. 168). They felt that clear national guidelines would perhaps help. Certainly the Department of Education and Science and HM Inspectorate think so; indeed, the latter has argued for a common curriculum at secondary level up to sixteen because of the variety of curriculum offerings, the lack of whole curriculum planning, and the need for national decisions in a political democracy to balance the autonomy of the school. But it would be wrong, at least at the secondary level, to see the fragmentation as somehow the fault of narrow, self-interested teachers. Not only do they operate under a variety of influences which limit their room for manoeuvre, but public examinations, based on subjects, are a major constraint, recently reinforced by the subject-based GCSE examinations. In the USA, legislation at both the State and Federal level often similarly defines the parameters within which schools can consider the curriculum[4].

There has, however, been a change of climate in recent years which has been a result of the pressures for accountability spelt out in Chapter 1. Teachers appear to be more willing to support the development of a common core curriculum (Venning, 1979; Wicksteed & Hill, 1979): a change that is mirrored by opinions in the 'Week by Week' column of *Education* (2 Nov. 1979: 11 Jan. 1980) which tries to reflect the current climate. The Great Debate, which we consider in more detail shortly, was largely responsible for this particular change. However this debate, and the ensuing documents, have given rise to a legal-formal or contractual accountability model rather than a partnership model for education, according to Lawton (*TES*, 7 March, 1980). There is also an increasing concern for the curriculum among teachers in other countries, although they often operate in more centralised education systems and have not been 'involved' in the kind of debate that has taken place in England and Wales[5]. The advent of a national curriculum in this country may change this situation.

This chapter, then, will consider the debate which has led to the change in climate, and the nature of the demands being made on schools and their teachers to review the curriculum. In particular it will consider the kind of guidance offered to schools on how to review what they are teaching, and also the issues raised by such an exercise.

The Great Debate and its Aftermath

Chapter 1 has already mentioned the impetus given to the debate by Jim Callaghan's Ruskin speech, and discussed some of the factors which led to accountability pressures. In the context of the debate about the curriculum, economic decline and supposedly falling educational standards were important elements. However, the evidence upon which basic standards were criticised was far from sound (Reid, 1978, chapter 1) and the level of analysis about, for example, a core curriculum was low (Lawton, 1980, p. 38). Nevertheless this speech, and the Yellow Book which formed its brief, helped to initiate the discussion on the common core curriculum. Lawton (1980) traces the stages of the debate, in which the Ruskin speech was followed by a series of regional conferences with participants invited by the DES. Two elements on the agenda of the conferences are of particular note: (1) Curriculum 5-16 - the aims and content of a core curriculum; (2) school and working life, i.e. education for awareness and understanding of the technological and industrial society. These conferences were then followed by a Green Paper (DES, 1977b) which contained a diagnosis of curricular problems in schools, namely, the lack of attention to basic skills and the lack of awareness in schools of the economic needs of the country.

The assumption of failure on basic skills training was subsequently shown to be incorrect when the two surveys by HM Inspectorate were published (DES, 1978a, 1979a), but then, as Reid (1978) argues, the DES seemed more interested in proposing solutions than in defining problems. The Green Paper also argued for a nationally agreed framework for the curriculum and also wanted the local authorities to co-ordinate the curriculum and its developments. This latter requirement brought a circular (14/77) to local authorities requesting information on the curriculum in their schools. The information collected was subsequently published (DES, 1979b); three topics are of particular interest. First, it appeared that there existed few formal and detailed policy statements, within LEAs, to guide schools in curriculum matters, and also that governors had little involvement with the curriculum. Indeed, only a quarter of the LEAs required heads to submit reports to governors and these only occasionally included curriculum items. Secondly, when the Department asked about the balance and breadth of the curriculum it found that few authorities encouraged schools to discuss the issues and it was mainly through routine visits of advisers that concern for balance and breadth was promoted.

The elements of the curriculum considered essential by LEAs were varied and some were reluctant to make any statement on this because they felt it the job of schools. When they did produce statements about the curriculum, about a half used general categories of knowledge, experience and skills (not related to particular subjects), and just over a quarter listed school subjects. The third topic of interest concerned what LEAs did to help schools promote preparation for working life. Sixty per cent claimed that this was done through traditional subjects, although few related this to actual school practice.

This initial investigation and the subsequent discussion (which we will come to shortly) obviously had the desired effect because the follow-up urging the development of curriculum policies at local level (DES Circular 6/81) showed movement on these issues. DES Circular 8/83 requested information on these efforts and preliminary results reported in *Better Schools* (DES, 1985a, pp. 12-13) showed almost a complete reversal of the situation found in the first survey. Most LEAs reported that they had a curriculum policy or were developing one; they consulted widely including with governing bodies; they now recognised the importance of 'breadth' and 'balance', and the need for relevance of the school curriculum to the world outside. On this latter point, however, they did not give details of how this was achieved in schools. (At the time of writing the full report of the survey has yet to be published.)

These circulars, therefore, provided the DES with the evidence to substantiate its concern for the curriculum and the need to arrive at a national framework, presumably to correct the faults it saw. At approximately the same time of the first circular (14/77) data from HMI surveys, and HMI statements on the curriculum (which we shall consider later), were being added to this evidence. However, before considering the statements on the curriculum eventually produced by the DES let us summarise some of the issues of the 'debate'. The centre piece was the desire to create a core curriculum for pupils in schools and to ensure that its content was both 'balanced' and had sufficient 'breadth' (concepts we shall return to later). Further, the DES was anxious to achieve national agreement on a framework for this curriculum. In contrast to the earlier stages of the debate, the concern was to make the common curriculum more than the 'basics' (something not altogether borne out in their subsequent pronouncements). Another issue, providing a constant theme, was the role of the school in promoting wealth creation. Although born out of a concern for the economic decline of Britain, such an emphasis provides a sad irony in the 1980s with massive youth unemployment. Thus the role of the school in promoting economic change was stated, but little debated, and reference was never made to studies which showed the difficulties of such a role[6]. True to Reid's claim (Reid, 1978) that the debate jumped to solutions, we now find that a major response to economic decline and youth unemployment has been the Youth Training Scheme organised through the Manpower Services Commission of the Department of Employment, in which the school sector plays little part. (See also OU, 1983b, Units 29 and 30.)

Whatever criticisms one may want to make of the quality of the evidence and analysis of the debate, it is hard to deny its effectiveness in changing the climate with regard to the control of the curriculum[7]. The DES has made the idea of a national framework more widely acceptable, and, as we shall show, is moving towards some kind of national prescription. It has also encouraged LEAs to exercise their responsibilities for the curriculum and encouraged those outside schools, such as governors and people in industry, to play a more important part in discussions about the curriculum. Finally, schools have been expected to initiate discussions and reviews of the curriculum — a change from the more usual state of affairs with regard to whole curriculum issues (a point we made earlier).

National Frameworks for the Curriculum

We now turn to statements on the curriculum that came out of the debate. These statements suggested that schools and LEAs should engage in an analysis of the curriculum and they offered possible kinds of analyses, as well as prescriptions for the curriculum itself. What they proposed, and the reactions to these proposals, are of interest to schools faced with the task of curriculum review.

The first attempt was put forward for consultation: *A Framework for the School Curriculum* (DES, 1980a). It posed questions about the core curriculum, gave an outline of such a core and stressed the need for schools to have written educational aims. The questions on the core curriculum concerned its nature, i.e. whether it should be a narrow core or cover most of a pupil's curriculum, and the way it should be expressed, i.e. in terms of school subjects or educational objectives. The core curriculum outlined by the document did in fact use school subjects: English, mathematics, science, religious and physical education, with modern languages being studied by most secondary school pupils. Other subjects were grouped under the general heading of 'preparation for adult life' and included: craft, design and technology; arts, including music and drama; history and geography; moral education; health education and preparation for parenthood and family life; careers education and vocational guidance. In addition to specifying what the core should contain, the framework laid down the percentage of the timetable to be allocated to some subjects, for example, English and mathematics were each to be allocated ten per cent. The document argued that a school would be more effective in achieving its aims if they were written down and it suggested six possible aims expressed at a high level of generality, for example: to develop lively enquiring minds . . . ; to acquire the knowledge and skills relevant to adult life and employment in a fast-changing world.

With such general aims it is not surprising that some of the reactions were as scathing as those of Max Morris, a former President of the NUT: 'As a pot-pourri of platitudes, a compendium of trite banalities . . . [the *Framework*] . . . would be hard to emulate (*TES*, 8 February 1980). Although many of the reactions were hostile, there was some welcome for the idea of a framework and for the consultation process[8]. Even Max Morris, despite his comments on the contents of the document, warned against belittling the importance of the debate on the curriculum. Besides general criticisms about the framework, some specifically focused on the undue emphasis on subjects[9], the neglect of a consideration of teaching methods[10], the specification of percentage time allocations, and the dominance of national needs as a criterion for selecting or determining the curriculum[11]. One interesting reaction was that in stating, for example, that science should be taught to all pupils in some form or other in the last two years of schooling for 10-20 per cent of the time (in addition to a broad course up to age 13 years), the DES was implicitly committing itself to increased resources, in terms of teachers and facilities.

It may have been such a realisation (along with the generally hostile reaction to the *Framework* document) that encouraged the DES to be less specific in its second attempt at producing a framework for the curriculum (almost a year after its first attempt). As before, this new document, *The School Curriculum* (DES, 1981b), emphasised preparation for adult life and the economic needs of the country, and repeated the list of aims claiming that they had been widely accepted during consultations. These aims were to be used as a checklist to test curriculum policies. Again LEAs were requested to draw up curriculum policies and schools were expected to set out their aims in writing. Schools were also expected to recognise that the curriculum could be described and analysed in a variety of ways. Two requirements guided the DES specification: the need for what is taught and how it is taught to reflect the values of society; the need for a broad curriculum (in terms of subjects). The document then outlined what the Secretaries of State for Education thought should be the curriculum in primary and secondary schools. The primary school curriculum was to go beyond the basics of English and mathematics, which in any case should be seen in the wider context of other subjects. Key elements identified included: multicultural aspects of Britain today; an understanding of the world; experience of elementary science work; music; and the personal and social development of pupils. In addition to these key elements specific mention was made of topic work, science, art and craft and French. The secondary school curriculum was described in much the same terms as in the previous framework, but time allocations were not specified.

The School Curriculum was distributed to every school in England and Wales, and perhaps for this reason there was a wider span of reactions, some of which seemed more positive. For example, of five head-teachers invited to give reactions in the *Times Educational Supplement* (10 April 1981), two were very positive, one somewhat neutral, and two hostile[12]. As before many recognised the importance of the document in initiating debate on the curriculum[13]. The problems identified by commentators, included those raised in connection with the previous document: the dominance of subjects[14], the neglect of teaching methods, and the implied need for increased resources. To these were added worries about the lack of justification of the proposals (Rigby, 1982), and the fact that the examination system was totally ignored[15]. A major critique of the document expressed concern about the nature of the analysis, not just in terms of the way the curriculum was described, but in terms of the view of culture that was used to select items for inclusion in the curriculum (White *et al*, 1981). It is the lack of quality of the analysis that provided the thrust of a swingeing attack by a committee of the House of Commons (Education, Science and Arts Committee, 1981), in relation to the limitation of subjects. Unlike the DES, this Committee took account of some of the literature in the field, including the work of HM Inspectorate (DES, 1977a), and some academics. They commended also the parallel work carried out in Scotland by a committee under the chairmanship of Munn, a Rector of a Glasgow high school (Scottish Education Department, 1977a). This (Munn) Report was thought by the Committee of the House of Commons to be altogether more sophisticated an analysis, with its recognition of the debatable nature of the fundamental principles underlying a specification of the school curriculum. Because of the perceived importance of the Munn approach and because it represents a parallel exercise at defining a national framework, we turn to a more detailed examination of it next.

The Munn Report examined the structure of the curriculum in the last two years of compulsory schooling in Scotland, and carried out its work almost at the same time as the Dunning Committee considered the aims, purposes and forms of assessment for the whole ability range. In fact the Dunning Committee reported first (Scottish Education Department, 1977b). Inevitably this committee had to consider the effect of public examinations upon the school curriculum. This it did in terms of the effect on the whole curriculum, and on individual subjects. It saw a role for internal assessment (internal to the school) in helping to release the school curriculum from total control by examination syllabuses originating outside of the school[16]. The Munn Report, therefore, started with an analysis of the present situation, which considered such issues as certificate versus non-certificate courses[17], the problem of lower ability children being pushed into 'O' grade examinations which they were not intended to cater for, the need to prepare pupils for life in a modern industrial society, and the importance of analysing the content, teaching methods, learning milieu, and informal aspects of the curriculum. It next considered the problem of designing the curriculum, and in particular the competing claims on the curriculum from society, from epistemology (i.e. theories on the nature of knowledge), and from the psychology of pupils. These competing claims usually emerged as community-centred, subject-centred and child-centred curricula, but the report argued that these could be reconciled. It did this by proposing four aims concerning knowledge, skills, affective development and the demands of society. These aims, it argued, should be used as criteria for determining the scope of the formal curriculum, which could further be expressed in terms of eight modes of activity: linguistic and library study; mathematical studies; scientific study; social studies; creative and aesthetic studies; physical activity; religious studies; morality. However, these are theoretical constructs which must be translated into an actual curriculum; inevitably this leads to a consideration of curriculum organisation, particularly subject-based versus 'integrated' or 'interdisciplinary' approaches. The report rejected integrated studies, although it nowhere defined what they are[18], and the curriculum it arrived at was again reduced to subjects. It proposed four compulsory subjects: English, mathematics, physical education, and religious and moral education. In the remaining three compulsory areas, i.e. science, social studies and creative arts, it proposed that pupils should study at least one subject which falls under these headings. Thus, for example, biology or food science could represent science, and geography or history could represent social studies. However, the Munn Committee realised that in the area of social studies, in addition to subjects such as history or geography, pupils would have to study units on political, economic, industrial and environmental aspects of life in modern society. Also for creative arts, a weekly period of music and art would be insufficient; rather, a rotational arrangement should be employed 'which allowed pupils to spend more time on music, say, for part of two years, with the opportunity for work in art and perhaps drama at other times' (paragraph 5.19). For each of the areas a recommended number of periods was given.

When considering assessment the Munn Report recommended that all subjects should be examined, with three levels of syllabuses to accommodate different ability groups. However, they stopped short of recommending a group certificate for the core areas, because this would effectively force their view of the curriculum on local authorities and schools[19].

The analysis represented by the Munn Report was indeed more sophisticated than that of the DES document; the fact that the former was drawn up by professionals rather than civil servants may have something to do with this. However, a number of criticisms can still be made.

Most notable is the observation that the reliance on subjects to express the actual curriculum can be seen as a rationalisation of its present form (Darling, 1978). Certainly the resulting curriculum looks rather dull compared with the initial considerations which offered the possibility of a refreshing new view. But even the more sophisticated thinking concerning the competing claims of the curriculum, and the eight modes of activity, have been criticised (Darling, 1978). How, the critique goes, can fervently-held views of the curriculum as represented by community-, subject- and child-based approaches be reconciled in a paragraph? It could well be argued that the committee under-played the ideological differences that exist between such approaches to the curriculum (an issue we shall return to later).

Finally, although the committee went to great lengths to argue the case for and against integration, have they not indeed simply rationalised the *status quo*? A major part of the argument against integration was based on the reaction of teachers rather than any theoretical problems[20]. Yet, in the context of the core curriculum, a number of well known 'practitioners' have argued for the necessity of a fundamental examination of the organisation of the curriculum, suggesting that the only way to achieve a sensible broad core is to integrate subjects[21].

HM Inspectorate's Reports

The DES documents on the curriculum can be contrasted unfavourably with the HMI equivalents (White, 1982b). The former take little account of the latter although much of the HMI's thinking has become known over the same period i.e. the late 1970s and early 1980s. As we noted earlier the surveys of both secondary and primary schools (DES, 1978a and 1979a) provided information on what was happening in schools, although they were restricted (in the case of the secondary survey particularly) to a subject-based analysis of the curriculum[22]. In the secondary survey the Inspectorate expressed concern for the balance, breadth, complexity (of options) and coherence of the curriculum. The primary school survey expressed concern for the range of work, i.e. too much emphasis on the basics, and the lack of continuity (a point we have noted already).

These surveys, although not published before the first major statement on the curriculum, must have influenced HMI thinking. The first document, *Curriculum 11-16* (DES, 1977a), was generally thought to be useful. In contrast to the later subject-based discussions of the

DES, this document proposed that the curriculum should be composed of eight areas of experience: aesthetic and creative; ethical; linguistic; mathematical; scientific; physical; social and political; spiritual. No justification was offered for these areas; neither are they identical to the six lines of development adopted by the Assessment of Performance Unit[23], which also involved HMIs. Of particular interest are those parts of *Curriculum 11-16* that include discussions of 'school and society' and 'schools and preparation for work'. The former includes a recognition of the conflict in schools between socialisation and the fostering of the autonomy of the individual, as well as the political and social assumptions and values implied in the curriculum. In particular the HMI discuss the role of schools in a changing society, arguing, for example, that schools have a limited role in social change, and rejecting the 'curriculum for violent change' (DES, 1977a, p. 9). Their discussion of preparation for work recognises that in the economic conditions of the early 1980s (which were evident in 1977), there is a need to prepare for unemployment. Later, these ideas on the curriculum moved beyond a public statement of the views of some of the Inspectorate and became the basis of a curriculum appraisal scheme in conjunction with five LEAs (DES, 1981a). In reviewing their curricula schools in these LEAs considered three areas: the education of the individual (in terms of subjects and the eight areas of experience); preparation for the world of work; education and society. In this context there seems to have been some unexplained change of thinking on the part of the Inspectorate because the eight areas of experience (in *Curriculum 11-16*) were seen as a way of considering a common curriculum, presumably satisfying all aspects of the curriculum *including* 'education and society' and 'working life'. In the report of the exercise with the LEAs (DES, 1981a), however, their scope is limited to 'education and the individual'. We will look at the details of the exercise in Chapter 8; for the moment it is worth noting that the review centred around an analysis of school subjects in terms of skills, concepts, and attitudes (expressed in terms of aims and objectives), and an analysis of the contribution of subjects to the eight areas of experience. It is also worth noting that Lawton (1980, p. 48) claims that the HMIs may be pushing a model of curriculum planning (based upon statements of aims and objectives) which is out of date — an issue we return to later in the chapter, and in Chapter 8. This model found full expression in the final document of the exercise (DES, 1983a), where a specification for an 'entitlement curriculum' was given. It was done in terms of what the specification should include, and a discussion of possible contents. Four elements of the specification are of particular importance here: a statement of aims relating to the education of individual pupils, and to the preparation for life after school; a statement of objectives in terms of skills, attitudes, concepts and knowledge; a balanced allocation of time for the eight areas of experience; and methods of teaching and learning which will achieve the objectives. It went on to give possible aims and objectives for the curriculum, but in the spirit of showing the process of curriculum appraisal that HMI, and the participating LEAs, hope will be attempted by schools.

Coinciding with the time of discussion on the national framework for the curriculum initiated by the DES, the Inspectorate issued a document giving their 'view of the curriculum' (DES, 1980b). This was a more pragmatic statement than *Curriculum 11-16* (DES, 1977a). Although it recognised that the eight areas of experience were important, the secondary school curriculum was discussed largely in terms of subjects because that is how secondary education is organised. The areas of experience seemed to be reserved for describing areas such as arts and applied crafts (aesthetic and creative experience), and history, geography, economics, social and environmental studies (social and political education). Despite the work of the surveys no reference was made to the importance of teaching method.

The latest statement (at the time of writing) from HMI is the culmination of their surveys (DES, 1978a and 1979a) and the *Curriculum 1 1-16* series (DES, 1977a, 1981a, 1983a). It employs what are described as 'two essential and complementary perspectives' (DES, 1985d, p. 13) as an overall framework; namely, the areas of learning and experience, and elements of learning. The areas of learning and experience are those identified earlier, except that they added one more: technological. They admit that these represent only one, and not original, point of view. The elements of learning are the skills, attitudes, concepts and knowledge outlined in the last *Curriculum 11-16* document (DES, 1983a). Only in the case of skills do they actually list what they think are the appropriate elements of learning. What they are offering through this framework are checklists to aid the development of a curriculum. In addition they elaborate several desirable characteristics of the curriculum; breadth, balance, relevance, differentiation, progression, and continuity.

Schools Council Statements

At about the same time as *The School Curriculum* was being prepared by the DES, the now defunct Schools Council was preparing its own document. Interestingly, despite DES and HMI representation on the Council, no connection existed between the two publications. *The Practical Curriculum* (Schools Council, 1981) was not in fact the Schools Council's version of a national framework for the curriculum, rather it was 'an incitement to critical self-evaluation' (p. 11) by schools. It provided no prescriptions for the substantive curriculum, except at the level of general aims, and these only by way of suggestion. The first major chapter of the document contains a discussion of various types of rationale that teachers could use for thinking about the curriculum. These include statements of general and specific aims, learning experiences, various forms of knowledge and areas of experience (e.g. the cognitive-based analysis of Hirst and Peters (Hirst, 1974) and the HMI areas discussed earlier), skills, and modes of expression (verbal and non-verbal). In addition values and attitudes are considered since they are apparent in both the formal and hidden curriculum. Each theme is offered as a suggestion about how schools could start planning the curriculum. The other chapters consider the mechanics of this planning (e.g. staff specifically responsible for it), as well as ways of monitoring and assessing the resulting curriculum[24]. In essence, as noted above, it presents guidelines for self-evaluation, and curriculum planning.

Central Directives

All of the documents considered so far have been intended as items for discussion or guidance to schools and local authorities. Even *The School Curriculum* (DES, 1981b), although issued to all schools, had no force of law. However, the DES, despite its history of neglect of the curriculum, started to move cautiously into this domain. The information collected from Circular 14/77 (see DES, 1979b) encouraged the DES to take further steps. Thus the 1980 Education Act made it a requirement for all schools to provide public information on the curriculum. As noted earlier this was extended by Circular 6/81 which urged LEAs to comply with the recommendations in *The School Curriculum.* These efforts by the government were given more force through the White Paper *Better Schools* (DES, 1985a), which outlined the aims that had been emerging through the previous documents. It picked up the principles (as it called them) enunciated by HMI, that is, breadth, balance, relevance, and differentiation. Although acknowledging that it was possible to analyse the curriculum in a variety of ways, the White Paper suggested that this was best done through subjects, particularly at secondary level. In fact even their proposals for the primary curriculum were largely described in terms of subjects (e.g. maths, language, science, history, geography, religious education, craft). *Better Schools* signalled the government's intention to offer a further statement on the organisation and content of the 5-16 curriculum. As we go to press the DES are in the process of drawing up details on various subjects; to date these include English, mathematics, and possibly technology. To follow up the concern in the White Paper for the definition of levels of attainment (DES, 1985a, p. 26), the government intend to introduce some kind of benchmark assessment, a point we made earlier, in an effort to improve standards.

In the USA a state defined curriculum, often enshrined in legislation, requires school district authorities to improve and develop the curriculum through a framework. One such framework, suggested by the California State Education Department (1977), is expected to contain the goals of instruction, an outline of the concepts and processes to be taught, the content objectives, the appropriate teaching strategies and learning activities, and the tests, student self-assessment and teacher evaluation required. There is obviously little room for the school to be directly involved in curriculum development at any level. This might well come to be true in secondary schools in England and Wales through the formulation of a national curriculum and the defining of national criteria for GCSE and the so-called benchmarks.

Issues

Having looked at some of the major developments in encouraging teachers, and others, to review the curriculum, we want now to consider the issues raised by such a review. In particular we shall discuss the nature of the evaluative activity being required, the type of analysis expected, the value issues involved in a review, the process of review suggested, and who is expected to carry it out.

First, the nature of the evaluation. It is clear that the focus is on what *ought* to be taught: the *intended curriculum*. This being so, the principal concern must be for the worth and value of the planned activities: something that requires an *intrinsic evaluation*. This type of evaluation can be contrasted with empirical evaluations, which most of the later chapters of this book consider, and which require a consideration of the curriculum *as experienced* by the pupils. Such a distinction is not accepted by all commentators, as we shall show, but where evaluating the intended curriculum is accepted, there are clearly a variety of ways of analysing it. We have already noted the criticisms about the use of subjects as an analytic tool, the neglect of teaching methods, and the lack of awareness of other forms of analysis on the part of, for example, the DES. Indeed the poverty of the DES analysis in *The School Curriculum* led the Committee of the House of Commons (Education, Science and Arts Committee, 1981) to advise headteachers to rely upon common sense rather than the analysis presented by the DES!

Many would readily accept the limitations of subjects as a basis for analysing the curriculum because, for example, they tend to emphasise cognition while ignoring affective aspects of education. On the other hand, the HMI's nine areas of experience, although offering an interesting alternative, appear to have a certain arbitrariness about them, especially when one (technological) is added with no explanation as to why. Halpin (1980), for example, questions their similarity with the APU lines of development which, because they were tentatively suggested, were specifically *not* intended as a curriculum model. If there is no particular justification for these categories, and they appear to be somewhat arbitrary, what faith can schools then have in them as a basis for review? The Munn Report (Scottish Education Department, 1977a) proposed a list similar to that of the HMI, and Darling (1978) criticised it for being similar to those proposed by Hirst and therefore following his view that education is basically about the development of the mind[25]. Such an approach would minimise affective elements of the curriculum; something the Munn Committee was anxious to avoid. In a rejoinder to Darling's criticisms, Kirk (1978), a member of the committee, points out the specific references in the report to the weakness of Hirst's approach, and the addition of appeals to the social usefulness of educational activities (something foreign to Hirst who was concerned primarily with intrinsic worth) as evidence of an attempt to look beyond a cognitive based curriculum[26].

A lot of course depends upon how these various 'areas' and 'modes' are translated into learning activities. Clarke (1979), having noted that the areas of experience are a good starting point but too generalised, suggests that they be elaborated by specifying for each, the basic skills, specific experiences and factual knowledge involved. He then goes on to outline some examples for the primary school curriculum. Skilbeck, in commenting upon the progress of the national frameworks (*TES*, 4 December 1981), suggests that in addition to setting out areas of knowledge, understanding and human activity firmly and clearly, the various kinds of learning experiences and learning situations also need defining. In making this request he is echoing the kind of analysis employed by the Curriculum Development Centre in Australia, where he was Director. This approach, whilst employing a similar list of areas of experience[27] to that employed in *Curriculum 11-16* and the Munn Report, avoids the criticism of ignoring teaching methods. Chanan has questioned the basic analysis of national needs employed by the DES (*TES*, 26 June 1980), as we have already mentioned; he goes on to propose a curriculum based on personal values. A person's ability to relate to wider issues means mastering relationships in the immediate community - initially the home, because family life is where personal and public life meet face to face. Chanan's argument is that with more than twice as many people who are non-working as are involved in manufacturing, their role in reinvigorating the community can, and should, be developed. Although this argument is not developed into specific proposals for the curriculum, if it were it would lead to a very different form from that of the DES[28].

It is worth noting that in the USA there is a long tradition of national commissions on the curriculum, as well as a considerable academic literature that has influenced British thinking. Van Til (1976), in reviewing reports up to the 1970s, concludes that the seven Cardinal Principles of Secondary Education, proposed by the Commission on the Reorganisation of Secondary Education in 1918, still apply. These principles dealt with health, a command of fundamental processes (e.g. writing), worthy home membership, vocation, civic education, worthy use of leisure, ethical character. He then traces four traditions on sources of curriculum content, which are similar to the three conflicting claims recognised by the Munn Report, namely: the needs of learners; demands of society and social realities; clarification of values for democratic life; structure of disciplines. These four traditions have varied in eminence over time and Van Til argues that the claims on the curriculum are no longer based on a single source - a conclusion in line with the Munn Report. From the interaction of the sources of the curriculum he identifies sixteen 'centres of experience'[29], but he provides no rationale or justification for them. Despite Van Til's apparent confidence in arriving at a model for the curriculum, Cowen (1981) says that currently the USA has no inclusion or exclusion principles for selecting curriculum content because: there is a lack of curriculum theory; the 'demands of society' as a principle has weakened; and the subject disciplines have also passed their time as a selection principle.

For a school seeking guidance the picture is a confusing one; a wide variety of analyses of the curriculum are available but with conflicting claims as to their usefulness. What is clear is that the DES, and perhaps even the Inspectorate, portray the task of curriculum review in rather too simplistic a fashion. Chapter 8 cannot claim to clear up the confusing array of approaches but it will offer some guidance, though with the definition of a national curriculum the role for the school in this is unclear.

The next issue is closely related to the value issues involved in curriculum review. *The School Curriculum* (DES, 1981b) took the simplistic view, saying that the values of society should be reflected in the curriculum. As mentioned earlier, the HMIs took an altogether more sophisticated view of the relationship of education to society and to social change, and like the Education, Science and Arts Committee (1981) saw a conflict between transmitting the values of society and preparing young people to change those values. Of course, transmitting values through the curriculum assumes a degree of consensus, the existence of which is questionable in a pluralist society (Becher and Maclure, 1978a). Such a problem is related to the different value positions represented by the three competing claims identified in the Munn Report, i.e. community-based, subject-based and child-based. It is not that the advocates of these approaches to the curriculum take different views of the nature of society, but that they fundamentally differ regarding the purposes of education. Skilbeck (OU, 1976, Unit 3) employs the idea of ideology (a system of beliefs and values of a social group) to describe powerful traditions which create educational theories. The three educational ideologies he considers, i.e. reconstructionism, classical humanism and progressivism, roughly correspond to the community-centred, subject-centred and child-centred curriculum respectively, although the community-centred curriculum can also be a form of 'instrumentalism' (OU, 1983b, Unit 2). The Munn Report (Scottish Education Department 1977a) claimed that these positions could be reconciled, but Skilbeck says of the three educational ideologies: 'each is a powerful force in contemporary educational thought and practice ... each can be seen as a comprehensive and well-articulated position' (OU, 1976, Unit 3, p. 24). Given such a statement, perhaps Darling (1978) was correct in questioning the confidence with which the Munn Report claimed that the conflicts between the traditions could be resolved. But at least the Munn Committee recognised the problem; something the DES and HMI largely ignored. What evidence exists, both in Britain and Australia, about the diversity of teachers' values (e.g. Ashton *et al*, 1975, and Kallenberger, 1981) also makes it uncertain whether the conflicts will be easily resolved. What is important is the recognition that curricular decision-making is a process of assigning value and particularly of *resolving* value conflicts (Kirst and Walker, 1971) - a practical rather than theoretical activity.

If curricular decision-making can be described in this way, then we need to consider whether the processes of review advocated are suitable for such a fundamental task. The approaches advocated by the DES, HMI and the Scottish Education Department follow a procedure very common in the USA, i.e. starting with a statement of aims and setting out areas, or whatever, that will satisfy these aims. Walker (1975) showed that when he monitored real curriculum decision-making, albeit in the context of a curriculum project, he found that statements of aims did not dominate. Again there is a considerable literature on the use of aims and objectives in curriculum planning that casts doubts on its efficacy. Chapter 1 has already made reference to the dominance of this approach in the USA, and Chapter 8 will consider some of the arguments for and against it. One of the major arguments against the approach is that it attempts to deal with curriculum problems involving value issues in a procedural way, i.e. by applying a suitable formula or technique (Reid, 1978, p. 41). Drawing on Reid's thinking, Halpin (1980) poses four questions to be asked about the approach to curriculum review advocated by the HMI in *Curriculum 11-16*. Although agreeing that this approach raises value issues (his first question), he thinks it of limited use in generating a range of curriculum alternatives (second question), that it ignores the effects of choosing particular courses of action (third question), and does not facilitate an examination of teacher's common sense beliefs and opinions (fourth question). Reid (1978) argues that for curriculum problems the process of deliberation is required: a process described empirically by Walker (1975), and which we shall examine further in Chapter 8.

This brings us to our final issue: who should carry out curriculum review? The assumption usually made is that it should be the teachers in schools who review the curriculum. With important value issues at stake it is difficult to deny the involvement of others. Governors of schools are the most frequently mentioned group and Circular 6/81 asked them to encourage schools to carry out a review[30]. *Better Schools* (DES, 1985a, p. 68) indicated the duty the governors would have in determining the curricular aims and objectives, and subsequent Education Acts have put this into legislation. Before asking whether others should be involved, however, it is worth asking if *teachers* are presently involved in curriculum planning. Keast (1980) states that curriculum planning should be seen as a right by primary school teachers, not just an activity for headteachers. In contrast, the Munn Report (Scottish Education Department, 1977a) assumed that headteachers would take the broad decisions after consultation. Thus subject departments and individual teachers are to be involved in forming curriculum policies rather than having rights over such policies. The international evidence of teacher involvement in curriculum planning indicates little possibility for ordinary teachers[31]. In Britain, where there has been a tradition of less direct central control, the climate created by the headteachers is likely to be the most important factor in determining teacher involvement.

Even if teachers are involved do they have the requisite skills? Bridges (1979) certainly doesn't think so because he sees the curriculum as a selection from culture requiring value judgements over which teachers have no monopoly of wisdom. Mills (1980) argues that both initial and in-service teacher education fails to prepare them for the task. Skilbeck (1981), in the Australian context, also wonders whether teachers are yet ready for the task, and states that the importance of in-service education and training has not yet been recognised.

Regarding the involvement of others, besides teachers, we are unlikely to have a Swedish style debate in Parliament, despite the fact that the community has a right to it, and that curricular decision-making is a political act (Becher and Maclure, 1978a). The Taylor Report (DES, 1977c) recommended a strong role for the governing board in keeping the school's activities under review; a position backed by the Education, Science and Arts Committee (1981) of the House of Commons, and as indicated subsequently incorporated into legislation. In Britain no systematic evidence exists of the role of governing bodies in reviewing the curriculum. In Victoria State, in Australia, Schools Councils (a form of governing body) do participate in review activities (Skilbeck, 1981), and in Chapter 6 we shall see an example of this involvement. The involvement of others in planning assumes, of course, that the curriculum that is laid down is compulsory, or mostly compulsory. It is perfectly possible, as Griffen explains (*TES*, 26 March 1982), to allow pupil and parent choice, but there is no evidence that his is other than an isolated example.

Conclusion

The idea of curriculum review has been brought into the schools' arena, though whether it will take off as a regular and meaningful exercise seems doubtful. Certainly the advice for carrying out a review, offered by official sources, is not altogether complete, and, as we have argued, it ignores work already done. Even more noticeably lacking is the support for such exercises; a point that became clear in the HMI-LEA curriculum appraisal activity (DES, 1981a), where advisers, for example, were unable to provide the support required. It remains to be seen whether contracts or staffing plans will take account of the work being required by central directives.

Whatever the problems for a school carrying out a review, there remains an ambiguity about where the focus of curricular control lies. Even if the DES does not grasp control, will schools be free to determine the curriculum? LEAs were encouraged to take a larger part in determining policies and ensuring schools follow them, but recent changes mentioned in Chapter 1 casts doubt on their future role. The predominant constraint is, of course, public examinations. Although most directly affecting secondary schools, this constraint has a backwash effect on primary schools. If, as Marland (1981) suggests, schools should develop new integrated subjects they will be faced with the task of getting them approved by the Secondary Examinations Council under the National Criteria for the various conventional subjects. For schools, there is also the additional constraint of curriculum-led staffing. While it may help protect the existing curriculum against falling rolls[32] it will also reduce the curricular decision-making capacity of the school. The question that must be answered is: will the exercise of curriculum review be a hollow one, resulting in schools simply justifying what they currently do, or becoming frustrated by their inability to follow through the consequences of their thinking?

Notes

1.   Garland (1981), for example, says that there are problems of balance, cohesion, sequence and progression as a consequence of the class teaching system. Clarke (1979) goes as far as to say that individual teachers following their own dictates are not likely to produce a balanced programme of work.
2.   A conclusion reached by HMI in their secondary survey (DES, 1979a, p. 42). In case studies of schools Weston (1977, p. 109) found that only senior teachers, and those with responsibility for planning at school level,

looked beyond their commitment to their own subject or to the aspect of the school that was their immediate concern. Similarly Mills (1980) found that less experienced primary teachers tended not to look beyond their own classrooms.

3.   In the USA in the 1960s, fragmentation was also seen as one of several shortcomings by Broudy, Smith and Burnett (1964). In 1978 the theme of one issue of 'Educational Leadership' (Vol 36, No. 2, November) was the 'patchwork curriculum' a reference to a lack of coherence and the fragmentary nature of the curriculum.

4.   California for example lays down frameworks in various subjects areas backed by State Legislation (California State Department of Education, 1977). Cowen (1981) claims that the 1958 Defence Education Act, which followed the launch of a Sputnik, assured the dominance of academic subjects in curriculum development for many years. (See also Pinar and Grumet, 1981.)

5.   Withers (1982), Skilbeck (1981), Musgrave (1979), and Cohen and Harrison (1979) report some decentralisation in Australia, although state education departments still retain the major control. A similar situation exists in Canada according to Watson (1979). In the USA teachers have lost control, but increased militancy may make them assert their rights through their contracts of employment (Cowen, 1981).

6.   Some of these studies (e.g. Foster, 1965) were carried out in developing countries where the governments are faced with investment choices, for example, rural development schemes versus education.

7.   Salter & Tapper (1981) examine the Great Debate and its aftermath from this stance, considering what it reveals about the bureaucratisation of educational power and the process of educational change.

8.   For example, Edwards in *Education's* 'Week by Week' (11 January 1980) and the National Association of Head Teachers' report in *Education's* 'Curriculum' column (18 January 1980).

9.   The reaction of the Secondary Heads Association report in the 'Curriculum' column, *Education* (18 January 1980).

10.   For example, John Tomlinson, chairman of the Schools Council, *Education* (29 February 1980).

11.   The NUT were worried about who defined the national needs (Reported in *Education's* 'Curriculum' column, 18 January, 1980). Others thought the analysis incorrect. For example Walter James, a professor of education, thought it strange that wealth production was being pushed just when Britain was experiencing economic decline (*Education*, 21 November 1980). Gabriel Chanan of the National Foundation for Educational Research argued that the emphasis on industry and manufacturing ignored the statistics which showed a minority involved in this sector. (*TES*, 26 June 1980.)

12.   Bob Doe, a reporter for *The Times Educational Supplement*, described reactions as a mixture of scorn and relief (3 April 1981).

13.   For example: Peter Mann (*TES*, 10 April, 1981); Santinelli, P. (*TES*, 17 April 1981; Malcolm Skilbeck (*TES*, 4 December, 1981). The latter thought that the impetus given to the debate on the curriculum had been underrated.

14. Peter Mitchell (*TES*, 17 April 1981) claimed that the dominance of subjects was responsible for inhibiting curriculum development and that despite its own advice the DES does not use a variety of analyses.

15. Solomon (*TES*, 10 April 1981) points out that the pressure of examinations limits the curriculum.

16. This was an important point made by Lawton (*TES*, 7 March 1980) in relation to teachers in Canada (and Withers (1982) in relation to some of those in Australia). Although there is a curriculum laid down centrally, at provincial level teachers carry out the pupil assessment themselves.

17. A certificate course is one which leads to a public examination – the Scottish Certification of Education, 'Ordinary' grade.

18. **Pring (OU, 1976, Unit 12), has spelt out several kinds of integration, which have quite different curricular implications. The Munn Report seems only to consider one of these: integration around themes.**

19. Perhaps this is the result of having separate committees considering assessment and the curriculum – a danger that faced the DES with the splitting of the functions of the Schools Council in such a manner.

20. Mary Warnock writing in the *TES* 'Personal Column' (18 June 1982) **hopes the Government will not emulate the Scottish system of teacher training where teachers are only qualified to teach a certain age group and subject, arguing that this is too rigid and out of date.**

21. **For example Marland (1981, Section V) argues that it is quite wrong to substitute a subject like biology for science when the former is a narrow specialism and the latter a broad foundation. The only way to ensure a suitable core, which leaves sufficient time for options, is to design special integrated courses. In particular Marland proposes a combined science and technology course for the core. Max Morris, not noted for advocating impractical theoretical ideas, also advocates a fundamental rethinking of** some subjects (*TES*, 8 February 1980).

22. **No specific reason is given for this decision, but it is implied that it is because subjects are familiar. However, they did consider personal and social development under a variety of headings: the formal subject curriculum, special courses geared to this development, the teaching methods employed in a school, the form of grouping used, and the general environment of the school.**

23. **We will consider the work of this Unit in Chapter 4. The six lines of development proposed by the APU were: aesthetic; language; mathematical; personal and social; physical; scientific (Kay, 1975). These, and those** of 'Curriculum 11-16', bear some resemblance to those proposed by Hirst (1965, 1974).

24. **The contents of this document resemble a much shortened version of Working Paper 53 (Schools Council, 1975b), for secondary schools, and, to a lesser extent, Working Paper 55 (Schools Council, 1975a) for middle schools.**

25. Hirst (1974) argues that liberal education requires the initiation into several forms of knowledge: mathematics; physical science; knowledge of persons; religion; literature and the fine arts; philosophy; moral knowledge. Apart from criticising the dominance of cognitive aspects of education Darling (1978) also says that the fact that this list has changed makes it arbitrary.

For a fuller consideration of Hirst's approach see Open University (1976, Unit 4). Pring (1981) criticises the APU lines and casts doubt on other such organisations of knowledge arising out of the philosophical literature.

26.   In reaction to such knowledge-based conceptions of education the campaign 'Education for Capability' was launched (*TES*, 30 Jan. 1981, and 5 Feb. 1982; *Guardian* 23 Feb. 1982) with the intention of promoting education directed towards action as well as understanding. However attractive that may seem to a government that has been concerned with wealth creation, it carries with it the possibility of promoting a dual curriculum (Open University, 1976, Units 9-10) with the less able being encouraged along the practical path. That this may be part of official thinking is illustrated by this extract from a lecture given by Sir James Hamilton , the Permanent Secretary at the DES:

> I am struck by the way in which representatives of teachers, the local authorities, employers and those concerned with curriculum development have been coming together under banners like 'Education for Capability' ... I have every sympathy with the proposition that a dilute form of the traditional academic curriculum does not necessarily offer the best preparation for adult life for the less academically able pupils, and indeed I believe that there is a strong case for giving the curriculum for all a more practical slant.
>
> (reprinted in *TES*, 23 April 1982)

27.   The areas of knowledge and experience defined by the Curriculum Development Centre are: arts and crafts; environmental studies; mathematical skills and reasoning and their application; social, cultural and civic studies; health education; scientific and technological ways of knowing and their social applications; communication; moral reasoning and action; value and belief systems; work, leisure and life-style. (Skilbeck, 1981.)

28.   Elsewhere Chanan (1977) has elaborated his ideas and envisaged a curriculum model made up of two types of activity: 'on the one hand a range of practical and cultural activities having close connections with the immediate community ... on the other a range of intellectual skills ...' (p. 165). He goes on to put this in concrete terms as a programme of activities.

29.   These centres of experience are: war, peace and international relations; overpopulation, pollution and energy; economic options and problems; governmental processes; consumer problems; intercultural relations; world views; recreation and leisure; the arts and aesthetics; self-understanding and personal development; family, peer group and school; health; community living; vocations; communication; alternative futures.

30.   Interestingly the two most important educational weeklies, *Education*, and the *TES*, disagreed in their interpretation of the new position of governors. *Education* said their role had been watered down (9 October 1981) whereas an editorial of the *TES* on the subject of Circular 6/81 was headlined 'More work for the Governors' (9 October 1981).

31.   In Australia, Cohen and Harrison (1979) report that few staff are involved. Watson (1979) is more optimistic about teachers in Canada although the Branches of Curriculum within state education departments are still the

main source of curriculum decisions. Cowen (1981) reports that USA teachers have lost their influence to those outside. Kirst and Walker (1971) report that although professionals control the curriculum in the USA, these are more usually superintendents and the school bureaucracy than teachers. Taylor *et al* (1974) found that primary classroom teachers in a sample of twelve schools had little influence over the school curriculum.

32. It will do this by calculating the requirement of teachers on the basis of a 'reasonable' spread of curricular options, thus helping small schools, which, on the basis of a teacher-pupil ratio calculation, would not be able to offer a full range of subjects.

Part Two

Strategies

4   Evaluation by Outsiders

Introduction

This chapter will concern itself with two basic approaches to evaluation by outsiders: the measurement of the 'products' or 'outcomes' of schooling, for example, through testing programmes; the independent observation of the processes of schooling by outsiders, for example by inspectors. For the most part the school has little control over these types of evaluation so we will consider the approaches in outline, concentrating on the issues raised[1].

The most controversial of outside evaluations involving outcome measurements are testing programmes[2] and public examination results. Schools can, and do, of course *use* tests for their own internal purposes - usually for screening children to give remedial teaching. Indeed Becher *et al* (1981) in their interviews with teachers in East Sussex found that teachers were likely to use such tests as an 'occasional independent check on their judgement' (p.65) i.e. as an external evaluation of their own assessment of pupils. Testing, as an *evaluation* procedure, is more likely to be conducted at a national or at a local education authority level. At the national level the concern is with the education system as a whole rather than with individual schools. However, local testing programmes can give information on individual schools.

In Britain public examination results have always been of internal interest to schools, although they have been used as only crude indicators in evaluating a school's performance. With the passing of the 1980 Education Act in England and Wales these results have to be published. It is this publication which gives them their force as a form of evaluation of schools, particularly as the intention of this part of the Act was to give parents information upon which to base their choice of school. Publication of examination results, therefore, qualifies as an outside evaluation because not only is the examination process controlled by outsiders (except in the relatively infrequent Mode III

73

school based examinations), but outsiders i.e. parents, can also pass judgement on the results.

The use of an outsider to observe what happens in a school has a long history in Britain through the process of formal school inspection. The idea of inspection started with national inspectors (Her Majesty's Inspectorate), but increasingly local inspectors are being used at local education authority (LEA) level. As we shall see, inspectors can provide evaluation at all levels of the education system: school, local and national level. We shall confine our discussion in this chapter to such 'officials' as HM Inspectorate, leaving the observation by 'consultants', more common in the USA, to Chapter 6 which considers combined strategies of evaluation.

Testing Programmes and Examination Results

According to House (1978) the importance of testing in the USA derives from two forms of educational accountability: at federal level, the requirement of system analysts for quantitative outcomes to measure the most effective educational programmes; at state level, the need for statements of objectives to judge teachers by testing students' perform-ance on those objectives (a scientific managerial approach). In its crudest form this approach is based on the idea that the outcomes that are tested (or assessed in the case of public examinations) are all important. Alternatively, the outcomes are assumed to be indicative of the quality of the educational process. It follows then that if the outcomes are poor, or lower than expected, the teacher is at fault, and should be held accountable. (Chapter 1 has already mentioned the classic case of California State being held accountable for not ensuring a minimum achievement for an individual student.)

Despite the fact that this may seem too crude a way to proceed this rationale has governed the operation of some testing programmes in the USA, most notoriously, that of Michigan State[3]. Such programmes are, as Chapter 1 pointed out, based upon a notion of contractual accountability. Even if you are not prepared to reject this form for professional accountability, as Sockett (1980, p. 19-22) does, you might feel that simply holding the teacher responsible for the results contravenes natural justice. Earlier in the same discussion Sockett (1980) argues that you can only hold the teacher accountable 'for what is within his control' (p. 15). Thus the test results must be interpreted in the light of such things as the ability of the students in the school and the resources available.

As with any accountability procedure it is insufficient just to indicate that a failure has occurred; information must be forthcoming on how to improve educational practice. In this respect testing has a poor track record, and its lack of impact at national and school level forms the substance of the major criticisms of it as an evaluation procedure.[4] However, it is fair to say that at local education authority level there is more evidence of its impact on change. (We shall examine this evidence later.)

The examples of approaches to the measurement of products that we will outline are:

1. national testing programmes (mentioned already in Chapter 1);
2. local testing programmes - such as those that a state in the USA, or an LEA in the UK, would employ;
3. the publication of examination results in the UK.

As intimated earlier it is only our intention to outline these here; there are many easily available descriptions and analyses in the literature (to which we refer).

National testing programmes

The National Assessment of Education Progress (NAEP), the national testing programme in the USA, aims to measure change in educational attainments as well as to develop the technology of assessment[5]. This technology will not only be of use to the programme itself, but can also be made available at state and local levels. Ten areas are tested, corresponding very much to conventional school subjects: mathematics, science, reading, writing, literature, social studies, music and art[6]. The schools are chosen as a representative sample, and neither individual students nor schools can be identified. A matrix sampling approach is used which results in no more than 12 students in a school being tested, and then on only some of the test material. Each subject area is tested at 4-5 year intervals, rather than annually[7]. At the time of testing, background information is collected relating to the students and schools: sex; size and type of community; parental education; colour. During some of the assessments 20 other variables may also be measured. The format of the tests themselves is mainly confined to pencil and paper exercises, and within these multiple-choice questions dominate, although science tests have used a wider range of exercises including practical work. The tests are described as objectives-related, that is, designed to test certain objectives. Items in the tests are not selected on the basis of how well they discriminate among students, i.e. they are not norm-referenced. Dissemination of the findings of the testing is diverse and includes sending out some 23,000 full reports and many more summaries.

In the UK the Assessment of Performance Unit (APU) fulfills a similar function to NAEP and indeed has similar aims. However, as Nuttall (OU, 1982, Block1) and Gipps (1982) note, the aim to measure changes over time was not in the original terms of reference although it appeared subsequently in publicity material. Unlike NAEP, the APU started with a cross-curricular model for the areas to be tested, proposing the six lines of development already mentioned in Chapter 3. To date mathematics, language and science have completed their initial round of annual surveys. Modern language surveys took place in 1983-5 and design and technology tests are being developed. For the measurement of changes of performance over time items were to be analysed using the Rasch model. This assumes that a test is trying to measure a single dimension of student ability - a trait - and that the difficulty of a test item is independent of both the other items in the test and the groups of students who answer it. In other words it is assumed that the difficulty of the item will be the same for any individual irrespective of his or her previous learning experiences etc. It is also assumed that an individual's response to an item will be completely independent of his or her response to any other items in the test. Conventional item analysis techniques (c.f. Chapter 8, *Curriculum Outcomes*) were intended to be used along with those based on the Rasch model. A light sampling approach is employed with the result that only a few students, in each of a representative sample of schools, are required to complete tests. Matrix sampling is also used, such that each student only takes a small part of the total battery of tests. Considerable effort has been expended to reduce the dependence upon written language when this is not the subject matter of the test, for example, in science use is made of oral presentations of questions. As with NAEP, the science tests exhibit the most imaginative types of questions, although Michael Marland praised those used in the first secondary language survey (*TES*, 19 March 1982, p. 20). The APU circulates summaries of its annual survey reports to all schools, but the full report which gives the results with little interpretative discussion, circulates less widely[8,9].

Local testing programmes.

The essence of these national schemes is that they provide a monitoring of the system as a whole and do not identify individual schools or students. Local testing schemes, in contrast, can give information on individual schools if they employ 'blanket testing' i.e. all children in the local authority are tested. The state testing programmes in the USA have been described in a survey by the Educational Testing Service (1973), which reported that, although there were plans for many states to test a wide range of curriculum areas (such as human relationships), few had developed the test technology sufficiently actually to carry out testing. This resulted in a narrow range of areas being tested. Many of the states have linked the testing programmes to the minimum competency testing mentioned in Chapter 1. The style of reporting of results varies. On the one hand Michigan, contrary to the original agreement with teachers, released individual school results to the public without taking into account the individual circumstances of schools. On the other California puts results in the context of pupil entry ability, a measure of socio-economic conditions of pupils, percentage of bilingual children, and pupil mobility.

Local authority testing in Britain is rarely used for accountability purposes. Gipps *et al* (1983), who surveyed LEAs, found that while most LEAs regularly conduct tests of reading there was no evidence to suggest a wide range of tests being administered, reading and maths being the most frequent. The most common reason for testing was screening for, say, those students who need remedial help. This means blanket testing, which was carried out by 52 of the 92 LEAs who gave information. None of the LEAs admitted publishing league tables of the schools' results, and rarely was any punitive action taken in relation to schools that were performing poorly.

Some LEAs in Britain saw an important opportunity in the formation of an item bank, linked to APU tests, upon which they could draw to generate tests. The Local Education Authorities' and Schools' Item Banking Project (LEASIB), operated by the National Foundation for Educational Research (NFER), offered such an opportunity. However, it was based upon the Rasch model, which, as we shall see later, has come under substantial criticism. The aim of providing national norms for any test supplied has been abandoned (Gipps *et al* 1983, p. 26) and no agreement has yet been reached on the use of APU test items by LEAs through the NFER bank.

Publishing examination results.

The requirement to publish examination results is, in Britain, laid down by law and the following information has to be specified:

1. the policy of the school in entering pupils into the examinations;
2. the examinations commonly entered for;
3. the appropriate year group taking the examination;
4. the number of pupils in the appropriate year group by subject, grade and total number in each year group.

The GCE and CSE examinations were conducted by a variety of Boards and, although subject experts tried to judge some standard of achievement, it was basically a normative assessment i.e. the same percentage pass the examination each year. This is a fact often overlooked in discussions on standards, as Choppin points out (*TES*, 6 February 1981, letters). Indeed there were problems about comparability of grades 'in different years, from different boards and in different subjects' (OU, 1982, Block 1, p. 35). (With the advent of GCSE examinations assessments were against criteria and grades awarded for the achievement of more or less specified performances.)

The law's requirement for information on entry is an attempt to take account of the variety of policies operated by schools. Such information is required, for instance, to compare the success rates of two schools, one of which only enters those who are likely to pass, and another which allows anyone to enter. However, information that the law does not require, and is often not available, is some account of the intake characteristics of the school. This poses a problem in that a school with high ability pupils would expect 'good' results but it may not be a 'good school' - a problem we look at under 'Issues' later in this chapter. In terms of sampling the curriculum, examinations do rather better than most testing programmes. However, they sample the pupils in a more selective way, because not all pupils take the same kinds of public examinations, and different criteria are used for each kind. A small percentage of pupils take no public examination and, if examination results are the sole criterion, there is no way of judging whether schools are effective in meeting the particular needs of this group.

Roles

Tests are defined and designed by people who are outsiders in relation to particular schools. Often consultation with insiders is inadequate. NAEP went through an initial consultation with teachers and the general public in an effort to arrive at a consensus on the goals of education. The tests were then developed by experts and submitted to lay people and subject matter experts for reactions. However, as might be expected, this consultation was far from adequate in the early stages of NAEP's life. First, the review of objectives only allowed lay people to suggest the *omission* of objectives that they found inappropriate, and attempts to add to or change objectives met with resistance (Greenbaum *et al*, 1977, p.49). Secondly, the process of arriving at consensual objectives meant that they represented 'the least-common-denominator' (Greenbaum *et al*, 1977, p.162). Thirdly, in generating assessment exercises from objectives the whole process took much longer than anticipated and initially reviewers were unhappy with the quality of exercises produced by contract 'item writers' (Greenbaum *et al*, 1977, pp.68-71).

The APU fairs even worse with regard to consultation; for example the six lines of development were not the subject of debate when they were initially proposed. Moreover, the consultative committee, a representative body intended to guide the work of the APU, was often ignored by those running the Unit (Holt 1981, pp.66-7). Burstall and Kay (1978, p.10) note that the positive response to NAEP testing may have been because critics were brought into the organising committee. However, such committees, at the national level, are unlikely to make individual teachers feel involved. Gooding (1980) surveyed teacher opinion and found that a majority thought there was insufficient consultation on the design of the tests, although a response rate of fifty per cent for the survey casts some doubt on how widespread this may be.

Teachers in schools being tested are thus powerless, since they have no control over the measures used[10] and are not in a position to dispute the findings (although this depends on how the results are used, and if, for example, they are published). It is, of course, possible for schools to use tests for their own internal evaluation, and indeed to operate their own testing programme[11]. Despite their lack of power and control, it is individual teachers in schools who must effect changes to improve education - if that is what the tests show to be necessary. Burstall and Kay (1978) report that, with regard to the NAEP programme, the impact on schools is poor. Local authority testing can have more impact, and in Britain advisers can follow-up any problems and support schools.

Changes designed to improve education can therefore be regarded as having two sources: those initiated by decision makers at local or national level; those initiated by teachers. We consider the use of test results by decision makers in the next section, and by teachers later when we consider criteria for judging testing as an accountability procedure.

Issues

Testing inevitably raises many issues, but we will consider five main ones: the validity of testing and other product measures; the technical problems; the possibility of curriculum backwash; use of test results to allocate resources; the release or publication of results.

The *validity* of product measures as the sole form of evaluation can be considered at a number of levels. First, at the most general level, testing, and other forms of assessment, represent education in a mechanistic way. Indeed Sockett (1980) goes so far as to call accountability based on prespecified results 'anti-educational'. Drawing on Pincoffs (1975) he argues that:

> Educational goals ... consist in the development of excellences. Excellences are indeterminate dispositions ... Wittiness, modesty, prudence and love of animals ... [are] examples. These cannot be defined prespecifically in behavioural terms as they would have to be for the tests (p.18).

Secondly, the earlier reference to NAEP's consensual goals reveals another problem with goal-setting. The 'facile consensual model of defining national educational objectives' means that deeply felt aims are neglected (Greenbaum *et al,* 1977, p.164). Thirdly, at a less general level, the particular model of the curriculum represented by the battery of tests may, or may not, be thought appropriate. The ten subject areas of the NAEP programme cover a good deal of the curriculum, but Greenbaum, *et al* (1977) argue that this was limiting[12]. The six lines of development of the APU offered a more attractive model, but as Chapter 3 argues, a somewhat arbitrary one. (For a critique for this model see Pring, 1981.) The subsequent change in the areas tested raises a question about the validity of the tests as a representation of the curriculum - a similar problem to that of the NAEP. Fourthly, at the level of individual test items, a question can be asked about how well they represent the learning that goes on in the classroom[13]. In defence of the tests employed by the APU, Foxam, in a letter to the *Times Educational Supplement* (10 October 1980), points out that the teachers whose pupils took the tests thought that the language in the written tests was appropriate. Holt (1981), in a review of all three of the APU test areas, has criticisms about each[14]. The independent appraisals of the maths testing (Cambridge Institute of Education, 1985) and the language testing (Thornton, 1986) do not directly comment on the validity of the tests. Both are generally positive, and Thornton notes that the testing is based upon an intellectually respectable view of language and uses assessment categories which 'break new ground' (p. 29). He also comments favourably on the test situation. Even if, in *general terms*, the curriculum model is adequate, and the test items valid, it may not match the *particular* curriculum experienced by the student who is being tested (Goldstein, 1981b).

The *technical problems* of testing have dominated discussions in the British literature on the APU, particularly the problems of the Rasch model[15]. This model, as indicated earlier, makes three assumptions: that ability is unidimensional (a trait); that item difficulty is independent of the other items in the test; that item difficulty is independent of the student i.e. it does not vary with the different learning experiences of students and hence it does not vary over time. As the intention was that items for a test were to be selected to fit the model, it was important to be able to test this model. But to test, for example, the assumption about item difficulty being independent of the student requires assuming that ability is unidimensional (Goldstein, 1981b); in other words it cannot be tested! Such tests are necessary because the model is not educationally very plausible (however statistically elegant and convenient it might be[16]). It seems unlikely that, all other things being equal, two students will find an item equally difficult when one has studied the topic that the item tests and the other has not. Similarly it is well known that an easy item following a difficult one appears to be more difficult (Nuttall, 1979). Both of these ideas contravene the model, which assumes that item difficulty is invariant under these conditions. In addition, the model creates some contradictions in use. First, we would expect over time that, for example, certain words would fall out of use and items related to these would appear relatively more difficult than those which use words still current (Nuttall, 1979). This also contravenes the model, or rather the model does not fit what common sense tells us. It certainly cannot, therefore, be used to measure change over time: one of the reasons for its use. Secondly, the trait assumption allows an item bank to be constructed so that users, such as LEAs, can construct a test appropriate to their circumstances. An 'appropriate test' will mean one which suits the curriculum studied by the pupils in question; but item difficulty does not depend upon what the pupils have studied so the whole idea of an appropriate test is non-sense - according to the Rasch model (Goldstein, 1981b)[17]. These difficulties led to the abandoning of this model.

Perhaps the most important issue, however, is the possibility of causing *curriculum backwash*. That it can occur nobody denies - witness the report of HM Inspectors on secondary education in England, in which they lament the narrowing effect on the curriculum of public examinations (DES 1979a). Burstall and Kay (1978, p.9) report that in the case of NAEP early opposition from teacher unions was partly based upon fear of a backwash effect and, indeed, it appears to have been a worry for those involved with setting up the APU testing programme (Kay, 1975). Critics of the whole APU testing programme, such as Holt (1981). saw it as a threat to teacher autonomy. Indeed Holt saw it as a mechanism for controlling the curriculum and even went so far as to suggest that the staff of the APU were concerned to promote desirable curriculum development (Holt, 1981, p. 65). Tall (1981, p. 193) argues, more moderately, that the Rasch model, because of its focus on traits, may inhibit new developments in teaching methods.

National systems of testing use light sampling methods and therefore the direct impact on the curriculum is unlikely to be large. But the selection of areas for testing (ten subjects in USA, and five in Britain) implies that certain elements of the curriculum are more important than others. In the USA, NAEP's use of conventional school subjects has been seen as a conservative influence, and the reduction to the 3Rs makes the backwash effect even more acute (Wirtz and Lapointe, 1982, p. 16). The APU would not have been accused of exerting a conservative influence with its cross-curricular model; however, the eventual selection of subjects could have a narrowing effect on the curriculum. In reviewing the curriculum backwash effect of the APU, Gipps (1982) reported little evidence of it, and a lack of mechanisms to bring it about. But her latest account of the APU (Gipps, 1987) indicates a more positive approach being taken. First, the APU has put more stress on disseminating survey information which has implications for teaching. Second, this is linked with teacher training work, for example the use of practical assessment materials. Third, there is a possibility that the

APU will be used to set attainment targets to raise standards with the result that teachers will teach to them, and inevitably the curriculum will be narrowed. Fourth, the need to develop grade related criteria for GCSE may give the APU a link with the examination system, if it is involved in their development. This link may give the APU a more direct backwash effect on the curriculum than the other three mechanisms above.

If the backwash effect is less direct in a national testing programme, local programmes, involving blanket testing of all pupils, have the maximum potential to cause an effect. Holt (1981) saw the setting up of LEASIB as the biggest threat to schools, allowing the APU to have more direct impact. As we noted earlier the developments of this work make this unlikely. The experience in the USA suggests that local testing programmes are usually of poor quality and their effects therefore more undesirable[18]. Gipps *et al* (1983) report little concern amongst primary school headteachers about adverse effects, though the programmes themselves lack clarity of purpose and use[19]. There is, according to them, no general worry in schools about LEA testing.

One of the attractions of a national testing programme is its supposed potential to help decision makers with policy formation, for example with how to allocate resources. The experience from the USA on the use of NAEP's results is disappointing and led Wirtz and Lapointe (1982), on the basis of all previous evaluations of NAEP, to conclude that: 'Everybody pretty much agreed that the results of National Assessment have never been very useful in a practical sense'. (p. 72). Greenbaum *et al* (1977) put it stronger when they said NAEP was so limited that it has 'virtually no capacity to provide the federal government, the lay public, or most educational policymakers with results that are directly useful for decision making' (p. 169). One of the reasons for failure is the need to measure more background variables, chosen to meet the needs of decision-makers; critics of NAEP think that more effort should be made to find out the needs of such decision-makers[20]. (This issue is taken up again in Chapter 11.) On an APU sponsored visit to the USA, Burstall and Kay (1978) drew the following lessons from the USA experience: that the APU should obtain information that is, on the one hand, of use to teachers and on the other to decision-makers; and that the information collected must be related to needs rather than being simply that which is easy to collect. However, after a number of years of operation, the APU does not appear to have been conspicuous in its success: most of the background measures are of little use, and there are difficulties in relevant measures (Gipps, 1982). Kelly (1987, p. 26) argues that the removal of the requirement to aid decision-makers would allay fears.

Another reason for the failure to use results is the lack of interpretation[21]. Since its inception the NAEP has been faced with the dilemma of deciding whether to report results in a descriptive fashion or to add interpretation. In a careful analysis of NAEP's attitudes and possibilities for action, Greenbaum *et al* (1977, p. 154) say that NAEP has a muddled policy and they conclude: 'its only really feasible potential - conceptually, economically, and politically - is that of description' (p. 159). Interpretations depend upon being able to link the background measures (class, size, socio-economic group etc.) to those of performance. However, Nuttall (OU, 1982, Block 1, pp. 16-7 and p. 43) has shown that this creates considerable problems for the interpretation of results in relation to, for example, class size[22]. However, in the more recent evaluation of NAEP, which seems preoccupied with the needs of researchers rather than policymakers, Wirtz and Lapointe (1982) maintain that more effort is needed to interpret results and suggest an independent council to carry this out. The APU has started along this course with the two independent evaluations of their surveys (Cambridge Institute of Education, 1985; Thornton, 1986).

Given the closer relationship between local testing programmes and decision-makers, and the use of blanket testing, such programmes have a greater potential for aiding policy formulation. Evidence from the USA, however, shows that such use is patchy, and only two states appear to have directly used test results (Educational Testing Service, 1973)[23]. We have already made the point that in Britain this seems unlikely (Gipps *et al*, 1983). Wood and Gipps (1982) pose an interesting dilemma for decision-makers allocating resources: do they give resources to the schools with poor results, thus penalising the good ones (from which the good schools may learn the best way to get resources), or do they reward the good schools and let the poor ones suffer?

An issue which has also caused controversy involves the release of results of individual schools. Of course, this applies only to local testing programmes, which employ blanket testing, and to the publication of public examination results[24]. The notorious case of Michigan shows this issue at its most stark. Becher *et al* (1981) point to some of the problems: it is not obvious what the real reasons are for poor results (e.g. poor intake); criticism of a hardworking school operating in bad circumstances undermines morale; and a high scoring school acts as a magnet and deprives other schools of high ability children.

Burstall and Kay (1978) report that estate agents in Michigan utilise test results - a graphic illustration of the last problem noted by Becher and his colleagues. While the law may require publication, the form this takes can reduce the damage that results cause; in this respect Michigan provides a contrast with California (a point made earlier). In relation to public examination results in Britain, Gray (1982) has documented the difficulty of interpreting the disputed results of two competing London schools, Highbury Grove and Islington Green, which sparked off considerable press comment and correspondence in early 1981. (For example, see letters in *Times Educational Supplement*, 13 February, 1981.) The major problems included the need to account for the differences in the schools' intakes, deciding which groups of pupils were included in the result statistics (e.g. whether sixth form pupils taking 'O' levels were included along with 5th formers), and the problem, for outsiders such as Gray, of getting hold of all the relevant statistics.

Judgement of testing programmes

We will confine our judgement to testing (for the purpose of monitoring) as this approach is primarily concerned with evaluating educational provision, whereas public examinations are concerned primarily with individual pupils and students. Many of the criteria put forward in Chapter 1 have already been indirectly considered in the discussion so far. We noted, for example, that control lay outside the school. National testing programmes are remote from schools, and even local programmes do not involve schools in planning, test choice or construction. We have also already considered the issue of methodological soundness and revealed doubts about the validity of the tests, at several levels, particularly with regard to the technical problems, and especially those of the Rasch model. However, there is no doubt that the APU has pioneered new testing methods.

Deciding whether testing programmes are economic in their use of resources is a more difficult problem. Nuttall (OU, 1982, Block 1, p.44) and Gipps (1982) estimate that the direct cost of the APU was £800,000 per year, which crudely would mean less than £30 per school. The annual budget of NAEP was once as much as 7.1 million dollars (about £3.5 million pounds), although by 1982 the figure was down to 3.88 million dollars. Despite this relatively small cost the Reagan Administration was encouraged to seek further savings and decided to put the whole operation out to private tender (reported in the *TES*, 28 October, 1982, p. 12). It is, of course, difficult to make any sense of these figures; in any case, as Nuttall argues (OU, 1982, Block 1 p. 44), what is important is the kind of results that are obtained for the money spent.

This brings us to a consideration of whether these programmes are capable of suggesting appropriate remedies. First, considering the issue at the level of teachers in schools, we have already cast some doubt on this in our discussion of 'Roles'. But it is possible that the APU's teacher training and dissemination efforts may have some effect. Regarding the USA state programme, the Educational Testing Service (1973) says that it is unlikely that even local testing can reveal anything startling about how teachers can improve their work[25]. It concludes that intensive analysis of individual schools and classrooms is required. Little evidence exists to indicate that tests help teachers; however this sad fact may not surprise many people. What is more surprising, when considering what advocates of testing have to say on this subject, is the lack of ideas on *how* such information *could* ever help schools. Consider, for example, this notion put forward by Wirtz and Lapointe (1982):

> Nothing . . . diminishes the recognition that the place to improve formal education is in the classroom and that what is done there is a local responsibility. Yet there is no question about the constructive effect of concentrating national attention on a common problem by reporting the situation in the country at large. (p. 6)

In other words, if the country gets a bee in its bonnet about some failing in schools, teachers will remedy the situation - hardly a sophisticated theory!

But it may be unfair to look for remedies at classroom level from such global data. Instead, it may be more appropriate to consider national and local educational decision-makers. Even here, as we have shown earlier, the evidence is overwhelmingly against the usefulness of testing, whether carried out on a national or local basis. What is worth considering is whether it *could* be of help if 'things were improved'. From our earlier discussion it is evident that opinion is divided amongst those who have tried to evaluate national programmes. Greenbaum *et al* (1977) say there is 'no capacity' to help decision-makers; Wirtz and Lapointe (1982) implicitly say there is, by recommending a doubling of NAEP's expenditure and its development to investigate 'causes' of the results reported (something that is very unlikely given the government decision reported earlier). However, it is this latter point that holds the key to understanding the different views, and, although a full analysis is beyond the scope of this book, it is worth exploring briefly. The thrust of the recommendations made by Greenbaum *et al* (1977) is that NAEP 'is not a short-term research or decision-making tool' (p.174), but that it should become 'a useful long-term census'. However, they realise that such an approach may jeopardise funding of the programme. Wirtz and Lapointe, on the other hand, concentrate on research problems in relation to policy development, recommending that specific studies be carried out in association with the general testing programme (a recommendation also made by Gipps (1982) in relation to the APU). Such special studies for *research purposes*, Greenbaum and his colleagues thought, could be done 'more precisely and less expensively by smaller studies' (Greenbaum *et al*, 1977, p. 169).

More central to the concerns of this book is the question of whether testing programmes are a suitable procedure for accountability. Certainly, on the criteria considered above, the answer would be 'no'. Wirtz and Lapointe (1982) however maintain that they are, by affirming the importance of NAEP's work in improving educational standards, although they rely more on judging the 'mood of the times' than on any careful analysis[26]. In contrast, after an analysis of the literature on social indicators and the reform of education, Greenbaum *et al* (1977) conclude not only that can NAEP not help with research hypothesis formation or policy guidelines, but that 'the prequisites of an effective large-scale system of social accounting demonstrates that no such system lies within reach in the field of education' (p. 186). They go on to argue that 'in the short-term the most likely approach to educational change is through enlarging the use of increasingly refined self-knowledge by particular institutions' (p. 186). This is a conclusion with which we would agree and indeed it provides a rationale for this book. That being said, it is undoubtably true that more empirical research is required into the effects on teachers of the APU's programmes of teacher training and dissemination.

Inspections

As we shall see later the basic premise underlying an inspection will vary with the circumstances of the inspectors. In Britain these are in a state of flux although there has been much discussion about the role of the inspector over a long period of time. Any inspection system, however, has a number of major elements:

1. an experienced professional, who has some independence from the school, observes the schools activities[27];
2. various aspects of school life are observed, through an informal visit or a formal team visit;
3. in a formal visit to an individual school a report is prepared for the education authority and the school;
4. inspectors are expected to have intimate knowledge and continuing experience of the classroom[28];
5. the inspectors' function is not just to pronounce judgement, but also to encourage and develop education[29]

Becher *et al* (1981, pp. 138-91) put forward the following strengths and weaknesses of visitation (which covers a wider range of activities than inspection) as an accountability procedure:

Strengths
1. inspection is commonplace and maintains public confidence;
2. teachers see it as natural justice (comparison with colleagues reduces isolation and gives them a yardstick);
3. it is more humane than testing - it can put a human face on any judgement, positive or negative;
4. it allows headteachers to approach awkward staff who have problems and reinforces the existing management structures;
5. extra resources may come to the school;
6. it is flexible and individualistic compared with testing;
7. it has more explanatory power because it involves direct observation and can hence lead to remedies.

Weaknesses
1. if it is to certify an institution then it can be superficial and impressionistic (i.e. subjective);
2. it can be susceptible to a headteacher who is good at public relations management.

Her Majesty's Inspectorate

The first example of inspection that we have chosen is the operation of HM Inspectorate in Britain. These inspectors, although originally instituted to inspect schools receiving grants from Parliament (DES, 1971, p.1) - a function now replaced by the task of reporting to the Secretary of State for Education on the quality of educational provision - have always had the aim of seeking to improve education in the institutions they visit (Browne, 1979, p.35). However, their history, from the first appointments in 1839, has been one of constant change and adaptation[30]. They have always spent considerable time visiting schools; in the nineteenth century there were regular visits, including during the period of payment by results (1862-1898) when the outcome of an inspection, involving assessing the children's performance, determined whether or not the school received funds. In the period of expansion of the Inspectorate after the Second World War the tasks diversified and regular formal visiting declined; in 1968 the Select Committee on Education and Science recognised this shift. However, the decline in regular formal inspection did not mean the abandoning of inspection but rather the development of a variety of types suited to particular purposes (Browne, 1979, p.37). Thomas (OU, 1983a, Block 2, Part 3), a retired HMI, lists four overlapping categories of present day inspections:

1. informal visits usually by one HMI;
2. 'reporting' or 'full' inspection followed by a written report to the Secretary of State and others;
3. area team exercises usually on a single issue, sometimes followed by an internal report;
4. national surveys followed by a public report.

The 'full inspection' is the traditional form, but one which is written about in detail least. Most accounts of the methods of inspection are by retired or practising HMIs[31], although those on the receiving end do describe the experience[32]. Thomas (OU, 1983a, Block 2, Part 3) notes that the basis of all the types of inspection are similar. Clearly a full inspection has a degree of formality because of its import and scale; thus it involves a team of inspectors, finite time (of the order of a week), a timetable of observation and discussion for each HMI, and a formal written report. A full inspection of a primary school will, of course, differ in scale from that of a large secondary school. Surveys, while using similar methods, require care in sampling schools (to aid generalisation) and efforts to standardise the data collected. But at the heart of all the methods, whatever their purpose or form, are two elements: observations of classroom, and discussions with teachers. Hopkins (1982) sees the main strength of the Inspectorate to lie in an 'intimate knowledge of the classroom scene'. This, he feels, can only come about by a return to the basic function of inspection.

What then is the nature of the observations made by HMI? Thomas (OU, 1983a, Block 2, Part 3) outlines the following kinds of observations and activities of HMI: observation of the exchanges between pupil and teacher, and pupil and pupil; discussion with pupils as a group, or individually; a look at current or past work of pupils; requests to pupils to do some particular piece of written work; discussions with teachers to find out aims and to check observations; examination of schemes of work and pupil records; a look at the quality of resources and how they are used. This is not intended to be an exhaustive list and throughout the observations the main questions in the HMI's mind are: Is the range of work suitable for the children? Are the levels of work such that children are managing increasingly complex information and relationships? Even in the more structured work of surveys HM Inspectors still rely upon informal and holistic methods rather than observation schedules (a topic we shall consider in *Part Three* in relation to observation methods).

Before 1983 the reports that resulted from full inspections were confidential and sent only to the LEA, the school's governors, and the headteacher. However, at the time of the inspection any comments made by the inspectors were discussed with any teachers who were implicated, the head, and possibly the governors of the school. Interestingly, in evidence to the Select Committee in 1968 the Senior Chief Inspector (Scotland) was asked: 'Do you in fact nowadays have any formal inspections in the old sense of written reports?' He replied, 'Not written reports. We gave up the written report quite frankly because we found it a waste of time. By the time a report reached the authority something was seriously wrong if all its recommendations were not already in operation' (Select Committee on Education and Science, 1968b, Minutes of Evidence, Examination of Witnesses, Q35.) In a following question the SCI (Scotland) also admitted that in translating recommendations into a written report the point was often lost; the discussions with the school and perhaps the LEA were the major reporting function[33]. Now all school and college full inspection reports are published as a matter of course. The Secretary for State for Education cannot withhold permission to publish and this is seen as an important sign of the independence of HMI. (This independence was illustrated most vividly over the publication of a survey of spending on education (DES, 1984a). It revealed a sorry state of affairs in schools which could be attributed to the cuts in educational spending - something that proved embarrassing to the government of the day. The publication of reports on full inspections of individual schools has become routine and no longer leads to any public debate of the rights and wrongs of such reporting. The *Times Educational Supplement* features reports on a particular page, picking out significant findings (both adverse and positive). Individual schools did enter into correspondence with the *TES* over its reporting of the full HMI report, and over the findings themselves. This at least testifies to the independence of HMI from the schools they inspect. (This also applies to LEAs who have equally taken issue with HMI reports on their provision of education.) It seems that the publication of these reports has by and large not proved such a worry to schools. When the publication of HMI reports on university departments of education was discussed (as part of the approval mechanism for teacher training courses of the Council for the Accreditation of Teachers' Education, CATE) there was initial resistance. These inspections were at the 'invitation' of the university department, but failure to allow an inspection would result in a course not being approved. Further permission for publication of the report was left to the department to give. The Universities Council for the Education of Teachers (UCET) debated this before agreeing to publication as a matter of course, though they were under some pressure from the DES, HMI, and, interestingly, from the Vice-Chancellors (individually and collectively through the Committee for Principals and Vice-Chancellors). It was agreed by both the DES and HMI that, since university teacher training represented excellence, they had nothing to fear, and other institutions could learn from the reports.

One thoughtful article by a headteacher whose school was the subject of an inspection pointed out the need for HMI to be scrupulous in their attention to details of factual accuracy (*TES* 1 February, 1985, p. 21). Not only can incorrect facts be used by local press to the detriment of the school, but such errors, and their refusal to correct them in published reports, cast doubt on the wisdom of this process.

These published reports and the surveys of particular aspects of education are periodically reviewed to give a judgment on the state of the education system in general. Naturally this judgement has to be tempered by the unrepresentative nature of the sample of reports that it draws upon. In the first six months this sample was of 106 reports (DES, 1984b). One of these summary reports was used to identify good teachers and good teaching (DES, 1985f), in the context of the White Paper *Teaching Quality* (DES, 1983b) and the discussion of teacher appraisal. (DES, 1984c, is the other such summary.)

LEA Inspection

The second example of inspection is that carried out by local authority inspectors. In essence the mechanics of inspections can be the same; what differs is the role of such inspectors and their experience of inspection. The 1944 Education Act gave LEAs the right to inspect schools, indeed, some LEAs inherited inspectorates from the School Boards which preceded them (Pearce, 1982). But the titles, size of teams and functions of inspectors vary among the local authorities. Thus some authorities employ a team of inspectors while others use a team of advisers or organisers. Bolam *et al* (1978) have published the most recent study of advisers[34] and they found that the least popular task, except among senior advisers, was the evaluation of individual staff. Further, although half were involved in general inspection few advisers wanted to spend more time on it (again senior staff were the exception). Bolam and his colleagues recognised, however, that since completing their research in 1975 the climate had changed and may have increased the demand for inspections. Some advisers, they thought, may turn to inspection to survive in a climate of education expenditure cuts. At present, the bulk of an LEA adviser's work involves helping teachers in a variety of ways, and, although this requires them to observe teaching, the act of inspection creates some tensions. Thus the issue of independence occurs again. This time the inspector is clearly associated with the authority that employs the teacher, and which is responsible directly for the quality of the education in the school. The most graphic statement of the dual role though some would call it an overstatement (e.g. Pearce, 1982), is that given by the National Association of Head Teachers (NAHT) in response to a document on the role of the advisory service issued by the Society of Education Officers and the National Association of Inspectors and Educational Advisers:

> For example, how can an adviser go into a school and give advice on procedures, and within weeks go in and inspect those same procedures in a censorial sense? How can a Head Teacher have the confidence to call in an adviser for consultation on a problem in his school when he is conscious that, as a consequence of that consultation, his school may be subjected to intense overtly critical scrutiny within a short space of time? (quoted in OU, 1982, Block 2, Part 3, p. 39).

This conflict of roles has of course its benefits, and in any case formal inspections are unlikely to be the norm. Local inspectors, like their HMI counterparts, favour informal routine visits. These will still contain an inspectorial element but will be much less tense. The benefits for the local inspector are that by their greater number (compared with HMIs - see Pearce, 1982) they can become more familiar with the schools, and by virtue of their advisory role they will have some responsibility for following up any findings of an inspection - whether it be formal or informal. In addition to this worry about the dual role, some teachers, and headteachers in particular, doubt the skills and experience of advisers. Whether or not one feels they are equipped to advise head-teachers[35] it is difficult to avoid doubting their skills at inspection. Except in a few cases, formal inspections will not have been frequent enough to build up the kind of collective experience that HMIs have. This is not to deny that local inspectors are skilled at informal observation, or able to give advice to teachers in particular areas of the curriculum. Nevertheless, we know even less about the inspection methods of these inspectors than we do of HMIs[36].

Roles

Inspection by its nature casts teachers and schools in a passive role. They are evaluated and yet play no part in defining the criteria, determining the methods, or controlling the process. For this to be acceptable to teachers they have to have confidence in the ability and independence of the inspectors: independence, that is, from the education authorities who are their employers. On the other hand the public would want inspectors to be independent of the school being inspected. HMIs fulfil both of these conditions, but this is not so for local authority inspectors. The HMI insistence on a formal written report for a full inspection also affects this confidence. Blackie, commenting on the evidence given to the 1968 Select Committee, claimed that those wishing to see reports abolished did not realise that 'the written report is a safeguard for teachers, and if abolished ... would almost inevitably lead to information being passed orally and, in effect, secretly' (OU, 1982, Block 2, Part 3, p.13). In saying this, however, Blackie ignored the evidence of his colleagues in Scotland who unequivocally denied any protection, adding, 'If we have a criticism of a teacher or if we feel that a teacher is weak in some respects ... the matter would be discussed very frankly with the teacher in the first place' (Select Committee on Education and Science, 1986b, Q38 Evidence)[37]. Whatever the form of the advice, the Inspectorate make it clear that the teachers are free to accept or reject it (DES, 1971, p.15-6; Browne, 1979, p.39). For the LEA inspectors confidence is lacking in both senses stated above. Even the reporting system can lead to worries: despite a written report the inspector can informally report the 'real story' to other officers of the authority. This may seem too unprofessional a view to have of them, but even discounting direct informal reporting, they cannot avoid using this information when, for example, they are involved in appointments and promotions. As indicated above the teachers and schools have no control over the criteria and methods, nor indeed the report. However, the DES (1971, p.26) speculates about the possibility of an 'agreed record' - a record of discussions between staff and inspectors.which should indicate that the different views expressed have been dealt with fairly. Whether or not this has been implemented is unclear. At the local authority level Dorset County Council (1980), in a booklet called *Looking at Schools*, talks of a joint-evaluation, which amounts to an inspection with the school agreeing to the report, but having no control over the process of the inspection. Hillingdon local authority have adopted a code of practice for 'in-depth visits' which lays down, at least in the case of secondary schools, negotiations over what is to be invest-igated and the plan of the visit. For all types of schools the headteacher has the right to append comments to the final report (Craddock, 1979). In a case study by Turner (1987) an account is given of an inspection which was to have built upon a self-evaluation, with the latter acting as an initial ground clearing and the provision of information. However, the inspectors ignored and even scorned the self-evaluation, seeing only their inspection as important.

Issues

Clearly two major issues concern the independence of the inspectors and their reporting methods; however, we feel that these have been adequately covered in the discussion so far. One remaining issue worthy of development concerns the quality of the methods of inspection used by the inspectors. These methods, as we have already indicated, are based upon an informal unstructured approach, although the HMI surveys employ a greater degree of structure. While it would be wrong to expect inspectors to use observation schedules (on the grounds that they do not allow the inspectors to keep an open mind on what they observe), it is quite reasonable to ask that they be explicit about the evidence collected and its basis. Thomas (OU, 1983a, Block 2, Part 3) gives a list of headings used in informal visits but these headings are very general e.g. 'curriculum', 'work seen'. The surveys have provided the most explicit statement of how, and on what basis, data are collected (DES, 1979a, p.67-70; DES, 1978a, p.206-218) Brown, M. (1979) gives a framework for observation of nursery and infant schools, to be used by LEA advisers during visits to schools.

Becher *et al* (1981, p.76) cite the following methodological criticisms of inspections: lack of empirical evidence on which they are based; impossibility of getting to know a complex situation quickly; failure to separate value judgements from evidence. When the HMI methodology is made explicit, as in surveys, then it tends to draw criticisms. Bennett (1978) in commenting upon the primary survey (DES, 1978a) complained about the lack of explicit theory on which observations were based, and that the theory which emerged[38], although respectable enough, had little empirical base. He was also concerned about the reliability of the data: for example, that no measure of agreement was given for observations made when pairs of inspectors were present in the same classroom. Bennett was also worried about the lack of allowance made for the impact that HMIs have when they visit a school (the term for this is 'reactivity', which will be discussed in *Part Three*). Perhaps, Bennett argues, the finding that so little use was made of exploratory methods in teaching was the teachers' reaction to the presence of HMIs. Nuttall (1980) questioned the secondary survey (DES, 1979a) in a similar vein, saying that HMI should employ the methodological standards of research. Nuttall concludes that in the end 'the only criterion for judging the adequacy of the reports' findings is one's faith in HM Inspectorate'. Thomas makes a similar point when he says the 'quality of their [HMI's] work depends on their personal attributes as shaped by experience' (OU, 1983a, Block 2, Part 3). This implies that both their background and training are important. Regan (1977) complains about the lack of statistics on their background but says there are still some subject areas where inspectors only have experience of grammar and independent schools. The evidence given by the HM Inspectorate (Scotland) to the 1968 Select Committee is however complete enough and shows a good spread of backgrounds[39]. Although for Scotland the main deficiency was only in the lack of HMIs with primary school experience, the Select Committee was concerned about the overall balance in England and Wales. The DES, however, saw no need to change its recruitment practices (DES, 1968). The comments, referred to earlier, by the NAHT on local inspectors' background experience indicate a more acute problem (see Note 35). Likewise, Jarmen (*TES*, 11 June 1982) a former adviser, expressed concern about the requirement for subject advisers to take on general advisory functions many of which they were not qualified to carry out. The Select Committee of 1968 suggested that secondment of HMIs to schools and colleges might be a useful experience. Although the DES said it was considering this (DES, 1968), it pointed out that there was a practical difficulty in the difference in salary scales. Again Regan (1979) makes the point that there is very little formal training, of any kind, in an inspector's career. Edmonds (1962) also says that this has been a problem throughout the 150 years of the Inspectorate. Again LEA inspectors suffer more acutely in this respect, perhaps because of their lack of corporate identity - each LEA's inspectors or advisers are rather isolated from those of other LEAs.

The publication of full inspection reports gives another source from which inferences can be made about the work of HMI, and here we will consider two critiques that have used them. First, Elliott and Ebbutt (1986a) consider the criteria used by HMI and question their lack of educative feedback to schools. This approach, Elliott and Ebbutt argue, stems from HMI's use of prespecified criteria and what appears to be the use of a check-list by them. The criticism that Elliott and Ebbutt make of this approach is three fold: values underlying judgements are not revealed; the analysis is atomistic and ignores the inter-relationships among features of a school's activities; and areas are inevitably ignored. The second critique of HMI comes from Gray and Hannon (1986), who argue that HMI judgements of individual schools are made against a 'national standard', i.e. comparing one school with another in an absolute sense. This ignores the particular contexts of individual schools, and the way they differ. Thus a school in an affluent area is usually praised whereas one in a deprived area will usually only get a 'satisfactory in the circumstances' judgement. These judgements take no account of the intake characteristics of particular schools, though HMI collect and report such data as social class and verbal reasoning scores at intake. They do not however use this data to temper their judgements, with the result that a school may be praised because of the intake characteristics of the pupils rather than because of anything it has done.

Judgement of Inspections

One of the great claims that inspectors would no doubt make is their *fairness* to both teachers and the public. To the teachers they offer a professional and sympathetic approach to evaluation; to the public they offer the evaluation of an outsider. However, this is premised upon a notion of their independence. As we have already argued, at the level of school, and indeed the LEA, HM Inspectorate have that independence. This is not so for local inspectors, although they would argue that their involvement helps in effecting change. In addition to independence, both teachers and public, and teachers in particular, will want to be assured of the inspectors' ability so that they can trust the judgements made. HM Inspectorate seem to command the respect of teachers, although as Becher *et al* (1981, p. 11) say, 'Sometimes this respect appears to be based on an assumption that inspectors must (because many teachers rarely if ever see them) be very busy and therefore very able people'. Again local inspectors do not seem to do so well in engendering trust. Whether HMIs or local inspectors are involved, the school still has to give over *control* of the evaluation to outsiders; it may only be willing to do this if teachers are assured of the kind of fairness discussed above. If, as HM Inspectorate argue, the recommendations they make are not binding upon the LEA then this may represent an acceptable blend of central and local control. However, in the case of both local and national inspectors, the school is likely to be bound by the LEA's response to recommendations, in which case the school still has no control.

The argument over where control should reside is often based upon the criterion that an evaluation should be capable of suggesting appropriate *remedies*. Although inspectors control the evaluation, they argue that they place great importance on discussions with teachers which increase the chance of changes taking place. HM Inspectorate are not in a position to follow such discussions up with any kind of sustained support. Local inspectors, on the other hand, can rightly argue that this is their great strength.

From the evidence that is available there seems to be some doubt about whether inspection is *methodologically sound* (though this is mainly based on what the inspectors fail to say rather than what they do say). Again a trust in their ability is their main defence. However, whatever that ability may be, inspectors cannot avoid the criticism that they fail to follow many of the practices that ensure rigour in research. (Whether or not *any* evaluator should follow such practices is an issue we shall explore in *Part Three*.)

Finally, we need to consider whether inspections are an *economic* approach. Most commentators, from the 1968 Select Committee onwards, argue that HM Inspectorate should not expand to the extent that it is able to carry out a full programme of regular inspections (Hopkins, 1982, is an exception). If it did, Nuttall and McCormick (OU, 1982, Block 2, Part 3, p. 17) imply that the costs would rise so substantially as to become prohibitive. On the basis of calculations about what local and national inspectors could manage by way of inspections, Becher *et al* (1979) go further and conclude that, 'It therefore becomes hard to see inspection becoming a routine form of accountability without at least doubling the number of inspectors' (p.57). They reach this conclusion as part of an argument for school-based accounting using criteria similar to those we have considered. On all of their criteria they conclude that a school-based approach is likely to be superior to either one based upon testing or inspection. It is not possible, however, to come to any conclusion about the usefulness of testing and inspection (outsider evaluations) without considering what is possible for schools to do themselves (Becher *et al*, 1979, go on to consider the merits of school-based approaches). The next chapter is just such a consideration, though one that takes as a starting point the professional development of teachers (Chapter 2) rather than the issue of accountability (Chapter 1).

Notes

1.   For those who want more details of each of these types of evaluation we give further references to the literature.

2.   We are using 'tests' and 'testing' to refer to standardised tests i.e. standardised with respect to the conditions of administration, and where scores are standardised against a group (OU, 1981a, Block 4, p. 48). Chapter 8 expands on this.

3.   In a recent evaluation of the National Assessment of Education Progress (NAEP) - the national testing programme in the USA - Wirtz & Lapointe argue that no-one questions the need to identify and measure standards (through measuring student achievement) nor that they should be used for accountability purposes:

> Teachers and school administrators continue, with considerable reason, to protest against being solely accountable for difficulties and failures to which parents and communities are at least accomplices. But the new rule is that the political community is to be represented in establishing the standards, and that the results of the measurements are to be reported in terms that parents, taxpayers, and people generally can understand. (Wirtz & Lapointe, 1982, p.4.)

Holt (1981) provides a vigorous critique of the national programme in England and Wales; Gipps (1982) gives a more measured and brief one, although the most complete evaluation is reported by Gipps and Goldstein (1983, forthcoming). The USA national testing programme, NAEP, has been the subject of several evaluations: Greenbaum *et al* (1977), the most detailed and critical; Provus *et al* (1974); Johnson *et al* (1975); Comptroller

General of the United States (1976); Wirtz & Lapointe (1982), which briefly reviews the previous evaluations. Burstall and Kay (1978) also provide a review of some of the evaluations of NAEP as well as evidence on state testing programmes gathered in a visit to the USA sponsored by the British national testing programme, the Assessment of Performance Unit (APU).

5. Four goals are mandated by legislation:
    1. To collect and report at least once every year data assessing the performance of students at various age or grade levels in each of the areas of Reading, Writing and Mathematics;
    2. To report periodically data on changes in the knowledge and skills of such students over time;
    3. To conduct special assessments of other educational areas, as the need for additional nationwide information arises; and
    4. To provide technical assistance to state and local educational agencies . . (Wirtz & Lapointe, 1982, pp. 68-69).

6. Wirtz and Lapointe (1982, p.16) report that these have been effectively reduced to reading, writing and mathematics - see note 5.

7. Wirtz and Lapointe (1982, p.16) say that the frequency has been reduced to once every five years.

8. Bob Doe reported that a year after the first primary mathematics survey was published only 4000 copies had been sold (*TES*, 17 July 1981).

9. The accounts of both NAEP and the APU are necessarily brief but there are numerous accounts of both systems available. Simon (1979) gives an early, but provocative, account of the setting up of the APU, its committees and working groups and what it sets out to do. Note 4 gives fuller references for accounts of both the APU and NAEP. The APU does not include Scotland in its testing programme, but Dockrell gives an account of the national surveys in Scotland in 1963 and 1968 (Scottish Education Department, 1979). For more general descriptions of testing in the USA and Canada see Forbes (1982) and McLean (1982) respectively.

10. Galton (undated) discusses strategies of co-operation and control of the APU by teachers, with control being the most important. He saw control being exercised either formally, through representation on committees, or more informally at school level. The latter, in his view, should involve teachers in developing their own assessment procedures. This would be more like a Mode III approach.

11. The Open University (1982, Case Study 5), describes a school's attempt at running a testing programme, although the information was of limited use for curriculum evaluation. Gray (OU, 1982 'Making more sense of examination results') describes how schools can use public examination results for their own internal evaluation.

12. They argue that the decision to use school subjects was never actually taken and that this limited NAEP to what schools teach rather than what they ought to teach. This latter point was also thought to be a limitation in the most recent evaluation (Wirtz & Lapointe, 1982), which generally does not agree with the conclusions of Greenbaum *et al* (1977).

13. Galton (undated) recounts a typical case of a teacher admonishing children who did not leave sums they could not do in a test - she would normally expect them to get each a piece of work marked before going on to the next.

14. Again Greenbaum *et al* (1977) have harsh words to say about the validity of the test exercises, although the team operating NAEP, in replying to Greenbaum and his colleagues (in the same volume), argue that they have improved the validity of the exercises: a point supported by the latest evaluation (Wirtz & Lapointe, 1982). The latest evaluation does not however support this statement with any evidence.

15. Strictly speaking there are both technical and educational criticisms, which interact (Nuttall, 1982a). Several accounts of these criticisms exist at different levels of technicality: Nuttall (1979) and Goldstein (1979b) give non-technical accounts; Goldstein (1981b) and Tall (1981) give slightly more technical accounts; Goldstein and Blinkhorn (1977) and Goldstein (1981a) give the most technical discussions.

16. Even this is in doubt - see Goldstein (1981a).

17. These criticisms of the Rasch model caused considerable controversy within the APU's Statistics Advisory Group, some of which spitt on to the pages of the *TES* (27 February 1981). This controversy, which eventually resulted in the model being abandoned, is documented in Gipps and Goldstein (1983, forthcoming).

18. Greenbaum *et al* (1977, p. 166-7) note the poor quality of some state and local testing programmes when they examine the NAEP's objective to forestall the development of less effective or misdirected attempts at assessment. A later study of state programmes, which Greenbaum and his colleagues had no access to, indicates that more state testing of verbal and mathematic achievement have problems with translating goals into objectives from which test items can then be derived (Edcuational Testing Service, 1973).

19. In particular there is a lack of thought about purposes, haphazard and minimal use of results, lack of co-ordination between LEA testing and school's own testing, and problems with the quality of standardization to produce norms.

20   Despite the requests for more information it appears that, even in the cases where NAEP collected more, the data remain unanalysed (Wirtz & Lapointe, 1982, p. 41).

21. A problem recognised by commentators on NAEP (Wirtz & Lapointe, 1982, p. 33) and the APU (Gipps, 1982).

22. Most of the evidence on class size points to large classes having better performance results than small classes. This contradicts what most people would expect. It cannot be assumed, however, that large classes are the cause of better results. It could also be that because remedial groups are small the performance of small classes is lower, or alternatively, that the best teachers are given the largest classes and it is these teachers who improve performance.

23. Some responses by states appear to be very crude. Florida, for example, has reinstated minimum amounts of mathematics and science teaching in the curriculum because of falling test scores in these subjects. California is also following suit (*TES*, 21 May 1982).

24. A recent controversy occurred in England when a councillor, who was not on the education committee of her local authority, failed to obtain the 11-plus results for schools in the authority. She threatened to take out a High Court injunction to get the results released (*TES*, 21 May 1982).

25. For example only one state in 1973 actually measured classroom variables (Educational Testing Service, 1973).

26. It will have become evident from a number of comments we have made that we consider the evaluation of NAEP by Greenbaum et al (1977) to be a more thorough and thoughtful one than that of Wirtz & Lapointe (1982). The latter evaluation presents little detailed evidence for their views and strangely does not address itself to some of the basic questions that Greenbaum and his colleagues did. In a review of Greenbaum *et al* (1977), Iwanicki (1978) claims that the validity of their criticisms depends upon one's philosophical position with respect to the structure of the educational process and 'one's view of what is technically, politically and economically feasible in the assessment process given the present status of social science measurement and research methodology' (p. 135-6). While we think this is largely true (Iwanicki's argument is too brief for us to be convinced), our view is that Greenbaum and his colleagues go further in producing evidence for their position than Wirtz and Lapointe.

27. Becher *et al* (1981) see this as the most obvious way of guaranteeing standards.

28. Hopkins (1982) argues that this is the most important guarantee of the quality of inspectors' reports and their credibility in the eyes of the education profession.

29. This is a point made by most pronouncements in which HMI trace their origins, e.g. Browne (1979) and DES (1971, p.2).

30. See Edmonds (1962) and Blackie (1970) for detailed accounts of the development of HM Inspectorate, and Regan (1977, pp. 103-120) for a brief account by an outsider to the Inspectorate. Hopkins (1982) gives a brief account by an ex-HMI, and DES (1983c; 1986) give official ones. Lawton & Gordon (1987) is the most recent complete account of HMI, to date.

31. For example Thomas (OU, 1983a, Block 2, Part 3) and Blackie (OU, 1982, Block 2, Part 3). Also see note 30.

32. See, for example, a satirical piece by 'Axegrinder' in the *Times Educational Supplement*, 24 April 1981, and an intriguing pupil survey of a school being inspected (Carding, C. *TES*, 6 June 1986, p. 20).

33. A former Senior Chief Inspector in evidence to the same select committee admitted that 'the formal report could disappear altogether without detracting from the exercise' (Select Committee on Education and Science, 1968a, Minutes of Evidence, Examination of Witnesses, Q207). The then current Senior Chief Inspector seemed to support the use of reports, but admitted that:

     If we really do have to say something critical about an individual person we say it very firmly to the person, but much more lightly to the head, and when it comes to the written reports it is a whisper. (Q74).

34. However, see Walker (1979).

35. The National Association of Head Teachers, again in response to the document on the role of the advisory service, did not pull any punches in criticising advisers in this regard.

36. Pearce (1982) gives the most explicit, but still far from satisfactory, account of their approach.

37.   There may of course be a difference of tradition between HMIs in Scotland and in England and Wales, because the Permanent Under Secretary of State (DES) also thought the report offered protection to the teacher (Select Committee on Education and Science, 1968a, Part I Examination of Witnesses, Q71.) See also note 33.

38.   The theory concerns the match of the work children are doing to their ability - see the main questions the HMI have in mind when observing (pp. 85-6).

39.   Curiously, although the Permanent Under Secretary of State (DES) promised the Select Committee a paper on the teaching experience of HMI in England and Wales (Select Committee for Education and Science, 1968a, Part I, Examination of Witnesses, Q9), only a paper on the previous experience of inspectors in one division was submitted, but not published. Perhaps a full analysis was too much work (in asking for it a member of the Committee said: 'I do not think we want to impose too much on you'. (Q. 43)).

5   Evaluation by Insiders

Introduction

The evaluation strategies outlined in Chapter 4 may satisfy the consumers of education that an independent check is being kept on the
work of schools, but, as the judgement we came to indicated, they
seem less satisfactory as procedures for assisting improvement in
educational practice. Even if more apparent than real, they carry some
threat of sanctions against teachers and schools who fail to perform as
expected however unreasonable, given certain contexts, that expectation might be. They can, therefore, evoke a defensive, sometimes
hostile, response from teachers that is anything but conducive to
creative effort in the direction of curriculum *improvement*[1]. Within
the profession the general feeling is that the greater the degree of
autonomy that can be given to teachers and schools, the more likely
are they to accept responsibility for educational provision and become
committed to improving its quality. This, as we saw in Chapter 1, is the
argument for a professional mode of accountability (see also Sockett,
1980). It is also the rationale for suggesting that evaluation has an
important role in promoting professional development and curriculum
improvement (see Chapter 2).

Proposals for Insider Evaluation

If, as has been suggested above, insider evaluation is primarily associated with curriculum improvement, it comes as little surprise that
proposals for particular approaches are directly or indirectly related to
models of curriculum design and development. Indeed, evaluation is
regarded as an important stage in 'rational planning' or 'objectives'
models of curriculum design, which rest on the assumption that education is a means towards ends. Accordingly, curriculum development
involves specifying educational goals and selecting appropriate learning

103

contexts in which those goals can be pursued. Thereafter, the task of evaluation is to ascertain whether or not the pre-specified goals (aims and objectives) have been achieved. It is customarily acknowledged that this model was first developed by Bobbitt (1918, 1924), clarified by Tyler (1949) and refined and elaborated by numerous others (e.g. Taba, 1962, Bloom, 1956, Block, 1971). The importance of finding ways to measure the achievement of goals encouraged some writers (e.g. Popham, 1967) to emphasise the need to specify aims and objectives in precise behavioural terms. This argument had a simple logic. If the achievement of specific goals is to be assessed, then they need to be observable; if they are to be observable they need to be framed in terms of specific student behaviours.

The arguments for and against this approach to curriculum planning and evaluation are well documented elsewhere (Stenhouse, 1975; Hamilton *et al*, 1977; Open University, 1976, 1983b). Suffice it here to say that there have emerged other groups of educationists who present alternative views. Some of these are in fundamental disagreement with the assumption on which the rational-planning or objectives models rest. In other words they deny that education is necessarily a means to an end, and argue instead that either the *content* or the *processes* of teaching and learning can have instrinsic educational value. Thus the teaching of certain forms of knowledge has been regarded by some (Hirst, 1965, 1974; Peters, 1967) as intrinsically worthwhile; whilst others have regarded certain principles of procedure, such as enquiry-discovery learning, in much the same way (Dewey, 1916; Bruner, 1960).

The critique of the objectives model and the erection of an alternative paradigm was the central theme of an important book by Stenhouse (1975). In this he pointed out that whilst the objectives model might be appropriate to those parts of education concerned with skills training and instruction (acquisition of information), it was of no help in the area of understanding (induction into thought systems). He argued that education for understanding can only be regarded as successful to the extent that it makes behavioural outcomes *unpredictable*. In this context, therefore, evaluation can only legitimately focus on processes. (This issue of what to evaluate will be developed further in Chapter 7.)

Stenhouse's argument, however, goes beyond proposing a process model for curriculum development and evaluation. According to him an emphasis on processes makes such great demands upon the teacher (an insight gained when he was director of the Humanities Curriculum Project) that any proposal for curriculum development should be regarded as tentative, having the status of an hypothesis to be tested by teachers in their own classrooms. For this reason he proposed a 'research model' that has as its central theme the notion that it is not sufficient that the work of teachers should be studied (either in terms of outcomes or processes), but that they should study it *themselves.* This is the concept of the teacher-as-researcher that we introduced in Chapter 2.

In relation to insider evaluation there is evidence in the educational literature that the three approaches to curriculum development outlined here (the objectives model, the process model, and the research model[2]) continue to have an influence on evaluation, at least in the UK (we will come to the USA and Australia later). In modified form the objectives model is still alive and well. Many educationists, administrators and teachers, especially those of a technocratic or managerial frame of mind, continue to argue that evaluation must be concerned with establishing educational objectives and then systematically monitoring, often by statistical methods, whether or not they have been achieved. This, for instance, is the stance taken by Shipman (1979) in the book he entitles *In-School Evaluation.* Avoiding the perennial philosophical question concerning what educational ends are most worthwhile, and what constitutes educational quality, he asserts that it is perfectly possible for teachers to agree 'working objectives' that can provide the focus for the development of an evaluation technology. His emphasis on systematisation, objectivity and the utilisation of indicators by which the achievement of objectives might be measured reveals a conformity to the classic, positivistic or behaviourist tradition[3]. As we pointed out earlier, the kind of model for insider evaluation that Shipman proposes has a long history and there is little evidence that it has been significantly displaced by newer alternatives. Undoubtedly its appeal rests on a simple logic that those inside and outside schools can readily comprehend; as such its influence should not be underestimated.

The influence of process and research models for curriculum development can also be detected in a number of proposals for insider evaluation. Among the most detailed derive, not entirely unexpectedly, from people like John Elliott and Helen Simons who at some time have worked with Lawrence Stenhouse[4]. Elliott's development of the research model will be discussed in Chapter 11 because it is very much concerned with strategies for action. Here we will confine our attention to an approach to evaluation proposed by Simons (1981). Although she argues mainly for *process* evaluation at *whole-school* level, her account is representative of a growing genre of writing on insider evaluation, which is generally opposed to the objectives approach (see also Adelman and Alexander, 1982; Elliott, 1979; MacDonald, 1978; Rodger and Richardson, 1985). According to Simons, evaluation in schools should possess the following characteristics:

1. It should aspire to reflect the *processes* of teaching, learning and schooling in order to educate judgements about the adequacy of educational provision and the quality of experience pupils have. Simons rejects product-efficiency models which pay attention only to outcomes, since some outcomes are beyond the school's power to influence (see the arguments outlined in Chapter 4).

2. It should draw on a wide spectrum of information sources: interview data, close description of observed events, documentary evidence, as well as test and examination results. In other words, evidence of processes and outcomes should be drawn from a *broad data base*.

3. It should examine the attitudes, values and assumptions that underly the kind of information that comes from various sources. In Simons's words it 'goes beyond the information given' to identify the interests which shape the 'facts'. For this reason it is considered important to gather the subjective judgements of participants as well as evidence of a seemingly factual kind.

4. It should encourage the flow of information in all directions: down the status hierarchy as well as laterally and upwards, as is more usual. In this sense it intends to foster the idea that the internal organisation of institutions should be open and democratic.

5. It should develop the kind of informal evaluation that teachers normally engage in, in order to gain some feedback on their practice.

6. It should focus on internal needs defined by the school and its teachers, not merely what outsiders consider to be important. This notion is based on the argument that unless teachers perceive issues to be relevant they are unlikely to be committed to their resolution. In this connection, Simons makes a special point of advocating the consideration of whole-school issues (a theme that we shall develop later).

7. It should be particularistic and small scale and concerned with the immediate problems of a given institutional context. It is likely to be less interested in universals and what may, or may not, be the general case.

8. It should be concerned, therefore, with evaluating educational situations in ways that provide information relevant to decision making and the analysis of policy options.

9. It should precede curriculum development rather than following after it; in other words, it should be formative rather than summative (Scriven, 1967; see also Chapter 11).

10. It should be initiated and managed by teachers inside the schools on the assumption that only if schools and teachers retain control of the evaluation process will they be committed to the implementation of any recommendations for action that arise.

11. It should recognise that evaluation is potentially very threatening to those whose practice is under scrutiny, so procedures need to be devised to protect the most vulnerable. These procedures are based on ethical principles concerning impartiality, confidentiality, negotiation, collaboration and accountability (which are expanded in Chapter 9). Again the assumption is that no genuine change will result if the confidence of practitioners is totally undermined.

12. It should also recognise that there is a need to protect such exercises from public scrutiny for a period so that teachers have time to acquire evaluative skills. For this reason Simons argues that self-evaluation should be isolated from accountability demands for a time, although she also believes that school self-evaluation could provide the most positive form of accountability procedure in the long term. Once more her argument rests on the potential of self-evaluation to influence change.

Examples of evaluations by teachers in schools

All that has been said so far has, of course, been at the level of advocacy. It has concentrated on the proposals of educational writers concerning approaches to inside evaluation that schools and teachers might be encouraged to adopt[5]. Very little has been said about what actually happens or, at least, there are still few readily available accounts of school evaluations conducted by teachers. Moreover, those published have never been analysed to see whether they reflect the theory. In Australia the Teachers as Evaluators Project has collected descriptions of school-level evaluations for inclusion in three bibliographies (TEP, 1978, 1979, 1980a). Nevertheless the project team was forced to admit that: 'Data about teachers and schools which have carried out school-level evaluations are fairly limited, particularly with respect to follow-up activities' (Teachers as Evaluators Project, 1980b, p. 8). Much the same is true of the UK, although a few case-studies of school-based evaluation activities are beginning to appear in the literature (see for instance, Ford Teaching Project, 1975; Cambridge Accountability Project, 1981; Holt, 1981; Nixon, 1981; Open University, 1982, Block 2, Part 2; Acland, 1984; Baker, 1984; Elliott and Ebbutt, 1986b)[6].

This apparent lack of evidence cannot, however, be taken to imply that school-based evaluation exists only in the minds of educationists. After all, if its purpose is professional development and curriculum improvement, there is no reason why schools and teachers should disseminate what they do farther than the bounds of their own school community. The question of what is going on 'at ground level' is none the less interesting and potentially important because schools that have experience in evaluation have much to offer those who are just beginning to establish procedures. It was for reasons such as these that in June 1981 we used the educational press to invite schools, colleges, and teachers to contact us if they had 'undertaken self-evaluation, self-assessment, self-monitoring or curriculum review'. We had some 200 replies, a large number of which were from LEAs and INSET providers who supplied us with policy documents or general literature. However, we also received a little over fifty responses directly from individual schools and colleges giving details of particular activities. Concentrating first on this small group we attempted a descriptive analysis of each activity and used these to compile what we called, rather cumbersomely, *A First Review and Register of School and College-initiated Self-evaluation Activities, in the United Kingdom* (James, 1982)[7].

Since our sample was self-selected it is impossible to say what proportion of the total number of self-evaluation activities it represents, or whether the range of activities is in any way typical. If in 1981 there were only a little over 50 recognisable activities of this kind, then educationists writing about school-based evaluation may have something to worry about. One assumes that there were considerably more, although it is interesting that some of those activities reported to us had already been reported elsewhere (i.e. in Cambridge Accountability Project, 1981; Holt, 1981; Nixon, 1981).

A few short descriptions of the kinds of activities reported to us may serve to illustrate some of their range and variety. In accordance with the main theme of this book the accounts given here are drawn from the school sector (primary and secondary) and concentrate on activities that were conducted at the level of the whole institution (although, in practice, the whole of the school may not have become involved). By way of qualification it should be noted that the descriptions are based mainly on documentary evidence; thus they lack the richness, and perhaps the verisimilitude, of 'in-depth' case studies. Certainly they are incomplete in terms of the kind of information we might have elicited through observation, interview and questionnaire. Four accounts follow. Obviously they cannot raise all the issues connected with insider evaluation so other examples are drawn on, but in less detail, in the final 'Issues' section of this chapter.

Quintin Kynaston School is an eleven to eighteen mixed comprehensive in North London. It was formed in 1969 by the amalgamation of two single-sex schools on the same site. For the first four years of the new school's existence the buildings were used much as they had been prior to amalgamation, but in 1974 organisation was rationalised to provide departmental areas with teaching rooms and adjacent resource bases. This re-organisation enabled the introduction of mixed-ability teaching in years one to three, in all subjects, and a decision to this effect was taken at a full staff conference in early 1974. The idea of co-operative course planning grew naturally out of this commitment to mixed ability teaching and in October 1976 a second staff conference embraced the idea that an emphasis should be placed on 'the learning process in all courses'. Since 1976 a number of working groups have met to consider ways of promoting effective learning across the curriculum. They include working groups on social education course development, mixed-ability teaching, language across the curriculum, numeracy across the curriculum, study skills development, multicultural and anti-racist education, and sexual differentiation in schooling. Their work is co-ordinated and reviewed by a Support for Learning Group (SLG).

Alongside the efforts of these 'across the curriculum' working groups there has been a commitment to review the work of courses, departments, and faculties. Again however the emphasis is on co-operative effort and, at the end of the 1979/80 year, the school set about producing review reports that would 'collectively reflect the ways in which staff plan and organise children's learning'. The format for these reports, agreed by the heads of department, invited consideration of course aims, course planning and organisation, co-operative planning and teaching, record-keeping and continuous assessment, finance, staffing, accommodation, timetabling, moderation and evaluation.

In the first instance reports were compiled for each course (e.g. 3rd year music, lower school drama, the pottery courses, CSE Mode I maths, upper school biology) by course co-ordinators. These were then collated by the head of department who sometimes added an overview. Individual department reports were then compiled into faculty reports by the head of faculty who again added his/her own comments. In most cases heads of faculty picked up general issues that had emerged during the reporting process e.g. public image, relationships between subject departments, staff support (or lack of it) for extra-curricular activities. The final collation was then made by the headteacher who again added comments on general issues and problems, and established the school's priorities for the next year.

The number of reporting levels involved almost every member of staff in writing one or other of the reports. According to the head-teacher the intention was 'to give as many staff as possible a sense of responsibility of teaching and learning', despite the fact that 'as in all schools we have a hierarchical structure of responsibilities'. When the final report was produced it was circulated internally amongst staff and presented to the school's governors and the section of the ILEA inspectorate most concerned with the school.

The commitment to whole curriculum planning and review represented in the final report suggested a need to investigate further the implications of whole school curriculum development. Thus the publication of the review reports was immediately followed by a proposal to mount a major three-year research project. The essence of the proposal was a request to the ILEA for funds to second one of the school's teaching staff for a period of seven terms, and for support in obtaining an outside consultant, secretarial assistance, and advice from various agencies including the ILEA's Research and Statistics personnel and university researchers.

The aims of the project were to be 'process-oriented' in that they were concerned with evaluating the process whereby the school promotes learning across the curriculum, and the extent to which policies (intentions) are 'part of the actual learning' being experienced by pupils. They were also 'development oriented' in that the findings were to inform action to 'improve the quality of the curriculum' and 'to identify priorities for in-service training'.

In terms of research procedure the project was envisaged as having three stages. In the first stage the Support for Learning Group would identify and publish the criteria to guide classroom observations. These were intended to cover areas such as language use and the acquisition of study skills.

Technical advice on classroom observation was to be sought from various advisory bodies, and agreement to the principle and procedures of the research was to be sought from teaching staff at a staff meeting. Other INSET and resources support was also to be organised at this point.

Observation was to constitute the major part of the second stage of the project. This was to involve lesson observation, and related discussion with the class teacher; analysis of teaching material, departmental policy documents, and student 'products'; discussion with course planning teams; monitoring learning outcomes and dialogue with students; involvement with INSET activities and dialogue with outsiders; and commissioning, training, monitoring and debriefing co-observers.

The third stage of the project was to involve reporting and discussion at the end of the observation period, although it was acknowledged that incidental feedback in the context of dialogue with teachers, students and outsiders was inevitable, and that smaller, interim reports to the SLG, as steering group, would be necessary. In addition to the production of reports, the research would also be expected to collect and disseminate examples of good practice.

In actuality this particular research project got no further than stage one. It became clear to the teachers that many of the objectives of the research model identified above could be achieved by building up skills of co-observation and self-evaluation within and between teachers. Further, self-evaluation was found to be most profitably focused in departments and on those structures which brought departments together to develop and evaluate whole-school policies. The idea of classroom observation encouraged some teachers to observe each other, and one group, for example, began some research on girls' talk.

By 1987 the SLG had been redefined as the Curriculum Review Group (CRG) and during 1984-5 had reviewed the 14-16 Curriculum to make it more accessible to all, and in particular to reduce gender and class disadvantages and increase its coherence. This resulted in a new curriculum structure, and the CRG is now reviewing the 11-14 curriculum. The Staff Development Group is exploring the possibility of extending the observation and self-evaluation process to review and sustain these developments.

Sir Frank Markham School is in the unusual position of undergoing expansion. Situated in Milton Keynes, it first opened its doors in 1979 as a purpose-built comprehensive for boys and girls between the ages of twelve and sixteen.

In 1980, after only one year's work with the 'entry' year of pupil intake (the 12/13 year olds), the seventeen existing staff were asked to submit a written appraisal of their work. Subsequently each was interviewed by the headteacher. In the following year, 1980/81, the staff had grown to 53 and two year groups of pupils were now in the school. The larger school required a more formal review procedure and a number of activities were initiated. In June 1981 a whole staff conference was convened to consider specific issues such as examinations, the needs of the less able, and the needs and demands of the older pupil. In addition, two review procedures were instituted: a staff review, under the aegis of the Deputy Head (Staff Development), and a curriculum review, conducted largely by the Deputy Head (Curriculum Development).

The *staff review of performance* was intended to 'look carefully at what we do now in order to do things better'. The exercise based on individual reports, attempted the previous year, had been modified to render the activity less threatening, and to reduce the workload placed on staff. Therefore, although a copy of suggested questions was issued to all staff individually, only the head of faculty was expected to submit a written report, on the basis of informal discussion with individual faculty members. Suggested areas for consideration included aspects of the school environment, communication, responsibilities and achievements, priorities and improvements.

These areas were framed in a checklist of questions, which covered issues of both individual and collective concern. For example:

What is the general appearance of our faculty/my room?
What visual evidence is there of the quality of children's work?
How noisy is the faculty/my room?
How do the children move to and from the faculty and within it?
Can we welcome a visitor at any time without worry?
Or what sort of worry?
Does everyone in the faculty know what is happening about
a) syllabus; b) money; c) timetable?
Does the head teacher know what the faculty thinks on major matters?
Who has responsibility for what?
What are my/our priorities for the coming term/year?
How far are my/our teaching aims hindered by: timetable structures; lack of resources; school policies; faculty policies?

(Sir Frank Markham School: internal document)

Each head of faculty's final report was duplicated and copies were given to each faculty member, the headteacher, and the appropriate deputy head. The headteacher then discussed each report with the head of faculty *after* discussions between the members of each faculty (other than the head of faculty) and the deputy heads. At first this procedure evoked a strong reaction from faculty heads who perceived the dangers of over-personalised accounts. Indeed some reports proved to be fairly personal, identifying the practices of individuals, whilst others dealt only with general issues.

In fairness to the senior management team the original staff review guidelines emphasised that information exchange would be two-way: reflecting also any adverse effect of school policy on classroom practice. Furthermore the deputy heads were expected to discuss their work with the head teacher, and a visit by two members of the LEA's advisory service was intended to provide an opportunity for the head to 'account' to his peers.

In the school year 1981/82, the staff review exercise was repeated, but once again with modifications. This time a decision was taken to place the process at the beginning of the school year. Although the faculty-based approach was retained, the scope of the activity was limited by stressing a group 'objectives-setting' exercise aimed at the forthcoming year. The intention was to change the tone of the activity from retrospective to forward-looking, thus emphasising its constructive nature and again reducing any threat (especially to senior staff).

During the academic year 1984/5 another system of staff review was introduced as a development of the earlier one. This was based upon an annual interview of all staff by the senior member of staff responsible for their work (for example a head of faculty). This was a formal process which focused on staff development by setting goals for the coming year. Guidance was given on the conduct of the interviews and a list of questions was provided to assist the tasks of reviewing the work of the teacher and setting targets. The teacher was also given time to prepare for the interview. At the time when this scheme was introduced it was recognised that schools would be required to have some such arrangement in the future. As we pointed out in Chapter 1, the school was right in its prediction!

In some senses a review of the work of staff, taken faculty by faculty, inevitably encompasses an element of curriculum review. However, in the summer term of 1981, the 'entry-year curriculum' was taken as a specific focus for evaluation. In this instance the issue of accountability was a principal and explicit motivation, and the need for *a curriculum review* was placed in the context of the need to provide information for the headteacher, the school governors, 'feeder' schools, and the LEA. The need to 'take stock' after the first year of the school's existence figured prominently, and recent publications from DES, HMI and the Schools Council regarding the whole curriculum (see Chapter 3) also gave impetus to the activity (although these documents appeared some time after the review had been initiated).

The exercise was divided into three stages. The first consisted of an analysis of curriculum content and teaching methods conducted by questionnaire. Perceiving a need for authority and direction if the exercise was to have credibility, the Deputy Head (Curriculum Development) took the lead in proposing sample questions as a 'cock-shy' for discussion. These were then debated by a working party of representatives from each faculty, who transformed them into 'a palatable form for staff to use'. The questionnaire which was eventually devised was designed to elicit information concerning:

1. Faculty/department aims/goals/priorities/intentions expressed in terms of concepts and/or skills. Teachers were also asked to assess the extent to which these concepts or skills contributed to the HMI eight areas of experience and their degree of relevance to pupils in terms of getting a job; personal development; subject development; leisure, and so forth.
2. Teaching and learning methods, including the proportion of class-time spent on individualised learning, small group work, or whole class teaching and the nature of homework tasks.
3. The nature of the results teachers believed they achieved (i.e. reported outcomes).
4. Methods of evaluation and subsequent action.
5. The degree to which the work of faculties/departments over-lapped, and the extent to which co-operation was desired[8].

Some guidance was provided to teachers completing the question-naire in order to familiarise them with the HMI eight areas of experience and to agree meanings of terms such as 'concept' and 'skill'. For some questions, particularly those connected with (1) above, teachers were asked to use a printed schedule and a 5-point rating scale for their answers. (A short section from the Maths report (Figure 5:1) illustr-ates its use.) Apart from the obvious element of subjectivity involved in scoring the contribution of subject teaching to various areas of the pupil's experience, some teachers seemed to have difficulty in ident-ifying concepts. Whereas the maths syllabus was organised around concepts (e.g. shape, plane, enlargement, volume), the humanities syllabus, for instance, dealt with topics (e.g. health and fitness, history

Figure 5.1 Extract from Maths Faculty Curriculum Analysis

MATHS

Concept or Skill	8 Areas of Experience								Relevance				
	Mathematical	Scientific	Linguistic	Socio-Political	Aesthetic/Creative	Ethical	Spiritual	Physical	Getting a Job	Personal Development	Subject Development	Leisure	Other
Concept (Cont.)													
Probability	5	5	5	4	1	2			4	1	3	5	4
Use of drawing instruments for simple construction	5	1	5	1	5	1			5	1	3	5	4
Circles	5	1	5	1	3	1			3	1	1	5	1
Skills													
Spatial awareness	5	5	5	1	1	1	2		1	1	3	5	4
Manipulation of numbers	5	5	5	1	1	1	1	1	1	5	1	5	3
Ordered thinking	5	5	5	3	3	1			1	5	3	5	3
Mental arithmetic	5	5	5	1	1	1			1	3	3	5	3
Ability to estimate length, weight, size etc.	5	5	5	1	1	1			1	3	3	5	3
Problem solving	5	5	5	1	1	1			1	3	3	5	3
Co-ordination and control	5	5	5	3	3	1			5	5	5	5	5
Clear communication of logical thought patterns	5	5	5	3	1	1			1	5	5	5	5

Note: *Rating scales*
1 = low importance/relevance
5 = high importance/relevance

and archaeology, ancient Greek, local studies) and these also tended to be listed under the 'concept' heading[9]. Nevertheless, once the questionnaire data had been collected and compared the Deputy Head (Curriculum) was able to present a summary report which included sections on:

the relative contribution of subject areas to the eight areas of experience; the nature and degree of relevance assigned to subject teaching; a selective summary of the skills taught by various faculties; an account of the way departments justified their teaching methods; an analysis of subject overlap; a description of evaluation procedures; and a department by department judgement of outcomes.

Among the interesting things to emerge from this first study was the way in which teachers equated formal evaluation exclusively with pupil assessment. They had no systematic means of monitoring the effectiveness of teaching and learning processes. Stage 2 of the curriculum review went some way, therefore, to provide more verifiable data. This involved classroom observation, by the deputy head, in the form of a shadow study of one class for the period of a week. The intention was to gain some insight into 'the whole curriculum at operational level'. Observation' gives more details of these). It is evident that the deputy record lesson format, materials used, pupil activities, teacher involvement and questioning, pupil responses, etc. (Chapter 8 on 'Direct Observation' gives more details of these.) It is evident that the deputy head soon realised that he had set himself an enormous task, despite the fact that he decided to focus on the work of three 'target' pupils. Nevertheless the exercise resulted in an evaluation report, which, like the report of Stage 1, contributed to the thinking of Stage 3.

Stage 3 was perhaps the most important of the project's three stages. Questions and issues arising in the course of the earlier work were collected into a discussion document to be considered by various groups of staff including the senior policy-making body, heads of department, faculty and tutor meetings, and appropriate working parties. Wherever relevant reference was made to *The School Curriculum* (DES, 1981b) and *The Practical Curriculum* (Schools Council, 1981) as well as the 'entry-year evaluation' study.

The document was divided into sections concerning curriculum content, overlap, teaching methods, relevance, and evaluation. Each contained a number of recommendations for consideration and future action. Among these a need for cross-curricular study featured prominently, as did various areas where curricular provision had yet to be developed (e.g. the tutorial programme, a 'life-skills' curriculum, curriculum provision for the able child). In addition, although the deputy head was clearly exhausted by the enormity of the task he had set himself, he had found the experience sufficiently valuable to recommend that all teachers should extend their understanding of curriculum evaluation and develop skills in addition to the testing of pupil outcomes. Indeed he went so far as to suggest that pupils might be involved in evaluating the curriculum in the future. His final recommendation, therefore, was that evaluation should become a continuous process in which all faculties and departments should be involved; that it should examine teaching and learning in all year groups; but that it should perhaps be less wide-ranging and more focused than this first effort.

In the year 1981/82 it became clear that the evaluation project had had a number of 'spin-offs', for instance:

1. teachers in 'feeder' middle schools were invited to read the study and two schools subsequently redesigned their humanities course to provide continuity with the curriculum at Sir Frank Markham;
2. working parties on able pupils, social and life skills, and community education had been formed;
3. a number of faculties had begun to follow up specific issues e.g. integration between science and maths, and art and recreation;
4. the Deputy Head (Curriculum) worked with the Head of Additional Studies Faculty to produce a framework for a study-skills course which would link with the work of all other departments;
5. the Humanities Faculty, having been rather disturbed by one or two things that emerged from the study, decided to meet in someone's house the day after the end of the Christmas Term. There it began a review of its work which continued, at intervals, throughout subsequent terms;
6. the exercise encouraged greater communication with governors (a number of whom read the whole study), and between the Deputy Head (Curriculum) and more junior staff (who seemed to be more willing to ask for help);
7. it also helped to take some of the 'sting' out of the staff review, and paved the way for further work e.g. the planning of an evaluation of the 12-16 curriculum with respect to areas of experience and skills.

The process begun in 1981 was continued and developed during 1983/4 and 1986. In 1983 the whole curriculum for pupils aged 12-16 was reviewed through the production of two important documents. The first was a 'Curriculum Digest' which contained a statement for all areas of the curriculum on aims, syllabuses and contributions to the areas of learning and experience identified by HMI. A Curriculum Co-ordinating Committee (CCC) was reponsible for editing this document to represent the work of each area in a standard format. The digest was circulated to all staff and to governors together with a questionnaire asking for comments under headings such as: organisation of the curriculum; aims of faculties/subjects; core and options in years 4/5. The CCC also drew up a questionnaire for teachers in charge of subjects/heads of departments/heads of faculty to be completed in collaboration with other staff. This second questionnaire covered a wide variety of issues including priorities in the aims, contributions and importance of the school as a community school, group work, special areas of the curriculum (e.g. health education, multicultural education), co-ordination of teaching across subject divisions, employment and in-service training.

These documents were discussed by the whole staff, by governors, and finally by the Senior Management Team, who proposed changes which were again submitted to staff for their views. This process of collecting and discussing information involved staff at all levels, although faculty representatives on the CCC played a central role. The changes decided centrally were structural and left changes in curricular content and teaching methods to faculties. For example, the school day and week were changed to increase the number of periods but reduce the amount of time pupils spent moving around the school between lessons. New courses which resulted from these changes began in September 1984 and parents were kept informed at all stages.

The shadow study, which formed part of the 1981 review, was repeated in 1986. The deputy head who carried out the original study was willing to repeat the exhausting exercise, even though he was also responsible for the CCC. The second shadow study was a true repeat of the first, although some of the schedules were changed. Thus comparisons could be made which revealed progress in some areas and decline in others. For example, the incidence of group work appeared to have declined although caution had to be exercised in interpreting results because there were inherent problems in sampling particular weeks for study (see Chapter 8). At the time of writing, changes proposed as a result of this study had not yet been implemented. Nevertheless, the whole review programme was testimony to the school's commitment to a continuous self-evaluation policy as integral to its decision-making process.

Priory Roman Catholic Primary School is to be found in Eastwood, Nottingham. Two infant and three junior classes cater for children from five to eleven although no class contains children with more than two years' difference in their ages.

In January 1981, the whole school embarked on work connected with a single language-based topic. The motivation for the project was:

staff recognition of a need to evaluate whether children made any real progress in their written work between 1st year infants and 4th year juniors; whether too much was expected too soon, and whether it is possible to decide an age when the average child could be expected to be competent in certain skills; whether the language curriculum throughout the school was sufficiently broad in terms of coverage or whether there was unnecessary duplication; whether the most able children were being stretched enough; whether there was any justification for 'setting' across classes for certain kinds of work; whether pooling teacher energy and resources on a common topic increased intrastaff awareness and co-operation, and co-operation and interest among children from different classes; and finally, whether whole-school topic work appeared sufficiently worthwhile in terms of children's learning experiences to warrant repetition at some future date. Described in this way the aims of the project appear to have been ambitious; the teachers believed them to be quite modest.

The initial stimulus for the work was a story: *The Shrinking of Treehorn* by Florence Parry Heide. This acted as the literature focus around which seven learning tasks were devised. They were not all preplanned; some of the later activities developed naturally out of those that came earlier. However, each task was intended to give children the opportunity to exercise a range of reading, writing and other language skills. Thus:

TASK 1 asked children to use their imaginations to predict the end of the story, both orally and in writing.

TASK 2 required simple recall in the act of narrating part of the story already told.

TASK 3 focused on sentence construction in the context of formal letter writing.

TASK 4 asked children to draft, revise and redraft a poem with a given theme.

TASK 5 was similar to TASK 4 but lots of class preparation was substituted for the individualised re-drafting process.

TASK 6 required children to write instructions and explanations relating to some game familiar to them.

TASK 7 demanded that they express their personal feelings in relation to the experience of being ignored or bored.

These seven pieces of work were designed to enable across-class comparison and analysis, but over fifty other topic-related activities involving art work, mathematics, science, music, environmental studies and various kinds of research were also suggested in order to give each class and its teacher a measure of autonomy over the way their work progressed. Clearly some of this work was beyond the scope of the youngest children, nevertheless the reception class joined in wherever possible and their teacher attended all staff meetings and discussions. Her comments were considered especially important since, not being quite so involved with the work, they were perhaps more detached.

Each of the main pieces of work was allocated approximately one week in the spring term of 1981. At weekly evening meetings staff discussed their observations of their own classes and took decisions regarding what seemed to be required in terms of teaching strategy, expectations, or reinforcement. In some cases these evaluations were formative in relation to the next main piece of work; thus when the task of story narration (TASK 2) did not appear to encourage children to use full stops, and capital letters, teachers suggested that formal and structured letter writing was more likely to help with the structuring of sentences. Observations on TASK 3 appeared to support this hypothesis.

At the end of the term and the completion of the topic, staff agreed that satisfactory progress seemed to be made from year group to year group in terms of the development of writing skills. They were confident that it was possible to make general statements about improvements across a year group, despite individual differences. However they also felt that they had been expecting most children to write in sentences at too early an age. Apparently all teachers of junior children 'found sentences the most difficult thing to teach; the most difficult thing for children to learn; the most irritating thing when correcting work; and decided that all hard work on sentences in the past had little effect.' Brought to the surface in this way, this problem supplied the staff of the school with a common concern to focus on in its future work. At the time of writing they are still working on this, although they no longer expect an immediate or easy solution.

Amenable to more immediate action was the decision to write into the syllabus certain activities concerning language skills. Staff agreed that unless this was done it was likely that some areas would inevitably be overlooked. In this way, as in others, the project directly contributed to the formulation of the school's future language policy. Unlike the other activities which we describe in this section, there was no outsider initiative, input or audience in relation to the efforts of this school's staff. A report of the work was typed by the school secretary but its informal style and the sometimes cryptic references to individual children make it clear that it was intended for internal circulation only. A slide show of the work of one class was presented to parents but this was a familiar procedure and not regarded as 'giving an account' or involving parents in the evaluation of *teaching*. The staff might have been helped by an outsider who could question those things that teachers generally take for granted (for instance, by asking what they meant by their habitual use of the term 'bright children'), or who could suggest an appropriate range of evaluative techniques. On the other hand, the staff felt that the project would have taken a different form and provoked different responses from teachers if an outsider had been present at meetings. In particular they felt that they might have tried to cover up their worst failings and made a public show of only their more successful work.

Even without any contribution from outsiders, the teachers at Priory School revealed a considerable capacity to innovate. They discovered for themselves the value of taking note of the way pupils write of their school experience; and by passing unnamed 'pupil products' around the staff group, they devised a way of cross-checking and standardising the assessment criteria that each was using in grading children's work.

Modest and unsophisticated though this activity may appear to the educationist there is little doubt that it issued in some constructive change in the school, not least, one suspects, in the degree of staff cohesion.

Combe Pafford School is situated in Devon, near Torquay. It is an all-age day special school for approximately 150 children who are classified as moderately educationally sub-normal (ESN (M)). There are fourteen teaching staff.

Since 1978 all teachers at the school have been engaged on a school-based, school-focused in-service training course. The initial motivation for this form of INSET arose from two main needs:

1. A need to revise the total curriculum by structuring curricular areas in terms of the skills, attitudes and values needed by ESN(M) children;
2. A need to introduce all staff to current educational theories and practice and to provide opportunities for staff to explore and make decisions about curricular practices in the light of theoretical considerations.

The decision to mount a school-based INSET course was taken by the headteacher in the knowledge that the school's teaching staff had much experience in classroom practice and were at a point when they could consider whole curriculum issues. Some, in fact, were engaged in degree work and were in a position to introduce ideas of a more theoretical nature to their colleagues. One of these was appointed the course co-ordinator. The decision to organise such a course was also motivated by the belief that this kind of INSET would have certain outcomes:

1. it would stimulate staff to re-examine their own work and that of their colleagues;
2. it would require total staff participation and therefore would act as a cohesive agent;
3. it would contibute to the professional development of the staff as a whole and increase the confidence of individual teachers;
4. it could help bridge the gap between theory and practice;
5. it could prepare staff for any further alteration in the role of the special school (re: the Warnock Report (DES, 1978b));
6. it could help staff to develop a common language for the discussion of curricular issues;
7. it would allow staff the opportunity to develop leadership skills in small group work.

The more specific decision to make the focus of the course an attempt to restructure the traditional content-based curriculum in terms of skills was justified in the following way:

1. We cannot hope to provide our children with all the knowledge that we would like them to have, but we can provide them with the 'study skills', which will enable them to further their knowledge, both in school and afterwards.
2. Knowledge can be exclusive (i.e. non-transferable) and impermanent. Skills, however, can be used in a number of learning situations. Skills, therefore, once acquired, have a greater part to play in the transfer of learning.
3. Skills, once learned, are less easily forgotten than areas of knowledge.
4. A content-based curriculum can impose constraints on a teacher. A skills-based curriculum can allow the teacher more autonomy in the choice of learning material, provided that the requisite skills are being practised.

5. A skills-based curriculum has a built-in mechanism for evaluating progress. The skills themselves become the 'tick-off'
   items which indicate a child's progress or lack of same.
6. During the past decade educationists have increasingly stressed
   the importance of a skills-based curriculum: Barrett, Bruner,
   Piaget and Bloom, to name but a few. (Combe Pafford School:
   internal document.)

This emphasis on skills was to be supported by the development of appropriate attitudes and values because it was felt that the
social, as well as the cognitive, development of the child should be
fostered; and because the education of attitudes removes the threat
of sterility from a skills-based programme.

Once the need and the rationale for the INSET course had been
established, the staff of the school proceeded to the next stage by
selecting a particular area to review. During 1980/81 the language curriculum was the main focus of attention. Concurrently the course co-
ordinator made an individual study of cnvironmental education and
submitted her work as part of the requirement for her M.Ed. degree.

The procedure for the consideration of each curricular area was
basically the same. An initial paper was put together by the headteacher
or the course co-ordinator. Normally this included a framework of
theoretical considerations or models supported by reference to the
available literature. This paper was then distributed among staff and
discussed in detail at a subsequent staff meeting.

The next stage of the process involved department (junior, middle
and senior) meetings where teachers attempted to break down the
curriculum area into the skills required by the children they taught.
At this stage ordering and progression became important. Written reports
from each department meeting were then put together in a paper which
was discussed and evaluated in a further 'whole staff' meeting. Eventually a final paper was produced, by the head and the course co-ordinator, which attempted to take into consideration all the findings of the
staff.

Towards the end of the school year, 1980/81, a number of such
curricular documents had been produced. Areas covered included
reading skills, comprehension skills, writing skills, social development
target-skills, oral language and listening skills, and environmental studies.
In 1981/82 the intention was to carry this kind of work into the mathematics curriculum area.

The 'product' of these staff discussions can perhaps best be illustrated with a single example. In the Autumn term of 1980, the work
involved examining reading 'as a response to graphic signals in terms

Figure 5.2 The Model for Discussion in the Autumn Term, 1980.

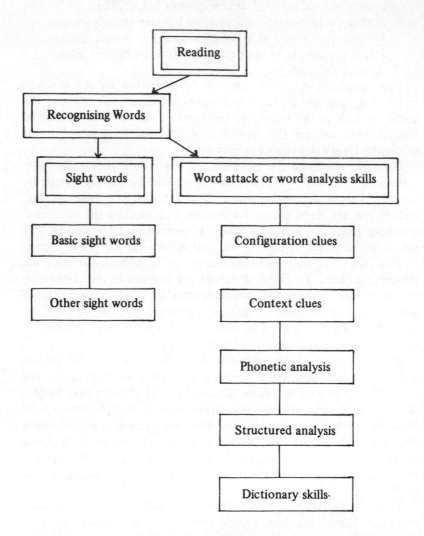

of the words they represent'. Teaching staff were thus presented with a model which they were asked to appraise (see Figure 5.2).

Following the agreed procedure each part of the model was examined by (1) the whole staff in the light of the total curriculum, and (2) by each department in the light of the idiosyncrasies of ESN children of different ages. After detailed and lively discussion composite lists of skills were identified, of which the following are two:

Sight Words
1. Symbol recognition - child can recognise a picture, word, letter, in isolation.
2. Symbol discrimination - child can recognise a picture, word, letter when occurring with other symbols a) dissimilar b) similar.
3. Symbol recall - child can remember what the symbol is whenever it is encountered.
4. Symbol transference - child can recognise the symbol whenever it occurs, regardless of type, context, presence of other very similar symbols etc.

Configuration Skills
1. Child uses left→right orientation appropriately.
2. Child can name everyday objects.
3. Child can name the picture of objects.
4. Child can name symbolic representation of objects.
5. Child can recognise shape of words by looking at length, number of letters, extenders and descenders, capitals, double letters, etc. Recognition, discrimination, recall and transference apply to the above.
(Combe Pafford School: internal document).

The procedure described so far falls quite clearly into the category of curriculum review (see Chapter 3). However other modes of evaluation were involved. The INSET course was itself evaluated 'primarily by subjective monitoring by observation, record keeping and frank discussion involving all members of staff'. Furthermore the development of a skills-based curriculum had a built-in assessment function: the lists of skills became the checklists of criteria (indicators) by which to assess children's progress.

Implementation of the skills-based approach can only, of course, take place after skills lists have been agreed and suitable environments selected in which these skills can be developed. We have evidence that an environment education programme of this kind had already been developed and implemented with middle-school and senior children with some success. In other areas the infancy of the programme meant that much had yet to be accomplished.

With a new INSET co-ordinator, the programme has developed since these early beginnings. The aims have remained the same, but the curriculum areas under examination have broadened. The skills-based approach has been used to develop lists of criteria for the production of records of maths skills and written English skills. So, for example, children can build up a record of their achievement in various mathematical operations and concepts. These recording procedures were the result of an INSET programme, carried out in the Autumn Term 1983, which included a consideration of assessment in general, as well as testing and referencing systems (see Chapter 8).

The earlier concern for attitudes and values was maintained in 1985 in response to a county-wide guide on moral and religious education. This led to a frank discussion of attitudes among teachers and resulted in a broad statement of aims and objectives for the school.

This INSET-based approach to self-evaluation was supported by TRIST (TVEI-related in-service training) funding, which also stimulated a concern for problem-solving within the curriculum. The new in-service funding arrangements under GRIST are allowing this work to continue.

A Typology of School Self-Evaluations

If one compares the examples described in the preceding section with the kinds of proposals for school-based evaluations put forward by educationists, then the differences are striking. In particular the theoretical issue of focus (e.g. whether to evaluate objectives, outcomes or processes) and the educationist's concern with research-type methodology (i.e. systematic data-collection and analysis) appear to be outweighed by more immediate practical issues concerning implementation of procedures. This is not to deny any concern with theoretical considerations but to emphasise that the question of what to evaluate and how to evaluate tends to be dictated by needs, purposes, and existing resources and structures. Indeed our evidence suggests that, with respect to 'objective', 'process' or 'teacher-as-researcher' approaches, school-based evaluations can represent a combination of two, or all three. For example, Quintin Kynaston School was interested in investigating certain cross-curricular issues and thus tended to focus on process. However the proposal for a teacher-researcher and the initiation of a number of classroom-research projects demonstrated a development of the school's activities along the lines advocated by Stenhouse. Sir Frank Markham School's curriculum review has involved stating departmental goals framed in terms of concepts, skills and the contribution to areas of experience, but this emphasis has been offset by the shadow study which was principally aimed at investigating curriculum processes. The experimental nature of Priory School's exercise is suggestive of Stenhouse's approach to curriculum and teacher development: 'The idea is that of an educational science in which each classroom is a laboratory, each teacher a member of the scientific community' (Stenhouse, 1975, p.142). Nevertheless appraisal of the extent to which the school had been successful in achieving certain objectives connected with language teaching is equally prominent. In our opinion, therefore, it is Combe Pafford School that comes closest to presenting a paradigm example of a particular approach to curriculum evaluation. The reason is not difficult to find. The staff's concern to reconstruct the curriculum in terms of *skills* meant, as Stenhouse (1975, p.80) pointed out, that an objectives approach was most appropriate. Thus the systematic analysis of the curriculum that took place provided a set of indicators by which teachers could subsequently measure success in attaining their curriculum objectives. In this case indicators were framed in terms of pupil outcomes.

Despite this evidence concerning the focus of evaluation, our four examples possess other characteristics which are at least of equal importance. Evaluation is distinguished from 'pure' research to the extent that that it is concerned with the identification of specific needs, the investigation of practice, the development of policy alternatives, decision-making, and the implementation of policy choices (see also Chapter 7). In the light of this it is hardly surprising that issues of organisation feature prominently in descriptions of actual examples. This aspect is often given insufficient attention in the literature on school-based evaluation, although such neglect is not always in evidence. For instance Simons' (1981) account of process evaluation in schools pays a lot of attention to organisational aspects and implications for action[10] (a reason for outlining her proposals in this chapter).

The importance of the organisational dimension was brought home to us when we attempted an analysis of the fifty or so insider evaluations that were reported to us in 1981 (James, 1982). Although we espoused a 'grounded' approach to the analysis of our data (see Glasar and Strauss, 1967), we inevitably had certain expectations concerning what school-generated accounts would reveal. Thus at the outset of our research we were interested in questions such as: What is being evaluated? How? For what purpose? Gradually we became aware that answers to these questions were in some way bound up with a question concerning the management of evaluation. Two distinct forms of organisation seemed to be evident: one we called 'rational management', the other we called 'collegial'. Evaluation with a rational-management style of organisation was closely linked with the management structure of the school and information tended to flow upwards through a series of policy-making levels or committees. In contrast, collegially organised evaluations attempted to avoid too close a connection with the school's management structure in an effort to secure the full and equal participation of all those involved in the activity. In this case procedures were usually developed to encourage information flow in all directions (see Simons' proposals for evaluation: point 4). Each style of organisation appeared to endorse a particular strategy of change: the rational-management style tended to be empirical-rational or power-coercive, whilst collegial evaluation aspired to be normative-re-educative (see Chapter 2.)

Further examination of our data revealed that this organisational dimension seemed to be related, in specific ways, to other dimensions that we had identified, for example: where initiatives had come from; who was involved in the conduct of evaluation; evaluation purposes (accountability, professional development, curriculum development or review); the focus of evaluation (antecedent conditions, including aims and objectives, processes, outcomes); methods (meeting-based or research-based); and the audiences for evaluation reports (internal or external). To summarise, it seemed that we had some evidence to suggest that:

A rational management style of organisation is more likely to be be associated with evaluation conducted chiefly by senior staff (heads of department and above), primarily for purposes of accountability or curriculum review, focusing particularly on antecedent conditions (e.g. aims, objectives, management structures), and using meetings and discussions as its main vehicle (usually discussions between heads of department and head-teachers, or heads of department and their departmental staff).

Collegially organised evaluations, on the other hand, are more likely to be conducted by staff at all status levels, primarily for purposes of professional or curriculum development. Antecedents, processes and outcomes all become foci but relatively greater emphasis is given to educational processes. Meetings and discussions again feature prominently but qualitative research is also an important method. (James, 1982, p.20).

On this basis, and developing a distinction between authority-based and responsiblity-based evaluations proposed by Brown, McIntyre and Impey (1979), we generated the following typology of evaluations by insiders. The labels attached to Type A and Type B were intended to suggest both an orientation towards certain interpretations of account-ability (contractual, professional, moral - see Chapter 1), and implicit strategies for change (power-coercive, normative-re-educative etc. - see Chapter 2).

TYPE A: Authority-based institutional self-evaluations.

Operational dimensions

Internal involvement and control:	senior and middle management.
Purposes:	explicit accountability and curriculum review.
Organisation:	rational management.
Focus:	antecedents and outcomes (input-output)
Methods:	meetings plus collection of mainly quantitative data.

Theoretical constructs

Mode of accountability to colleagues:	legal-formal (explicit)
Socio-political perspective:	positivistic or systems theory.
Evaluation tradition:	systems analysis, objectives, management or technology models.

TYPE B: Responsibility-based institutional self-evaluations

Operational dimensions

Internal involvement and control:	all status levels
Purposes:	professional development and curriculum development
Organisation:	collegial
Focus:	processes
Methods:	discussions, plus collection of mainly qualitative data.

Theoretical constructs

Mode of accountability to colleagues:	moral (implicit)
Socio-political perspective:	interpretative or humanistic

Evaluation tradition: the transaction or process
model (also responsive,
illuminative, democratic,
ethnographic.)
(Source: James, 1982, pp. 25-26)[11]

It goes without saying, that our analysis remains at the level of hypothesis, derived as it was from the data of a self-selected, and possibly atypical, sample of schools. Nevertheless, it suggests that the organisation of evaluation might be a fruitful area of further research; and that particular attention needs to be paid to the implications of various evaluation strategies for the management structures of schools, and vice versa. In particular, the impact of, and on, leadership style is worthy of attention. Although not explored in the Review described above, there was plenty of circumstantial evidence to suggest the influence of a charismatic headteacher in some collegially organised self-evaluations. In Chapter 2 we noted the implications for evaluation of the dilemma that Hoyle (1975) identified as the root of innovation problems i.e. that curriculum innovation requires change in the internal structure of the school, but that this too is a major innovation. Since systematic evaluation by insiders is itself still in the category of innovation, the 'creativity' of the school system is crucial to its success. However, it seems that a preoccupation with methodology among evaluation theorists has tended to deflect attention from this important organisational dimension. (The issue of organisation is taken up again in Chapter 9.)

The Contribution of Records of Achievement to School Self-evaluation

Some interesting responses to our request for information on school self-evaluations, which supplied the data for the review described in the preceding section, referred to pupil self-assessment schemes. At first we attributed such responses to misinterpretation of our request because such schemes focus on individual learners rather than classrooms or schools. In retrospect, however, we realised that some of best examples of feedback on curriculum and teaching were embedded in reports of processes in which pupils discussed their self-assessments with teachers (James, 1982, p. 99). Of necessity pupils discussed their experiences and achievements in context and thereby described, and often evaluated, the curricular opportunities available to them.

Pupil self-assessment and recording is a feature of the many pupil profiling or records of achievement schemes which have burgeoned in the UK in the 1980s, although prototypes have been around for a decade or more. The rapid growth of profiling as an educational idea, even a movement, was given particular impetus by the publication of a DES policy statement on records of achievement (DES, 1984d) and subsequent funding, through an educational support grant (ESG), of nine pilot schemes involving twenty-two LEAs. Moreover, the government of the day expressed a commitment to establishing national guidelines for records of achievement by 1988 with a view to having a national system, for all pupils of secondary school age, in place by 1990.

The significance of this development for curriculum evaluation in schools arises from the fact that an examination of the suitability of curriculum provision is an explicit purpose identified in the DES statement of policy:

> The recording process should help schools to identify the all round potential of their pupils and to consider how well the curriculum, teaching and organisation enable pupils to develop the general, practical and social skills which are to be recorded. (DES, 1984d, p. 3)

The schemes that have been developed both with and without DES funding very considerably. Some concentrate on personal experiences, achievements and qualities (the pastoral dimension), whilst others incorporate subject-based and/or cross-curricular assessments. Some record achievement in relation to pre-specified criteria generated by a project team (e.g. using comment banks), whilst others are open-ended and decisions about what to record emerge in teacher-pupil dialogue. Some promote personal recording and self-assessment by pupils whilst others rely more heavily on teacher assessments discussed or 'agreed' with pupils. Some systems are generated by individual schools on whom the burden of validation rests, whilst others are developed by LEA or consortia teams, in which case an examination board might take major responsibility for validating some components of the record, e.g. graded or staged assessments.

Despite these differences there are a number of basic principles held in common. Recording processes are intended to involve pupils of all abilities, not just those for whom conventional examinations are inappropriate. Formative processes are considered as important as the production of a summative statement. In relation to the formative side, opportunities for one-to-one discussion between teachers and pupils are regarded as vital in order to agree the record, but also to diagnose areas for improvement and set targets for the future. On the summative side, it is generally accepted that final documents of record should contain only positive statements.

Both similarities and differences among records of achievement and other profiling schemes (such as those devised in relation to the Technical and Vocational Education Initiative (TVEI), the Lower Attaining Pupils Project (LAPP), the Certificate of Pre-vocational Education (CPVE), the City and Guilds of London Institute (CGLI), and the Business and Technical Education Council (BTEC) diploma courses) have implications for the kind of contribution they might make to curriculum evaluation, and especially school self-evaluation. However, since most schemes have a formative role with a diagnostic and remedial function it would also be reasonable to expect this to have an evaluative function in relation to the curriculum, as implied in the DES policy statement. Preliminary analyses of school case study data by the national team evaluating DES-funded pilot schemes (PRAISE, 1987) indicate that feedback from pupils, and sometimes parents and employers, on curricular provision is virtually unavoidable. This occurs especially in the context of teacher-pupil dialogue which, as indicated above, is integral to most schemes.

What is not clear, however, is how such information should be analysed, communicated and used to inform curricular decision-making at group and whole-school level. For the most part, pupils, and parents if invited, will offer feedback on individual experiences of teaching and learning. This information can be used to make decisions about changes in curriculum and teaching to match the needs of the individual pupil (Harlen, 1978 - see also Chapter 11). Indeed this is the thrust of the DES statement quoted above. Whether the same kind of information can be used to evaluate curriculum and teaching as it applies to whole teaching groups is more problematic. In all probability the sum of comments on individual experience will provide sufficient evidence of group-related patterns for it to be regarded as a valid basis for judgement and action at class, department or even whole-school level.

A greater problem may be whether teachers are able to communicate and act on the information generated during the recording process. Whilst some individual teachers may be able to act on feedback regarding individual pupils (and it is debatable whether they can), structures for communicating information which goes beyond the immediate context are rare (PRAISE, 1987). This could be a stumbling-block for the whole records of achievement initiative since failure to respond adequately to information and opinion with a wider reference could undermine the whole recording process by destroying credibility with both pupils and parents who will expect change.

One interesting aspect of pupil self-assessment elements in records of achievement systems is that although the onus of change is on the learners they may not be able to act because of the way learning is structured. It is often claimed that goals for learning and criteria for assessment should be communicated to pupils at the start of units or modules of work, in order that pupils may be motivated to change their behaviour to ensure that the criteria are met. However, in order to meet learning targets they may also require additional information, resources, or special opportunities. These in turn may demand changes in curriculum, teaching and organisation to meet individual needs which, for various reasons, teachers may not be able to deliver. Teachers may find it particularly difficult to change their classrooms from an organisation premised on whole-class teaching to an organisation designed to support individualised learning.

(Some technical aspects of records of achievement are examined in the section on curriculum outcomes in Chapter 8.)

Insider Evaluation in the United States, Australia and elsewhere

The discussion so far has focused on the literature and evidence of insider evaluation currently available in the UK, although links with early curriculum planning models originating in the USA have been acknowledged. At the very beginning of this chapter, for instance, we pointed out the influence of Tyler (1949) and Bloom (1956) on the development of objectives-based models of evaluation. Similarly the ideas of Americans such as Stake (1967), a programme evaluator, have influenced the development of strategies for process evaluation, especially that of Simons. (Stake's framework will be dealt with in more detail in Chapter 7.)

In the United States itself, however, there appears to be little evidence that models for programme evaluation, which pay attention to curriculum processes, have anywhere been adapted to serve the purposes of insider evaluation of schools[12]. School-level evaluation continues to be dominated by models derived from psychology and the objectives model of curriculum design, and much of the 'testing' that this entails is, in any case, developed and conducted by outsiders (see Chapter 4)[13]. The accreditation procedures developed by a number of regional associations (described in more detail in Chapter 6) involve self-evaluation but even here the criteria for the evaluation are generated outside the individual school, and the school's self-study is audited by a group of visiting professionals. On the whole it appears that the fierce debate at national and state level concerning accountability has not been conducive to the development of strategies for evaluation by insiders (something we noted in Chapter 3), neither has the fact that the major initiative for curriculum planning lies outside the schools. If teachers and schools have no role to play in curriculum development there is little incentive for them to engage in activities whose major rationale is a potential to facilitate change.

In Australia the situation is rather different. As in the UK, the notion of insider evaluation is gaining acceptance and has perhaps reached a more advanced stage of implementation. It is interesting, therefore, that this situation may have come about for reasons which are almost the reverse of those in the UK. In Britain the growth of support for self-evaluation seems to represent an attempt to bolster teacher autonomy in the face of attempts to increase central control (see Chapter 3). In Australia the relaxation of state control of the curriculum over the last decade has given greater responsibility for curriculum development to individual schools. Until recently curricula in Australian schools were prescribed by state bodies; details were set out in syllabuses for various subjects and the system was regulated by external examinations and state education department school inspectors. Now that control over these matters is passing to individual schools or regions, curriculum evalution has had to take on a new role: not only is school-based evaluation expected to provide a mode of accountability but it is also, and principally, expected to supply the basis for curriculum improvement.

In a review of the evaluation policies of Australian states the Teachers as Evaluators Project (1980b) has remarked on an apparent agreement about the nature of school-level evaluation.

A common stand is the emphases on self-evaluation for school improvement; generally viewed as a co-operative venture, supported at the system level by the provision of resources. The Schools Commission reinforces this approach, viewing school-level evaluation as a school-initiated change process designed to yield information for in-school use. Although this information may also be used at the system level for decision making, primarily the system's role is to provide encouragement for the evaluation process by the provision of resources, dissemination of information and supplying of a climate in which schools are encouraged to act. (p.5) [14].

Since 1977, the Teachers as Evaluators Project, sponsored jointly by the Curriculum Development Centre and the Educational Research and Development Committee in Australia, has been trialling processes and materials to support curriculum evaluation in schools. The project's early experience was that there was not a lot of material on insider evaluation available to Australian teachers. More recently, however, exchange visits between UK and Australian educationists has resulted in a cross-fertilisation of ideas that has undoubtedly contributed to a sympathetic development of practice in the two countries [15].

Evidence of insider evaluation in other countries is rather thin. A survey of what was described as School Based Review (SBR) for school improvement, conducted for the International School Improvement Project (ISIP, 1983), identified only 28 SBR projects in 12 countries with membership of the Organisation for Economic Co-operation and Development (OECD) - Britain and Australia accounted for half of these.

Issues

Levels of evaluation

Much of the emphasis in this chapter has been placed on the role of evaluation in both curriculum development or improvement and professional development, which we, like Stenhouse (1975), have assumed to be closely interrelated. Our other main emphasis has been on evaluation of the whole school, or an issue or policy which concerns the whole school. All four of our case studies fall into this category of institutional evaluation. However, as we pointed out in Chapter 2, the question of whether evaluation at whole-school level can effectively contribute to curriculum improvement and professional growth is not entirely unproblematic. There are arguments for and against at both a practical and theoretical level.

Simons (1981) makes a strong case in favour of studying the school as a whole. Firmly maintaining that the chief rationale for school-based evaluation must be educational and professional (she regards account-ability demands as secondary, at least while the school is establishing its procedures) she supports her case with the following six assumptions:

1. that better understanding of the organisation and policies of the school could improve the opportunities and experiences provided in classrooms;
2. that systematic study and review allow the school to determine, and to produce evidence of the extent to which they are providing the quality of education they espouse;
3. that a study of school policies can help teachers identify policy effects which require attention at school, department or class-room level;
4. that many policy issues (remedial education, for example) cut across departments and classrooms and require collective review and resolution;
5. that there are many learning experiences (field work and extra-curricular activities, for instance) which do not take place in the classroom and which require the co-operation and appraisal of the whole school;
6. that participation in a school self-study gives teachers the opportunity to develop their professional decision-making skills, enlarge their perspectives, and become better informed about the roles, responsibilities and problems of their coll-eagues.

(Simons, 1981, p.119-120).

Considerations such as these were very much in evidence in our four examples, particularly the activities conducted at Sir Frank Markham School.

It may be that whole-school evaluations are particularly appropriate in larger institutions with complex organisational structures. In this respect Simons's emphasis on aspects of policy-making takes account of the kinds of conditions necessary for the development of the 'creat-ive school' (see Chapter 2).

Convincing as Simons's arguments may appear, the discussion in Chapter 2 implied that they are not universally accepted. There are those, like Stenhouse, who argue that the quality of education is un-likely to be improved through evaluation of whole-school policy issues. According to this view education is concerned with the ex-periences of learners and these can only be enhanced if attention is paid to them directly. In other words, if curriculum evaluation is to contribute to educational improvement it must focus on individual classrooms, each of which is in some senses unique (Stenhouse, 1975, p.143). This basic tenet is shared by Elliott (1979), who nevertheless acknowledges a need to understand structural and organisational constraints on classroom action (Elliott, 1980b). Moreover, Elliott recognises that in certain contexts (e.g. accountability demands), the conduct of departmental or whole-school evaluation is unavoidable. As a kind of compromise, therefore, he suggests that whole-school accounts can be compiled from the sharing of individual classroom evaluations (Elliott, 1979b).

It can, of course, be argued that the two opposing views concerning the worth of whole-school evaluation are grounded in different theoretical perspectives: one declares that institutional structures are worthy of close attention because social systems constrain the actions of individuals (the structuralist perspective); the other focuses on classroom action because individuals are believed to have power to influence change in social systems (the interactionist or humanistic perspective). At a more pragmatic level, the limited time available for curriculum evaluation in the total work of any school makes some judgement about priorities a necessity. Whole-school evaluation built, as Elliott suggests, on evaluation across individual classrooms would demand an enormous amount of time and considerable skill from every classroom teacher. If, therefore, whole-school evaluation is judged to be a priority it may be more feasible to begin, not in individual classrooms, but with a school-wide issue that is of general concern. This whole-school approach may be particularly appropriate when the purpose of evaluation is to review the whole curriculum, in the sense discussed in Chapter 3, or to respond to accountability demands (see Chapter 1). On the other hand, it is interesting that of the four evaluations we chose to describe, two eventually adopted an approach similar to that advocated by Elliott (i.e. Priory R.C. School and Quintin Kynaston). The fact that they were principally interested in improvement of classroom practice, albeit throughout the whole school, may have had something to do with this[16].

Participation and control

It is reasonable to assume that *classroom* evaluation should be carried out by the individual classroom teacher, on his or her own initiative. Evaluation at whole-school level, however, presents problems.

Questions concerning where initiatives come from, and who should be involved in conducting the evaluation, are important because they have implications for the various purposes which insider evaluations seek to serve. In our examples, with the possible exception of Priory R.C. Primary School, headteachers and senior staff are prominent. Whether they initiated the activities is in some cases difficult to detect, but they undoubtedly assumed a key role in maintaining momentum.

The involvement of those with administrative responsibility is obviously vital to the success of any evaluation at whole-school level, since it is they who can provide the organisational structures for teachers' meetings, data collection, the presentation of reports and, most importantly, the implementation of policy decisions. On the other hand when a whole-school issue or policy is the focus of attention, it is conceivable that many of those whose practice is implicated will neither initiate nor conduct the evaluation. In our four examples there is evidence that where an initiative was taken by senior staff they consulted all the teachers in their schools. Nevertheless, one cannot escape the impression that in some evaluations the involvement of junior staff is minimal.

The issue of who *participates* in the process of evaluation is important, therefore, not only in terms of democratic ideals, but because it is likely to influence the outcomes of the exercise. Whatever its specific purpose (e.g. accountability, professional development, curriculum review), all evaluation is aimed at stimulating change, if change is shown to be needed. But teachers who have little or no part in the conduct of evaluation in their schools may well be resistant to any suggestion, by others, that they need to change some aspect of their practice. In effect, an approach to school-based evaluation, which involves the evaluation of a school-wide issue, by only a small proportion of the school's staff may place this elite group in an outsider-insider relationship with others. From the point of view of its potential to encourage change, it may therefore be judged in much the same way as evaluation by outsiders (see Chapter 4), and some combined strategies (see Chapter 6). (The issue of who are the insiders in insider evaluation will be returned to later in this section.)

If, as implied here, it is important for the implementation of recommendations that those whose practice is implicated should be involved, or at least have confidence in the evaluative process, then procedures need to be devised to ensure that they have a reasonable degree of *control* over the activity. In developing a concept of 'democratic evaluation' MacDonald (1977a) proposed that evaluation should be guided by the principles of *confidentiality, negotiation* and *accessibility*. Similarly, he saw the key justificatory concept of democratic evaluation as the 'right to know'. However since one group's 'right to know' may conflict with another's 'right to privacy', the principle of negotiation is in some senses superordinate, because it requires all stages of the evaluation process (including access to, and release of, data) to be agreed with all those likely to be affected by it. (Principles of procedure are dealt with more fully in Chapter 9.)

Threat

Underlying the issue of control is the assumption that evaluation is likely to threaten people in such a way as to inhibit change. Threat can manifest itself at two levels: in avoidance of direct observation of curriculum-processes, and in reluctance to share observations and judgements of practice with others. With regard to the latter, the traditional insularity of the teaching profession presents an obstacle that may not be overcome unless schools which exhibit a 'closed' style become more 'open'. The major shift in the internal organisation of schools that this would require reminds us again of Hoyle's (1975) point about the fundamental dilemma of innovation i.e. that innovation in curricular practice calls for innovation in organisation.

In our examples of insider evaluations there are indications that all four schools are towards the 'open' end of the organisational spectrum, and that dialogue between all levels of staff is encouraged. If teachers feel threatened in sharing their observations with their colleagues it is not very obvious. However, our examples are based on accounts from relatively senior members of staff who may be unaware of the feelings of their more junior colleagues. After all, inexperienced teachers may not feel that it is in their interests to reveal their difficulties to staff who have some influence over the future shape of their careers. In other words, the issue of threat is just as likely to emerge in insider evaluations, as it is in evaluations which involve outsiders. In fact, as we noted earlier, school-based evaluations which involve senior staff visiting the classrooms of those who are more junior (as at Sir Frank Markham) shift the meanings of 'outsider' and 'insider'. In these circumstances senior staff may well be perceived as 'outsiders', and the exercise become one of legal-formal accountability in much the same way as local inspections (see Chapter 4). The identification of 'authority-based institutional self-evaluations' (James, 1982) as a major category of insider evaluations suggests that this experience may not be uncommon.

Significantly, the deputy heads at Sir Frank Markham School recognised the degree of threat associated with their review procedures (especially the staff review) and much of their effort went into modifying their strategy in ways designed to increase the confidence of their colleagues.

The other common manifestation of threat i.e. avoidance of direct observation of curriculum processes, is also illustrated in our examples. If education is essentially concerned with the learning experiences of pupils it is remarkable that they provide so little evidence of systematic *direct* observation of educational transactions, in the classroom or elsewhere. Most of the evaluative activity in the four schools concentrates on curricular intentions or 'reported' observations. There is some use of (or the intention to use) research-based techniques, but methods are mostly an extension of traditional practice in that they involve teachers in meeting-based discussions of the aims and strategies they espouse, and routine observation and outcome measures[17]. (The methodological implications of this will be discussed below.)

Of course, the suggestion that direct observation is avoided because of feelings of threat is purely inferential, albeit supported by the reflections of teachers who have engaged in school-based evaluation elsewhere (James and Ebbutt, 1981; OU, 1982, Block 2, Part 2). The implication following from this is that the choice of evaluation focus in the four schools was a negative rather than positive decision: based on what teachers were prepared to do, rather than what they ought to have done. In their defence it needs to be noted that each school's activity was in some sense a curriculum review, thus intrinsic evaluation (or deliberation) was as important as empirical evaluation, if not more so. (See Chapter 3, and the discussion of intrinsic and empirical evaluation in *Part Three*.)

Whatever may have been the case in our examples, we would suggest that threat is an important, if not overriding, issue in school-based evaluation. For this reason it may be appropriate to consider an intermediate stage between the kind of informal, unsystematic and impressionistic evaluation that all teachers engage in as part of their natural practice, and full-blown, formal, systematically validated, research-based evaluation (an issue that is revisited in the section on 'Skills' in Chapter 9).

Methodological Soundness

The tendency for educationists, especially those with a research background, to advocate research methods as a basis for evaluation is no doubt grounded in the knowledge that evaluations need to have credibility. In the context of accountability, when the audience is external, this need is particularly acute. The solution has usually been seen to lie in the methodological soundness of the procedures chosen (see the criteria in Chapter 1), and in particular their validity and reliability. In this respect, whether quantitative or qualititative techniques are selected there are certain prescribed canons of procedure (which will be elaborated in *Part Three*).

A preoccupation with the methodological soundness of data collection and analysis has however tended to draw attention away from the fact that this is only part of the total evaluation process. The other part involves judgement concerning the worth of educational provision, the development of policy options and subsequent decision-making. This part of the process ultimately involves value issues which require deliberation; as such it too requires a procedure which, as we shall see in Chapter 8, can be considered in terms of technique.

In this sense, those who conduct research in their own schools are obliged to go through the deliberation process (in order to erect criteria and make judgements) if the activity is to be called evaluation. In whole-school evaluations the forum for such deliberation is likely to be the staff meeting or working party. In view of this, the importance attached to meetings and discussions in our four examples, and in the Review from which they were taken (James, 1982), is not without justification. Indeed, as suggested above, it is more reasonable to suggest that deliberation can proceed without formal research (i.e. on the basis of shared experience) than it is to suggest that formal research can serve any useful purpose without deliberation.

Time

As Simons (1981) points out the development of evaluative skills (research, deliberative or decision-making) is likely to take a lot of time. In many schools it would require teachers to take on roles with which they are not at all familiar. The expectation that teachers and schools will engage in a fully-fledged evaluation at the first attempt is therefore almost totally unrealistic (a criticism that can be levelled at some of the LEA schemes described in Chapter 6). Almond (in OU, 1982, Block 2, Part 2, Appendix) maintains that an incremental approach to evaluation is best. (His detailed suggestions are given in Chapter 9.)

A sense of unease about the amount of time evaluation can take, and doubts about the value of its outcomes, stimulated Holt's (1981) lively critique of the research-based school self-evaluation movement. In his opinion the exhortation to systematic self-critical reflection on practice diverts time and attention from the 'real' business of curriculum development and action. His criticism goes further than suggesting that there is simply not enough time for this kind of retrospective analysis of past activity. He believes it is fundamentally wrong-headed. Subscribing to the idea that teaching is a form of art or craft, he believes that no amount of analysis will enhance the practice of teaching because: 'Teaching depends on *practical* knowledge, and so does curriculum development. And practical knowledge "can neither be taught nor learned, but only imparted and acquired" '. (Holt, 1981, p. 141.)

Flattering as this kind of statement may be to teachers, one cannot resist the impression that those outside our schools will construe Holt's exhortations as yet another attempt to bolster professional mystique. However, Holt is chiefly mistaken in that he believes evaluation to be a 'big science', and as such separate from practical reasoning and deliberation. This is perhaps understandable given the methodological pre-occupations of much of the evaluation literature. In contrast, the accounts of evaluations to which we have access suggest that schools and teachers have little doubt of the priority of deliberation[18].

The role of outsiders

In our investigations of school-initiated evaluations (James, 1982) a number of activities reported to us involved someone outside the school (i.e. 14 out of 29 whole-school evaluations). These outsiders ranged from university lecturers and researchers, through local authority advisers and teachers' centre wardens, to the occasional governor, parent or teacher from another school[19]. The nature of outsider involvement was equally diverse although inevitably limited in some way by their existing roles (of which more later).

Some of the issues already raised in this section suggest that external help may be very desirable. For instance, the credibility issue forces us to enquire whether evaluations conducted by insiders alone can be even moderately free from bias. Given their insider status it is questionable whether teachers can ever detach themselves from what has become familiar in order to subject it to critical scrutiny. Here then is a role for an outsider who can help to 'render the familiar strange' and raise teachers' awareness of issues they take for granted (see also Chapters 8 and 9, and McMahon, Bolam, Abbott and Holly, 1984b, pp. 44-47).

In relation to one primary school's attempt at self-evaluation, Ray Shostak, formerly a teachers' centre warden, has described how he acted as 'agent provocateur' and 'ignorant observer' (see Open University,

1982, Block 2, Part 2). In this context he also acted as a consultant by advising on various classroom research techniques and providing other resources. In many ways his involvement was little different from the kind of involvement that inspectors claim in relation to outsider evaluations (see Chapters 4 and 6). The difference lies in the conditions under which the outside involvement was negotiated. In Shostak's case the control of the evaluation process lay entirely with the school, and he defined his role simply as 'facilitator' or 'process helper'. In no way did he see himself in the role of final arbiter or judge. In fact the only condition he required of the school's staff was that, if he was being asked to commit his time, they should be equally prepared to commit theirs.

The involvement of an outsider in ways such as this may not only improve the methodological soundness of an approach, and therefore increase its public credibility, but also lessen the burden on teachers in terms of the commitment of time, and the pressure to acquire evaluative skills quickly. It could even reduce threat if a trusted outsider acted as an 'honest broker' in an exchange of views between the more powerful and the less powerful in the status structure of the school - a role that Shostak assumed on one or two occasions.

In our view it is likely to be people such as advisory teachers who emerge as especially suited to take on the role of outside helper in school-based evaluation. Unlike other groups their sole responsibility is to provide a service to schools without exercising any authority in relation to them. This, combined with their local knowledge and their access to resources, makes them an obvious choice.

An alternative would be to involve lecturers and researchers from universities and colleges. Our evidence suggests this is frequently the case; indeed school-based evaluation is often first stimulated by a teacher's participation in an in-service, diploma or degree course (James, 1982). Once again the advantage of engaging researchers and lecturers as collaborators, consultants and 'critical friends' is that they too have skills, expertise, resources and some time that might be devoted to the support of schools. Most importantly, they have no position of authority in relation to schools, so they should pose no threat (although they may pose a threat of an intellectual kind). In some ways however they may be less free to give schools the kind of unconditional help that they most want. It would be an unusual academic who has no preconceived views about the best approach to school-based evaluation, or who has no need to account for his research time in terms of 'research products'.

This emerged as a significant problem in our involvement, as outside researchers, with a research project involving both Open University 'academics' and teachers at Stantonbury Campus (see OU, 1982, Case Study 2). The long and tortuous history of the project, an evaluation of interpersonal education at the school, was characterised by a tension concerning whether deliberation over school aims and approaches should precede research (the teachers' view), or whether research into what actually happened should precede judgement (the academics' view). There were also differences of opinion concerning the most appropriate research techniques (quantitative or qualitative). Significantly the proposed publication never materialised - a circumstance that worried the academics significantly more than it did the teachers! Perhaps the reason for the delay is to be found in a teacher's comment that: 'the school has found the process [of research] more educative than the research findings' (OU, 1982, Case Study 2, p. 39).

It is interesting that the experience at Stantonbury was, at about the same time, being almost exactly mirrored in another school (Melbourn Village College, Royston). The teacher who conceived the Melbourn project describes events in the following way:

A new appointment to the senior management of the school introduced to the school's varied operation a shift towards more instrumental attitudes. Lest any energy a teacher might spare for increasing his or her professionality be dissipated on what I considered at the time to be relatively trivial matters rather than fundamental matters of an enriching and animating nature, I rather hurriedly set in motion a scheme that would enable any teacher who so desired to become a research student - to investigate an aspect of his teaching that was problematic to him. Twelve teachers so desired. There was no reason that any teacher should have misunderstood the purpose or scope of the project at this stage. However, in my own mind, the project was taking a more distinct form. I pictured teachers being counselled on the identification of a suitable subject for investigation, receiving advice on the appropriate investigative techniques, and working for each other in a group as sounding boards, critics, advisers, assistants, guinea pigs, or whatever. I envisaged us putting together a collection of papers at the end of the project and either publishing them or circulating them locally. I recognised the need for an expert as consultant. I anticipated that he would be necessary for his familiarity with the literature, current research, and investigative techniques, for the injection of academic rigour, and for his own insights on students' research based on wide experience. My own tutor at the X ... Institute had been A ... We have met from time to time over the intervening years. I put to him my idea of a Course Consultant for a school-based research project and he said B ... was the ideal person. B ... came out to Melbourn and we dicussed the matter. He showed an interest and agreed to sound out the Institute on the feasibility of the project. Bureaucracy then played a part. In order that the services of B ... and his colleague C ... could be secured, the project had to be put on some kind of formal footing. The most appropriate slot was the Institute's Courses of Further Professional Study. Though a certificate was not an important feature of the project nor a factor in the membership of the group, the idea of certification was not unattractive. A meeting with D ..., the Secretary for Courses and Conferences, was arranged and the project became a course leading to a Certificate of Further Professional Study with a finite programme and 'compulsory' elements. The project's character was already changing. It was at this point too that a fundamental conceptual misunderstanding took place. 'School-based' (geographical) was confused with 'classroom-action' (methodological). Because I and my colleagues at that time were not even aware of a methodology called 'classroom-action', the misunderstanding did not become evident until it was too late to make a fresh start - and, in any case, 'classroom-action' by then, because of the skill and enthusiasm of the consultants, did seem to have some appeal, so the notion was 'gone along with'. This basic misunderstanding coloured the subsequent progress of the course.

Though classroom-action research is clearly rich and rewarding, its superimposition on the original energy that initiated the project together with the formalisation of the project into a C.F.P.S., had the effect of transforming the role of the students from active to passive. The students appreciated their dependance on direction and instruction in classroom-action research techniques. Exercises were set. Responsibility for action passed away from the students. I perceive this only with hindsight. The consultants clearly were not likely to take on that responsibility because that is not the role of consultant; I did not take it on as I was in the role of fellow-student and had my own research work to motivate. And there was no institutional coercive factor within the school to demand, however gently, a commitment. No one took on the responsibility, with the result that any small gaps of time set aside for the project rapidly filled up with other more immediate school tasks. That the teachers so readily unconsciously converted their role to a passive one may have some connection with a prevalent secondary school learning/teaching mode - the establishment of a contract involving clearly-defined and well-packaged puzzle-style assignments. Weightier priorities, arduous routine work loads, heavy extra commitments already made, and hurried assumptions on my part about other teachers' attitudes to personal research, and about the role of consultants also contributed to this eventuality. My assuming resulted in my failing to *ensure* that the members of the project and the consultants pictured the operation of the project as I did. In any case, bearing in mind the original description of the project as a mutually-supportive group of individual research students, I would not have been party to its conversion to a listen-and-obey task-orientated course.

That so many of the teachers did actually complete the 'compulsory' commitment to the course - the time element - and did produce a written contribution - albeit a contribution that most of the teachers found utterly unsatisfactory and unsatisfying - must be due to a variety of factors. Among these I would include high on the list the wish not to 'let down' a friend and colleague - me, the feeling of guilt at having set out in good faith and then come close to capitulation, the earnest wish to respond to the efforts of the consultants, and the professional urge to complete what investigation had been embarked upon.

(Farnell, 1981, pp. 2-4)

The problems of establishing the purpose of school-based research or evaluation, defining the roles of those involved and ultimately deciding what is to be done, whilst maintaining the kind of atmosphere conducive to creative effort are here writ large. Whilst outsiders with a background and experience similar to Melbourn's consultants can undoubtedly assist teachers in the acquisition of skills and the validation of findings, there is a need to clarify the expectations and purposes of the enterprise. Before introducing new strategies and techniques it is perhaps wise to work on some of the processes with which teachers are already familiar: deliberation over curricular aims and intentions, for instance. (The introduction of rigour into the process of deliberation is discussed in Chapter 8, and the role of the outsider in the provision of skills is taken up again in Chapters 6 and 9.)

Apart from advisory teachers and college personnel, it might be possible for schools to attract outside help from advisers, governors, parents, teachers in other schools, or members of the local community. Providing they possess the necessary experience, skills, and most importantly, time, they might be as helpful as any of those already mentioned. In one of the examples recorded in our Review and Register (James, 1982), a school was assisted by its Chairman of Governors. Being also a graduate computer personnel trainer he was able to suggest a self-assessment format borrowed from his own industry. Of course the other roles that advisers, governors and parents represent in their relations with schools can create a certain amount of anxiety, if not threat, so their involvement also needs to be considered carefully by all parties. (The involvement of local authority advisers is discussed in Chapter 6.) As we pointed out earlier the role of the outsider, in evaluations initiated by insiders, may differ very little from the roles of some of the outsiders described in Chapters 4 and 6. The principal difference lies in the assumption that schools should retain overall control of the process. In this sense it is quite distinct from other kinds of school evaluation. However, as we have also noted, the other roles of outsiders, such as researchers or advisers, may intrude to such an extent that the issue of who is in control is not at all clear. One way out of this situation is for insiders to negotiate a form of contract with outsiders whereby they establish the conditions under which the evaluation is to proceed. There is no suggestion that this should be legally binding; merely that it should be made explicit orally or in writing. Such a contract might cover:

1. the purposes of evaluation;
2. the roles of both outsiders and insiders;
3. the approximate anticipated duration of the activity and the time commitment required of all participants;
4. an agreed overall strategy and, if relevant, an outline of the methods to be employed;
5. arrangements regarding resources;
6. procedures to be employed to safeguard confidentiality, impartiality, and control of access to, and release of, information.

At various points in this section it has been noted that evaluation at whole-school level can place some of those within the school in the role of outsiders. When evaluation is conducted on a department by department basis the involvement of teachers from other areas of the school, as observers, is particularly likely. In Sir Frank Markham School, for instance, the deputy head who conducted the shadow study was in some senses an outsider in relation to the classrooms he chose to observe. In situations such as these the negotiation of a contract along lines similar to those given above could help to ensure that teachers (and pupils) whose work is being monitored feel able to retain control over the process. In the case of Sir Frank Markham School the shadow study was only conducted after consultation with a working party representing all faculty areas.

Of course, teachers may well feel that to agree a contract in so self-conscious a manner is needlessly cautious. In response we would point out that sometimes schools and teachers need to be protected against themselves, or at least made aware of ways in which information may be misused. In our view outsiders with a more global view of evaluation practice have a moral obligation to ensure that teachers are cognisant of the possible repercussions of their self-revelations.

Conclusion

By way of conclusion we would like to commit a few paragraphs to an appraisal of curriculum evaluation by insiders in relation to the criteria set out at the end of Chapter 1. Unlike approaches to school evaluation which may go little further than the production of a report for an external audience (as some of the LEA schemes described in Chapter 6), strategies of evaluation which are initiated and controlled by insiders are principally action-oriented. In other words, they usually respond to a particular institutional need and are intended to generate policy alternatives to guide future school practice. The fact that the evaluation is the result of the school's own initiative usually stimulates a commitment among staff that is perhaps the best guarantee that findings and recommendations will be acted upon. As we pointed out in Chapter 2, it is often argued, though not proved, that evaluation by insiders possesses the most effective model of change. In terms of the criteria set out in Chapter 1, this form of evaluation (or accountability scheme, if this is its purpose) is the most likely 'to be capable of suggesting appropriate remedies'. However commendable their motives may appear to be, evaluations conducted by outsiders are almost inevitably associated with an element of coercion and so may evoke a defensive response within the school.

It is hardly necessary to repeat, however, that whilst internal *participation* in the evaluative process may be important for action, an inbalance of *control* in favour of insiders is unlikely to be endorsed by those outside schools. Not only will it be regarded as unfair, but the credibility of the exercise will be called into question unless those with a legitimate interest are in a position to judge the methodological soundness of the approach. In theory there is no reason why insider evaluation should be any less rigorous than any other strategy, but in order to be credible a school's methods would need to be made public so that their reliability and validity could be checked. In order for this to happen the work of the school would need to be presented in a way that is intelligible to additional, possibly lay, audiences. The schools we chose to illustrate the insider approach had all produced written accounts of their activities. These documents, although not obviously prepared for general public consumption, provided the kind of evidence that could well be verified by 'triangulation' (a cross-checking procedure discussed in Chapter 7).

The issue of time, dealt with in the previous section, drew attention to the considerable cost, both in time and energy, that this approach is likely to demand, particularly while insiders are establishing procedures and developing evaluative skills. It is doubtful, therefore, whether the criterion of economy (see Chapter 1) can be easily met. In Sir Frank Markham School, for instance, the burden that the curriculum review exercise had placed on one deputy head was particularly heavy. Of course, as we pointed out earlier (and will develop further in Chapter 9), it is quite possible to plan evaluation in such a way that it proceeds by small incremental stages. This kind of strategy is also likely to ensure that evaluation becomes part of the routine professional work of teachers and schools.

Whatever the potential for educational improvement, and however convincing the arguments that problems of credibility can be overcome, there remains one additional difficulty connected with insider evaluation. The insider's familiarity with a particular context may cause teachers unwittingly to ignore certain problems that an independent outsider would wish to identify. Even the help of an outsider in the way suggested in the previous section, might not ameliorate this situation, because it requires that outsiders be involved from the very beginning, in the analysis of needs. In school-based evaluation outsiders are rarely brought in until a later stage, and it is usually regarded as axiomatic that the analysis of needs should be the responsibility of the school.

In summary then, the advantages and disadvantages of evaluation by insiders are finely balanced, and it is perhaps not too far-fetched to suggest that teachers considering this approach will need to decide whether they want to be considered autonomous professionals first, and democrats second, or vice versa.

Notes

1. It is interesting, however, that the results of the University of London Institute of Education's study on testing in schools and LEAs indicates that many primary headteachers are not opposed to LEA testing programmes per se; where they have a choice of 'blanket' testing of all the children in their school (the LEA may only require a light sample) they do so.

2. **An alternative classification is offered by Holt (1981) who distinguishes output evaluation, procedural evaluation, and process evaluation. Output and procedural evaluation can be subsumed under our 'objectives model' category, since both require the pre-specification of criteria or indicators of educational quality. Procedural evaluation is not necessarily linked to outcome measures, however.**

3. In relation to institutions of higher education, Sizer (1979) presents a case for performance indicators which reveals an even stronger managerial orientation than Shipman's. (See also the discussion in Chapter 1 in relation to the Green Paper (DES, 1985b.)

4. **Stenhouse's research model has informed a number of action-research projects which incorporate the notion of the self-monitoring teacher (e.g. the Race Project, directed by Stenhouse himself; the Ford Teaching Project and the Teacher-Pupil Interaction and the Quality of Learning Project, both directed by John Elliott.) It has undoubtedly also had an influence on the concept of self-evaluation in its most specific sense:** involving a teacher's own evaluation of his/her own classroom practice.

    The relationship between research and evaluation will be considered in Chapter 7, and action-research will be described in more detail in Chapter 11.

5. **It is interesting, therefore, that many of these advocates have made their recent careers in 'outsider' evaluation and research in schools.**

6. **Stenhouse (1982) makes the point that accounts of in-school evaluations are also available, if not easily accessible, in the form of Master's Degree theses.**

7. This is an occasional paper in two parts. The first part (the Review) is a theoretical analysis, including an across-case comparison of over 50 activities reported to us. The second part is a register, with brief descriptions of individual activities, including names and addresses of teachers and schools with whom contact is invited.

8. This review has a number of similarities with the HMI/LEA exercise (DES, 1981a) discussed in Chapter 3, of which they were aware.

9. **This same problem was encountered in the HMI/LEA exercise (see Chapter 3 and note 8 above).**

10. The 'process' label that she gives to her model is in some ways a misnomer because it is not exclusively process oriented. It calls for a wide data-base including outcome measures, and it is concerned with very much more than the question of what to evaluate.

11. Theoretical issues concerning socio-political perspectives and evaluation traditions will be discussed further in Chapter 7.

12. Atkin (1978) reports an exercise in institutional self-evaluation that is internally initiated and controlled, but this involves a university, not a school. Significantly perhaps the university is that of Illinois at Urbana-Champaign, where Robert Stake holds a Chair.

13. To some extent the dominance of testing may be a myth. Minimum competencies testing is the main element in this regard, since NAEP and most state evaluations activities involve only light sampling.

14. An interesting example of the way in which one state (Victoria) has set out to support teacher-initiated and school-based developmental research projects is described by Ingvarson (1979). In 1978, the Victoria In-Service Education Committee (VISEC) invited submissions from teachers' work groups (not individuals, since collaboration was considered vital) for funds to support the study of classroom-based problems. Proposals needed to indicate that there was a support structure for the project in the schools and that some form of external, long-term support had been obtained.

15. Brief case studies of evaluation studies at Australian schools and colleges are to be found in Davis (1981).

16. One of the major distinctions between two recent Open University Courses, P234: 'Curriculum in Action - an approach to evaluation,' and E364: 'Curriculum Evaluation and Assessment in Educational Institutions', is that the former concentrates on classroom evaluation, while the latter considers evaluation, whether of classroom activities or school policies, at the level of the whole institution, culminating in a discussion of school policy on evaluation.

17. This general observation is supported by other examples in the Review and Register from which these examples are taken (James, 1982).

18. An edited extract from Holt's book appeared in the *TES* on 20 November 1981. Letters from teachers published on 11 December 1981 suggest that their perceptions of the value of school self-evaluation are very different from Holt's. Interestingly two of the five letters criticising Holt's view were from teachers formerly at the school from which he drew his one example.

19. Significantly perhaps we have no evidence of procedures being initiated, devised or conducted with the assistance of pupils, except as informants.

6   Combined Strategies

Introduction

Given the lack of public confidence in public institutions in general, and in professionals like teachers in particular, the self-evaluations portrayed in Chapter 5 are unlikely to be seen as credible *accountability* procedures. While teachers may ask for a professional model of accountability to be applied the reality will not be clear cut. Depending upon the model of change that is endorsed self-evaluation has, however, a strong case for claiming that it leads to improvements[1]. This contrasts with outside evaluations such as testing, which show little evidence of leading to change but which have a mystical credibility as accountability procedures in the eyes of the public. The use of local inspectors, as one form of outside evaluation, offers more hope for improvement than other forms, but they too have a credibility problem. What is required of an evaluation is a balance on the criteria for judging an accountability procedure, particularly those concerned with control and fairness. In this respect local inspectors have an advantage because they are close to the school, but detached from it. Thus it is possible to envisage a whole range of approaches to evaluation which combine external and internal evaluations. The most appropriate form will depend upon the particular context in which it is used, but any combined strategy must attempt to sustain professional development and hence, so the argument goes, lead to improvement, while ensuring a credible procedure. Becher *et al* (1981, p. 92) examine what they call 'audited self-assessment' (i.e. a combination of self-evaluation and outside evaluation), and note that although several arrangements have been suggested few have been tried out in practice. In this chapter we therefore present some examples and use them to explore the issues that must be resolved in combining strategies. The examples we have chosen are: local authority evaluation schemes, GRIDS (Guidelines for Review and Internal Development of Schools) a validation or accreditation model, and an audited self-evaluation. The speculative nature of this chapter means that it is inappropriate to come to a judgement on combined strategies and its format is therefore different from that of the previous two chapters.

Local Authority Self-Evaluation Schemes

This is a combined strategy because it is usually based upon a self-evaluation which is in some way initiated by a local authority. In some cases the self-evaluation is mandatory - an ironical state of affairs! Over the last few years there has been a growth of such schemes and, in a survey conducted in 1981, Gordon Elliott (1982) found that forty-one LEAs in England and Wales had agreed guidelines for self-evaluation in their schools. (Although he collected only 31 examples of such schemes.) About forty other LEAs were at the time discussing the topic. Not surprisingly there is a considerable variety of such schemes, and some, such as those of Kent and Lancashire LEAs, are curriculum review exercises like those explored in Chapter 3. Despite this variety, these schemes exhibit a number of major characteristics:

1. They are initiated by the LEA (although they may not involve LEA officers) and it may be mandatory for a school to take part.
2. The schemes often use a set of guidelines, or a checklist, to guide the self-evaluation (e.g. ILEA, 1977).
3. The school carries out its self-evaluation, usually on its own, but sometimes with the help of advisers.
4. Often there is a formal reporting procedure to governors, LEA officers and the education committee of the authority.
5. The self-evaluation may be required to be repeated at regular intervals of about four to six years[2].

These characteristics do not apply to all the schemes, and indeed some do not involve a self-evaluation phase. The Solihull LEA (1979) checklist, for example, in its original form, provides a checklist of questions the purpose of which is to identify issues of concern to the staff. The teachers fill in a questionnaire and the questions that are most highly rated are taken as the subject of an in-service day. Chapter 4 has already mentioned the example of Dorset County Council (1980) who carry out joint-evaluations which give a minor role to the school in the evaluation activity. However, there has been no comprehensive review of the details of the various schemes, although Clift (1982), Elliott, G. (1982), Nuttall (1981) and OU (1982, Block 2, Part 1) contain brief descriptions of a selection of them[3].

LEA schemes: issues

Many of the issues arising out of these schemes relate to the self-evaluation element, so here we will only discuss those which relate to the schemes themselves. Firstly there is the problem of conflicting purposes: accountability (contractual) verses professional development (identified by Nuttall, 1981, pp. 22-24). None of the authors of the schemes would deny that they aim to foster professional development and hence improvement in education, but, as Nuttall (1981, p. 21) notes, a tension may exist between the aim and the method. There is also the likelihood that some schemes were introduced to stem a tide of cruder forms of accountability, for example through testing (Brighouse, 1982), and they were therefore 'sold' to teachers on the basis of professional development. Procedures which require a formal report to the Education Committee of an LEA illustrate how contractual accountability can dominate, leading to a ritualised process. This relates to the arguments in Chapter 2 about models of change: if a procedure is imposed it may not bring forth the required change. Indeed this was underlying several of the issues discussed in Chapter 5 (particularly 'Participation and Control'). On the other hand education committees may not be reassured without a report, although Nuttall (1981) suggests that perhaps the needs of those outside schools are for more modest descriptive accounts rather than searching critiques.

The second issue also derives from the reporting procedure: the threat to teachers of exposure. Although no one would want to deny the right of the public or its representatives to know about inadequacies, is it realistic to ask teachers to bare their breasts so that someone can stick a knife in? Some LEAs have recognised this problem by assuring teachers of the strict confidentiality of reports, although this has sometimes had unfortunate consequences. In the case of Oxfordshire, for instance, a governing body was only allowed to see the report produced by its school one hour before discussing it; it was then required to return it immediately after the meeting (OU, 1982, Block 2, Part 1, p. 38).

The requirement for a report also causes a problem for the LEA, because it needs to cope with the volume of reports it receives. This is our third issue. Clift (OU, 1982, Block 2, Part 1, p. 31) calculates that

Oxfordshire, which initially wanted a report from its schools every four years, would receive, on average, one report every two and a half working days as long as the scheme runs! If an LEA is to avoid engendering cynicism, and hence a ritualistic operation of the scheme, it must overcome this problem. The introduction of more structure (i.e. making a report more like a response to a questionnaire), as suggested by Clift (OU, 1982, Block 2, Part 1, p. 31) is likely to be counter-productive because it may encourage an even more cursory treatment of the process of evaluation.

Our fourth issue concerns the kind of questions and topics that schools are asked to deal with in the evaluation, particularly in the various booklets that accompany the schemes. These questions and topics usually represent the collective wisdom of a group of advisers and heads, who have met to draw up the booklet. To this extent they cannot be criticised anymore than the kinds of questions that local inspectors bear in mind. In fact Salford developed its scheme from the questions advisers would generally ask when they visit a school. Doubt has been raised about both the validity and reliability of these schemes (OU, 1982, Block 2, Part 1), but given the difficulties of either defining what 'quality in education' actually is and of finding empirical indicators of it[4], perhaps the judgement of a group of professionals is justified[5].

It would be reasonable to question the sense in which LEA schemes are a 'combined strategy'. We would justify their inclusion here, rather than, say, in Chapter 5, as a form of insider evaluation, partly because of the initiative of the LEA and its subsequent requirement of reporting, and partly because they often envisage a phase where outsiders are involved. Some schools in Oxfordshire have asked local industrialists and educationists to visit them and 'audit' the self-evaluations which they have conducted as part of the Oxfordshire Scheme. Even without this deliberate attempt to audit the report the fact that advisers, who know the school, can comment on a report provides a kind of validation of its authenticity. Oxfordshire also sends a member of the education committee to the school whose report is to be discussed (Norman, 1982), and, although the prime intention is to give the committee a better 'feel' for the school, it also provides a low key audit. Our next 'example', however, presents a more formal process for auditing a self-evaluation, arising out of validation or accreditation.

GRIDS

As the title indicates (Guidelines for Review and Internal Development in Schools) this is basically a procedure for self-evaluation. We have included it in this chapter because it is usually initiated by the local authority advisers etc. In some senses it is like the LEA schemes which are not mandatory, and provide only guidance and support. GRIDS is funded by the School Curriculum Development Committee (and Schools Council before that), with a central team who develop materials and promote the activity in LEAs and schools. They work with local authority advisers in introducing it into schools, although of course individual schools do take on GRIDS through off the shelf purchases of the material. The important aspect of GRIDS is that it is a complete process for evaluation, not just a list of questions, as in LEA schemes. The handbooks, available for both primary and secondary schools (McMahon *et al.*, 1984a and b), give a step-by-step approach to the review process (see Figure 6.1). Detailed advice and examples are given on what to do at each stage along with suggested data collection instruments (e.g. a survey sheet for the survey of staff opinion in stage 2). Initially the GRIDS method was based upon key principles, such as: that the review is for internal school development not to produce a report for accountability purposes; to consult, involve and generally give the teachers control over the review process; to involve outsiders (e.g. as external consultants) in giving help and advice. These match with the 'responsibility-based institutional self-evaluation' type outlined in Chapter 5. However, since its inception there have been some changes, particularly with the issue of accountability. Some of the schools who piloted the material involved governors, and reports were prepared for them. This has led the central team to develop guidelines for the involvement of governors. This brings it closer to the kind of combined strategy that is the focus in this chapter.

The initiation of the GRIDS procedure by advisers through head-teachers may lead to conflict with the principles of teacher control. For example, some heads have taken on GRIDS with only minimal consultation of staff, others have decided the priorities which are taken up from the initial review (see Figure 6.1) despite staff opinion. However, this has not been because of autocratic behaviour by the heads, but their concern to act as leaders, not just chairs of a staff meeting. It does nevertheless represent a considerable improvement over many of the LEA schemes, both in its philosophy of involving teachers and in the advice it offers on how to carry out a review.

Figure 6.1   The five stages of the internal review and development process

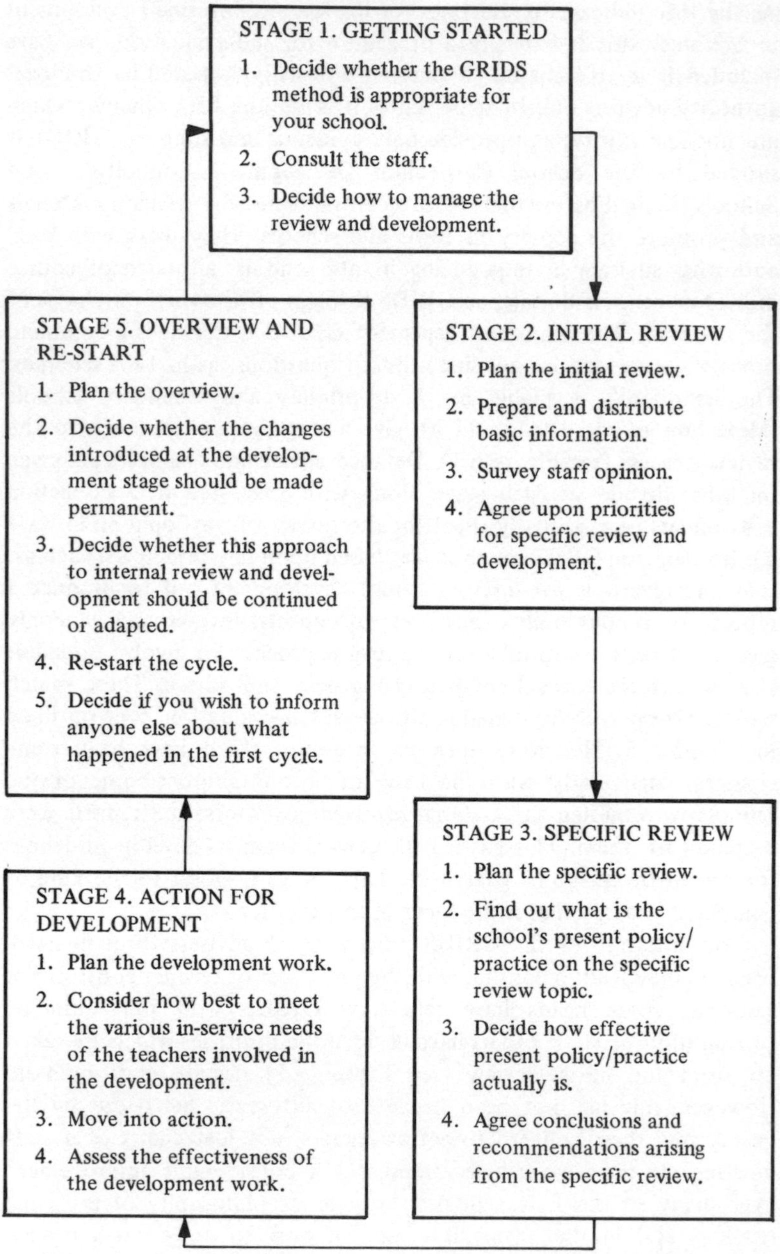

STAGE 1. GETTING STARTED

1. Decide whether the GRIDS method is appropriate for your school.

2. Consult the staff.

3. Decide how to manage the review and development.

STAGE 5. OVERVIEW AND RE-START

1. Plan the overview.

2. Decide whether the changes introduced at the development stage should be made permanent.

3. Decide whether this approach to internal review and development should be continued or adapted.

4. Re-start the cycle.

5. Decide if you wish to inform anyone else about what happened in the first cycle.

STAGE 2. INITIAL REVIEW

1. Plan the initial review.

2. Prepare and distribute basic information.

3. Survey staff opinion.

4. Agree upon priorities for specific review and development.

STAGE 4. ACTION FOR DEVELOPMENT

1. Plan the development work.

2. Consider how best to meet the various in-service needs of the teachers involved in the development.

3. Move into action.

4. Assess the effectiveness of the development work.

STAGE 3. SPECIFIC REVIEW

1. Plan the specific review.

2. Find out what is the school's present policy/practice on the specific review topic.

3. Decide how effective present policy/practice actually is.

4. Agree conclusions and recommendations arising from the specific review.

Validation / Accreditation

The idea of applying the validation model was put forward by Becher and Maclure (1978b, pages 233-6) when they considered the Council for National Academic Awards (CNAA) as supplying a model which could be used by schools. In proposing the CNAA they pointed to three principles of the validation process: that it is a regular and formal procedure; it is essentially peer evaluation; and it involves a thorough evaluation. McCormick (1981) has cast some doubt on these principles as they apply to the CNAA's procedures in higher education, but nevertheless the spirit of the audit, as represented in such a model, is a useful one. An alternative example, which appears to be more relevant, is of the accreditation procedure found in the USA. What follows is a necessarily brief description of the procedure; a fuller account can be found in OU (1982, Block 2, Part 4).

Accreditation of schools is operated by a number of associations which cover various geographical areas of the USA, and has a tradition stretching back to the late nineteenth century. These associations are self-regulating bodies made up of the schools that have been accredited. They accredit an institution rather than a qualification, in contrast to the CNAA's approach prior to the Partnership in Validation proposals (CNAA, 1979). The first stage in the accreditation procedure is a self-study conducted by the school using guidelines approved by the association. These guidelines are similar in conception to the booklets used in some of the LEA schemes described above. However, they are much more substantial, giving guidance on how to organise the evaluation, for example the formation of committees, as well as what to evaluate. Some of the associations have their own guidelines but many recommend those produced by the National Study of School Evaluation (NSSE), an umbrella organisation for the associations. The NSSE produces two types of guidelines: one composed of questions and statements that are mainly answered by completing a five-point rating scale (NSSE, 1978); one composed of a set of open-ended questions (e.g. NSSE, 1975). Incorporated into some of the associations' guidelines (or provided in a separate book as in the case of NSSE) are instruments to be used for data collection during the self-study, for example, a questionnaire for teachers to complete. On the basis of these guidelines a report is completed[6].

The self-study is then followed by a visit from a team made up of teachers, state or district education office representatives and other educationists (such as university staff). The accrediting association is responsible for choosing the team, but the principal of the school has the right to veto any member. Team members usually use the self-study as a help in evaluating the school, and observe the classrooms and talk to staff and students. Although they evaluate the school in its own terms, i.e. given its kind of students, environment and objectives, they have to bear in mind a set of standards which are to be met for the school to be accredited. The standards are phrased in fairly general terms and can be classified into three types: those which are concerned with the consistency of the curriculum and the aims of the school; those defining the nature of the curriculum, for example, the kinds of subjects that should be available; those specifying certain procedures that should be in operation, for example, procedures for developing the curriculum. Interestingly, in the USA context, none of the standards involve outcome measures, such as test scores. Naturally the team does not have to follow the standards slavishly and can use its collective judgement on the overall quality of the school. On the basis of this judgement, contained in a report to the association, the school will be accredited (or not, as the case may be). Even if the school is accredited any aspects which require action will be followed up in the next year when the principal makes an annual report. The accreditation procedure is normally only repeated every seven to ten years, so the association relies upon annual reports from the principal to indicate that the school continues to maintain its quality.

We feel the above example of accreditation has some interesting features for those in other countries wanting to construct an audited self-evaluation[7]. But, as with any international comparison, there are aspects unique to each country. For example, there are no self-regulating bodies at school level in England and Wales which could take on the task of organising the visits etc. Scotland, however, with its General Teaching Council, has experience in approving qualifications and acting as a self-regulating professional body. Moves to start a GTC in England have still come to nothing even though there have been efforts in this direction[8].

The formality of accreditation may also make it unattractive to, say, British teachers, and so we next turn to an Australian example of an audit in which the school had more control over the process.

Huntingdale Technical School

This example of an evaluation carried out in a school in Melbourne,

Australia, was initially reported by Delves and Watts (1979) and further elaborated by McCormick (OU, 1982, Block 2, Part 4). It took place against the background of a reaction against inspections some years earlier, which brought evaluation nearer, but not under, the control of the schools. Huntingdale was an innovatory school which had agreed, with the State Education Department, to an evaluation after a few years of operation; the continued freedom to innovate was thus given in return for an evaluation. The governing body of Huntingdale, called the School Council, was widely representative, including elected members of parents and students, nominated members from a voluntary community group, the local government and the Education Department, as well as the principal and some members of staff. The School Council had overall control of the evaluation and set up a committee to look after the running of it. Thus the school controlled the evaluation, although here 'the school' extends beyond the usual idea of staff and students.

The first element of the process was a self-evaluation resulting in a document containing a wide variety of material, some drawn from existing papers etc., and some being specifically produced. The material included:

1. discussion papers written by individuals and groups on general philosophical ideas and issues of school operation and organisation;
2. reviews of individual departments;
3. surveys, some conducted by outside researchers.

Some of the accounts were purely descriptive, others were openly critical, although never of individuals. The next element of the evaluation consisted of a visit by a Planning and Review Board (PARB), set up by the School Council and including educationists from university departments, officials from the Education Department and people from other educational agencies in Australia. (One overseas member was John Watts, former Principal of Countesthorpe College in Leicestershire.) Some members of PARB were familiar with the school, and one was sceptical of the school's approach. The Board spent a week in the school observing and discussing with teachers and students, having previously received a copy of the self-evaluation report. They made a point of holding open meetings to reassure staff of their approach and made a final verbal report at the end of the week. Each member of the Board commented on an aspect of particular concern and a written report was produced by transcribing a recording of these verbal reports.

This visit was followed by a seminar held by the School Council and attended by a wide variety of people. The seminar drew upon the self-evaluation and the PARB visits as inputs to the whole evaluation process. The seminar was well prepared and written resolutions, backed by proposals from the evaluation, were debated. The resulting decisions were documented in a report of the seminar. Evaluation was thus seen here as integral to decision making and policy review.

General Issues

In combining inside and outside strategies of evaluation in an audited self-evaluation several issues have to be resolved: its prime purposes; who controls it; the nature and role of the visiting team; the nature of the information collected; the action to be taken as a result of the evaluation. The way these issues are resolved will determine the form the evaluation takes[9].

We have already discussed the conflict of purposes in the LEA self-evaluation schemes, and suggested that it is unlikely that the issue can be satisfactorily resolved. The reporting procedure is the element which is crucial in determining which purpose dominates: an open and full report to outside audiences i.e. a public report, emphasises con-tractual accountability; confining the report to professionals emphasises professional accountability (and hence professional development).

A second issue concerns the balancing of control. The notion of a combined strategy of evaluation is promoted because it offers an approach in which the locus of control can be near enough to the school to ensure involvement of the staff[10], but far enough away to be a credible procedure. We have already expressed scepticism about the possibility of self-regulation being acceptable, as in the case of accreditation in the USA or the CNAA in Britain, and about the prospects for a General Teaching Council, in England and Wales. The example of Huntingdale Technical School, in which the School Council controlled the evaluation, offers a viable solution to the problem of balance. In Britain the Taylor Committee (DES, 1977c) envisaged a role for the governing body in the review of the 'life and activities of the school'[11]. This was reinforced by the Education, Science and Arts Committee (1981, paragraph 4.21) which suggested that the governing body should not only be responsible for setting the aims of the school (a Taylor Report recommendation), but that a public statement of these aims could act as a basis for a regular self-evaluation by the school. The 1986 Education Act consolidated these suggestions in defining the roles and tasks of governors. Any implementation of these kinds of recommendations will place considerable importance on the nature and role of the visiting team: our third issue, to which we now turn.

Who actually appoints the team will be a major element in the control of the evaluation. If the school or the governing body do not appoint the team then it is important to consider some right of veto for the school over appointments, as is the case in the accreditation procedure. Nevertheless, whoever controls appointments, it is the composition of the team that will determine the form that the evaluation takes. As mentioned earlier, one of the principles that Becher and Maclure (1978b) stated was that an audit along the lines of a CNAA validation offered the possibility of *peer* evaluation. This implies that the visiting team should be composed of experienced professionals. This could, therefore, involve teachers from other schools. The criticisms against using local inspectors (Chapter 4) could thus be avoided. However it is important that staff from another geographical area are used (a procedure followed by the accrediting associations) in order to reduce the possibility of disparaging comments circulating on the local professional grapevine. This independence *from* the school should, however, be balanced by knowledge *of* the school, as it is unlikely that a visiting team could gather sufficient information in the time usually available. This is the argument used by local advisers and inspectors for their involvement in evaluation, and was evident in the choice of some members of PARB, in the Huntingdale example. A team must be put together to combine these various criteria for its composition.

No less important than its composition is the way it operates, in particular, what use it makes of the school self-evaluation and how it reports. The Huntingdale example illustrates an evaluation where the self-evaluation was a central focus for the visiting team, although it was not prevented from taking up issues it felt were of importance[12]. Some accrediting associations, on the other hand, focus more on the prescribed standards and indeed the visiting team do not even receive a copy of the self-study before going to the school. In contrast, the idea of an audited self-evaluation is that it focuses on validating the school's own evaluation, although the report of the visiting team will determine what the prime purpose of the evaluation is i.e. contractual accountability or improvement. In the case of Huntingdale Technical School's evaluation the PARB report was one element in the whole evaluative process: something which contrasts with the reporting of the accreditation process. However, although the initial accreditation process depends upon the visiting team's report, subsequent follow-up is based upon the principal's annual reports, thus achieving some kind of compromise.

Our fourth issue, on the nature of information collected, echoes another of the Becher and Maclure (1978b) principles, namely, that of 'thoroughness'. Clearly all evaluations should aspire to this, but it is likely that with an audited self-evaluation a policy will have to be agreed, within the education authority, about how the self-evaluation and visit will be conducted. It is important, at this authority level, to strike a balance on the amount of guidance provided. For example, there is quite a contrast between the impressive self-evaluation conducted at Huntingdale, without guidance, and the somewhat excessively structured checklists in the accreditation self-study[13]. Experience and skill will of course determine how independently schools can operate free of guidance. The comments in Chapter 5, on the role of outsiders, and the support they can give regarding the development of evaluative skills, apply equally well to the self-evaluation element of a combined strategy; so too, the comments on the methodology of inspections apply also to the visiting team's approach.

One interesting idea arises out of the accreditation procedure which could well be used elsewhere. Often it is not clear what the incentives should be for teachers involved in a self-study. In accreditation, however, teachers can register for a post-graduate qualification and their work in the self-study counts as credits towards the award. In addition the supervisor of the teacher can act as a consultant for the school. The example of Melbourn Village College, given in Chapter 5, indicates that this approach can have its disadvantages.

The final issue that determines the nature of a combined strategy, which we shall consider, is the action to be taken as a result of the evaluation. This is part of a larger problem to which we will return in *Part Four*; here we will simply be concerned with the effect of the involvement of outsiders, firstly in the visiting team, and secondly in the reporting. Phrasing the issue as 'action taken as a *result* of the evaluation' poses a distinction between the evaluation and development process. This is clear in the accreditation example, but less so in the case of Huntingdale. For change to be effective it is necessary for the visiting team's reports, particularly, to be part of an improvement process. The involvement of local advisers in the visiting team allows them to be part of the follow-up to the visit, and to support any developments[14]. If the visiting team's report is the sole basis for action then we have another form of control issue, since this may put the school in a defensive position. This is particularly acute if the report leads to sanctions. In the LEA evaluation schemes some authorities, for example Dorset, specifically exclude sanctions taken against individuals in order to encourage honesty in the process[15]. However, in cases where contractual accountability is the dominant purpose some form of 'protection' for schools is necessary. For example, in accreditation schools can appeal against the decision to refuse accreditation; the ground for appeal being, 'alleged departure from established procedures, bias, injustice, misapplication . . . of standards, or for the presentation of additional evidence' (North Central Association, 1980b, p. 43). Alternatively, but less satisfactorily, there is the 'agreed record', proposed in regard to HMI Inspections and the 'agreed report' in Dorset's joint-evaluations, mentioned in Chapter 4.

Any policy for a combined strategy which involves a self-evaluation and a visiting team evaluation must take account of the above issues. The lesson from the LEA schemes for evaluations is the importance of wide consultation, not just among head teachers, but with ordinary teachers, parents and the community. With the uniform instruments of government for schools established in the 1980 Education Act, and strengthened in the 1986 Act, there is the prospect of satisfactorily, and most effectively, accomplishing this through the governing body at the level of each school[16]. We recognise that some early commentators in the accountability debate, for example MacDonald (1978, p. 143), have rejected the combining of school self-reporting systems (based on the process evaluation presented in Chapter 5) and external reviews (of the kind carried out by inspectors). However, such stances were not grounded in any empirical evidence (because there was little available). From the experience of the examples contained in this chapter, we feel such a combination of approaches is possible, although the issue of control is crucial. No doubt advocates of 'process evaluation', such as MacDonald, or Simons (1981), would go along with a combined strategy, such as illustrated in the Huntingdale example, if control resides with a governing body. Indeed MacDonald (1978, p. 142) was anxious for an improved role for school governors, albeit only with regard to receiving school reports.

Notes

1. We have argued in Chapters 2 and 5 that evaluations seen primarily as part of professional development are based upon a model of change

which, although it has a great deal to commend it, has not been empirically validated. Although we still feel that the issue of how change takes place is an open question, in this chapter we do not question the link between professional development and change.

2.   Nuttall (1981, p. 17) uses some of these characteristics to classify a selection of LEA evaluation schemes.

3.   More important than descriptions of the schemes are case studies of their implementation; see The Open University (1982, Case Study 1), Norman (1982), Poad (1981), Howells (1980), and Clift, Nuttall and McCormick (1987).

4.   Early studies in the USA by Coleman *et al* (1966) and Jencks *et al* (1972) indicate that schools make very little difference: to put it crudely, pupil performance (in standardised tests or public examinations) is dependent, not upon what school the pupil attends but upon the pupil's characteristics on entry to the school (e.g. social class and verbal reasoning quotient). Rutter *et al* (1979) seemed to refute these findings by identifying certain elements of the school process which did 'make a difference'. However, there has been considerable controversy surrounding the validity of the conclusions of the Rutter study (e.g. see Tizard *et al*, 1980). John Gray (1981) reviews this study and others, in the light of the earlier USA evidence, to see what the research does and can reveal. He concludes that the Rutter study comes up with answers similar to previous research, and also notes:

> The school factors that have been measured add modest or trivial
> amounts to our understanding of differences in performance
> between schools.   (Gray, J., 1981, p. 66).

One of the 'further unanswered questions' Gray identifies is contained in the following statement:

> 'we have only limited knowledge of whether educational practitioners can identify more effective schools'(Gray, J. 1981, p.66).

So we are a long way from being able to show empirically, first, whether schools make a difference, and secondly, if they do, what aspects of schools are significant.

5.   The way such checklists are arrived at, and who is involved, is not unimportant, however. Lyn Gray (1981) briefly outlines the development of a primary school checklist by a local authority, involving advisers, headteachers and consultants from a management centre. The lack of involvement of ordinary teachers is a common feature of the development of such checklists (Elliott, G., 1982, Appendix 2). However, the Schools Council (1982) is developing guidelines with teachers alone, i.e. without LEA officer involvement. It has of course previously sponsored such review guidelines - see Ashton, Kneen & Davies (1976). Harling (1981) gives a short checklist of questions for staff of a primary school who have a curricular or phase responsibility. Higham (1979) gives an example of a teacher produced schedule for evaluating a History department.

6.   A survey of teachers and administrators who had taken part in a self-study (Saisi, 1976) revealed that the third most important factor in aiding self-study was effective guidelines ('Evaluation Criteria', NSSE, 1978). In addition the survey revealed that other important factors were to do with organisational support and co-operation (within the school) and an atmos-

phere of trust. Among factors impeding the self-study were: that it inter-
fered with teachers' professional duties; that there was insufficient time;
and (ironically) ambiguous guidelines. A question asking for general
feelings concerning the initiation of self-study in the respondents' schools
showed that the highest ranked feeling was that it was a waste of
professional time and energy. The next highest ranked feeling was that
self-study was accepted as a professional task! Saisi (1976) does not
however reveal sufficient of the survey details to judge the strength of
opinion in the different elements.

7.   We are aware, however, that the credibility of accreditation may be fading;
     this is suggested in the entry on accreditation in Anderson, Ball & Murphy
     (1975).

8.   CATE has already taken over one of its functions by approving courses of
     initial teacher training.

9.   See McCormick (1981) for a fuller set of questions which have to be asked
     in deciding the form of an audit.

10. Again, as argued in Chapters 2 and 5, this involvement is thought to offer
     the best possibility of leading to improvement, which, as Note 1 says, we
     still think is an open question. However, at the very least such involvement
     will, as Chapter 5 implies, help to avoid resistance to change.

11. Sallis (1979), arguing from the parent's perspective (and also as a member
     of the Taylor Committee), saw the need to have a partnership, among the
     various interested parties in education (including the parents and comm-
     unity), as a way of moving beyond consumerism.

12. This points to the difficulty of the involvement of outsiders in an identifi-
     cation of problems, noted in the penultimate paragraph of Chapter 5.
     Clearly the visiting team can raise problems not attended to by the school
     self-evaluation, but this may be too late to be constructive. In the case of
     Huntingdale this is less likely to be an issue because the School Council
     laid down criteria for the evaluation (see OU, 1982, Block 2, Part 4, p. 33).

13. But see the ambiguous evidence of the survey of teachers presented in
     Note 6.

14. Dean (1982) gives a range of roles and tasks in evaluation for an adviser.

15. Dorset's scheme says that none of the evidence would lead to disciplinary
     procedures. This does not of course preclude informal sanctions such as
     non-promotion.

16. Even before this Act a survey by ACE (Advisory Centre for Education,
     1979) indicated a growing involvement of governing bodies in decision
     making in general, and a growing interest in the curriculum in particular.

Part Three

Techniques

7   General Approaches

Introduction

To suggest that evaluative techniques should be selected according to their capacity to illuminate particular problems may appear to be stating the obvious. However we suspect that choice of methods is often fairly arbitrary and governed more by what is convenient, or what is compatible with the existing skills and interests of the evaluators, than what is best suited to the problem. In the context of curriculum evaluation in schools this contingency is understandable since evaluations are rarely carried out by professional evaluators. It is little wonder then if a scientist inclines towards the use of an experimental model, a mathematician chooses statistical techniques, a keen photographer makes a photographic record, an English teacher favours case study (even fictionalised case study), or a senior manager spends most of his evaluation time creating committee structures for staff consultation.

In relation to evaluation by insiders (Chapter 5), Simons (1981) suggests that the relative lack of expertise needs to be acknowledged so that evaluative skills can be built on those that teachers already possess. In general the literature on techniques for evaluation has neglected to take account of the degree of skill that might reasonably be expected of evaluators, and the practical needs and purposes that characterise different evaluation contexts. In other words, much that has been written has been excessively academic and remote from concrete situations. This is particularly true of literature which concentrates almost exclusively on evaluation models (e.g. OU, 1976, Units 19 and 20; Hamilton, 1976). Even Davis (1981), in a book entitled *Teachers as Curriculum Evaluators*, seems to have been seduced into allowing a large number of models to structure his discussion. In an effort to avoid following this trend we have organised this chapter around a number of issues that arise when considering the choice of methodology. Since models rarely help evaluators to decide what to do *in practice*, they are only introduced when they seem to offer a

171

solution to a particular problem[f]. (Indeed many models arose as responses to specific problems.) However, whilst our treatment of models is not exhaustive, we have chosen to concentrate mainly on *theoretical issues* in this chapter - those of a more practical nature are dealt with in Chapter 9.

We begin with a reconsideration of what evaluation is for and the question of focus (i.e. what to evaluate), before moving to a consideration of the 'how' of evaluation. There we discuss the theoretical and methodological strengths and weaknesses of a number of approaches and debate the distinctions between research and evaluation, and description and judgement.

What Evaluation is For

In *Part One* we examined a number of contexts in which evaluation was perceived to have a role. It was suggested that in various forms evaluation might provide a mode of accountability (Chapter 1), promote professional development and institutional improvement (Chapter 2), and facilitate curriculum review (Chapter 3). In *Part Two* we examined a number of ways in which strategies for evaluation seek to fulfil these purposes. At various points we argued that a strategy that satisfies one purpose (e.g. accountability) may not necessarily satisfy another (e.g. professional development). If this is so we need to consider whether it is possible to provide a general definition of what evaluation is for.

Most definitions of evaluation derive from programme evaluation and focus on the provision of information for 'decision-makers'. Thus:

... we may define 'evaluation' broadly as the collection and use of information to make decisions about an educational program.
(Cronbach, 1963, p. 672)

Educational evaluation is the process of delineating, obtaining and providing useful information for judging decision alternatives.
(Stufflebeam, *et al*, 1971, p. 43)

Evaluation is the process of conceiving, obtaining and communicating information for the guidance of educational decision-making with regard to a specified programme.
(MacDonald, 1973, pp. 1-2, quoted in Stenhouse, 1975, p. 112)

> Curriculum evaluation is the process of delineating, obtaining and providing information useful for making decisions and judgements about curricula.   (Davis, 1981, p. 49)

Clearly definitions of evaluation have undergone very little change over the past 20 years. What has changed is the conception of who the decision-makers are. Although Cronbach (1963) identified three types of decisions for which evaluation is used (i.e. course improvement, decisions about individuals, and administrative regulation), the preoccupation with programme evaluation in the 1960s and early 1970s, both in the USA and the UK, meant that decision-makers were usually assumed to be programme sponsors or project teams. With the evaluation of curriculum projects, such as the Humanities Curriculum Project (HCP), the focus began to change and the *consumers* of educational programmes, i.e. the teachers and schools, came to be regarded as the key decision-makers. In the last analysis the implementation of innovation depended on their judgement and action. Today the situation is even more complex and the role of the decision-maker may be assumed by members of many different groups according to particular evaluation contexts. Thus, politicians, administrators, inspectors, the electorate, parents and governors may be considered the decision-makers in accountability contexts, because they have the power to restrict or expand the resources and support received by schools. In terms of curriculum review, however, the headteacher and staff may be the chief decision-makers; whilst in the context of professional development decisions about practice are likely to be made by individuals or groups of teachers.

The emphasis on decision-making as the central purpose of evaluation assumes that there is something that calls for judgement and action. This takes the discussion back a stage: to deciding what the problem is. As Reid (1978) points out, this issue is often neglected in thinking about curriculum and evaluation. In some contexts the problem may not be very specific; it could simply be a perceived need to review practice in order to ensure that everything is as it should be. If the appropriate decision-makers are satisfied, their only decision would be to encourage 'business as usual'. Some accountability and curriculum review exercises might be conceived in these terms, although it is unlikely that practice would fulfil aspirations in every respect. In most situations there is 'some room for improvement'.

Other evaluations are likely to focus on a specific need - an approach which is familiar in the context of formal, full inspections (see Chapter 4), and curriculum development and INSET. However, if needs are to be the focus of attention, then some kind of needs-analysis instrument may be required to begin evaluation, particularly if the activity is to be conducted by insiders. Support for this suggestion derives from the Schools and In-Service Teacher Education (SITE) Evaluation Project, which monitored the considerable problems experienced by schools in developing school-focused INSET programmes. Regarding needs analysis Baker (1980) states:

> The methods used in most cases lacked sophistication; no formal models of needs analysis technique were used (cf. Houston *et al*, 1978). From questionnaire and interview responses the [SITE] evaluators concluded that the needs analysis was conducted in a superficial way in many schools and the validity of the 'needs' was questionable. This may be seen in the nature of the requests made to the Project Co-ordinators which often merely indicated broad areas (e.g. mathematics or language) with no attempt to specify detail. (Baker, 1980, p. 184)

In the quotation above, Baker refers to the source of one model of needs analysis (i.e. Houston *et al*, 1978). An adaptation of the Nominal Group Technique (Hegarty, 1977; O'Neil, 1981) could provide another. This technique can be used to identify and prioritise issues, of which needs may be one. It could also be used for data collection, using teachers as the data source, and in curriculum deliberation and review. (The details of the technique are given in Chapter 8.) The most significant feature of the technique, however, is the procedure devised to ensure that priorities are genuinely those of the whole group, not merely the most vociferous or powerful. In other words it aims to protect the expression of individual views in the process of identifying and formulating a consensus view. Among LEA schemes in the UK, the Solihull document (Solihull LEA, 1979) offers an approach to school evaluation which goes some way towards this kind of analysis. Teachers are invited to rate aspects of their school's work according to a scale of priority of need. They are then encouraged to use their personal assessments as a basis for whole staff discussion and planning (see also Chapter 6).

What to Evaluate

Once needs or policy issues have been identified, the next step is to decide what aspects of curriculum or organisation are likely to provide the most relevant information for decision-making. The issue of focus (i.e. what to evaluate) has already been raised in Chapter 5, because insider approaches can be distinguished by their response to this issue. In this respect evidence (James, 1982) suggests that insider evaluations are roughly of two kinds: those that focus on educational aims and antecedents (prior conditions) and outcomes; and those that focus primarily on educational processes. A similar distinction holds for other strategies of evaluation. For example, examinations and testing programmes focus exclusively on pupil outcomes, while many LEA checklists appear weighted towards the evaluation of procedures (i.e. antecedent conditions - see OU, 1982, Block 2, Part 1). Inspections, however, traditionally purport to be as much concerned with processes as with outcomes and in-school procedures.

Holt (1981) observed similar variations in focus. In relation to school self-evaluations, both insider and outsider initiated, he distinguished three evaluation types: *outcome* evaluation, *procedural* evaluation, and *process* evaluation. The major assumption underlying outcome and procedural evaluations is that it is possible to pre-specify goals, the achievement of which will be the measure of educational quality. Goals may either be framed in terms of pupil learning outcomes or in terms of what 'ought to' happen if a school is functioning properly. Although the term 'objective' is usually taken to refer to desired student behaviour, both of these forms of evaluation require intentions to be pre-specified.

There are, of course, those like Shipman (1979) who believe that the formulation of working objectives is the only way to proceed. He argues that the tasks of teaching and learning, and educational provision in general, must be defined if they are to be operationalised. Moreover, such definitions must, of necessity, include an indication of what is to be considered success and failure. These indicators subsequently become the criteria and standards by which curricula may be systematically judged.

The simple logic of the objectives model for curriculum evaluation is beguiling since it is difficult to find fault with the idea that education should be judged according to whether it measures up to stated intentions. No-one would deny that teachers and schools are expected to have aims and objectives for their work; indeed this assumption is embodied in the 1980 Education Act. What is at issue, however, is whether the evaluation of outcomes or procedures against stated intentions or objectives is the best way to tackle curriculum evaluation. As we pointed out in Chapter 5, there are those who argue that it is not. We do not intend to rehearse all their arguments here but merely point again to those we consider to be especially important. First, it is possible to regard curricular processes as having intrinsic value. For this reason, they are worthy of attention in their own right i.e. without reference to objectives or outcomes, If, as Jencks *et al* (1972) have suggested, education is ineffective in improving the life-chances of the 'culturally disadvantaged', then it is perhaps important to evaluate whether the school experiences of pupils are, at least, enjoyable and satisfying in themselves. (This is a point made by Clift (OU, 1982, Block 2, Part 1, p. 21).) Secondly, as Eisner (1979) points out:

> The outcomes of educational programs are not completely predictable, and hence to evaluate only for those goals one has intended can lead one to neglect equally important, and at times even more important, outcomes that were unintended. Using objectives to serve as criteria for evaluating educational programs has an important function to perform, but a conception of evaluation that limits itself to what has been preplanned in terms of goals or objectives is likely to be educationally thin. (Eisner, 1979, p.174).

Finally, and most importantly, whilst the use of objectives as criteria for evaluation permits judgement of success or failure, it is incapable of assisting in the diagnosis of reasons *why* a curriculum has succeeded or failed. In other words, the objectives model for evaluation is unable to provide the kind of evidence from which curriculum development can proceed. The only kind of action it can stimulate is the continuation or discontinuation of an *existing* programme or practice. Thus, according to Stenhouse (1975), 'The crucial criticism of the objectives model is that it assesses without explaining ... Hence the developer of curriculum cannot learn from it' (p.120).

As we noted in Chapter 5, these criticisms of the objectives model have given rise to a number of alternatives which can broadly be termed 'process' models of evaluation (e.g. Simons, 1981). These direct attention to the 'curriculum-in-action' (Elliott, 1979; OU, 1981b). However, this change in focus does not obviate the problem of establishing criteria by which effective 'processes' may be judged. In the absence of any empirically validated and generally accepted indicators of educational quality (an issue raised in Chapter 6), evaluators who choose to focus on processes still frequently turn to stated intentions (if not more specific objectives) as bench marks for examining actual learning experiences[2]. Thus, it is not unusual for 'so-called' process evaluations to be centrally concerned with 'performance gaps', or gaps between teachers' 'theories-in-action' and their 'espoused-theories' (see Elliott, 1976). As such these may not be so dissimilar from more sophisticated versions of objectives approaches to evaluation i.e. those which pay some attention to what happens between input and output, or those which consider process objectives as well as outcome objectives[3].

In 1967 Robert Stake proposed a framework for evaluation that still provides perhaps the most comprehensive answer to the question of what to evaluate. The first and conceivably most important distinction to which Stake draws attention is that between description and judgement - the two separate but complementary activities of evaluation. Leaving judgements aside for the moment, we want to look briefly at the kinds of data that he suggests it would be important to collect in order to describe a curriculum or programme fully, prior to judging its worth. He presents his analysis in the form of a 'description matrix' - see Figure 7.1 (Stake, 1967, p. 533, reproduced in Stenhouse, 1975, p. 108, also OU, 1982, Block 2, p. 65). First, he distinguishes three aspects of the educational process:

1. *Antecedents,* that is, 'any condition existing prior to teaching and learning which may relate to outcomes' (Stake, 1967, p. 528). Examples might include environmental factors, school procedures or pupils' interests or prior learnings.

2. *Transactions,* such as the interactions that occur between teachers and pupils, pupils and pupils, pupils and curriculum materials and tasks, or pupils and the physical, social and educational environment.

3. *Outcomes,* which are to be interpreted in the widest sense to include outcomes that are 'immediate and long-range, cognitive and conative, personal and community-wide' (Stake, 1967, p. 528).

Secondly, he proposes that in relation to each of these aspects, data should be collected concerning both *intents* (he avoids the behavioural connotations of terms such as 'objectives' or 'goals'), and *observations*. This renders six categories of potential data: intended antecedents, observed antecedents, intended transactions, observed transactions, intended outcomes and observed outcomes. (These constitute the six

Figure 7.1 A representation of the processing of descriptive data (Stake, 1967, p. 533)

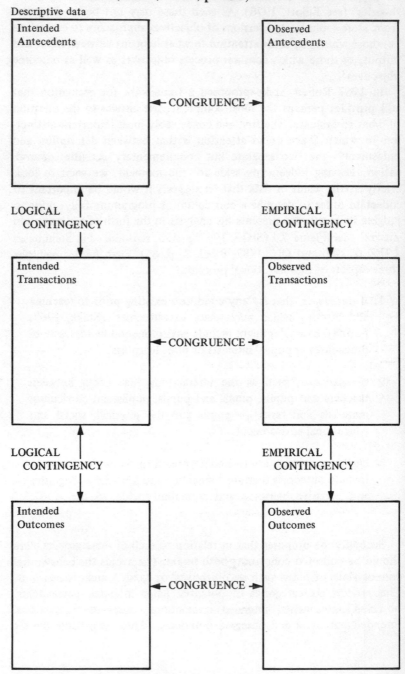

cells of Stake's 'description matrix'.)

The next task is to establish the nature of the relationship between, for example, data relating to intended transactions and data relating to intended outcomes, or between data relating to intended outcomes and data about observed outcomes. In order to assist this kind of analysis, Stake introduces two further concepts: *contingency* and *congruence*. Moreover he further distinguishes *logical contingency* from *empirical contingency*. *Logical contingency* relates to an assessment of how far intentions relating to antecedents (e.g. assumptions about pupils' prior learnings) are logically coherent with those regarding transactions (e.g. the kind of learning tasks that are planned) and intended outcomes (e.g. the results that are expected). Often this kind of assessment requires some form of philosophical analysis. As we noted in Chapter 3, this is sometimes referred to as *intrinsic evaluation*: a term used by Scriven (1967) to denote a judgement of the structure of an educational programme itself, for example, its design and assumptions. Similarly, the appraisal of *empirical contingency* can be referred to as *empirical evaluation*. In this case, the analysis of contingency between antecedents and transactions, and transactions and outcomes is based on the data of observations (i.e. empirical evidence). For example, classroom processes can be examined for (1) the extent to which they fulfil expectations arising from evidence of pupils' prior learnings, and (2) the degree to which observed outcomes can be regarded as genuinely unanticipated.

In contrast to this description of contingency, Stake's notion of *congruence* concerns the relationship between intents and observations. In particular it involves an analysis of how well what actually happens fulfils what was intended. Thus observed transactions can be compared with the transactions that were planned; observed outcomes can be evaluated against intended outcomes; and actual prior conditions can be compared with those whose existence had been assumed.

Clearly, Stake's framework presents us with a nearly exhaustive account of what it is appropriate for evaluation to focus on. In some senses, it encompasses aspects of both the 'objectives' and 'process' models for, although Stake puts much emphasis on 'process' (transactions), he does not reject the data of input or product. (Unlike Scriven (1971) he considers the goals or intents of teachers or programme developers as important.) However, by its very construction, his framework implies that intentions are, or can be easily made, explicit. It therefore seems to ignore the 'hidden' intentions or 'theories-in-action' (Argyris and Schon, 1974) that can only be revealed by a close study of practice. It is a perceived need to focus on these, as a preliminary to consciousness-raising, which is often the main rationale for process evaluation.

How to Evaluate

Although Stake distinguishes six kinds of data relevant to educational evaluation, and a number of different forms of analysis, he favours an holistic, rather than atomistic, approach. In other words, he believes that it is the dynamic relationships among the various elements of an educational programme that really count. Moreover, in order to portray the full complexities of any educational experience he regards a 'broad data base' as essential: a notion supported by Parlett and Hamilton (1972) in their advocacy of 'illuminative evaluation', and by Simons (1981) in her proposals for process evaluation in schools (see Chapter 5). According to this view it is permissible, indeed desirable, to draw on the whole range of data sources from standardised tests, through 'systematic' observation schedules, inventories and pre-coded question-naires, to unstructured interview and participant observation. The principal criterion for their selection should be their capacity to inform judgements about a particular activity. In general this kind of eclecticism is more acceptable in the context of evaluation than it is in the context of 'pure' research. The distinction between the two is contested but evaluation is usually distinguised from research by its interest in practical problem-solving, rather than theory generation. Therefore, specific methods are chosen more for their potential usefulness in situations where decisions are required, than for their agreement with a particular research paradigm[4]. This is not to suggest, however, that evaluators can afford to be any less rigorous in their approach. If evaluation in schools is to have public credibility, and if it is to provide the basis for action, then it needs to be demonstrably valid, reliable and, as far as possible, free from bias.

The debate about the distinction between evaluation and research draws attention to the fact that approaches to evaluation have been influenced by the research literature; indeed many of the specific techniques used in evaluation (see Chapter 8) are derived from research. The difference is that in evaluation the choice of technique is not necessarily *theory-led*: a factor which permits the kind of eclecticism mentioned earlier. Given this methodological link it is worth spending a little time considering the principal features of different research approaches.

Theoretical considerations

Recent research in both the social sciences and education has been characterised by a number of styles derived from two fundamentally different perspectives: what, for the sake of argument, may be termed the positivist approach and the interpretative approach. The positivist approach assumes that the social world, like the natural world, is governed by laws that can be investigated by systematic observation and experiment. By using scientific methods in much the same way as they are used in the natural sciences it is thought possible to establish certain objective social *facts*. There are, of course, strong practical and ethical objections to the manipulation of individuals that experimentation would require, so most social research in the positivist mode has been directed towards the production of accurate correlational evidence, which, if not possessing the predictive value of the cause and affect relationships discovered in controlled experiment, nevertheless possesses a generalisability arrived at from statistical inference. The standard research procedure is therefore to generate *a priori* hypotheses, to define operational categories of observation, to develop 'objective' methods of data gathering, and to conduct appropriate statistical analyses. In the field of educational research, and in relation to its application in evaluation, this classical paradigm has been variously labelled: 'scientific' or 'hypothetico-deductive', emphasising the testing of *a priori* hypotheses; 'nomothetic', emphasising the search for general laws; 'experimental', 'agricultural' or 'psychometric', indicating methodological links with approaches to research in the natural sciences, agriculture and psychology. In terms of social and educational *theory*, the positivistic emphasis on quantification and generalisation has tended to create an image of the individual as subject to powerful forces which constrain uniqueness and render his or her actions *predictable*. This is especially true in some fields of social research where explanations of individual action tend to be at the *macro* level i.e. located within the interrelated structures of society. Such explanations have given rise to a number of 'structuralist' or 'functionalist' social theories.

This image of the individual and his or her relation to the social world has not gone unchallenged however. For instance, among social theorists there are those who argue that social systems are the meaningful creations of individuals, and as such should not be reified i.e. treated as 'objects' which have a life independent of their members. (This is a major objection to Hoyle's (1975) conception of the 'creative school' - see Chapter 2.) Thus social phenomena, rather than being 'facts' to be counted, explained or predicted, are regarded as 'actions' that need to be interpreted and understood in terms of intentions, motives, reasons etc. This alternative to the positivist paradigm is frequently called 'interpretative' (sometimes 'humanistic'): a generic term which subsumes a number of approaches whose main differences lie in their view of the act of interpretation. Therefore, phenomenology, symbolic interactionism, ethnomethodology and analytic philosophy (approaches developed in sociology, anthropology and philosophy; some of which are linked), all emphasise the need to give accounts of what a person is, or does, in terms of what he, or his fellows, *thinks* he is, or does[5]. For this reason, inquiry tends to be *idiographic,* seeking to discover the unique features of the particular case (hence 'case study') rather than establishing general laws regarding behaviour (as in *nomothetic* inquiry). This shift in focus also favours an alternative to the hypothetico-deductive mode of theory generation. Instead of being concerned to 'test' *a priori* hypotheses, there tends to be greater emphasis on the *generation* of hypotheses during the research process. Of course, all scientific research that is 'inductive' goes through this process at some point, but in interpretative approaches hypothesis generation and the 'discovery of grounded theory' (Glasar and Strauss, 1967) are relatively more important than the testing of hypotheses for predictive purposes. In other words, *understanding* is regarded as more important than prediction.

Attractive as the interpretative paradigm might appear to those who are unsympathetic to positivism, it does not, however, escape criticism. Dissatisfaction with the implicit conservatism of interpretative approaches, which, by focusing on the way people see themselves and others, tends to ignore the question of what they *might become,* has encouraged some social scientists and social philosophers (particularly those of the Frankfurt School of Critical Theory) to argue a need for interpretations that actively criticise and transcend peoples' own understandings of themselves. The approach is still interpretative or humanistic in that it seeks to improve understanding of the *meanings* that people attach to their existence, but *explanation* does not remain at the *micro-level* i.e. at the level of the individual or group. Instead it attempts to relate micro and macro levels of analysis. In other words, analysis of the personal constructs of individuals is subjected to a kind of meta-analysis which is usually accomplished by reference to some macro-theory, such as Marxist social theory or Freudian psycho-analytic theory (some of the members of the Frankfurt School were psycho-analysts). In this way critical theorists demonstrate their active concern to challenge peoples' assumptions, through consciousness-raising, in order to increase their degree of autonomy. According to Jurgen Habermas (1972), who is currently perhaps the most influential member of the Critical School, this approach, unlike the others, is action-oriented in that it is informed by an 'emancipatory interest'.

In some measure all these approaches to social research have influenced the development of general approaches to educational evaluation. Much of the early programme evaluation, particularly in the USA, was conducted along classical 'scientific' or 'experimental' lines. The elegance of the research design derived from Fisher (1953) was eminently attractive, so the obvious answer to the question concerning how to evaluate seemed to be: administer pre-tests to pupils, submit them to different experiences, then measure the results by post-tests. The practical and ethical problems associated with the 'true' experimental method are now well recognised but there are still those who argue for a broadly-based 'scientific' approach (Bynner, 1980)[6].

In 1972, the shortcomings of the experimental paradigm were forth-rightly spelt out by Parlett and Hamilton, who accused the traditional-ists of assuming that educational programmes were little different from agricultural or horticultural 'treatments' and could therefore be evaluated in the same way. Arguing that evaluation should be more concerned with description and interpretation than measurement and prediction they proposed a social-anthropological approach. They called this 'illuminative' evaluation, because they believed that decisions could only effectively be made on the basis of an in-depth understanding of how curricula operate in specific situations. Two kinds of understandings were considered particularly relevant: an understanding of the *instructional system* i.e. how formalised curricula plans relate to particular teaching arrangements; and an understanding of the *learning milieu* i.e. the complex social-psychological and material environment in which pupils work. The task of illuminative evaluation, therefore, was to elicit the interactions in and between the instructional system and the learning milieu.

As is characteristic in academe, Parlett and Hamilton's (1972) formulation of 'illuminative evaluation' has also come in for a fair amount of criticism. For instance Parsons (1976) criticises the approach on a number of counts. First, and perhaps rather unjustly, he claims that advocates of illuminative evaluation neglect to acknowledge links with interpretative social science and, by emphasising its utility in decision-making, attempt to absolve it from a research critique. Secondly, and more tellingly, he argues that an almost exclusive concentration on method, especially data collection, has contributed to the almost total omission of any consideration of the role of formal theory. In so far as extant theories can help to 'make sense' of the data of particular circumstances, he feels that they should have a place in the illuminative approach. Thirdly, he suggests that the emphasis on the provision of information for decision-makers 'here and now' is implicitly conservative. By accepting the perspective of participants, evaluators corroborate the *status quo* where they should perhaps be challenging it. In this sense then, illuminative approaches to evaluation can be context-bound and ahistorical.

There are elements in Parsons's critique which are very reminiscent of the critique of some *purely* interpretative approaches by Critical Theorists who are interested in *causality*. It is interesting, therefore, that in educational evaluation, as in social research, a third tradition has emerged and there are now a number of educationists who are beginning to promote the concept of educational action-research as a way of bringing theory to bear on interpretative forms of evaluation - thereby admitting the possibility of emancipation (Kemmis, 1981a; Brown, Henry, Henry and McTaggart, 1982; Elliott, 1982b)[7]. (Since the distinctive focus of action research is on action, rather than specific techniques of data-gathering and analysis, it will be dealt with in more detail in Chapter 11.)

Earlier in this chapter we suggested that approaches to evaluation, and in particular the choice of methods, could be eclectic because, unlike social research, evaluation is not theory-led. In the light of the above discussion this assumption is rendered problematic. Social scientists would no doubt argue that in so far as evaluative approaches are derived from social science, they carry with them a certain amount of *implicit* theoretical baggage. Thus, any attempt to combine different approaches may be tantamount to attempting a reconciliation of fundamentally opposed views of, say, the relation of the individual to society. In response to this we would suggest that while this may create difficulties at the level of interpretation and explanation of findings, it creates no serious problems during the stage of data production. Thus an eclectic approach can be defended in that eclecticism generally refers to *methodology* rather than theory, and few methodologies have a *necessary* relationship to particular theoretical perspectives. Positivism tends to favour quantitative methods, whilst interpretative approaches incline towards qualitative methods, but there are exceptions. For instance, whilst much research in archaeology, palaeontology and history is positivistic it is often constrained to use the evidence of single cases because this may be all that is available. Since the 'problems' that educational evaluation seeks to solve are those of policy or practice *any* method that illuminates the issue can therefore be helpful, and as a general rule 'the more, the better'. In this respect it is significant that Parlett and Hamilton (1972) suggest the collection of data by a variety of methods including those more usually associated with the experimental approach[8]. Even among social scientists who are primarily interested in developing formal theory (i.e. doing 'pure' research) there are also those who strongly advocate a multi-method approach. Webb *et al* (1966), for instance, suggest that no single measure can possibly tap every parameter. Instead they argue that 'the most persuasive evidence comes through a triangulation of measurement processes' (p.3). As we shall see later, *triangulation* is a useful validation procedure because it permits data collected by one method to be cross-checked by data collected in another way. In the next section we look a little more closely at some of the issues related to this choice of methodology.

Methodological considerations

As the above discussion implies, much of the debate surrounding general theoretical approaches to research and evaluation concerns what kind of findings are considered most important. The classical 'scientific' or 'experimental' approach aspires to be *nomothetic,* emphasising the need to establish rules or laws that are generalisable. On the other hand, the various 'interpretative' or 'illuminative' approaches tend to favour the *idiographic* mode of explanation because they seek to describe and explain the *unique* circumstances of the single 'instance'. Notions of typicality or representativeness are less important, therefore, and the only kind of generalisation that is appropriate is that which occurs when hypotheses generated in one 'case study' are seen to be relevant to another (a kind of 'snowball' effect).

These different conceptions of what research or evaluation is trying to achieve give rise to different views about the kind of data it is appropriate to collect. Thus, although all methods derived from social and educational research share certain things in common, for example, a conception of sampling, analysis and criteria for methodological soundness, their treatment of these aspects of the research process may differ considerably. In this respect, a major distinction relating to methods or techniques is between those that are *quantitative* and those that are *qualitative*.

In quantitative research *representativeness*, the criterion for generalisability of findings, is achieved in a number of ways: by studying the total target population (e.g. all 16-year-old boys and girls studying science), or by selecting a *sample* whose characteristics purport to represent those of the target population. The selection of a sample can also be accomplished in two ways: by truly *random* selection (as in tombola), or by ensuring that certain important variables appear in the sample by sub-dividing the population into appropriate groups (e.g. children in different socio-economic groups, or schools in different geographical regions) before selecting randomly. This latter, known as a *stratified sample*, is commonly found in educational research. Sampling need not, of course, simply apply to people or institutions. In the structured observation of children over time, variations of *time sampling* are frequently used (see the section on 'Direct Observation' in Chapter 8); and in assessment procedures the questions in examinations frequently represent a *sample of subject or topic content*. In all these modes of sampling, the principle of representativeness applies and is, as we shall see later, the basis of a technique's 'content validity'.

In qualitative research, sampling occurs in the process of analysis and the search for explanations. As concepts, categories and hypotheses begin to emerge in the study of a particular case (e.g. school, class or child), the researcher seeks data from other events, situations and groups, which may help to clarify, refine or falsify his/her perceptions. Since sampling and analysis are so interwined, and data selection is guided by its capacity to inform theory, this process is called *theoretical sampling*. Linked to this notion is that of *progressive focusing*. This is also part of the process of analysis in qualitative research and refers to the successive refinement of categories of observation as the relevance of particular issues becomes clearer. Finally, in the construction of theory from observation across cases or 'instances'; what ethnographers call *analytic induction* is also involved. This is very like hypothetical-deductive method in classical 'scientific' research but uses single cases rather than groups to test or 'falsify' hypotheses[9],[10].

As in qualitative inquiry, quantitative analysis involves the development of categories and dimensions. Likewise, both approaches require that these should be clearly defined, mutually exclusive and, as far as possible, exhaustive in that they account for all the data. However in quantitative inquiry the definition of categories *precedes* the data collection proper, although they are usually tried out and refined in a 'pilot study'. Furthermore the whole process is more familiarly known as *classification*. If more than one variable pertaining to the persons, situations or events being observed are identified, classified and, if necessary, calibrated, then it is possible to conduct correlational analyses and calculate statistical 'significance' (the basis of statistical inference). For example, in evaluation contexts it might be important to discover whether there is any significant correlation between the socio-economic status of parents and the scholastic attainment of their children[11,12].

As we have already implied, when a decision has to be made concerning the relative merits of using qualitative or quantitative research techniques in evaluation contexts, the judgement will usually be based on how important generalisations are considered to be. Both qualitative and quantitative approaches enable comparisons to be made between people and events, but this is the *chief* objective of quantification which aims to formulate generalisations which are applicable to the *total* target population. Inevitably, however, the reduction of a 'case' to a limited number of dimensions that are identifiable in other cases, has the effect of sacrificing an investigation of what is unique in order to discover what is common. In some circumstances this may be desirable or necessary, particularly in the area of pupil assessment where 'placement' is regarded as important. In other situations the reverse may be true. For instance, again in relation to pupil assessment, a qualitative account of an individual's educational experience and attainment (for example, through the compilation of a record of achievement) may, in some circumstances, be regarded as more valuable than a list of results in graded tests or examinations. Similarly, in order to understand the reasons for, say, a school staff's resistance to any initiative in the area of school-community liaison, it may be necessary to explore the unique combination of situational factors that affect the work of the school (e.g. parental support, local resources, teacher attitudes and skills, school organisation and pupil intake). In other words, in some cases a qualitative approach may be better able to supply the kind of information required for decision-making.

This brings us back to the point with which we began this section: in evaluation it is quite acceptable, indeed necessary, that a choice of methods should be dictated by utilitarian values. The evaluation 'problem' needs to be kept always in mind, so that techniques are chosen according to their power to illuminate the practical issues involved in present and future action. This does not, of course, mean that such techniques can forego the kind of rigour expected of research. As we pointed out earlier, if evaluation is to have any credibility then it needs to demonstrate what Nuttall has described as the criterion of 'methodological soundness' (see Chapter 1 and OU, 1982, Block 1, Part A).

Validity and reliability

In all research approaches emphasis is placed on the *validity* and *reliability* of methods. In other words, researchers are expected to demonstrate that the observations they actually record and analyse, match what they purport to be recording and analysing. This is the concept of validity. Secondly, they need to ensure that random fluctuations in recorded observations are avoided. This is the concept of reliability. Both concepts subsume a number of variants, or types, of validity or reliability. Reliability is the easiest to describe so we begin with that first.

Basically reliability is concerned with *consistency* in the production of results and refers to the requirement that, at least in principle, another researcher, or the same researcher on another occasion, should be able to *replicate* the original piece of research and achieve conparable evidence or results. Reliability can therefore be of two kinds:

1. *Inter-judge reliability*, which refers to the degree of agreement between two researchers in recording their observations of the same or similar phenomena;

2. *Intra-judge reliability*, which refers to the consistency of a researcher's observations on different occasions.

As with reliability, validity is concerned with 'errors' that may occur in the research process. This time, however, 'systematic errors' (i.e. biases), rather than 'random errors', are the focus of attention. Although the validity of a method is basically the extent to which the observations recorded are those that the researcher set out to record, the concept is rather more complex than this statement suggests. It is quite usual to distinguish several kinds of validity:

1. *Face validity*. This is validity at its simplest (and weakest) level, since it merely requires that a measure etc. *looks* as if it measures what it purports to measure.

2. *Content validity.* Sometimes referred to as the principle of 'inclusiveness', this concerns the requirement that the data produced cover all the relevant subject matter. As Deale (1975 p.30) points out, this is a very important aspect of validity for the teacher who is interested in the construction of classroom tests or examinations, since it requires that the test covers the syllabus adequately.

3. *Criterion-related validity.* This refers to the agreement between, say, scores on a test and some other criterion, say, teachers' estimates of ability or examination results. This type of validity can be further subdivided into: (a) *predictive validity*, which requires that the measurement successfully predicts behaviour or results: and (b) *concurrent validity*, which requires that the measurement agrees with another measurement of known, or assumed, validity.

4. *Construct validity.* This is a very important concept in test theory. In this context, 'Construct validation tests the degree to which the test fits the full range of theoretical predictions about an intervening variable whose very existence or usefulness may be merely a hypothesis of the tester' (OU, 1979, Block 8, p.6). In other words the measurement must reflect the construct (e.g. intelligence, anxiety) in which researchers are interested - it should not be testing something else. Similarly, if the theory predicts the construct as a unitary *trait*, analysis should not be able to partition results into a number of independent factors.

5. *Internal validity.* This term is of a rather different order from those above, since in some respects it subsumes them. Basically it refers to the soundness of an explanation (i.e. whether what is interpreted as 'cause' produces the 'effect'), and the appropriateness of the research design and measuring instruments for producing this explanation.

6. *External validity.* This contrasts with 'internal validity' and is concerned with the generalisability of findings. Again this can be subdivided. *Population validity* is a strength of survey research because it is concerned with generalisations to populations of persons, whereas *ecological validity* is a strength of ethnography because it refers to generalisation from one set of conditions (e.g. case, setting, culture) to another[13].

The importance of validity and reliability in the context of research, is that they increase the replicability of research design, and thus the verifiability of research findings. In experimental research in the natural sciences, the process of replication has a central role; advances in scientific knowledge are achieved as much by the falsification of previously held theories as by the discovery of new theory[14].

In education and the social sciences, replication is more difficult. Human behaviour is never static, and since it would be unethical and unnatural to control certain variables, no study can ever be replicated exactly. This is true whatever methods or research designs are employed. Nevertheless the need for findings to be credible remains and has encouraged researchers to seek other ways to render their work valid and reliable. Although something of an over-simplification, establishing the *validity* of results appears to be the larger problem for quantitative approaches, whereas problems of *reliability* dominate qualitative approaches.

One validation procedure for quantitative measures, such as examinations, is to ask 'experts' to judge which skills, objectives or content each question is measuring. This is content validation and it is achieved primarily through intrinsic analysis. Standardised tests, on the other hand, rely primarily on construct validation. This is achieved by demonstrating that the measurement produced conforms with prediction from theory concerning the properties of the construct[15]. As for reliability, this is encouraged by aggregating many assessments or measures of the phenomena under observation, and allowing (statistically) for a margin of error. Even precautions such as these do not however eradicate all sources of error or bias. Consider, for example, the administration of a supposedly validated 'pencil and paper' test to a group of primary school children who are normally taught in informal classrooms. The procedure of sitting alone and in silence and producing written answers may be so unfamiliar that it seriously distorts both their performance and the kind of curriculum that they have actually experienced. In other words, the distortion created by the unnatural setting may invalidate the results produced by an instrument which, in all other ways, conforms to the requirements of classical test theory.

In qualitative approaches the fact that there may only be one 'instance' of the phenomenon being researched, and that its appeerence may be fleeting, makes the application of a battery of measures difficult. However the idea that different kinds of data can be collected about a unique event, and that these can subsequently be used to cross-check one another, has provided the basis for the principal validation procedure used in qualitative research. This is known as *triangulation*.

According to some researchers who use qualitative, and particularly ethnographic, techniques, triangulation is itself beset by problems of validity (see Bloor, 1978). For instance, there is no absolute guarantee that a number of data sources which purport to provide evidence concerning the same construct, in fact do so. As an alternative to triangulation, therefore, procedures have been developed for establishing some kind of correspondence between the views of the researcher and the views of those being researched[16]. In view of the apparently subjective nature of much qualitative interpretation, validation is achieved when others, particularly the subjects of the research, recognise its authenticity. One way of doing this is for the researcher to write out his/her analysis for the subjects of the research, in terms that they will understand, and then record their reactions to it. This procedure is known as *respondent validation* (Bloor, 1978). In the field of educational research it was used by the Cambridge Accountability Project (1981) and in our analysis of school-initiated self-evaluation activities (James, 1982).

The major threat to the validity of both quantitative and qualitative research approaches lies in the concept of *reactivity*. This refers to the tendency of any research procedure to distort the reality that it seeks to investigate. The conditions under which classroom tests are administered (see the example above), examinations are conducted, an inspector makes a visit, or a teacher makes an audio-recording of classroom talk all have the effect of changing the natural setting and creating bias in the analysis of observations. This problem is particularly acute for positivist approaches and supplies the basis for their main ethical critique. Interpretative, and especially ethnographic, approaches on the other hand aspire to be 'naturalistic' and deliberately try to avoid creating artificial conditions for observation. Even so, it is a rare participant observer who can enter and leave the research field without creating any disturbances (an issue that will be dealt with more fully in Chapter 9).

The ethnographer's usual solution to the problem of reactivity is to adopt a reflexive stance. *Reflexivity* demands that researchers constantly monitor, not only their own interactions with the groups being investigated, but also their own roles and reactions to what they observe. In other words they make a conscious effort to make explicit anything that could bias their interpretations of events. Sometimes they can be assisted in this by first recording their observations using low inference descriptors (i.e. those that record behaviour and which do not infer mental states or make judgements), or by audio- or video-recording. Although still selective, the use of the latter enables initial impressions of what is going on to be checked (triangulated) against at least some of the raw data. However this advantage needs to be weighed against the disadvantage of the additional intrusion into the natural setting, which may actually increase reactivity.

The problem of reactivity and the process of reflexivity reminds us that observations are always subjective in some degree. This has often been cited as an objection to interpretative and qualitative approaches in research and evaluation, although most people now agree that even quantitative and positivistic approaches cannot be regarded as 'objective' in any absolute sense. Even in the natural sciences, a number of philosophers have demolished the logical empiricist view of science as an objective progression towards the 'truth' (Kuhn, 1962, 1970). Similarly, in educational and social research, it is now recognised that so-called 'objective' tests are limited in the sense in which they are objective. As Nuttall has pointed out (OU, 1982, Block 1, Part C), only the *marking* of such tests is objective in that rules can be devised to enable non-specialists or computers to carry out the task. Everything beyond that has an element of subjectivity: the choice of what to assess, the choice of test items, the choice of criteria to evaluate performance.

Given the unavoidable element of subjectivity in any research design, the idea of the reflexive account is perhaps relevant to all approaches. Therefore, whatever research tradition a particular study derives from, it is always important to make explicit the assumptions on which categories of observation and interpretation are based and to explore possible sources of bias. Only by reflexivity will the research process be open to the kind of public critique that will enhance its credibility.

The fact that the major part of this section has focused on research approaches assumes that the information gathering and analysing stages of curriculum evaluation conforms to one or other research paradigm and can be validated accordingly. It should perhaps be pointed out, therefore, that this view of the relation between evaluation and social and educational research is by no means universally accepted. Eisner (1980), for instance, argues that evaluation methods derived from social science (even qualitative social science) have not had the impact that was expected. He proposes therefore that evaluation should be regarded as an artistic activity having two dimensions: (1) educational connoisseurship, and (2) educational criticism (Eisner, 1979). The first should be concerned with appreciation i.e. the ability to discern subtle qualities, whilst the second should act as a 'midwife to perception'. In practical terms he implies the need for accounts of education which are evocative as well as analytical[17]. Although Gibson (1981) does not totally reject the idea that the methods of artistic criticism might yield some illumination of school and classroom processes, he roundly castigates would-be curriculum critics for: (1) assuming, wrongly, that a curriculum is a work of art and can be treated as one; (2) making erroneous assumptions about the nature of criticism and ignoring its sheer variety; and (3) assuming that those who aspire to be critics should see *themselves* as artists for whom an artistic use of language is a necessity. According to Gibson this last assumption has had disastrous results since it has encouraged accounts of curricula that are self-centred, narcissistic, apparently omniscient, grandiloquent in style and self-consciously searching for effect. (It is important to bear this last criticism in mind when considering the style and form of case study reports (Chapter 10), and particularly those that employ fictional approaches (Walker, 1981).)

If we examine what evidence there is regarding the practice of curriculum evaluation in schools (i.e. *Part Two* of this book), the connection with either artistic criticism or social and educational research is not altogether obvious. Only pupil assessment tests, and examinations developed by outsiders (see Chapter 4), seem to have adopted a strict research-type methodology (of a quantitative kind). Other forms of curriculum evaluation seem to bear little explicit relation to any formalised procedures borrowed from elsewhere since their main activity involves either discussions and meetings where experiences can be shared and judged, or the exercise of individual 'professional judgement' (see the accounts of the school-based exercises in Chapter 5, and the inspections in Chapter 4).

Given this reality, the argument for including a substantial section on research procedures in this chapter (and Chapters 8 and 9), rests on the perception that even if the process remains unarticulated, *all* evaluation includes the collection and processing of observations and judgements. In the light of Gibson's objections to curriculum criticism, as it is presently formulated, we would suggest that the methods of research still have much to offer, not least because they hold the promise of rigour. If educational evaluation aspires to be acceptable to a wide audience then it cannot be regarded as totally exempt from the normal checks and balances that regulate research[18].

However, a significant difference between evaluation and research (apart from the former's concentration on practical rather than theoretical problems, as mentioned earlier) concerns the location of the principal data source. In the context of most educational and social research the researcher identifies his data 'out there' in the social world.

Although he may consider himself part of that social world he rarely regards himself as a primary data source. In curriculum evaluation, particularly self-evaluation or curriculum review, teachers who conduct evaluations may themselves be a chief source of information. Thus one of the tasks of evaluation is to elicit the information of their own and one anothers' experiences, and to scrutinise the assumptions and values that they embody. In this context the sharing of accounts in discussions is a legitimate form of data gathering and analysis[19]. The important point, however, is that there should be a deliberate attempt to reveal value positions in order to make judgements which, as far as possible, are free from coercion or bias. In some respects this conception aspires to the characteristics of what Habermas (1972) describes as the Ideal Speech Situation (the grounding for Critical Theory). According to him, this is a form of dialogue which has been so successfully freed from ideological or power interests that rational considerations alone dictate the outcome of exchanges between individuals or groups. Similar processes of deliberation and dialogue have already been discussed in relation to curriculum review (Chapter 3) and will be developed further in Chapter 8 (see particularly the section on the 'Intended Curriculum').

Judgement

The importance of dialogue and deliberation is not, however, exclusive to particular kinds of evaluation, such as curriculum review. As we pointed out earlier, by reference to Stake's (1967) framework, judgement is an essential part of *any* curriculum evaluation. In that judgement involves the development and application of criteria of worth (or quality) then some form of deliberation is unavoidable, and should be conducted with the same degree of care and reflexivity as the stages of data gathering and analysis. It now strikes us as a little strange that the definitions of evaluation given at the beginning of the chapter emphasise the activities of information - gathering and decision-making but say little, or nothing, about the act of judgement itself. Yet valuation is the very essence of the whole enterprise.

According to Stake (1967): 'To be fully understood, the educational program must be fully described and fully judged' (p.525). This does not mean, however, that the evaluator should be the final judge of a programme's worth. Some evaluators believe that they should judge (e.g. Scriven, 1967), while others have suggested that the evaluator's role is to provide the descriptive data from which others (the decision-makers) can form judgements. Stake's emphasis on 'portrayal' (Stake,

1972) suggests that he inclines to the latter, although he poses 'portrayal' as description and therefore the alternative to 'in-depth' analysis, rather than an alternative to judgement. However, he clearly espouses the view that the evaluator has the responsibility to 'process' judgements (Stake, 1967). In other words he regards the subjective judgements of various individuals and interest groups as relevant 'data', and as much part of any portrayal as data of more 'objective' kinds.

This idea has been developed further by MacDonald (1977a) in his concept of 'democratic evaluation'. Unlike bureaucratic evaluation which serves the interest of government agencies, programme sponsors and policy-makers, or autocratic evaluation which serves the interests of the academic research community, democratic evaluation 'recognises value-pluralism and seeks to represent a range of interests in its value-formulation. The basic value is an informed citizenry, and the evaluator acts as a broker in exchanges of information between different groups' (MacDonald, 1977a, p. 226). Simons' (1981) emphasis on discovering the values and assumptions underlying practice in schools (see Chapter 5) is also in this tradition.

In school-based evaluation, unlike large-scale programme evaluation, the evaluator and the decision-maker may be one and the same person or group, in which case the debate about whether or not the evaluator should judge is somewhat academic. Nevertheless Stake's ascription of equal importance to the complementary (and arguably inseparable) activities of description and judgement remains relevant, as does MacDonald's suggestion that evaluation, if it is to be truly democratic, should recognise value-pluralism within the school, and in the wider community.

Discussion of who should make judgements has tended to distract attention from a much more fundamental question about the nature of judgement itself. Of course, the issue of judgement may be intractable and we are not entirely convinced that the following discussion throws very much more light on the question. We have no evidence that the ideas which are adumbrated have anywhere been put to practical use, although we are attracted to the possibilities.

The lack of clarity with which terms are used may be partly responsible for the problem. Terms such as values, standards, criteria and objectives are used almost interchangeably (we fear we may also be guilty) and contribute to widespread confusion about what the act of judgement involves. In an article on the origins and functions of evaluative criteria Sadler (1985) has therefore made a welcome attempt to cultivate some order in this conceptual (mine-?) field. First he distinguishes criteria from standards by saying that criteria refer to dimensions relevant to an evaluation whilst only standards refer to particular levels used as reference points for positive or negative attributions of worth. For example, judgement about a curriculum package might rest on criteria concerning congruence with the aims of the school, suitability for a particular target group of pupils, or cost. Standards, however, would involve notions of sufficient congruence, sufficient suitability and acceptable costs; implying qualifying levels which would act as cut-off points for acceptance or rejection.

Most formal evaluations have reference to one of two bases for judgement: they are either relative or absolute (Stake, 1967). According to Sadler, relative judgements have reference to criteria alone because the case is compared with the distribution of other cases on a certain criterion. The cases are ranked (X is considered better than Y) so a specified cut-off point is not relevant. In contrast, absolute judgements have reference to both criteria and standards because the case is compared with what authorities define criterial quality to be. In this instance notions of sufficiency and acceptability are brought into play.

Interestingly the rest of Sadler's article concerns the identification of criteria rather than standards. Perhaps he too finds the problem of standards intractable. Are they, as MacDonald (1978) suggested, merely subjective and idealised distillations of the past? Witness the complaint: 'Standards were higher when I was at school'. Or are they in fact relative in that the best past performance becomes the qualifying level for the judgement of all future initiatives? Or is there a sense in which standards are, or should be, objective or absolute and agreed through rational discourse? The last seems the best alternative although the skills required to generate such standards are very much those of the philosopher.

Sadler is more helpful on the subject of criteria. He argues that criteria are organised hierarchically and that most criteria for educational judgement are at the middle and lower levels of a three-tier system because they include reference to content. However they are also linked with higher-level or backstop criteria which represent underlying values.

It occurs to us that this organisation is well illustrated in the framework for product evaluation developed by the Secondary Science Curriculum Review. The products in question were the curriculum proposals (materials, teaching strategies, assessment schemes etc.) developed by teachers' working groups. These were evaluated (a quality control exercise) at local, regional and national levels using a set of criteria developed by members of the central team (Ebbutt and West,

1984). The criteria were arranged hierarchically with each of four general criteria subsuming a set of criteria with greater specificity in terms of content. (See Figure 7.2 for an example.)

Criterion 2

The product must be compatible with the Central Team's view of increasing educational opportunity

There ought to be recommended assessment and reporting procedures included and, whether summative or formative, these ought to match the aims, content and teaching strategies

The product ought to identify the needs of and make special provision for enhancing the participation of girls

The product ought to be varied and stimulating to both teachers and students

The product ought to make special provision for the expression of cultural diversity

The product ought to make special provision for students with special needs

The product ought not (implicitly or explicitly) to erect undesirable stereotypes

The way in which the product is organised ought to facilitate students' cognitive growth

Provision ought to be made in the product for extending pupils up to and beyond some minimum entitlement

The product (including diagrams) ought to be appropriate, clear and unambiguous with respect to the intended audience

The language in the product ought to be accessible by the intended audience

Figure 7.2 An example of criteria used to evaluate SSCR products
(Ebbutt and West, 1984, p.13)

In this example, although 'increased educational opportunity' is at a level of generality it is not content-free therefore it is not a 'backstop criteria' as such. Underlying it is the generic value of 'justice-as-fairness' (Rawls, 1971). For this reason the SSCR's general criteria can be described as middle-level and their associated sets of specific criteria are lower-level.

Sadler goes on to portray the specification of criteria as having three phases. The first is the primary evaluative act which predates any criteria as such. This recognition of worth is best expressed in the observation: 'I can recognise quality when I see it, but I can't say why'. This kind of valuation is holistic and arises not from reason but from the interaction of underlying values with the context of experience. In other words primary valuation is existential in character.

The second phase of criterial specification is entered when having recognised value from the ground up, as it were, the abstract value is then 'decomposed' downward again to yield criteria with content. (This is never a purely abstract exercise because it always has reference to the existential context in which the primary valuation took place.) According to Sadler: 'Criteria are useful for making, and necessary for substantiating, value claims because they determine existentially the content of the axiological [i.e. underlying] values by clarifying them and interpreting them' (p. 296). Thus criteria have reference to content and are explicit whilst underlying values are abstract and often implicit, which would explain why underlying values are often taken for granted and have to be read-back from the stated criteria (as in the SSCR example given above).

A third phase, following on from primary valuation and criterial specification, is the act of prescription in which criteria are converted into objectives: 'Objectives are criteria that have been arrested and formulated in such a way as to allow them to function as ends-in-view' (p. 293). In this way they become foci for action. Stemming from this, Sadler further points out that the conception that evaluation is simply the process of measuring the extent to which pre-specified objectives have been attained is a very natural one because it brings the valuation-criteria-objectives relationship full circle.

However, he also points out that explicit, specified criteria, which are by nature atomistic, are rarely able to capture the holistic nature of the valuations in which they originate. In other words, the whole is likely to be more than the sum of the parts; indeed there could be alternative and contradictory sets of criteria derived from the same generic value. (McIntyre, 1981, in a seminal study of moral theory, gives the example of principles of *just acquisition and entitlement* (capitalist ideology) in contest with principles of *just distribution* (socialist ideology), both having appeal to the superordinate virtue of justice.) Sadler concludes:

> . . . while any set of criteria for educational evaluation should in general be made explicit, complete prior specification is undesirable in principle. The case for this assertion rests on four grounds: (a) decomposition of value principles is always partial; (b) criteria emerge from experience and cannot be deduced from value principles; (c) not all criteria *can* be made explicit; and (d) there are criteria for using criteria (e.g. principles that demand the suspension of one criterion in favour of another). (p. 297)

For all these reasons, Sadler is prepared to give some credence to the concepts of connoisseurship and criticism, developed by Eisner (1979) and Willis (1978). These are premised on acceptance by non-judges of holistic evaluations by others either because they can interpret the judgements of the connoisseur in the light of similar experiences of their own, or because they simply accept that the judgments are authoritative.

Unfortunately and perhaps not unexpectedly, Sadler does not go so far as to suggest ways in which this analysis could offer practical guidance on the conduct of evaluations in schools? However, we think it is possible to extrapolate a number of suggestions:

1. It is important to recognise that prior specification of criteria may be a shibboleth, and that it is quite legitimate to collect information in relation to the area of evaluative interest in a fairly open-ended way.
2. There is also a need to acknowledge that individuals will make intuitive holistic judgements on the basis of the information they gather or receive (Sadler's primary evaluative act). However, they should be encouraged to articulate and clarify judgements (gut-feelings), for themselves or for a group of colleagues.
3. These articulated judgements can then be examined for their underlying values by asking the question: 'Why is it that I think that such a thing is good or bad?' This should lead into a consideration of whether these underlying values are really worthy of support or whether they are mere prejudices. The process is akin to consciousness-raising and is only likely to be effective for the

individual if others are involved, such as a 'critical friend' (see Chapter 5) or collaborative group (see Chapter 11).
4. Once values and judgements have been scrutinised, they can then be formulated as criteria with content and used as the basis of formal judgement. As Sadler points out, such criteria might indeed become objectives in that they can be used as guides for future action, although, for the reasons quoted above, he avoids the implication that they should necessarily become the criteria for future judgement.

Although this process may look complex it is actually naturalistic in that it merely argues for evaluators to make explicit what they usually do intuitively. By so doing, formerly hidden criteria can be placed in the forum of public debate without requiring any artificial pre-specification of indicators of quality which distorts experience and denies the reality of value pluralism.[20]

In many ways the whole process is little different from the process of deliberation described in Chapter 8. Like Walker's (1975) observations of group reflection on proposals for action, judgements can be made in a self-conscious and ordered fashion, although, as with deliberation, this is probably most effective within the structure of collaborative groups. There is a difference, however. Whereas action requires agreement, consensus is not necessary for judgement. For example, the staff of a school could remain divided about the worth of an initiative even after rigorous scrutiny of their judgements; it would be quite legitimate to present competing valuations (c.f. MacDonald's, 1977, conception of the evaluator as 'honest broker'). It is only at the point when decisions have to be made about one course of action as opposed to another that some judgements have to be rejected in favour of others. This activity brings into play another level of judgement. Whether or not the evaluators have made judgements themselves, this category of judgement is usually the preserve of the decision-makers alone (although independent evaluators sometimes make recommendations). Who the decision-makers are and how they might go about this task is, of course, a management question (which is touched on briefly in Chapter 11). The point here is that in this respect, as well as those explored by Sadler, the act of judgement, in relation to educational evaluation, is complex and multi-faceted.

In essence, throughout this discussion, we have been forced to return to the concept of intrinsic evaluation which requires the skills of the philosopher. If, as Stake suggests, all evaluation requires both systematic description and systematic judgement, the task posed for teachers and others, who seek to evaluate educational practice is considerable. If their judgements are to be regarded as credible, fair and thorough they undoubtedly need to extend their roles both in the direction of curriculum research *and* in the direction of deliberation, and what Habermas calls 'practical reasoning'. In this regard deliberation comes closest to, and research furthest from, the usual working methods of teachers. In Chapter 8 we will look specifically at what is known about teachers' use of these methods; then we will return to the general issues surrounding teachers as evaluators in Chapter 9.

Notes

1. A very brief readable 'tour' of evaluation models is provided by Taylor, D. (1976). Another is to be found in Lawton (1980).
2. However, at least one writer (Scriven, 1971) has argued that evaluation should be 'goal-free'. According to him knowledge of the goals that a particular programme is expected to achieve is likely to distort the evaluator's perception and prevent him/her noticing unintended effects, which might be the programme's most significant outcomes His emphasis on effects, however, still makes his approach a version of outcome evaluation. Interestingly Scriven also argues that it is the evaluator's responsibility to make judgements. However, lacking statements of programme goals he has to find alternative criteria by which judgements can be made. Scriven's solution to this problem is to propose a 'lethal checklist' of thirteen programme needs which he claims to be independent of audience values. Failure to meet any point leaves the quality of the programme in doubt. In school-level evaluation the objection to this approach is fairly obvious: the criteria of the school are merely replaced by those of the person doing the evaluating, with no absolute guarantee that they are any more objective.
3. Eisner (1969) draws a distinction between 'instructional objectives' and 'expressive objectives'. He claims that it is perfectly appropriate for teachers to plan activities to provide pupils with opportunities to increase their experience and enable them to exercise personal choice. However, since the outcomes of these activities must, by their nature, be unpredictable, Eisner believes a new term is required. The notion of 'expressive objectives' is especially appropriate to the Arts (Eisner is an art educator); an equally appropriate alternative, with a somewhat wider sphere of reference, might be 'process objectives'.
4. However, courses like DE 304: 'Research Methods in Education and Social Sciences' (OU, 1979) also encourage the view that research methods should be chosen according to 'fitness for purpose'.
5. See OU (1977) Units 7 and 8 for an account of the ethnographic approach to the analysis of schooling, and see OU (1979) for fuller accounts of distinctions between experimental, survey and ethnographic research approaches.
6. Bynner (1980) argues for a multi-faceted research approach combining qualitative and quantitative elements without the necessity for a random-

ised control. (See also Campbell and Stanley (1966) for a classic formulation.) There is evidence that this model is still employed in the evaluation of educational programmes. For instance, curriculum modules developed by the Health Education Council's Dental Health Study were evaluated in this way (in 1982/84). The Study's Director argued that this form of evaluation has the greatest credibility in the eyes of the programme's sponsors, many of whom are only familiar with 'scientific' or 'medical' models.

7.   Action research, in the social sciences, has a long history. It was pioneered by Kurt Lewin in the USA in the mid-1940s. However Kemmis (1981a) points out that there is considerable evidence to suggest that Lewin was well aware of developments in Critical Theory taking place in Germany at the same time. In other words the link between the two developments may be actual as well as notional.

8.   Parlett and Hamilton (1972) suggested the collection of data from four areas: (1) observations (2) interviews (3) questionnaires and tests (4) documentary and background sources.

9.   See Bloor (1978) for an ethnographer's account of his attempt to put the analytic induction method into practice, and the difficulties he experienced.

10. There appear to be more accounts of how to collect qualitative or ethnographic data, than there are about how to analyse them. Glasar and Strauss's (1967) classic book is still one of the most helpful, as is one by Patton (1980). The Open University (1979) Course DE304: 'Research Methods in Education and the Social Sciences', also has two blocks (6 and 7) devoted to data analysis, including ethnographic data and statistical inference. See also Hammersley and Atkinson (1983) for a very lucid account of analytic induction and other methods associated with ethnography.

11. For a discussion of issues connected with the use of educational measurement procedures in evaluation contexts, see Choppin (1981).

12. In discussing participant observation, the ethnographer's principal technique, Becker (1958) suggests three stages in the analysis of data that are not unlike those of quantitative research: (1) the selection and definition of problems, concepts and indices; (2) checking the frequency and distribution of phenomena, and (3) construction of social system models. The inclusion of Stage 2, encourages the researcher to make quasi-statistical statements such as: 'every child reported that ... ', 'no one asked questions ... ', 'some proportion of the group were observed ...'. According to Becker it is quite acceptable for a participant observer to draw on this kind of quantitative support for a conclusion. However he also emphasises that analysis in participant-observation research is carried out concurrently i.e. important parts of the analysis are made whilst data is being gathered. In this sense, his approach conforms to the ethnographic model (theoretical sampling, progressive focusing, analytic induction) and is unlike survey research.

13. A more detailed description of these various types of validity and their relative strengths and weaknesses in experimental, survey and ethnographic research can be found in OU (1979, Block 8, 'Evaluation of Research'). See also Deale (1975) pp. 29-38 for a discussion of validity and reliability in pupil assessment.

14.   Popper (1963, 1972) has argued that no observations are 'pure' in the sense that they are theory-free; they are always interpretations in the light of previously held theories. Therefore scientific effort needs to be directed towards the critique of existing theory, and the evaluation of knowledge (c.f. Kuhn's (1962) 'paradigm shift').

15.   One of the problems with so-called IQ tests is that the construct 'intelligence' remains at the level of hypothesis. Thus, all that can be said with confidence is that 'IQ tests test what IQ tests test!'

16.   Shutz (1953) suggests that three conditions should be fulfilled if interpretative inquiry is to satisfy the requirements of social scientific theory. These he calls the postulates of: (1) logical consistency, (2) subjective interpretation, and (3) adequacy. The second postulate insists that second-order constructs (i.e. the researcher's) must include a reference to the subjective meaning an action has for an actor (first-order constructs). The third postulate suggests that it should be possible to translate theory back into the commonsense knowledge from which it was derived in such a way as to allow those being researched to criticise the researcher's formulations and assess their plausibility.

17.   This view of evaluation as curriculum criticism is also elaborated in Willis (1978).

18.   This is not to suggest that research methods need necessarily be only those of social scientific research. Stenhouse (1979a), for instance, has suggested a role for the methods of the historian.

19.   An approach adopted by Lewy (1977). The 'sharing of accounts' approach is explored further in a brief case study of a primary school's evaluation activity (OU, 1982, Block 2, Part 2).

20.   A note at the end of Chapter 6 indicated that there have been a number of attempts to establish process criteria which could act as indicators of educational quality (see Jencks *et al*, 1972; Rutter *et al*, 1979; Olson, 1970; Sizer, 1979). While there is undoubted agreement that a school is successful in so far as it is educationally effective, what constitutes educational quality is always likely to be contested. The best that can be achieved in this respect is a 'working consensus' between teachers, or teachers and other interested parties. The search for absolute criteria appears therefore a vain hope, if not a waste of time.

8   A Review of Specific Techniques

Introduction

Whatever general strategy is adopted for evaluation in a school it will eventually require the use of particular techniques. Furthermore, although some strategies place emphasis on certain techniques (e.g. testing), the choice is often open. The spirit of the book thus far has been to encourage schools, and those involved with them, to take a broad view of strategy (hence the argument in Chapter 6). Much the same applies to techniques. The major research approaches discussed in Chapter 7 have given rise to a wide range of techniques for carrying out data collection and analysis; therefore teachers, and others, should be prepared to make use of those that are appropriate to the evaluation problems they face. Stake's (1967) description-matrix acts as a reminder of the range of potential data sources, so we shall use its categories as the framework for this chapter. However, as we have already noted, evaluation is not synonymous with research in its choice of problems, ultimate purposes, and, perhaps most importantly, in its concern for data collection.

In discussing his 'description-matrix', Stake reminds us that evaluation need not be only an empirically based activity (as indeed we pointed out in Chapter 3). We have therefore chosen to consider techniques, which cover both empirical and intrinsic evaluation, under four basic headings:

> Observed curriculum
> Curriculum outcomes
> Intended curriculum
> Curriculum context

In the case of the 'Observed curriculum' and 'Curriculum outcomes' we focus on data collection and analysis techniques, but the 'Intended curriculum' and 'Curriculum context' are treated somewhat differently.

The evaluation of 'Intended curriculum' is considered to require intrinsic evaluation, and, because the techniques for this are not well-defined, we explore the nature of such an evaluation, as well as the techniques that are necessary. Although the other headings speak for themselves, 'Curriculum context' is not obviously related to Stake's data matrix. Here we have in mind his idea of antecedents, although we choose to use 'context' to emphasise the pervasiveness of conditions which provide a context for teaching and learning, but which may or may not be central to it. For example, the architecture of a school is an obvious, though little studied, aspect of curriculum context (Wallace, 1980).

Where we deal with data collection and analysis there is a large research tradition to draw upon. We do this mindful of the methodological issues raised in Chapter 7, but make no attempt to be comprehensive - that is a job for books on research methods. Instead, where certain techniques are commonly used, for example, the techniques of interviewing, we consider the main elements of the method and any experience of its use in evaluation, and by teachers, in schools. This latter experience is not extensive and where information is lacking we discuss the issues that we consider relevant to schools. As this chapter is essentially a *review* we attempt to offer a guide to these issues, and to the literature. Although a number of texts are available, which cover aspects of the four areas we have chosen, they are often specific to one or two aspects (e.g. Hook, 1981; Gronlund, 1981), general in their treatment (e.g. Harris, Bell and Carter, 1981; Ford Teaching Project, 1975, or not addressed primarily to teachers (e.g. Lewy, 1977). The growth in interest in teacher-as-researcher has led to a number of books being written specifically to help teachers with research methods etc. (e.g. Walker, 1985).

We bear in mind throughout the constraints and limitations of the situations teachers find themselves in, but postpone a general discussion of these practical issues until Chapter 9. However, the fact that we give details of a wide range of techniques is not necessarily a recommendation for any one of them (although our preferences will be obvious), nor do we suggest that teachers should become familiar with all of them. The review is intended to *aid* the choice and development of appropriate techniques: appropriate, that is, to the problem being investigated.

The Observed Curriculum

Introduction

This section is predominantly about data collection techniques and draws upon the traditions of both nomothetic and idiographic inquiry. We have not treated them as competing traditions, although the discussion of some issues may be cast in this light, but rather as sources of different kinds of information. The section is sub-divided to reflect the preoccupation with *direct observation* of behaviour (e.g. in the classroom) and *indirect observation* through, for example, the reconstruction of behaviour from accounts of participants (i.e. teachers and pupils). To some extent this is an artificial boundary, not least because it simplifies certain theoretical traditions within research, but we use it for convenience and try to remain aware of the sensitivities of the traditions. Finally, the curriculum can be observed in the classroom, the school's corridors, or even perhaps in pupils' homes, although most experience of using techniques concerns classrooms. Direct observation, therefore, has tended to focus on the classroom and this is reflected in our treatment of it. Indirect observation is appropriate inside and outside the classroom. It is particularly useful for those situations, often occurring outside the classroom, which are not directly observable. In other words, this section on observation does not attempt to balance the discussion on evaluation at classroom and institutional level. Thus, it is hoped that the section on 'Curriculum context' will help correct any bias towards the classroom level that occurs in this section.

Direct Observation

Introduction

The increasing concern for observation among evaluators, usually those associated with curriculum projects, has come from those of the 'illuminative' camp who are concerned with the processes, rather than the products, of learning. Thus experience of observation techniques mirrors the methodological debates of the two major research traditions discussed in Chapter 7. In classroom research this finds expression in two approaches: structured (systematic) observation; unstructured (informal) observation[1]. We turn to each of these approaches before considering the special problems that teachers experience in observing, i.e. as true participants who become observers.

Structured observation

This entails recording classroom behaviour against pre-specified categories and representing the occurrences of these behaviours in a tally of frequencies, or as a sequence. This provides quantitative data which can be used for the comparison of classrooms: a practice common in nomothetic research. As might be expected structured observation has a longer research tradition in the USA than in Britain[2] and consequently many systems for such observation exist[3]. Many of the systems are based upon Flanders' Interaction Analysis Categories (Flanders, 1970) which codes seven categories of teacher talk (e.g. 'praises or encourages' and 'asks questions'), two of pupil talk (e.g. 'responds to teacher' and 'pupil initiates talk') and one of silence or confusion. This system reflects a formal teaching approach where whole-class teaching dominates. General writings for teachers in this area reflect two traditions: that relating to student (pupil) assessment, for example Gronlund (1981) and TenBrink (1974); and that relating to observing young children (again with an emphasis on assessment), for example, Boehm and Weinberg (1977); Cohen and Stern (1978); Good and Brophy (1978) and Goodwin and Driscoll (1980). In the British context Galton (1978) has documented a collection of over forty systems, which, in contrast to those developed in the USA, are concerned with more flexible types of classroom organisation[4]; indeed a major focus is the primary classroom[5]. Many of these focus on pupil activity, pupil-teacher contact and the proportion of time the pupil spends 'on the task'.

There are in fact a variety of ways that structured observation systems can be described but all systems must resolve the following issues:

1. the purpose of the study;
2. how the schedule is derived;
3. its focus - pupil, teacher, or both;
4. the number and type of categories;
5. the frequency of recording;
6. the period of observations;
7. the number and selection of persons observed.
   (adapted from Bennett and McNamara (1979, pp. 36-7).

Eggleston, Galton and Jones (1975) used 'purpose' as one dimension of a conceptual map for structured observation research, isolating three distinct kinds: process - to produce a description; comparative - to compare one class or teacher with another; process-product - to relate behaviour to measurable change in outcomes. Each of these is relevant to evaluation although process studies are the most likely to be within reach of schools[6]. The focus of the study and the number and type of categories in the system relate to what behaviour is to be sampled. This sample can be classified according to how the schedule was derived: inductively, starting with a wide focus of relevant behaviour and ending in theory relating this behaviour; from an explicit theory of classroom behaviour which is operationalised into categories; or based on curriculum objectives that prescribe which behaviours are important. (This forms the second dimension of the conceptual map developed by Eggleston, Galton and Jones (1975).) The sampling of behaviour also provides the basis for three common types of systems:

1. sign system - a list of mutually exclusive but non-exhaustive behaviours from which either the occurrence of a behaviour is recorded (no matter how many times it occurs), or a frequency count is made in a specific observation period;
2. category system - an exhaustive list of mutually exclusive behaviours from which a frequency count and the sequence of occurrence can be derived;
3. rating scale - a judgement involving a high level of inference expressed as a point on a scale[7].

The behaviours listed in sign and category systems should be directly observable with a minimum of inference: an important guarantee of reliability.

Clearly the frequency of recording for each of the above is different: sign systems depend upon the occurrence of the event, no matter *when* it occurs; a category system encodes behaviour at specified time intervals; a rating scale is usually marked once (for each scale) in a period, such as a lesson. Unfortunately this area of sampling, of both time and events, is characterised by the use of a wide variety of terms. Some of these are synonymous, others exhibit subtle differences, but few writers in this area seek to unify them. (No doubt some people will disagree with our attempt!)

Event-sampling[8] occurs when a tally-mark is made each time a behaviour occurs - the sequence of behaviour is therefore lost. For example, taking two categories of behaviour, the record might be:

Teacher asks a question   ⊬⊬⊤ ╷
Teacher praises or encourages   ╷╷╷

Instantaneous sampling[9] requires a single category to be chosen at regular intervals to represent the behaviour at that moment. This is a discontinuous form of recording which maintains the sequence between instances. For example, using the same behaviours as above, recorded each minute, would give a record thus:

Category	Minutes
	1 2 3 4 5 6 7
Teacher asks a question	| | | . | |
Teacher praises or encourages	| |

Interval recording [10] means that at regular intervals a record is made of the behaviour that has occurred during that interval. This gives a continuous record but the sequence within the interval is lost. (The effect of this will depend upon the length of the interval[11].) The period of observation, its length and when it occurs is important to sample the behaviour adequately[12]. Sampling among pupils can be accomplished in four ways: by random sampling; by observing them all; cyclically, by observing each for ten minutes until all are covered; by point-time sampling i.e. observing until behaviour is identified, then moving on (Boehm and Weinberg, 1977).

In developing structured observation systems, reliability and validity are naturally important considerations. Reliability is one of the important strengths of these systems, being ensured by well defined (i.e. unambiguous) behaviours to be encoded. The aim is to reduce the effects of any particular observer, such that if two observers encode the same behaviour they will, within certain limits, produce the same record of categories. Reliability can, therefore, be expressed as a correlation between the two observers (inter-judge reliability)[13]. Similarly, the reliability of a single observer recording the same behaviour at different times can also be measured (intra-judge reliability). For teachers acting as observers of their own teaching some kind of recording (e.g. audio-recording) of the behaviour will be necessary to carry out such a check. As we shall see later, critics of structured observation are concerned about its validity, which depends, in part, upon the descriptive and explanatory value of the concepts underlying the schedule (McIntyre and MacLeod, 1978). Provided that satisfaction is achieved on that count, it is possible to consider five questions posed by Hurwitz (1979) concerning validity[14]:

1. Do the aspects of classroom behaviour the system purports to measure actually differ from classroom to classroom? (Construct validity).
2. Are the aspects of classroom behaviour the system purports to measure relatively stable in one classroom? (Construct validity).
3. How do measurements of the aspects of classroom behaviour the system purports to measure relate to measures of other aspects of classroom behaviour that are logically or theoretically related or unrelated? (Construct validity).
4. Does the system fully measure the aspects of classroom behaviour it purports to? (Content validity).
5. Do the aspects of classroom behaviour the system purports to measure fully exist in actual classrooms? (Content validity).

(Bennett and McNamara, 1979, p. 112)

Naturally all the sampling decisions outlined above (behaviour, time, period etc.) affect the validity of the observation system in recording representative behaviour in the classroom. As Chapter 7 has already intimated validity and reliability overlap; any interpretation of behaviour that an observer has to make while encoding is a threat to the validity of the system as well as affecting its reliability[15]. Thus rating scales are weak in this respect. Validity is also threatened at the stage when inferences are drawn i.e. when analysing the recorded behaviour, but here triangulation can be used (see Chapter 7 and 9)[16].

Although most observation systems are developed for research purposes, advice does exist on how teachers can choose one that is suitable from those in existence, or develop their own. Hook (1981) and Boehm and Weinberg (1977) give advice and examples specifically for teachers, drawing upon the traditional research literature where appropriate[17]. Harris, Bell and Carter (1981) offer some general advice but with few examples. Gronlund (1981) has advice on rating scales, but as noted earlier, this is directed towards student assessment. One important idea that is particularly relevant to teachers observing their own classrooms is that observation systems need not be used for 'live' recording i.e. encoding by an observer present in the classroom. Instead they can be used to analyse classroom behaviour which has been electronically recorded, on audio- or video-tape.

Unstructured observation

In contrast to structured observation this approach looks at behaviour in a holistic way: not as discrete occurrences (or categories). Instead observation is progressively focused, and an attempt is made to look at behaviour from the actors' (i.e. pupils and teachers) point of view[18]. This concern with such things as pupil intentions contrasts with structured observation which considers only observable behaviour. For the purposes of evaluation it is worth distinguishing between unstructured observation, which uses ethnographic methods, and ethnography itself. The latter is concerned with developing theory about social systems (including schools and classroom): something that is not a central concern of evaluation[19]. However, features of the research approach used to develop this theory, such as progressive focusing and reflexivity, are important for evaluators, particularly those working within their own school. (We will return to this point later in this section.)

For participant observation, the main form of observation in ethnography, the taking of notes based on direct observation is fundamental. Naturally the literature of ethnography, in both educational and other settings, contains accounts of this technique; here we will be concerned only with the literature which tries to address the needs of teachers.

Field notes are the ethnographer's principal tool for recording direct observations. Elliott (1978), Ford Teaching Project i.e. (1975), and Harris, Bell and Carter (1981) give general descriptions of field notes for teachers and Adelman and Walker (1975) give advice on observing a classroom in the context of initial training. Patton (1980) gives a detailed account of field notes made by professional evaluators (as opposed to researchers) although these are generally outsiders to the institution or programme being investigated. Only Hook (1981) addresses teachers directly, and in some detail, including examples of field notes.

However the assessment tradition and the study of young children in the USA bring a useful and analogous approach: the use of *anecdotes*. These are systematically gathered, factual descriptions of meaningful incidents and events, recorded as close to the event as possible. Gronlund (1981) gives helpful guidelines on writing up anecdotes[20]. The concern in assessment, however, is with recording a representative sample of behaviour. In evaluation it may be just as important to consider unexpected or exceptional events, as well as those that are meaningful to the observer.

The making of field notes is similar to recording anecdotes but, in addition to behavioural descriptions, they may contain the inter-pretations and impressions of the observer. To improve their validity they should be made as soon after the event as possible. This is difficult for a teacher but, as Elliott (1978) suggests, it might be possible for a teacher to make a record in a hiatus of teaching. Teachers in the Ford Teaching Project (1975) suggested that the topic being recorded should be selected by the teacher; thus it could be anything of interest. How-ever, this raises some problems. First, in evaluation there is always a problem concerning whether an observer should start with an 'open mind' or with a particular focus. Secondly, the selection may not only be based upon undisclosed criteria, but also involve teacher bias. Apart from these special problems for teachers observing their own lessons, any observer has to decide whether to take notes during the observation period or afterwards. The former has the advantage of being immediate and spontaneous but takes time away from observation with the consequence that events may be missed. Writing notes after the observ-ation period allows the task to be accomplished without distraction. However, although an overall impression of the lesson can be conveyed, events can be forgotten or selectively recalled. A compromise is to note down single words, to trigger the memory and supply a sequence, which can then be elaborated later. More general disadvantages of field notes are that: they cannot capture conversation easily, though some say they should (Patton, 1980); they are difficult to analyse; they are subjective. On the other hand they have the advantages of being simple, not requiring an outsider, and being easy to look over (acting as an *aide mémoire*).

Notes can be made to cover a long peiod of time, such as a day, and be collected over, say, a school term or year to form a *diary*. Obviously in this form they are more selective, although they can be structured to record certain issues - usually referred to as a 'log'. Hook (1981) dis-cusses the use of *item-sampling* cards as a way of systematically attend-ing to issues. The teacher keeps a card for each of several issues felt to be important. At the end of each day one of the issues is chosen to be written about. Issues can be randomly chosen each day by shuffling the 'pack' of cards. Both Armstrong and Enright (in Nixon, 1981) give examples of diaries, although Armstrong's consisted of field notes written up after the lessons he observed (as participant observer) in the classroom of another teacher; Enright, on the other hand, was usually the only teacher in her class.

Structured and unstructured observation compared

Naturally there have been methodological debates between the two traditions and these have engaged a number of British writers in the late 1970s[21]. Those favouring unstructured observation have been on the offensive for the most part, although McIntyre and MacLeod (1978) have countered criticism and defended systematic (structured) observations. Their defence serves as a useful summary of the debate so far[22].

1. *Category systems have a narrow conception of the classroom*[23].
McIntyre and MacLeod counter this by saying that some of the proponents of unstructured observation seem to imply that they 'know' what are the significant events that category systems miss. Nevertheless McIntyre and MacLeod concede that the use of pre-specified categories does miss some data which are not recorded and, therefore, that great reliance is put on the descriptive and explanatory power of the concepts underlying the system.

2. *Category systems provide only a partial description of classroom behaviour.*
In response to this, McIntyre and MacLeod argue that any observation will be partial. Unstructured observation does not, in their view, make explicit the reasons for choosing a focus on certain events. This contrasts with the explicit choices involved in structured observation[24].

3. *Category systems, particularly those reflecting the supposedly formal classrooms of USA, are inadequate for a range of contexts.*
For example, a system which emphasises teacher talk is unsuitable for categorising pupil behaviour in groups. However, nowadays a wide range of systems exist to cover a variety of contexts. At another level McIntyre and MacLeod recognise that no system can cope with elements of a context that are not publicly shared in our culture, e.g. jokes between a teacher and pupils based on a past incident, but, they argue, such occurrences are rare and therefore not a serious problem[25].

4. *Structured observation reveals a lack of concern for the meanings that are attached to behaviour by pupils and teachers.*
This is a central concern for observers using an unstructured approach, and McIntyre and MacLeod do not deny that it is a limitation. However,

they argue that some inference can be made from observable behaviour. In any case, other techniques exist to get at these meanings, for example, by interviewing[26].

5. *The concern for quantification is unnecessary, particularly for those who are interested in teachers researching their own classrooms.*
McIntyre and MacLeod argue that even unstructured observers quantify by using statements such as "the majority of the pupils . . . ", but these statements are vague. Systematic observers, on the other hand, make precise statements and use statistics to support them.

Although McIntyre and MacLeod counter adequately many of the criticisms of structured observation, some of the debate reflects the different conceptions of research outlined in Chapter 7. McIntyre and MacLeod seek no hegemony for structured observation, since they make quite clear what it can cope with, and expect *other approaches to be used where other kinds of information are required.* They go on to discuss what it can be used for. With an emphasis on observable behaviour, they acknowledge that structured observation is not suitable for studying the perceptions of pupils and teachers. In this respect, for them, two questions are of importance: why do pupils learn what they learn? why do teachers teach as they do? For the first question they suggest three kinds of evidence: pupils' reports on classroom behaviour; pupils' thought processes while in the classroom; observable events in the classroom. However, they claim that pupils' reports may not relate to influences on learning i.e. on *how* they learn, and at present there are no adequate procedures for finding out what pupils are thinking. This of course leaves observable events as the best kind of evidence. In considering why teachers teach as they do, McIntyre and MacLeod say that only through overt behaviour or by controlling observable characteristics can teachers influence pupil learning. Teacher accounts of their behaviour are insufficient. Neither of these two questions necessarily requires structured observation, only attention to overt behaviour.

Interestingly few critiques of unstructured observation exist[27], although Power (1977), in considering studies of science classroom interaction, has this to say about unstructured observation: 'the ethnographic approach shows signs of becoming yet another new religion. Its prophets are often more concerned with denouncing the evils of the scientific establishment than with clarifying and resolving the problems of the interpretative paradigm' (p.21)[28]. By emphasising the meanings attached to behaviour Power argues that ethnographic research reduces reality to 'what goes on inside people's heads [and] leads to a neglect of the ways in which classroom interaction is shaped by external constraints ... whose consequences are present whether or not they are perceived by teachers and pupils. Furthermore, while patterns of inter-action may be in part the product of participants' definitions of the situation, there is the possibility those participants might be falsely conscious' (p.22). (See also the critique of purely interpretative approaches outlined in Chapter 7.)

The teacher as observer

False consciousness is made doubly problematic when one or more of the participants i.e. the teachers, become observers. It is to this special case of observation that we now turn. Because most of the literature reflects the concern of researchers, who come from outside the school, few writers have considered the special problems of teachers as observers in their own classrooms. For example, if a teacher with-draws from teaching to observe, then the situation will have been changed by that withdrawal[29]. Although Stenhouse (1975) was an advocate of teachers researching their own classrooms he did not offer much guidance, except by way of rejecting structured observation. The major detailed text which specifically addresses the concerns of teachers carrying out observation is from Deakin University (Hook 1981)[30,31]. The Ford Teaching Project material, which pioneered the use of research methods appropriate for teacher-researchers, contains only general guidelines and is to some extent biased towards a part-icular form of curricular change - focusing as it does upon questioning strategies. Harris, Bell and Carter (1981) are similarly brief, although very comprehensive. Nevertheless, they give little consideration to methodological issues. Boehm and Weinberg (1977), although focusing upon younger children, provide detailed advice on observation. As mentioned earlier, Adelman and Walker (1975) give advice within the context of initial teacher training, but this does not include any con-sideration of structured observation.

It is of course recognised that teachers already routinely observe, although there is a need for this to be more systematic as well as continuous (Adelman and Walker, 1975; Anderson, 1979). This recog-nition emphasises the 'participant' element of 'participant observation' and implies that only the teacher can make informed judgements in the classroom (Ford Teaching Project, 1975). It also implies that the teacher has access to reasons for action[32], and is unique as an observer in being in the classroom over a long period of time[33]. However, this involvement gives rise to difficulties; teachers are indeed participants, but with a specific role which excludes them from some of the action associated with the 'pupil culture'[34]. We have already noted the problem of withdrawing to observe, and consequently changing, the situation - a conflict between two roles, i.e. of teacher and observer[35]. Pupils may be unsure how to interpret the teacher's behaviour and hence problems of reactivity may be created for the 'observer'. As we shall see later, electronic recording is a way of reducing this effect because it postpones observation.

Associated with the role problem is one of bias. At the simplest level a teacher's observation may suffer from the 'halo effect' i.e. existing knowledge of the situation may be used to be even more selective. For example children from poor families may talk less and therefore be noticed less (Boehm and Weinberg, 1977); or boys may be treated differently from girls (Delamont, 1981). At another level it is suggested that teachers may be more likely to make a biased interpretation of behaviour (Hook, 1981, pp. 29 and 31). Even more profound is the problem of 'false consciousness' noted by Power (1977). It is possible for a teacher to misconstrue a pupil's behaviour, as indicated by the action (s)he takes as a consequence of that behaviour (Good and Brophy, 1978). The Ford Teaching Project (1975) teachers and researchers talked of misguided intuition, and how sound evidence needed to be gathered as a basis for action. Reflexivity is of course the ethnographer's device to counter problems of bias and hence to counter the criticism on selection of focus made by McIntyre and MacLeod (1978) (see the earlier discussion). With regard to structured observation, the use of pre-specified categories helps to reduce bias (Eggleston, Galton and Jones, 1975, p. 56); and making explicit the basis of the category system is a form of reflexivity. On a more positive note, efforts to reduce bias will help to make teachers more aware and to make their tacit knowledge more explicit (Anderson, 1979).

Recording techniques

This brings us to a consideration of recording techniques which allow either selection of focus to be delayed, or repeated access to the recorded behaviour: both important in countering problems of bias. For teachers acting as observers such recordings are not treated as the only source of data, but as an aid to reconstructing the lesson (Elliott, 1978, p.79). Adelman and Walker (1975, p.129) take the view that recordings should accompany participant observation and, therefore, that notes should still be made.

Audio-recording is the basic method for a teacher because, by being less obtrusive, it is easiest to do while teaching (OU, 1981a, Block 3, p.23). Moreover, if the teacher is present then having all the information recorded is less important and, it is argued, teaching is mainly verbal anyway (Elliott, 1978, p.80)[36]. Teachers in the Ford Teaching Project went so far as to say that audio-recording was the most important research tool, and Bassey and Hatch (1979) abandoned video-recording in favour of audio-recording while developing a structured observation system for use by teachers. When a radio microphone is used, or a cassette tape-recorder is carried by the teacher, then all the talk within range of the microphone can be recorded. However, disadvantages include: the cost of equipment, pupil reticence, although this can be reduced by having a recorder present before it is required; the time required for transcription; the cumbersome nature of recording equipment. Above all the transcribing time is a universal cause for complaint!

Advice on use of audio-recorders, covering such things as suitable equipment and microphone positioning, can be found in the following texts:

Anderson (1979), which is a prescriptive guide to recording;
Open University (1981a, Block 3, pp. 25-9), also a guide drawing, in part on examples from the experience of two teachers;
Bassey and Hatch (1979), which gives brief details of the equipment and arrangement they used;
Hook (1981, pp. 237-9), which gives general details and problems of recording;
Boydell (1975), which presents brief discussion of problems of recording.

Video-recording is another possible technique but Bassey and Hatch (1979) claim that, in their case, it was not worth the effort. However, if non-verbal behaviour is required, if the observer is ignorant of the situation e.g. not a teacher, or if the recordings are to be replayed to young children in order to gauge their perceptions, then video-recording will be necessary. Although it gives a more complete record of the classroom behaviour (depending of course on the technical qualities of the equipment), it nevertheless has a number of disadvantages:

1. the camera gives a selective view, especially if more than one is used since this requires cutting between cameras[37];
2. analysis of the recording is complex[38];

3. the equipment is costly and cumbersome[39];
4. reporting data thus collected is difficult.

Details of video-recording for classroom observation are not usually given in texts on the subject. For example, OU (1981b, Block 3) discusses it only in the most general terms, and Hook (1981), although presenting much useful information on the use of video, gives few technical details in contrast to his treatment of still photography. Bassey and Hatch (1979) give the most detailed practical advice drawing on their particular experience, and Adam and Biddle (1970) describe, in general terms, how they used a two-camera set-up for research.

The use of still-photography, especially if synchronised with an audio-recording, is a useful compromise[40], but it requires an outsider if the behaviour of the teacher is to be recorded - unless a pupil operates the camera. Using half-frame slides and audio-recording, Adelman and Walker (1975) are the best known exponents of this technique. Although it is highly selective, depending heavily upon the judgements of the cameraman, the uncertainty or ambiguity inherent in still photographs or slides appears to be a useful device to get pupils and teachers to talk about the lesson subsequently. However it takes some time for reactivity to be reduced. Technical details of this technique can be found in Adelman and Walker (1975)[41]. Still-photography is covered in some detail in Hook (1981) and to a lesser extent in OU (1981a, Block 3).

Analysis

This is treated differently in structured and unstructured observation approaches. In constructing an observation schedule some thought must have already been given to analysis. After collecting the data, whether it be in the form of a tally of frequencies or a sequence of categories, analysis can be carried out. For unstructured observation the analysis begins while collecting data and continues through progressive focusing. At intervals, and at the end of the investigation, the data will be reviewed and a more reflective analysis produced[42]. If observation schedules are used to analyse pre-recorded behaviour, e.g. behaviour recorded on video as opposed to being recorded 'live', analysis can be carried out from different angles using several schedules (or modifications of the same one). Nevertheless, whichever way they are used, analysis is a mechanical activity in the first instance involving, for example, the calculation of various indices. In the Bassey and Hatch (1979) seven-category system the percentage frequency of 'teacher questions', or 'direction giving' can be calculated, or the number of long and short interactions counted. Determining what these indices mean is, of course, a creative process of speculation and judgement. Bassey and Hatch (1979), however, give some guidelines for evaluating teaching through a series of questions such as:

> Consider the differences between long and short interactions. Is it the case in your classroom that short interactions mainly serve to keep everyone busy, while long interactions are more valuable as teaching events? Would it be desirable to have more long interactions?   (Bassey and Hatch, 1979, p. 137)

McIntyre (1980, p. 18) argues that simple frequency counts are unlikely to be indicative of effective teaching. More important, he argues, is how the event (being counted) is related to those preceding and following it.

The much maligned Flanders' Interaction Analysis System has a well developed procedure for analysis which goes beyond simple frequency counts to offer a matrix for modelling how the verbal interaction proceeds. This requires the production of a record of the lesson as a sequence of categories. Any change, for example, from category 5 (teacher lectures) to category 6 (teacher gives directions) can subsequently be represented as a count in a cell of the matrix. Flanders has also developed models of lessons, such as 'short question, short answer' and 'creative inquiry' which can be identified from the completed matrix.

As noted above, structured observation implies starting with some ideas about what is likely to be found. For teachers just beginning evaluation, however, this approach may presume too much. The approaches of qualitative evaluation become important therefore, and since audio-recording is regarded as such an important tool we shall focus on its analysis. Transcription of the recording is the first step. Not only does this provide data to work on, but the process itself stimulates ideas for analysis. However a balance has to be struck between obtaining a complete transcript, which is very time consuming (e.g. 10 hours to transcribe 1 hour of tape), and the more manageable task of producing a partial transcription. Anderson (1979) gives advice to the beginner which involves making a progressively more detailed transcription ending up with only a small portion of the recording being 'completely' transcribed[43]. Thus transcription should start with an attempt to obtain an overview (OU, 1981a, Block 3, p. 30) prior to focusing on particular aspects or events. Whatever criteria are used for such select-ion[44] it is important that they are noted as a part of reflexivity. Such a note may include the frame of mind of the analyst: a factor which could affect the transcription (OU, 1981a, Block 3, p.31). The trans-cription can then be used to make the familiar strange. For this reason it is important not to 'doctor it'; speech is usually fragmented and 'messy' (Atkinson, 1981). In contrast to those working on the Ford Teaching Project, some writers emphasise the importance of looking at the organisation of talk and hence recommend a close inspection of the transcript[45]. They counsel against expecting major concepts, such as 'social control', to leap out from the data (Atkinson, 1981, p.101) and advise building up the analysis from the technicalities of talk at the level of each utterance, upwards to a consideration of episodes within the lesson[46].

When the data are taken from field notes, on their own or along with an audio-recording, the general guidelines for qualitative analysis can be used. Patton (1980) provides guidance for those involved in evaluation, rather than research[47]. The stages he identifies are:

1. finding a focus for the analysis - stemming from the concerns of the decision-makers and having begun in the data collection;
2. organising, checking and, for safety's sake, even copying the data;
3. producing a qualitative description or narrative;
4. developing inductively categories, labels and typologies;
5. carrying out a logical analysis on these categories to search for further cross classifications;
6. expressing these categories etc., where appropriate, through metaphors[48];
7. speculating about causes, consequences and relationships.

James and Ebbutt (1981, pp. 90-1) describe the problems for a teacher analysing data and they suggest the use of index cards for categories that evolve, allowing cross-referencing and searching for patterns.

Observation outside and across classrooms

The literature on techniques for this type of observation is much less extensive, although of course what has been said so far about unstruct-ured observation, particularly field notes, is relevant[49]. Here therefore, we will briefly describe two studies both of which employed structured observation: one concerned the 'teachers day' and the other involved a 'shadow study' of three pupils.

The study of the teacher's day (Hilsum and Cane, 1979) was concerned with teachers' commitments, rather than with teaching or relationships with children. This employed a continuous record of all the teachers' behaviour in time, sequence and duration. All activity was encoded, and the number placed on a sheet which divided each minute of the day into 5-second intervals, allowing several codes to be entered in each interval. Entries were made such that the duration of an activity could be measured. Teachers also completed a precoded 'diary' indicating how long they spent on certain activities out of school. The schedule also allowed qualitative notes and comments to be recorded.

A shadow study is where pupils are almost literally 'shadowed' continuously for a period: usually a day or up to a week. It is a technique often used by HMI[50]. Usually the observations are unstructured but in the case we consider (i.e. Sir Frank Markham School, 1981 - see Chapter 5) they involved the use of schedules. Three pupils of high, average and low ability, from the same class, were shadowed for a week. For each lesson a series of schedules was completed, covering such topics as: lesson format (e.g. lecture, question and answer, group work); materials used; pupil activities (e.g. reading silently, copying, listening); teacher questions. Some of the schedules required a rating relating to, for example, how bored the pupil appeared. In addition to the schedules, a brief qualitative description was written for each classroom, the target pupils' tasks, the classroom atmosphere, pupil confidence and homework done by target pupils. The observer was the school's deputy head and he was naturally aware of the intrusiveness of his presence and problems of sampling - the latter in terms of sampling the pupils and sampling during the period of observation[51].

An alternative to this structured approach would have been a qualitative study which attempted to capture the flavour of the week for each pupil and which would have included interviews. Nevertheless, the structured study revealed many ideas that could be followed up in detail.

Issues

A dominant issue concerns which approach is most appropriate? Although many writers advocate the use of unstructured approaches by teachers, examples do exist of teachers having usefully employed structured observation[52]. Our position is similar to that of McIntyre and MacLeod (1978) in that we would recommend whatever appears to be the most appropriate technique for the particular evaluation. While it is not possible to rehearse the full range of contingencies that might arise it is worth considering a few of the factors involved in deciding on an appropriate approach. Obviously if the observation takes place in a number of classrooms in a school, with the intention of comparing them, then structured observation is suitable. In this sense it is an hypo-thesis-testing rather than hypothesis-generating study. Teachers have, after all, wide experience of individual classrooms and therefore look-ing across classrooms could be productive[53]. They can use their exper-ience to create pre-specified categories, perhaps with more descriptive and explanatory power than those created by researchers (cf. Note 26). On the other hand where their understandings of classrooms are still implicit, then unstructured observation and narrative descriptions may be more useful[54].

Another consideration is the problem of bias. We have already shown how the two approaches deal differently with this. The part-icular problems experienced by teachers as observers, and to which we have already referred, may place a severe burden upon their reflex-ivity, resulting in a considerable volume of field notes, only a small proportion of which record observable data[55]. The use of an outside observer (to be considered, further in Chapter 9) and the use of audio-recording are, of course, alternatives to employing structured observa-tion to reduce bias. Ainley and Lazonby (1981) describe the use of a structured observation schedule used by an outsider, combined with a teacher's report of the lesson. This report was subsequently used to validate the schedule[56]. The problem of volume of field notes raises perhaps the most important issue for a teacher involved in evaluation: that of data overload. It is, of course, an issue for all techniques, whether of observation, assessment, or whatever. However, with the need to collect observable data from classrooms which, by their nature, are fast moving and complex, the issue is magnified. The obvious advice in such a situation is of course to start simple, say, with field notes made after lessons, then moving on to audio-recording and/or paired observation later.

Indirect Observation

Introduction

The techniques in this section are needed when behaviour cannot be directly observed, as is the case when it occurs infrequently or in private. Even where behaviour is public, and not infrequent, the observer may simply not be present. Thus events have to be reconstructed from accounts of them. However, these techniques go further than this; they provide information on motives and attitudes towards certain events, as well as attitudes, values and beliefs in general. Advocates of a 'scientific model' of research see such methods as a poor second to direct observation[57]. However, as we pointed out when discussing direct observation, researchers such as Delamont (1976), from the symbolic interactionist tradition, see the revelation of attitudes, values and beliefs as central to their methodology[58]. As was the case in direct observation, 'structure' is a key in characterising the techniques. Although the methodological argument about structure has its parallels here, it seems less polarised in the literature, thus allowing for a more pragmatic choice. If as a researcher you are clear about what you are interested in finding out you can be specific and employ a degree of structure[59].

The techniques we consider here are interviews, questionnaires, pupil diaries, and unobtrusive measures. Interviews and questionnaires are treated more extensively because they are of more obvious use in evaluation[60]. They are also basic techniques in social science research, and as such command an extensive literature. Although schools present challenges to researchers and evaluators, they are no less difficult than those faced by other social researchers who carry out, for example, interviews connected with issues such as rape and police brutality (Smith, 1981). However, despite the extensive literature on techniques in general, comparatively little exists which specifically deals with teachers working within their own schools[61].

Interviews or questionnaires

Researchers from the survey tradition (e.g. Smith, 1981) see questionnaires as self-administered structured interviews, and as such treat them very much the same. Naturally the respondent to the questionnaire cannot ask for questions to be clarified (and hence questions have to be simpler and clearer), nor can the interviewer probe the responses; motivation and interest have to be maintained by design devices rather then the formation of a personal relationship. Ethnographers, on the other hand, regard an unstructured interview as having a distinctive approach that is integral to participant observation. Apart from these methodological conflicts, those in schools need to consider additional issues. For instance, young children or poor writers can only be interviewed (Wragg, undated), and pupils may prefer to reveal sensitive information about their teacher's work anonymously, through a questionnaire (Ford Teaching Project, 1975). There is also a sampling issue, which involves deciding whether or not all the pupils in a school are to be involved in the evaluation, and how many teachers are available for interviewing. At the level of a single class the population is small and a questionnaire to all the pupils may be unnecessary; besides, interviews with a good sample are likely to be better (Elliott, 1981a). With target groups such as parents, who are widely (geographically) distributed, then questionnaires are attractive. Whatever technique is chosen, it should not be entered into lightly. Interviewing pupils, although a seemingly obvious thing for a teacher to do, not only requires personal skills, but presents problems of role (both of which we will consider below).

Interviews[62]

Types

We have already mentioned structured and unstructured interviews; these provide points on a continuum of types. At one end there are structured interviews with precisely worded questions and pre-specified responses (like a questionnaire); at the other end there are unstructured, non-directive interviews with the respondents (interviewees) dictating the topics to be discussed. Each of these represents the paradigm of the two research traditions. Between them lie variously described compromises:

1. The focused interview, which takes a particular pre-specified situation or event as the subject of the interview, then, using a set of general guidelines, tries to explore the respondent's perceptions of that situation or event (Hook, 1981, p.138-9)[63].
2. The semi-structured interview, which involves a carefully worded set of questions and pre-determined responses combined with open-ended questions allowing respondents to formulate their replies. These the interviewer must note down. (Wragg, undated)[64].
3. The informal, conversational interview, which presupposes nothing about what may be learnt. The interviewer follows the respondent's flow of ideas and makes notes after the event (Patton, 1980)[65].

As noted earlier, there is a much more flexible use of interviews within the two research traditions. For example, Smith (1981, pp.175-9) discusses the 'depth interviewing' (equivalent to the 'focused interview') of rape victims as part of a survey approach. Obviously this required the interviewer to follow the respondent's topics. In general, where hypotheses are clear then the interview can be structured (to test them); where they are to be developed, then it should be unstructured[66]. 'Unstructured' does not, of course, mean 'unprepared' and it would be inexcusable for an interviewer to go into an interview devoid of issues and topics of interest. Even where the interview is exploring the uniqueness of an individual the interviewer must have criteria to judge what to follow-up and what to leave.

Another type of interview exists which does not fall neatly into this structured-unstructured continuum i.e. group interviews. These can be conducted with varying degress of structure, but one important element is the interaction of respondents. These are often advocated for evaluation in schools and we will deal with them separately later.

Interview questions
The nature of the interview is crucially dependent upon the kind and sequence of questions asked. For structured interviews, a schedule is drawn up with questions and pre-determined responses; for unstructured interviews, guidelines would be prepared containing a loose collection of topics to ensure coverage and provide a degree of structure to the interview[67]. Whether working from a schedule or following the respondent's flow of ideas, the interviewer has to pay careful attention to the questions asked. It is beyond the scope of this book to give details of all the advice available, but we will outline the issues discussed in the literature[68].

The most important feature is whether the questions are open or closed. If the classification of a clearly understood dimension is required, then a closed question is used. If the respondent's knowledge of the topic, or conception of the issue, is unknown, then open questions are required (Smith, 1981, pp.156-7). Of course both types can be used in an interview, but Patton (1980) warns against getting deeper into the hole of dichotomous questions (e.g. ones requiring yes/no responses) while conducting unstructured interviews.

A second feature of interview questions concerns their wording, and here much advice is available[69]. Patton (1980) identifies the following issues:

1. singularity, i.e. questions should contain only one idea[70];
2. clarity, e.g. the vocabulary should be at the correct level[71];

3. neutrality; the interviewer must not express an opinion on the responses by the way he or she reacts. Nor should leading questions be used, except where they are used to indicate to respondents that seemingly unacceptable behaviour can be discussed[72].

Follow-up and probing questions require particular care so that more details can be obtained, a topic elaborated, or a response clarified. Smith (1981, p.171) gives a list of non-directive probes to encourage further response without leading the interviewee along any particular track (for example, 'How do you mean?').

This brings us to the third feature: the sequence of questions. Probing questions can follow a closed question, representing a simple sequence. With a structured or semi-structured interview a careful sequence can be built up. For complex issues a battery of questions can cover the various aspects[73]. With an unstructured interview the interviewer should not 'jump about' in covering various topics. Adelman and Walker (1975) suggest going from unstructured to structured questions, but others (e.g. Smith, 1981) only propose a general framework for sequence, for example, a 'warm-up' at the beginning using non-controversial descriptive questions and similar kinds of questions at the end to allow the respondent to 'cool down'[74]. Clearly, not all of this kind of advice on sequence is appropriate to unstructured interviews, for which no general rules can be laid down.

Conduct of interview

The sequence of questions is, of course, an aspect of the conduct of the interview; for structured interviews this is predetermined. Whichever kind of interview is being conducted, it is important for the interviewer to establish a relationship with the respondent (OU, 1981a, Block 3, p.50). A variety of words are used in the literature to describe the general attitude to be adopted: 'sympathetic', 'neutral', 'at ease', 'friendly'. Respondents should be made to feel that their responses are valued by, for example, being able to talk about their interests. They should also feel confidence and trust in the interviewer. The rapport that should result is particularly important in an unstructured interview; but both kinds require what Laffeur (Davis, 1981, p. 138) calls 'attending behaviour', i.e. making sure that the verbal and non-verbal behaviour (e.g. eye contact and body language) of the interviewer indicate interest[75].

This relationship is naturally established at the beginning of the interview. The opening remarks should also explain the purpose of the interview: how and why the respondent was selected and the confidentiality attached to the information collected (Hook, 1981, p.147)[76]. These considerations are just as important for teachers interviewing their own pupils since they are establishing another kind of relationship, i.e. other than that of teacher and pupil[77]. This is of course contrary to the normal way a participant observer works[78]. Pupils, like respondents in any study, should also be told who is conducting the study - the staff as a whole or just one teacher. Establishing and maintaining the relationship requires interpersonal skills. Regarding this Smith (1981, p.176) says that novices should reflect on three things: inclusion - the extent to which they feel part of or excluded from the interview; control - their perception of their degree of control over the interview; affection - how they feel towards the interviewee. If the interviewers don't feel they have the right to ask the questions of interest (because, for example, they are personal) then they will be ill at ease and this will be transmitted to respondents. Interviewers lose control if respondents take over, for example, when the latter start asking questions. The use of a schedule or guide helps maintain control, but without this, i.e. for an unstructured interview, interviewers need to exercise considerable skill[79]. Affection allows respondents to express feelings normally suppressed in formal relationships: a particular problem for teachers interviewing their pupils. Interestingly teachers may come to an interview with pupils *without* examining their right to ask questions. Assuming their normal controlling role, they are unlikely to establish the kind of relationship they require for the interview[80].

In addition to verbal devices for probing, mentioned earlier, the interviewer needs to use non-verbal behaviour to encourage responses (Simons, 1977), for example, when maintaining a silence after a response in the hope of encouraging elaboration. Finally the interview ought to end with an opportunity for respondents to ask questions[81].

Recording interviews

When a schedule is used then this provides the interview record, along with any notes of responses to open-ended questions. For unstructured interviews an audio-recording is an obvious consideration. This provides an accurate record without memory distortion, and allows verbatim quotations to be made in any analysis (Simons, 1977, pp.129-30). In addition it saves distracting scribbling during the interview (Hook, 1981, p.150) and allows more attention to be paid to the respondent (Patton, 1980). However, transcription is a major problem, although not such an acute one as in recordings of classroom observation. Patton (1980) quotes a 4:1 ratio of transcription time to recording time, but perhaps he assumes secretarial support; Wragg (undated) quotes a 7:1 ratio. The recorder can of course be intrusive and inhibit respondents, particularly if they are worried about confidentiality. The Ford Teaching Project team suggested using a cassette recorder with built in microphone, and keeping it, or a separate microphone, out of the respondent's line of vision. Young children can be allowed to play with the tape recorder to ensure familiarity.

Audio-recording does not however mean that note-taking should be neglected. Notes may be needed for the next interview, in advance of transcription (Simons, 1977, p. 130), or as a back-up in case of a bad recording (Hook, 1981, p.150). They also aid the conduct of the interview by helping the interviewer to monitor what is being discussed, for example, by acting as a reminder to follow-up a lead given when a topic is finished, so avoiding any interruption of the respondent's flow. They also allow the interviewer to deflect the respondent's eyes to give both of them some 'space' to think (cf. Stenhouse's (1978) side by side interview). Finally notes are useful in analysing the interview, particularly when transcription is made in long hand.

Interview analysis
Texts that address interviewing as a technique for evaluation have little to say on this issue. Some consider analysis as a general research issue using the kind of approach we discussed for direct observation, based on Patton (1980)[82]. Content analysis is advocated as an analytic technique (Wragg, undated), and we will look at this later. For the moment we will consider the cautions that are usually given (Simons, 1977, p.130-131).

1. Criteria for selection must take account of the conditions of the interview and the respondent's understanding of the purposes of the research.
2. Any inferences made must be accompanied by details of the context of the interview to allow others to judge them.
3. Care must be taken about whose categories are being formed - the interviewer's or respondent's (cf. Chapter 7).

Whatever approach is used some kind of check is required, preferably by a third person[83]. Wragg (undated, p.17), suggests a sandwich model: a first rapid read of all transcripts to decide how the analysis should proceed, followed by the main analysis and then another re-read to see if anything has been missed. This is what Glaser & Strauss (1967) called the 'constant comparative method'.

Structured interviews, like structured observation, require the analysis to be planned before collecting the data, so that specific hypotheses can be tested. Such analyses require statistical techniques either of a simple descriptive kind (e.g. tabulations of responses), or of a correlational kind. In this respect, the analysis of structured interviews resembles that of questionnaires.

Interviewing in schools
Little experience is published on this topic in the field of evaluation; the Ford Teaching Project (1975) being the major source[84]. Indeed most writers discuss the issue from the outside researcher's point of view (e.g. Simons, 1977). As we implied earlier, when we discussed the teacher's conduct of a pupil interview, the crucial issue concerns the adoption of a new role. As in direct observation, teachers must 'step back', but remain attentive, so that pupils will talk freely. In other words they must cast themselves in the role of learners, not teachers. Furthermore, pupils need to be told that their teacher is adopting this new role, although they may still find it confusing or difficult to believe[85].

All that we have said so far about interviewing applies equally to schools, but here we list some of the additional hints given by the Ford Teaching Project (and others)[86]:

1. pupils may need help in overcoming their reticence[87];
2. maintain informality and avoid constant reference to a clipboard or notes;
3. questions must be at the right level, but also be circumspect, i.e. avoid direct questioning;
4. be watchful of pupil boredom, but do not misinterpret non-verbal cues (e.g. shrugging of shoulders); they may be signs of pupils having difficulty in expressing themselves.

Sampling of pupils is a particular problem in schools: not simply in terms of who is sampled, but who does the sampling. Teachers who select their own pupils for interviews, introduce a possible source of bias.

One approach to interviewing, mentioned earlier, is group interviewing. This is of relevance to schools because pupils experience classrooms as a group as well as individuals. Adelman and Walker (1975) recommend interviewing groups of two or three pupils for twenty minutes or less. The Ford Teaching Project team employed what they called 'multiple interviewing', which involves an outsider in audio-recording and observing a lesson, interviewing the teacher before and after the lesson, interviewing the children, and finally interviewing the teacher and children together. Group discussions are also useful for senior staff. For instance, if they are conducting interviews with junior colleagues they can hold a group interview, which may help to reduce the importance of their own role. Similarly, if they are to be interviewed themselves, then including them in a group may overcome the problem of having to ask direct questions (and getting the 'official' answers)[88]. There are of course difficulties with group interviews, not only of transcribing them, but also problems of validity and the fact that individuals within the group may not share one anothers' values[89].

Pollard (1982b) describes his problems of interviewing as a teacher-researcher, for example, the limitation of having to do it mostly at lunchtime. An interesting strategy he employed was to involve children in the research by forming an interviewing team. He gave them a general brief on what he wanted to know, then asked them to record interviews with other children. Later in the study he 'entered' some interviews half way through, thus using the child-interviewer to break the ice. This enabled him to pursue, more specifically, his research interests. The Ford Teaching Project team employed a similar technique, using children to chair recorded discussion groups, without an adult being present (Elliott and Walker, 1973). In a study of children's perspectives on classroom interaction, Davies, B (1980) describes a conversational interview involving children in which interviewer and interviewees discover each other's conceptual framework. Part of Davies's framework was, of course, concerned to understand the children's frameworks. The children aided the interviewer in this by, for example, replaying the recorded conversation and drawing attention to what they saw as important. For a general guide to interviewing children see Rich (1968), who, although in the social work and counselling tradition of interviewing (e.g. for assessment), nevertheless writes for the inexperienced. In contrast to most texts, this deals specifically with children and young people.

Validity and reliability of interviews
Both interviewers and respondents are sources of bias: the former through the questions they ask, or their perceived role and presence; the latter through their conception of the interview, their memory of the event, their ability to answer and their motivation in taking part in the interview[90]. Obviously the points made above about questions

and the conduct of the interview will help to improve validity and reliability. As with direct observations, structure aids reliability and can minimise interviewer bias. Unstructured interviews require reflexivity. For example, there is a need to include details of context (including the interviewer's state of mind) along with any inferences, a point noted above. If the reliability of an account is suspect, as in the case of a confused recall of an event, the account can be treated as a perception of the event and, therefore, as a different kind of data. A similar approach can be taken to group interviews where, because of peer group pressure or support, individuals may give different responses from those they would make if interviewed alone[91]. Thus one kind of interview is not regarded as more reliable than another; they simply give different kinds of data.

Questionnaires

Although the skills needed for producing questionnaires are different from the interpersonal skills required for interviewing, they are no less demanding. Many questionnaires, including those produced by academic researchers, are poorly constructed and of doubtful validity and reliability. In saying this we are not referring to 'questionnaires' designed to *measure* psychological traits or some sociological construct, for example, measures of 'curiosity', 'teacher dogmatism' (Cohen, 1976, pp. 30 and 158 respectively) and 'classroom environment' (Fraser, 1981)[92]. These are usually subjected to a validation procedure. However, their concern for specific research problems often makes them inappropriate for evaluation[93].

The major effort must go into constructing the questionnaire and here all the advice, referred to earlier, on question types, wording and sequence in interviews applies[94]. As in a structured interview, a variety of pre-specified responses can be used: dichotomous; multiple-choice; scales (e.g. Likert scales: 'strongly agree', 'agree', 'neutral', 'disagree', 'strongly disagree') and rankings[95]. These can be combined with short or free (i.e. not limited) answers to open-ended questions. However, for ease of analysis there should be more closed than open-ended questions. The contrast with interviews comes with the concern for design. This is the (poor) substitute for the interviewer's sympathy, noted earlier. Youngman (undated) gives some useful hints in this respect, including advice on the use of headings, to indicate themes of questions, and attention to appearance, e.g. spacing, type face, separation of instructions and questions, consistent positioning of responses. For those with access to good reprographic facilities, photo-reduction is a useful method of improving appearance. Clearly length is an important element of design and a balance must be kept between the desire to collect 'interesting information' and the effect on the motivation of respondents. Youngman (undated, p.22) interestingly suggests leaving the pages unnumbered to reduce the impact on motivation! All this applies to rather formal questionnaires, but there is undoubtedly a place for the 'Write about half a page of sensible comments about the English lessons I've given you this year' (Tony Evans, *TES*, 23 April 1982) kind of exercise, which promises some revealing insights.

Unlike interviews, questionnaires can be examined by others, and tried out on potential respondents, to test the questions and the overall design. This offers a form of validation as well as giving some insight into the analysis. In fact the problem of analysis sould be an important consideration in constructing a questionnaire; a feature of this technique is its usefulness when there is a clear evaluation problem that can be translated into a set of questions. The categories of responses should be exclusive and exhaustive and be given numerical codes to make the analysis routine. The responses can be tabulated for each question and where necessary two questions can be cross tabulated to look for relationships[96]. Responses to open-ended questions can be subjected to content analysis, perhaps involving frequency counts.

Pupil diaries

Under direct observation we treated teacher diaries as a form of notes, assuming that the evaluating teacher was taking them. However, asking all teachers, or a sample of pupils, to complete a diary is a form of questionnaire designed to reconstruct events which the evaluator cannot observe. An example might be teacher or pupil out-of-school activities. (We have already discussed an example of a teacher diary.) Shipman (1979, p. 107) sees this technique as a way of evaluating extra-curricular activities, particularly participation. Pupils, he suggests, can complete a diary noting down which clubs, and so forth, they participate in, and when. This they could do over a period of two or more weeks, sampled in two terms of the year. Obviously this is a very selective diary. In contrast, Cohen (1976, pp. 85-90) shows how researchers have collected information through non-specific diaries, which ask pupils to record all they do, within time intervals covering out of school hours. In one case this was used to study television viewing (but wanting spontaneous information); in another it was used to look at pupils' overall activities. In this latter example (Birmingham University, Survey of Children's Habits) pupils were also asked to record who they did the activity with, and where. The activities were coded using 92 categories.

Pupil diaries of in-school activities can be given in a questionnaire form with pre-specified categories such as 'listening to teacher dictation, copying from the board, listening to other pupils etc.' (Robertson, 1980, p.97). In effect, this becomes an observational schedule, and, provided the categories are straight forward, a sample of pupils can be asked to complete these across, say, a day's lessons. This is an alternative to at least part of the structured shadow study discussed above (Sir Frank Markham School, 1981, Stage 2).

Unobtrusive measures

All the techniques of direct and indirect observation discussed so far cause various degrees of reactivity and require efforts to reduce it, or to be reflexive about its effects. Unobtrusive measures are an attempt to obtain non-reactive observations, thus they rely upon data being collected without the participants being aware of it. The classic text on these measures (Webb *et al*, 1966) considers three basic kinds: physical traces, archives and simple observation. The latter is more properly considered under the heading of direct observation, although the kinds of situations Webb *et al* had in mind (e.g. a researcher wandering up and down Regent Street noting down people's conversations) require a degree of anonymity not available in schools. A teacher will be *recognised* as a participant (and hence the ideas of participant observation are relevant), and an outsider who observes will be *noticed* as an outsider. Neither will be unobtrusive nor non-reactive. Below we give examples of the other two types of measures[97] drawn from Bouchard (1976), Hook (1981) and Shipman (1979)[98].

Physical traces
These include wear or dirt on library books to indicate amount and type of use; graffiti to indicate prejudice (or sexual preoccupation - in toilets!); broken windows or furniture scratches to indicate pride in school or pupil morale[99]; the area of staff notice boards covered with memos to indicate level of written communication; displays around the school (to indicate values e.g. honours lists, works of art) and in the classrooms (to indicate attitudes of teachers).

Archives

These might include documents such as minutes of meetings, committee reports, memos to staff, letters to parents, the school prospectus, school annual reports, school and LEA files, records such as pupil records, collections for charity, complimentary letters and letters of complaint, attendance registers, records of choice of school by parents.

It can be seen from the above lists that some of these items produce quantitative measures, e.g. frequency of occurrence, and some require some kind of content analysis, as in the case of documents. As Shipman (1979, pp. 120-1) points out two problems exist: what do the measures indicate? what criteria are applied to judge the level? Under 'physical traces' we have suggested what the measures *might* indicate; but they are guesses, a fact that emphasises the need to use them in conjunction with other methods[100]. Any measure produced, for example the number of chairs broken per term, has no absolute meaning (except in financial terms!) and the criterion for judgement must be drawn from a comparison between schools, or classrooms, or over time. Unlike the research in the social sciences reported by Bouchard (1976), most of the discussion of unobtrusive measures either remains buried in studies, along with other kinds of measures, or remains at the level of suggestions (e.g. Miller, 1978). Therefore little in the way of concrete guidance is available, particularly with respect to issues of validity and reliability[101].

Content analysis

This is an umbrella-term used to cover the kind of analysis conducted in a variety of circumstances. Its origins lie in mass-communication studies where, for example, it is used to determine newspaper bias in the treatment of election candidates, or to analyse propaganda during a war. Holsti (1968, p.601) defines it as a 'technique for making inferences by systematically and objectively identifying specified characteristics of messages'. Although it is a research technique in its own right, to be used when no other technique is available (e.g. on documents), it is increasingly applied to data produced by other methods. (We have already mentioned it in relation to the analysis of interviews and questionnaires.) For example, it can be used on data which are unstructured:

1. documents in a school - curriculum materials, minutes of meetings, memoranda or letters, notice board contents;

2. interview transcripts;
3. open-ended responses in questionnaires.

Holsti's definition indicates that analysis is carried out by using categories to code the data. Like structured observation a clear definition of categories is required, which must have theoretical relevance. There is no point, for example, in counting the number of people who speak in a meeting (as recorded in the minutes) unless it is thought that this is an indicator of, for instance, 'participation'. The analysis does not have to be quantitative (although there is some discussion of this in the literature[102]) because it is not essential to count the frequency of categories. The appearance or non-appearance of a particular category may be sufficient.

The technique of content analysis is also commonly used to deal with open-ended responses to questionnaires. The task is to reduce the data in some meaningful way on the assumption that a survey of opinions, or whatever, is sought. The first step is to read through the responses and take note of the categories that seem to be important. Their importance derives from what the question was intended to elicit. At the simplest level, for example, it might be important to note a view for or against a particular topic or lesson. Having produced a list of categories, the next step is to attempt to define the category, followed by the coding of each response. Some responses may not fit, or it may emerge that a category needs further sub-division. In other words, a revision of the categories may be necessary, which consequently requires the responses to be recoded. Thus it may be necessary to go back and forth between the data and categories several times to code the responses satisfactorily[103]. This kind of technique is systematic in that an effort is made to obtain a reliable and valid categorisation of the data. Validity derives from the relevance of the categories and reliability from the precision of their definition, with the inevitable trade-off between the two. It is perfectly acceptable to look at latent (i.e. hidden) meanings, for example, any sex-bias exhibited in a response. In this instance an inference is being made from the category to some general notion i.e. bias. However, the category, which should indicate how bias is recognised, must be clear. It is useful to get someone else to code the data using the categories developed.

Some examples of documentary analysis will be given later when we consider the analysis of curriculum material ('The Intended Curriculum'). Other examples of the use of content analysis as a technique in its own right include the analysis of interview transcripts. For instance, it could be used to discover whether a pupil had achieved some level of under-standing, perhaps of 'conservation of volume'[104]. It can also be used to analyse the errors pupils make in written work, for example, in their spelling, or at a higher level in terms of misconceptions. In relation to this latter example it is not essential to count the number of errors, only to look for their existence (appearance/non-appearance). The over-all process, therefore, requires the statement of a problem, the definition of categories, the choice of a unit to categorise (units of context) such as a sentence, passage or book, and some system of enumeration (Krippendorff, 1981). This latter term refers to frequency counts, length of time occupied, space taken, intensity (of feeling), and appear-ance or non-appearance. Thus, for example, political bias can be judged by the amount of *space* given to a particular point of view, or the *number of times* a political party is mentioned, or the *time* it is given on the television, or the way members of the party are treated (favour-ably/unfavourably). The standard text in this area is Holsti (1969), although Holsti (1968) gives a good summary. Unfortunately most examples come from communications studies and few from educa-tion[105], although readability, one element in such studies, is of relevance (cf. 'The Intended Curriculum').

Curriculum Outcomes

Introduction

Chapter 7 showed the importance that has been attached to outcome measurement as part of evaluation, and its dominance as a model for evaluation. Given this importance, it is surprising therefore that test materials, addressed to teachers and dealing with assessment, contain little advice on curriculum evaluation. Writers frequently include curriculum evaluation as an important purpose of assessment, along with, for example, 'selection', but give little concrete advice on how to use assessment for evaluation[106]. Most texts that we have looked at recognise the multi-purpose nature of assessment information, and an important aspect of this is 'diagnosis'[107]. In the USA this is typically part of the concept of mastery learning (e.g. Gronlund, 1981; Bloom, Hastings and Madaus, 1971; Block, 1971). This is based on the notion that mastery is achieved in small units of learning. Assessment is used to diagnose whether a pupil has achieved mastery in a unit. If she has, then she moves on to the next; if she has not then remedial help is given.

(We will return to this topic later.) In Britain diagnosis is also a concern, but not connected with ideas of mastery. Harlen, Darwin and Murphy (1977) and Muncey and Williams (1981), for example, are concerned with matching the curriculum to individuals, through assessing what pupils have learnt. This implies that evaluation is integral to learning, because the teacher constantly monitors individual pupils and adjusts the teaching accordingly. While this is an important kind of evaluation, it seems more appropriate to consider this, as Shipman (1980) does, as part of the organisation of learning. In addition it is based upon an individualised approach to learning, whereas our major concern is with larger elements of teaching and learning, and with groups of pupils rather than individuals[108].

What, therefore, are the differences between the use of assessment information for evaluation and the assessment of individuals? A common concern of assessment is with ranking individuals, for example, within a class. Such ranking can be useful in certain circumstances, but generally in evaluation we want to know what a pupil or class understands, so that if problems arise teaching can be improved. As we shall see later, this requires scores or grades obtained in assessment to be interpreted differently[109]. This leads on to the fundamental difference between norm-referencing and domain or criterion-referencing. In ranking an individual, the knowledge or understanding of that individual is compared with a group (e.g. class, year group) with less concern for *what* it is that the individual actually knows; this is norm-referencing. When an attempt is made to say what the pupil knows then the concern is with domain-referencing. We have chosen to use 'domain-referencing' rather than the more common term 'criterion-referencing' because the latter is specifically associated with mastery learning and getting learners to reach a certain criterion (e.g. eighty per cent of correct sums on a mathematics test)[110]. There are circumstances, which we shall consider later, where both kinds of information will be useful for evaluation[111].

So, to what areas of advice can schools turn for guidance on using outcome measures? First, we would agree with Shipman (1979, p.19) that a lot of the technical and quantitative aspects of assessment are probably useless, and discussions of methods of assessment are overtaxing and beyond the interest of teachers, for the purposes of evaluation. Therefore, although evaluation using outcome measures can only be as good as the measuring instruments used, we feel it it generally only worth considering new methods of assessment to improve the assessment of individuals (for selection, diagnosis etc.). Their use for evaluation is a bonus, and we review them in this spirit. Again like Shipman (1979), we feel it is worth using the assessment information that has already been collected in the school and we look at what the literature says in this respect. However, given the difficulty of producing good assessment information, we also look to that which can be produced outside the school, i.e. standardised tests and public examinations[112].

Assessment procedure, design and construction [113]

Most of the advice on the design and construction of assessment procedures is addressed to secondary school teachers and, in Britain particularly, this includes advice on constructing examinations (e.g. Deale, 1975). There is little on assessment in primary schools, perhaps because they use informal and individualised teaching methods and standardised tests[114]. Authors who stress the multiple purposes of assessment also stress fitness-to-purpose, although they discuss uses of assessment only in general terms i.e. they do not relate purposes, methods, and ways of analysing results (e.g. Deale, 1975). Advice for design and construction follows a common series of steps:

1. produce a statement of objectives preferably in behavioural terms (i.e. indicating the behaviour pupils should be able to exhibit);
2. create such a statement to describe a whole topic or content area;
3. choose the method of assessment (e.g. written test, oral examination, practical activity);
4. from the objectives, derive items (questions etc.) to test these objectives;
5. if the assessment procedure is not an 'objective' test[115] then construct criteria and instructions for marking;
6. put an assessment procedure or test together which represents (i.e. samples) the whole topic - this will depend upon the number of items, their type and upon pupil choice;
7. try the questions out before using for assessment - something rarely possible in a school.

This procedure reflects the need to operationalise when trying to measure (e.g. if you are concerned to measure size this has to be operationalised into a particular property of size, e.g. length, in order to measure it).

Drawing up objectives to cover the whole topic (Step 2) requires some way of describing the domain being measured. Commonly three kinds of domain are recognised: cognitive, i.e. dealing with thinking; affective, dealing with feeling; psychomotor, dealing with manipulative skills etc. Bloom (1956) edited a volume containing a taxonomy of objectives for the cognitive domain, which is organised in hierarchical levels, from 'recall of knowledge' at the lowest level, to 'application' and 'evaluation' at the higher levels. The objectives are expressed in terms independent of any particular content and can therefore be used for any subject or topic[116]. This taxonomy was drawn up by groups of teachers and contrasts with Gagne's (1970) approach which is based on a psychological theory of learning. His, too, is hierarchical with stimulus-response connections at the lowest level, and problem-solving at the highest. Although this hierarchy of learning has an empirical grounding, Gagne recognises that it may well change as theory develops. Gerlach and Sullivan (1969) also contrast with Bloom in insisting upon using only statements of overt behaviour - Bloom's taxonomy is intended to describe mental processes. Eggleston (1974, pp 246-7) recommends an approach which is somewhat of a compromise and involves levels of performance in 'understanding': at the lowest level are 'initiating, duplicating and repeating', and at the highest, 'creating, discovering, reorganising' etc. Clearly the variety of ways of describing objectives implies that none qualifies as being more authoritative than another; thus they should be used as tools to help describe the domain of interest[117].

A description of the objectives, created in the ways suggested, leads to a specification for the assessment procedure in which each item, question or activity can be 'allocated' to test a particular objective. It is also possible to analyse an assessment procedure retrospectively to determine the objectives it assessed. In practice it is likely that both prospective planning and retrospective analysis will be employed.

Choosing a method of assessment (Step 3) requires consideration of the mode of presentation of the questions and activities, as well as the way the pupil will respond. Thus young children might be given a visual presentation with an oral question and the person administering the test could then tick 'yes' or 'no' on an answer sheet. USA texts limit their discussion to written tests (e.g. Gronlund, 1981; TenBrink, 1974)[118]: these divide into objective tests (i.e. objectively marked tests) and essays (or free response questions). Objective tests include questions which range from low-level 'yes/no' questions, through multiple choice questions, up to a high-level interpretative exercises requiring the use of evidence to identify relationships and evaluate assumptions (see Gronlund, 1981). Essay or free response questions can require short answers or extended answers (any length), and the pupil chooses the form of the response within the bounds of the instructions. These instructions can range from highly structured to open. The feature that distinguishes objective tests from those involving essays is that in the former the pupils *choose* the answer and in the latter they *supply* it. The concomitant of this for the assessment designer is that, compared with the essay, the objective test requires more thought in its construction, and less in marking. The ease of marking makes it useful for assessing a large group of pupils. Nevertheless the essay still requires careful preparation, particularly in the preparation of marking criteria. Other advantages and disadvantages that need to be weighed include the difficulty of constructing an objective test but its high reliability, compared with the essay's ease of construction but low reliability[119]. The general argument used to justify the use of essays is their capacity to assess high-level learning, although Ingenkamp (1977) doubts that there is any evidence to justify this. Besides, objective tests can be used to test high-level learning in certain subject areas[120]. One advantage of using objective tests for evaluation is the relative ease of analysing wrong choices made by pupils in a group, and representing these numerically. However, these are limited to predicted errors, whereas essays can give insight, not only into misconceptions, but into the knowledge and ideas that teachers were not aware pupils possessed. Also, although using content analysis on long essays is time consuming, it can produce a satisfactory measure of the errors that pupils make.

Other methods of assessment are less common, but oral and aural assessment should become increasingly important, in Britain, in the light of criticisms of excessive amounts of written work, made by the HMI (e.g. DES, 1979a). Although such assessment can test unique skills (generative i.e. speaking - for oral; and receptive i.e. listening - for aural), Ingenkamp (1977) says that oral assessment, in particular, is of doubtful value because of difficulties in conducting the oral test. However, these difficulties (for example with reliability) are less important in evaluation, and attempts to introduce or increase the development of oral and aural skills would be worth evaluating[121]. Practical and project work are assessed as part of teaching and learning and, unlike most methods, allow some assessment of the process of learning. This is particularly so if some kind of checklist is employed, such as those discussed in the section on 'Direct Observation'.

In designing an assessment procedure, validity and reliability are major concerns. When choosing an assessment method to fit the particular objectives being measured, then *face validity* is the most obvious form of validity to consider first. For example, if the intention is to assess practical skills, assessment based upon a written response will have low face validity. However, the most important form of validity is *content validity*. It is this that is being checked when a specification is being drawn up because the intention is to check that the assessment procedure reflects the content and objectives being measured. The major problem lies in sampling from the content and objectives: an issue we shall return to. As we have indicated earlier, reliability is less of a worry in the context of curriculum evaluation (Lewy, 1977, p. 218) because group scores are of more interest. The techniques for measuring reliability will be considered later, although they are unlikely to be within reach of most schools. However, the need to reduce bias from three main sources is important:

1. in relation to the pupil - by measuring on more than one occasion;
2. in relation to the test - by sampling items to represent the objectives (more than one item per objective);
3. in relation to marking - by structuring the item, or the marking, and having more than one marker.

Published examples of the construction of assessment procedures are inevitably confined to research studies, but three are worthy of consideration by teachers: first the work of the Observational Research and Classroom Learning Evaluation (ORACLE) researchers in assessing study, and other, skills (Galton and Simon, 1980). They were concerned to produce assessments of performance that would reflect normal classroom activity better than standardised tests. This example is particularly interesting because it shows prospective planning and retrospective analysis in action. To assess study skills the team worked with teachers to develop exercises that the teachers thought represented the study skills practised in their classes. They then analysed these to see what each was measuring (retrospective analysis). This descriptive analysis was followed by a trial assessment against all the criteria, conducted by the teachers; and finally an assessment against a selection of the most adequate criteria. In order to assess abilities not covered by conventional tests (for example listening skills, originality, acquisition of information from methods other than reading) the teachers devised structured activities. They did this by setting out their aims, developing their critieria of behaviour from these aims, and designing the tasks to assess them (prospective planning).

The second useful published example was reported by Wood and Napthali (1975). They used repertory grids (see note 60) to determine the constructs that teachers used in assessing pupils. They then pooled all the constructs from various teachers and asked the teachers to rank them - to find those that were most commonly used. They concluded that what was required was to anchor these constructs in observable behaviour. The third example, from Black and Dockrell (1980), did just this, although they were exclusively concerned with the affective domain. They asked a group of teachers to consider an assessment such as that of 'effort' and to operationally define points on the scale of measurement (in fact several agreed definitions for each point) in terms of specific behaviours [122]. We feel that it is important to reiterate our initial qualification that the work involved in carefully constructing assessment procedures may not be warranted for evaluation alone[123]. Not quite so much care is necessary for evaluation because the concern is with groups, rather than individuals.

Basis of comparison

We have already indicated that the kind of referencing used in measurement (norm or domain) affects the way scores are interpreted. It also affects the design of the assessment procedure[124]. Both kinds of measurement require the same basic steps in design and construction, outlined above, but norm-referenced measurement requires empirical selection of items or questions. (The Rasch model was the basis of one such procedure - discussed in Chapter 4.) The differences will be examined below by looking at the different assumptions and procedures adopted by each kind of measurement.

Norm-referenced measurement.

A basic assumption of such referencing is that some general or specific achievement is being measured which has a unidimensional nature - a 'trait'. Thus 'mathematics ability' can be a trait as can 'ability to do algebra'[125]. This trait is represented by a single score and each item in the test contributes a small piece of information to this measurement. So, although the first stage must be to ensure that the test has content validity, this is insufficient in itself; the scores achieved by pupils must also be considered. If each item in the test is contributing to the measurement of this unitary trait then pupils' scores on one item should correlate with their total scores on the test. It also means that the scores on each item can be added together because they are measuring the same thing, and that the total score will be more reliable i.e. subject to less error[126]. Such a correlation will ensure that pupils will be discriminated if items scored correlate with total score i.e. their marks will be spread out with less likelihood of pupils achieving the same score. This correlation is therefore referred to as the *discrimination index*. An item should also be moderately difficult, i.e. half should get it correct and half get it wrong; the measure for this is the *facility index*, an indication of what percentage of pupils get the item correct[127]. These assumptions underly recommendations on the way to treat scores, made by the texts addressed to teachers (e.g. Deale, 1975; Gronlund, 1981; Satterly, 1981), although they invariably recommend simplified techniques. The assumptions mean that a test is defined in terms of the group that takes it and they are used to establish its *construct validity* i.e. that, in this case, it is measuring a single trait, verified by empirical means. An individual pupil's score under this referencing is therefore only meaningful in relation to a group, and preferably a large group representative of a population, say, of all eleven-year-olds[128]. One further assumption is that the ability (trait) is normally distributed over the population in question (e.g. eleven-year-olds)[129]. This is a relatively safe assumption to make when the sample is large and representatively or randomly selected. Thus, after designing and constructing a test, it is tried out and the facility and discrimination indices are calculated for each item. If they fall within acceptable limits they are retained; those that do not are rejected[130].

Domain-referenced measurement.
Measurement based on this referencing puts content validity first: items are judged appropriate primarily according to whether they test a particular objective or domain. We can therefore make no assumptions about how the scores will be distributed. For example, if the teaching is good then pupils will, by and large, achieve the objectives; items will not discriminate between students, and they will be easy (high facility index, low or even negative discrimination index). Hambleton *et al* (1978) argue that relying upon content validity has its problems:

1. the domain being tested may not be well specified and, in any case, this specification assumes a highly structured subject such as mathematics[131];
2. items may not be a random sample (or a representative sample)

of all possible items that measure achievement of the objectives;
3. items relate to specific aspects of some ability and a profile of
scores is more appropriate than a global score for, say, mathematics ability.　　　　　(Ingenkamp, 1977; Pilliner, 1979, pp. 38-9).

Hambleton *et al* (1978) drawing upon the USA literature, and
Ingenkamp (1977) drawing upon the European, suggest various ways of
ameliorating the first two problems: (1) ask experts to rate the items as
representative of the domain; (2) ask experts to match items against
objectives (disagreements represent poor content validity); (3) ask
groups of item writers to produce items in parallel to match the same
objectives. Hambleton *et al* (1978) also argue that it is crucial to employ
empirical tests of the construct validity of *scores* (not content validity
of *items* alone). In the case of criterion tests associated with mastery
learning, it is difficult to use conventional item analysis because most
pupils get the items correct (high facility index); hence there is no
discrimination (low discrimination index) and the variance of scores
is low. It is however suggested that item analysis may be used to check
for flawed items. Thus, those items which are supposed to measure the
same objective should correlate; if they do not, then construct validity
is not established for these items *in this group* (norm-referencing is a
group dependant procedure). We therefore arrive at a point where the
difference between the two tests diminishes with respect to how they
are constructed[132]. The assumption of a lack of variance in scores does
not necessarily apply to evaluation (e.g. when the teaching has had
mixed results) and hence the analytic techniques of norm-referenced
measurement can be applied, to check flawed items.

Hambleton *et al* (1978) are optimistic that enough theory and
practical guidelines exist to construct good domain-referenced tests,
although Ingenkamp (1977), surveying the European situation, notes
that despite the universally high regard in which they are held, few
examples of such tests exist[133]. The advent of GCSE will add to the
store of domain-referenced assessment. Whatever the situation is like for
professional test constructors, the technology involved is certainly
beyond the reach of schools in terms of time and statistical support[134].
Moreover, few schools are likely to be content to restrict themselves to
objective-type tests, and the same technology does not apply to all
kinds. Where it does (e.g. for norm-referenced essay examinations), the
statistics become even more complex (see Nuttall and Willmott, 1972).
Later we examine how published tests can be used.

Ipsative comparison

Before moving on it is worth saying a word about ipsative comparison: a (jargon) concept which has emerged recently, mostly in association with pupil profiling. Derived from the Latin *ipse* meaning 'self', the reference is to the individual and the basis of comparison is the differential achievement of the same individual in relation to different criteria or domains; or to the differential achievement of the same individual on the same criteria over time. In the first instance performance in a number of areas is presented in such a way that strengths and weaknesses can be compared. 'Profiles' of pupils, sometimes represented in bar chart form, can be produced from scores on batteries of standardised tests. For example, results from the *Richmond Tests of Basic Skills* (Hieronymus, Lindquist, and France, 1974), which provide a battery of eleven tests each designed to assess performance in a different domain, can be represented in this way. (Clift, Abel and Simpson; 1982, cast some doubt on the extent to which they are assessing unique domains, as we will shortly explain.) Comparing performance in one domain with performance in another then becomes an easy matter, merely requiring scanning across scores. Using information in non-statistical form for similar purposes is more difficult. This is well illustrated in relation to profiles of a very different kind which are associated with records of achievement initiatives. (See Chapter 5 for a brief description.) These may cover many areas of a pupil's curricular and extra-curricular experience, but only positive achievements are recorded and often in a non-standard prose form. Most diagnosis of strengths and weaknesses is accomplished orally in teacher-pupil review sessions; however, strengths should be clearly evident in written records, although identification of areas of relative weakness may require 'reading between the lines'. The City and Guilds of London Institute (CGLI) profile (adopted by some TVEI profile schemes) allows for shading on a scale against which are written qualitative descriptions of grade levels for each of the fourteen criteria. Alternatively, the profile can be represented by scores on each of the criteria, indicating the levels of performance reached. (See McCormick, 1987, for examples.)

Ipsative comparison, in the second sense, is accomplished when individuals are assessed, or assess themselves, against standards set by their own previous performance. This is a feature of graded or staged assessment systems (sometimes incorporated into records of achievement, for example, in the Oxford Certificate of Educational Achievement's 'G' components in English, maths, science and modern languages) which, through a conception of levels of achievement within a domain provide the basis for comparison of present with previous performance.

Rowntree (1977) distinguished assessment of individuals against previous performance as a seperate and distinct basis for comparison, although it can be argued that both forms of ipsative comparison described above are ultimately reducible to norm- or criterion/domain-referencing. This occurs because at some point performance has to be described against criteria, as in the CGLI example above, or against other pupils' performance.

Identifying the reference base of open-ended components in records of achievement, notably in the personal record, is more difficult. In some cases the criteria appear to be generated with reference to the individual rather than the group. This is best illustrated in schemes where statements of achievement are extracted from relatively unstructured prose accounts of experience compiled by pupils, often in the form of diaries or logbooks. Since the choice of what to record rests largely with the pupil, the criteria 'belong' to the individual and may have little relationship to criteria used by others. In this sense they are genuinely ipsative. In practice, however, most summative statements of achievement are written in discussion with teachers, who are likely to guide selection on the basis of an implicit or explicit set of criteria which is more or less applicable to whole teaching groups. Indeed the preliminary, and as yet unpublished, evidence of the PRAISE evaluation of pilot schemes suggests that most teachers find the analysis of free accounts unmanageable and move rapidly towards structuring pupil accounts in a way designed to provide information on pre-specified and group-referenced criteria. (We are both members of the PRAISE team.)

Interestingly, in investigating the ways in which teachers and pupils make profile assessments, the PRAISE evaluation team has also produced some evidence that habits of norm-referencing die hard. Whilst ostensibly engaged in the task of judging performance against a criterion, some teachers, and pupils in the context of self-assessment, make tacit comparisons with others in the teaching group, especially where levels of performance on a criterion are to be indicated. In other words, there is a tendency for pupils to be placed, or to place themselves, in some rank order in relation to their peers before making a judgement about whether a criterion has been achieved or a specified level reached. This is often a consequence of broad criteria which cover a large domain and hence require an impressionistic and holistic assessment. (For example, 'craftsmanship' in relation to CDT.)

In summary, therefore, it may be that the only case for ipsative comparison as distinct from norm- or domain-referenced comparison is in circumstances where the criteria themselves can be, and are, derived ipsatively i.e. not pre-specified by reference to a generalised domain, but formulated from the data of individual performance and experience. This may be especially appropriate in curriculum areas like the creative arts, where teachers find it difficult and often unacceptable to pre-specify outcomes, although they would willingly retrospectively analyse what has been achieved, or help pupils to do so. In cases such as these, statements of achievement, and hence the basis of comparison, are likely to have a much stronger reference to the individual than to some notional group. On the face of it, ipsative forms of assessment, with strict reference to the individual, are even less useful in the context of curriculum evaluation than are forms whose reference is a group. However, insofar as the curriculum is experienced by individuals, teachers may do well to attend to any implications that individual patterns of achievement may have for curriculum and teaching, whether this be conceived in terms of group or individual provision. But this takes us back to the problem we identified in Chapter 5, namely that it implies that the teacher responds at the level of the individual pupil in adapting his or her teaching to the pupils' needs.

Using routine assessment information [135]

Given the difficulties of constructing assessment procedures, noted above, schools will have to rely upon their internal system of assessment, although they should utilise the general principles outlined. One important idea is to improve the content validity of current assessment by clear specifications, say, through retrospective analysis, and ensuring face validity through choosing an appropriate method of assessment. Colleagues could, for example, act as experts in judging the match of items to objectives, or agree behavioural descriptions for rating scales. In such a case, with a focus on content validity, a domain-referenced test could be constructed. (Item statistics could still be used to help eliminate flawed items if the test could be trialled. If not, then the scores of flawed items could be excluded from the test totals -see Kibblewhite (1981) for a graphical approach.)

Let us turn, therefore, to the kinds of analysis or use that can be made of a domain-referenced assessment procedure, at the level of an individual class, and within a particular domain. The basic task is to see if the class is meeting the objectives measured by the assessment. In other words, are most of the pupils achieving the objectives; are all of them achieving the major objectives; is any particular group failing to achieve the objectives (e.g. boys or girls, ethnic groups, social class groups)? The assessment procedure can also be analysed to determine common errors or misconceptions: for essay questions by content analysis and listing or tallying errors; for objective tests by counting the errors (i.e. those items with low facility indices)[136]. The action taken on the basis of this kind of analysis will obviously depend upon the stage at which the evaluation is conducted. Something will have to be done for the individuals involved (a diagnosis function), but a reconsideration of the teaching approach may also be necessary[137].

This diagnostic function, both in relation to individual learning and in relation to teaching, is a chief purpose of many records of achievement and other profiling schemes. It is especially prominent in those systems which incorporate assessment on specified criteria derived from teaching objectives for curriculum modules or units of work. The assumption is that assessments made can be used as a basis for diagnosing strengths and weaknesses then setting targets for future improvement. Target-setting mostly refers to learner targets, but there is usually also an assumption that the same process will also help schools identify strengths and weaknesses in curriculum, teaching and organisation (DES, 1948d, p.3). Certainly, the PRAISE evaluation team has evidence that schools regard pupil records of experience and achievement as providing a check on what is taught, whilst recognising that such things as out-of-school experiences are beyond their curricular control. The same might be said of personal qualities, which feature in many recording systems, except that it is within the power of the school to devise curricular opportunities in which personal qualities can be demonstrated.

Of course, there is always a danger in regarding pupil achievements as directly attributable to curriculum and teaching. Prior conditions, such as social background and previous educational experience, and contextual influences, such as peer group pressure, an individual's state of health, or even the weather, can be equally decisive.

The claim that assessments can be analysed for the purposes of diagnosis rests on a prior assumption that the assessment procedures themselves are reliable: that there is no bias in the recognition of achievement or in the allocation of marks or grades in tests. Deale (1975, pp. 36-8) suggests ways of reducing bias in routine marking which, in the context of the process of recording achievement, can be applied to simple assessments of whether or not a criterion has been met or a quality or achievement demonstrated. Deale's suggestions are related to the two major sources of bias:

1. Intra-marker bias - by producing a model answer or having clearly distinguished criteria (e.g. argument of the essay or facts covered). If neither of these is appropriate then impression marking may be used.

2. Inter-marker bias - by standardising the marking (e.g. by discussing criteria, marking samples, comparing marks and agreeing upon a standard); by obtaining a second opinion on responses which are difficult to mark; by asking one person (e.g. Head of Department) to act as a moderator, to sample the responses and check uniform standard among markers.

When the analysis is to be carried out at the level of a year group (again within a subject or domain), rather than an individual class, particular care must be exercised to reduce the inter-marker bias that may occur when marking say, a common task or test. At this level it is possible to compare classes within the year group. If the classes are comparable (e.g. parallel mixed-ability classes or classes within a homogeneous ability band) then the strengths and weaknesses (on certain objectives) of each class can be determined. The teachers dealing with this year group can therefore discuss appropriate steps to remedy any problems. Obviously it is also possible to consider how other groups (e.g. boys and girls) are faring, either across the year group as a whole, or within each class[138].

So far we have assumed that the information obtained relates to particular objectives (domain referencing). However, it may be that insufficient confidence exists in what the assessment procedure is measuring in detail; there may only be confidence that it is measuring, say, mathematics ability. In this case norm-referenced measurement is appropriate, provided the items conform to the limits discussed earlier (see note 130). Pupils' total scores, or more particularly the mean scores of subgroups (e.g. boys and girls), can be examined, to see if they deviate from what is expected. If classes within a year group are of comparable ability then scores obtained from different, but equivalent, assessment procedures can be standardised so that the mean scores and the spread of scores will be the same for each class[139]. Although it will be obvious that no comparisons can be made between classes (because the means are all the same), it is possible to compare sub-groups that cut across the year group - again boys and girls, social class etc. Even here there are difficulties because, for example, those low on a social class scale would normally be expected to perform less well compared with the year group as a whole. If, on the other hand, special efforts were being made to compensate for this expectation, the mean standard scores (see note 139) would indicate success or otherwise.

The assumption of comparability of assessment procedures of a group of teachers teaching in parallel is suspect, even within a subject[140]. An alternative is to use a common test (i.e. common to a whole year group) to scale the marks of other assessment procedures (e.g. homework or class tests) so that they can be compared directly[141]. This allows the comparison of class performance (across a year group) on different elements of the subject (e.g. practical work), to see, for example, how the approaches of individual teachers compare. However, this approach assumes a good correlation between the common test and the assessment procedure being scaled.

Throughout we have confined our discussion to comparisons within a particular subject or domain. Shipman (1979, p. 27) suggests that comparisons can be made across subjects by working out the percentile scores (see note 139) in each subject, for pupils in a class[142]. Ingenkamp (1977, pp. 28-30) casts doubt on this assumption, from the point of view of severity of marking, for which, of course, the standardising of scores is supposed to compensate. Christie and Forrest (1981) go further and argue that in the arena of public examinations there is no reason why it should be assumed that different subjects are comparable. We take the view that there are already questionable assumptions being made for within-subject comparisons and that to assume between-subject comparability at the group level is going too far. The most useful group to use for this kind of norm-referencing is the year group[143], and to standardise each class score to a common year-group standard, in all subjects, seems to be expecting too much.

Externally-referenced assessment

Internal assessment, as we have described it above, poses problems for the achievement of a standard against which to compare pupil performance. Furthermore, norm-referencing at the class or year-group level relies upon dubious assumptions about the distribution of ability. Externally referenced assessment, with a norm based upon a large sample of the population (e.g. all eleven-year-olds), offers, within limits, a stable standard. The information obtained is crude, usually a global score for, say, mathematics ability, but it can be a useful indicator if considered together with other information available from internal assessment. Thus norm-referenced, standardised, achievement tests are a possible external reference.

The task for the school or teacher is to choose a suitable test. Jackson (1974) is the major source of advice on standardised tests for British teachers[144]. The crucial consideration is the content validity of the test, in other words, does it match the objectives of teaching? This requires a detailed analysis and Nuttall (OU, 1981a, Block 4) advises against taking a test developer's word for what it tests, if for no other reason than that content validity is context specific. He also suggests that face validity should be considered by asking whether pupils will be accustomed to the test situation. A second concern, in choosing a test, is the information provided in the test manual, in particular:

1. validity - Jackson (1974) says that predictive and concurrent validity are important, but Nuttall (OU, 1981a, Block 4, p. 50) disagrees;
2. reliability;
3. standardisation norms, i.e. what the standardisation was, how it relates to the pupils to be tested, and the date of standardisation[145].

We have already noted that few criterion-referenced tests exist, but because they are more specific, they need careful attention regarding content validity.

As we said at the beginning of this section, little advice is offered on using assessment information for curriculum evaluation. This is reflected in a lack of examples of the use of standardised tests by schools for evaluation[146]. Such examples are important because, as Nuttall (OU, 1981a, Block 4, p. 49) notes in the context of the *Richmond* tests, test developers claim that their tests have uses without providing empirical evidence of such applications. A case study of a school using the *Richmond Tests of Basic Skills* revealed some problems in this regard (OU, 1982, Case Study 5). This school tested a whole year group on entry to the school, and again a year later (the test has age related norms). The intention was to see if the year cohort had progressed more than expected. The test battery provides both an aggregate test score and eleven subscores in areas such as vocabulary, language skills, work study and mathematical skills. However, it was found that the subtests of the battery produced high correlated scores; hence a single factor appeared to lie beneath the total score, thus calling into question the legitimacy of the use of subscores as indicative of separate abilities[147]. The total score did however indicate general trends, but provided only the crudest of information. Comparisons can be made year on year for the same groups, and between different year groups, assuming that there are grounds for comparability between the groups in question i.e. same distribution of ability. Sparshott (Fairbrother, 1980), for example, used a cognitive ability test to show how different departments in a school varied - but it is unclear from the details what the validity of this is.

All this emphasises the need to consider global test scores only as indicators; if they produce an unexpected result, then further information is required to make sense of it. Shipman (1979) quite rightly advises teachers to look for other causes of change, for example, a change in intake, or even a national change in, say, 'reading' standards. However, he also advises that small changes should be ignored because of the unreliability of test scores and the way of accounting for absentees.

The group (class etc.) scores on each objective from a criterion (domain)-referenced test could also be used to see if a class or year group is doing worse than expected. This implies a kind of norm-referencing, but of a kind that can be combined with judgements about the comparability of the objectives, and related test items, with the teaching.

Although in Chapter 4 we cast some doubt on the use of public examination results as a means of evaluation, they can have a role in providing an external reference for use by a school. The major issue in interpreting these results, which was identified in Chapter 4, is the need to take into account a school's pupil intake characteristics, for example, social class and previous schooling. In addition the school's policy on entering pupils for the public examinations will affect the results (Shipman, 1979). For example, a school may let everyone take the examinations and get a maximum number of passes, but a high failure rate; or let only those pupils who are certain of passing sit the examination, hence achieving a high pass rate (low number of failures). Each of these alternatives represents different objectives for a school, and they need to be clearly set out before using results to help in evaluation. For example, restricting entry benefits only the able pupils, whereas open entry gives more pupils the opportunity to gain a pass. The initial problem is to get the data into a usable form and then tabulate it for analysis. Shipman (1979) suggests starting with a few simple tabulations and working up to more complex ones as needed. He also suggests a basic tabulation (p. 71) giving the following information for each pupil: Verbal Reasoning Quotient (VRQ) and reading age; and the grade attained in GCE or CSE, for each subject. John Gray (OU, 1982,

'Making More Sense Out of Examination Results', p. 14) also gives a simple table for demonstrating the relationship between performance of intake on a standardised test (like VRQ) and fifth-year examination results. The pupils are grouped into five intake bands and the examination results are presented separately for GCE and CSE, as well as in a combined total score[148].

There are a variety of comparisons that can be made. First, the total score for each intake group can be calculated and compared with previous years. In this respect trends are important, although several years' results will be needed to indicate 'typical' performance. These trends can be shown graphically (OU, 1982, 'Making More Sense Out of Examination Results', pp. 14-15). Secondly, subject comparisons are possible although low numbers entered for some subjects, girl and boy differences, and lack of comparability of subjects (and perhaps subject department entry policies) make them suspect. According to Shipman (1979) it is more appropriate to compare single subjects over time. As with internal assessment it is possible to look at various subgroups of the year-group (i.e. the fifth year) including ethnic and social class groups (Shipman, 1979). However, if these subgroups have also to be divided into intake groups (e.g. by VRQ) the numbers in each are likely to be small[149]. Finally it is also possible to compare schools, although this requires data to be collected at the local authority level. (See John Gray, OU, 1982, 'Making More Sense Out of Examination Results', pp. 15-20; Gray, McPherson and Raffe, 1982; Plewis *et al*, 1981; Shipman, 1979, pp. 91-100.)

As we said earlier, these results can only be used as indicators, and, like all assessment information, they tell schools nothing about *what* is wrong. Teachers must provide the diagnosis, with help where appropriate from others, and they have to solve whatever problems exist. An analysis of examination results can, however, be a catalyst to curriculum discussion.

Qualitative and idiographic approaches to learning outcomes

The concern for information on what is wrong when pupils score less well than expected, takes us back to our earlier discussion of the organisation of learning. If teachers are prepared to teach by listening (Easley & Zwoyer, undated) and observing, they are likely to gain insights into children's thinking that directly help the children and improve their teaching generally. Earlier we said this was not a main concern in this section, however, it does open up an alternative path.

Thus far we have focused on learning outcomes; but what of learning processes? It is fair to say that our review of classroom observation has only dealt with these in the most global terms: reflecting the concerns in the literature with classroom processes or the learning milieu (Parlett and Hamilton, 1972). The discussion of learning outcomes is, in part, an attempt to correct this imbalance. However, as Kemmis, Atkin and Wright (1977, Chapter 7) argue this is based upon a view of attainment which stresses subject-matter and outcome behaviours. Put crudely, we assess pupils' cognitive structures (for that is the product of learning) by assessing how well they match subject-matter structures. This ignores what Kemmis, Atkin and Wright term the pupil's 'private knowledge'. We cannot do justice to their argument here[150], but, in keeping with those we have already mentioned who stress close observation of learning, it emphasises the pupil's cognitive structure and how that can be developed. One approach to this requires looking closely at how a pupil interacts with the learning task in order to make inferences about the pupil's cognitive structure. Another is the clinical interview technique used by Piaget (1929), to which we have already referred[151]. Further consideration of these approaches demands an examination of qualitative measures of learning.

The requirements of such an examination are exactly the same as for the assessment methods we considered earlier, but this time expressed in terms of learning, not subject-matter. Thus, what is needed is:

1. a description of the learning;
2. techniques to assess the learning.

Regarding the former, the proposals of Kemmis, Atkin and Wright (1977) are more exciting than of immediate application, particularly as the implementation of their ideas is in computer assisted learning and, therefore, not confined to schools. They do, however, point to the importance of stressing pupil learning: something which some 'illuminative' evaluators drifted away from in their concern with the learning milieu. Kemmis, Atkin and Wright (1977) applied their ideas in the evaluation of the National Development Programme in Computer Assisted Learning and developed a typology of student-computer interactions. They were then able to describe particular computer assisted learning projects according to the kind of interactions in which they resulted. Although they argued for an idiographic approach to such evaluation, giving examples of particularly successful (or unsuccessful) instances of interactions, rather than quantitative summaries, they did use quasi-statistics to describe the programmes. Naturally, the use of a computer means that not only are all the inter-actions clearly defined and observable (through the inputs to, and outputs from, the computer), but the computer can store them. The situation in a conventional classroom is, of course, quite different.

The principle of close observation is, however, no less important in the conventional classroom, and Armstrong (1981) provides an example of such an approach. (Some of his observations did not take place in the classroom.) He observed children over a considerable period making detailed notes each day which, along with samples of their writings, paintings etc., provided a study of pupils' individual growth in understanding. (Nixon, 1981, contains a study of one of these children.) Armstrong pursued this research while on secondment from his secondary school as a participant observer in another teacher's classroom (in a primary school), and was well aware of the difficulties of doing this under normal circumstances. His work does, however, point to the need for idiographic inquiry because only a few pupils can be studied by one person at any one time. In this sense his approach differs from those we referred to as stressing the organisation of learn-ing. Armstrong was developing insights about pupil development through close and detailed study, rather than looking at the performance of the teacher, as has been the case in many qualitative evaluations (see also Chapter 11).

Other recent examples of investigations of learning outcomes using qualitative approaches include the detailed work of researchers inquiring into children's learning in science. The Children's Learning in Science Project (CLISP), based at Leeds University, first analysed wrong answers in APU scripts (Driver, 1982 and 1983), then explored children's misconceptions in relation to a limited number of key concepts (e.g. plant nutrition, energy, particulate nature of matter) by eliciting explanations directly from pupils. At about the same time, researchers at Surrey University and in New Zealand were pursuing similar themes in similar ways (e.g. Pope and Gilbert, 1983; Osborne, Bell and Gilbert, 1983; Watts and Zylberstejn, 1981). All were interested in pupils' cognitive structures and the match with accepted theory about the structure of science and science teaching. They concluded that 'what children learn from interaction with a phenomenon . . . depends not only on what they abstract from the situation, but also on the mental constructions they bring to it' (Millar and Driver, 1987).

Drawing on a constructivist perspective in the work of cognitive psychologists such as Piaget, Bruner and Kelly, they interpreted the evidence as indicating that children's misconceptions in science derive from prior sets of ideas, schemes or internal mental representations, which children use to interpret and interact with new situations. The researchers judged that the fit with ways in which science is taught is not good; both the old content approach and the newer process approaches assume that the child's mind is a *tabula rasa* on which knowledge has merely to be written. The second phase of the CLISP project has attempted to tackle the pedagogical implications of these conclusions by supporting teachers in developing strategies for 'starting where the children are', but moving towards better scientific under-standing. In essence the approach is a psychological one.

In this example the basic research was conducted by professional researchers using fairly sophisticated techniques, including clinical interviews (Piaget, 1929) and repertory grids (Fransella and Bannister, 1977). Despite their advantages in terms of time, skills and support, their inquiries were of necessity restricted to small samples of pupils and a few science concepts. The possibility of teachers engaging in similar inquiries is therefore remote, despite their potential value for planning of curriculum and teaching. The research skills needed are considerable but time and opportunity are likely to be even more difficult to find. Teachers who organise learning on an individual basis may be able to find time to talk with pupils at some length; another opportunity could be provided by one-to-one review sessions which are a key element in records of achievement schemes.

The DES statement of policy on records of achievement (DES, (1984d) emphasised that schools need to make internal arrangements for 'appropriate' discussion between pupils and all teachers in contact with them. In principle recording processes are expected to provide opportunities for all teachers to explore the learning of individual pupils in order to diagnose difficulties and set future targets, as well as to fulfil the requirement of compiling a record of experience and achievement. In practice, at least at the time of writing when many records of achievement schemes are in their infancy, one-to-one review sessions involving all teachers are still a long-term objective. Formal arrangements for reviewing are in many instances confined to form tutors. They are in a position to explore general progress with pupils, but not to discusss specific learning outcomes in subject lessons, without going beyond their competence (PRAISE, 1987). Undoubtedly, discussion of specific learning does go on in review and recording sessions, but, as yet, we have no evidence of in-depth analysis of pupils' cognitive structures by teachers to compare with the examples given above.

Other outcome measures

We have devoted most of this section to assessment information and, more particularly, to the assessment of cognitive learning. While this is justified in terms of its importance within schools, other measures are worthy of consideration. Here therefore we consider non-cognitive assessment and measurement as well as two other outcome measures: 'staying-on' and the 'destination of leavers'. Non-cognitive learning includes such things as feelings, emotions, awareness, values, beliefs and attitudes. Some of these can be investigated using the methods outlined in 'Indirect observation', for example, by using interviews and questionnaires. Here we are concerned with enduring aspects, like attitudes, which can therefore be measured[152]. The inter-relationships of non-cognitive aspects are complex. For example, Oppenheim (1966, pp. 109-110) describes a variety of levels, with beliefs at the most superficial, and attitudes, values and personality being at successively deeper levels. The inter-connections occur both within each level and across levels. This complexity means that a single question in a questionnaire will not be sufficient to tap the underlying attitude. Although non-cognitive aspects are enduring, they are also learnt and hence it is legitimate for the school to measure them. However, teachers must be clear about the connections between the attitudes in question, and the ways in which teaching brings them about (Brown, S., 1979). Of course there exists a debate about whether non-cognitive learning outcomes should be assessed at all. However, since the concern in evaluation is with the group and the teaching, not the individual, we feel that the ethical issues are less contentious.

One major problem for schools, however, concerns *how* these aspects of learning are to be assessed. Many of the techniques used (e.g. Likert, Thurstone and Guttman scales[153]) are more usually research tools requiring resources for construction and validation. Ingenkamp (1977) is quite scathing about teachers' judgements in this area:

> At the moment, however, we have the disquieting situation in which teachers make their judgements like amateurs in the field of those objectives which are often regarded as the most important.
>
> (p. 81)

He sees a need to operationalise the aspects being assessed so that they can be expressed in terms of overt behaviour. As we have already noted, Black and Dockrell (1980) show that it is possible for teachers to do this regarding, for example, 'effort': a common feature in a school's non-cognitive assessment[154].

The two other outcome measures that we wish to deal with here i.e. 'staying-on' and 'destination of leavers', were suggested by Shipman (1979) as ways of evaluating the 'Wider aspects of school life'. 'Staying-on' can be regarded as a vote of confidence in the school, although in these times of high youth unemployment (which may force pupils back to school) and government youth training schemes (which may encourage them to leave early) the validity of 'staying-on' as an indicator of 'confidence' is uncertain. It may, however, be worth calculating the figures, and Shipman (1979, pp. 114-5) suggests two ratios: lower sixth/preceeding fifth form; upper sixth/fifth form two years previously. These can be compared with national statistics. The 'destination of leavers' is of course a true outcome measure (!) and, if Department of Employment categories are used, leavers destinations can be compared with national statistics[155]. Such measures may not, of course, represent an evaluation of the school itself, but of the policies of the school in helping pupils to get jobs[156]. A useful measure employed by one school was to discover the destination of its leavers one year after leaving school.

Conclusion

We are conscious that in spending some considerable time, in this section, on two kinds of referenced measurement, i.e. norm and domain (criterion), we have spent less time on self-referenced. However, we feel this is more relevant to the organisation of individual learning than to evaluation, which we have taken to be concerned with groups[157]. In addition we have said nothing explicitly about Mode III assessment, which combines internal and external standards. We have omitted this for two reasons. First, Mode III entries are a small number of the total examination entries (Torrance, 1982). Secondly, we regard it as important, as Torrance (1982) does, for professsional development and we have therefore referred to it in considering the 'Intended Curriculum'. It is, of course, more than a device for professional development because it brings together teaching, learning and assessment; however, in the context of evaluation we feel that professional development is its major contribution. Moreover, Nuttall (1982b) is pessimistic about its future in any combined 16-plus scheme (where GCE and CSE examinations will be combined).

Our attempts to make sense of the field of assessment left us with two thoughts. First, we wondered about the ethics of saying, as many writers do, that one of the important purposes of assessment is curriculum evaluation, without also saying how it should be done[158]. For example, no-one explains how the assumptions relevant to grading are relevant to evaluation. Secondly, in view of the difficulties in using assessment information, we wondered why assessment is regarded as such an obvious technique. After all, many full-time curriculum evaluators went to great lengths to construct assessment devices, and were clearly less than happy with the use of the results (see note 137).

Intended Curriculum

Introduction

In Chapter 3 we explored the kind of curriculum review that is being advocated as a form of intrinsic evaluation to be carried out by schools. Although we ended on a pessimistic note, doubting whether such a review would be a meaningful exercise (because of the constraints imposed from outside, the rights of teachers to carry it out, and their qualifications to do so), here we consider the techniques that could be employed. Bearing in mind the limited room teachers have for manoeuvre, we argue here that curriculum review is an important exercise for teacher development[159]. If teachers have so little experience of looking at the whole curriculum (a point made in Chapter 3), it is an essential task irrespective of whether or not it leads, at least initially, to dramatic changes in the intended curriculum. This section will therefore consider curriculum review and planning - the process and kinds of analysis involved - as well as the analysis of curriculum materials. Because it is presented as an argument covering 'disputed territory' it does not itself have the features of a review and therefore does not resemble the other sections of this chapter.

Curriculum review and planning

We have combined 'review' and 'planning' because statements emanating from the DES, HMI, and indeed the Munn Report, deal with both aspects often without distinguishing them. 'Review' is characterised by the following quotations:

> Every school should analyse its aims, set these out in writing, and regularly assess how far the curriculum within the school as a

whole and for individual pupils measures up to these aims.

(DES, 1981b, p. 5)

Only if a school has clearly formulated objectives and some such set of criteria or checklist ... is it likely to be able to assure itself ... its concept of secondary education essentially holds good for all pupils.   (DES, 1980b, p. 13)

This use of aims or the 'areas of experience' as a checklist, or set of criteria, is also combined with ideas of planning:

It is a checklist [of areas of experience] ... for curricular analysis and construction.   (DES, 1977a, p.6)

When schools come to plan their detailed programme of work they need to be able to measure the adequacy of these pro-grammes by reference to more specific objectives ...

(DES, 1980b, p. 3)

Using aims etc. as criteria for review and for planning are different, though of course not unrelated processes. However, the above quotations show that both the DES and HMI casually lump them together. Of course, what these documents say is less important than the kinds of activities they stimulate and guide, and so we turn next to actual examples of curriculum review activities.

The first is drawn from the HMI-LEA scheme, introduced in Chapter 3. In particular, we look at the activity in the Cheshire local authority, since it is the best documented and includes an independent evaluation. This authority asked its schools to look at four areas, one more than the HMI initially proposed: education of the individual; preparation for the world of work; preparation for society; personal relationships. For each of these areas the authority produced 'instru-ments' to aid the review procedure (Cheshire Education Committee, 1981). There is not sufficient space here to examine all these instru-ments in detail so a selection will be made. The central element of the exercise, noted in Chapter 3, was an analysis of subject disciplines using a three-dimensional model for education and the individual (concepts, skills and attitudes; progression of these through the five years of schooling; the disciplines in relation to the total curriculum). The first two dimensions were covered by instrument E1 which asked each subject department to list: their aims; their objectives in terms of concepts, skills and attitudes and content/knowledge; their teaching method, assessment and evaluation. The resulting lists were collated within the school and could then be analysed using suggested strategies, such as the following:

Concept objectives
(1)   are the same concepts being explored by more than one subject during the same/different years? How well are they correlated? Action: bring appropriate subjects together.

(Cheshire Education Committee, 1981, p. 29)

The third dimension was investigated by means of each subject department rating and ranking the contribution of its subject to the eight areas of experience proposed in *Curriculum 11-16* (DES, 1977a)[160]. Schools were recommended to analyse their results by displaying the rankings on matrices showing subjects with high or low commitments to particular areas of experience. This could again lead to 'action' that involved bringing departments together to see how they could correlate or reinforce their efforts.

'Preparation for society' was examined in two parts: first, the general framework (school policy; structural aspects e.g. school council; educational activities e.g. holidays; community involvement; relations with parents and governors); and second, the subject contributions. The first instrument (S1) used was in the form of a questionnaire requiring short open-ended responses[161], this was sent to the senior management teams and heads of year and house. Questions posed for analysis included, 'Does the extent and balance of educational extension activities meet pupils' needs effectively?' (Cheshire Education Committee, 1981, p. 57).

From the above descriptions it is evident that the recommended form of analysis required the use of the instruments (checklists) as lists of criteria against which to judge the intended curriculum[162]. There was also a large element of data collection, both at the school and local authority level. Unfortunately there are insufficient details of the work of other local authorities to judge whether this was the main approach, however, the review of the whole exercise (DES, 1981a, pp. 21-2) reveals that a Nottinghamshire school's English department used aims as a starting point for producing objectives and learning units.

It is also worth considering the approach of schools that were not part of the HMI-LEA exercise, but who took some inspiration for their approach from HMI and DES documents. Sir Frank Markham School's first stage evaluation (see Chapter 5) was similar to the Cheshire exercise and used the eight areas, and lists of concepts etc., as criteria to judge its curriculum. However, the combination of this kind of activity with a study of the curriculum as experienced by pupils makes it a more useful study, although some of the questions raised (in the third stage) about, for example, the balance of the eight areas of experience are similar to those in the Cheshire curriculum reappraisal.

In the HMI-LEA exercise the HMI were reported as having expected other models to be used, besides the checklist of eight areas (DES, 1981a, p. 68). This implies that there were other important issues that the schools may not have considered. The unquestioning acceptance of the checklist by the schools may also be a symptom of a neglect of the fundamental issues upon which it is based. The reported evidence of what happened, and teachers' perceptions of it (Cheshire Education Committee, 1981; DES, 1981a; North West Educational Management Centre, 1981; Wrigley, 1981), indicate three important and related aspects of the exercise.

1. The importance of raising awareness.
The over-riding impression, from the evidence, is of a worthwhile and stimulating exercise which generated much debate and discussion about each of the aspects considered (e.g. subject analyses; eight areas; world of work). It revealed areas that school staff had not thought about very much and helped correlate subject departments' efforts[163]. There was disagreement about the depth of the analysis achieved, but there is no doubt that it increased awareness, both at the level of what colleagues were doing[164], and at the level of the nature of the issues involved in curriculum review. Interestingly it increased solidarity, particularly within departments.

2. The use of checklist instruments.
Much of the debate, about whether the analysis was sufficiently penetrating, centres around the instruments used by Cheshire. For example, the rating of subjects in terms of the eight areas of experience was seen to be meaningless; its significance lay in the debate that surrounded the task of agreeing a rating. Indeed the meaning of the 'areas' was an important topic for debate: something that revealed considerable confusion and lack of consensus. The checklists and questionnaires were generally thought to produce too much detailed information, and therefore to be of limited value in themselves.

3. The outcomes of the review.

Some teachers thought it an artificial exercise, not reflecting either classroom activity or the issues of importance, and the amount of curriculum change reported seems limited. However, the LEA benefited from the creation of a curriculum model upon which it could base future policy on staffing resources[165]. For the schools the discussion activity was *itself* important. In the conclusions to the 'official report' from the local authority great play was made of this, as the following quotation illustrates:

> It can now be recognised that the process of re-appraisal has amounted to a large scale in-service training programme . . . This form of re-appraisal is essentially a process of self-evaluation for a school: it does not purport to give answers to all the many curriculum questions likely to arise. Its major value is that it provides a focus for staff attention.
>
> (Cheshire Education Committee, 1981, p. 21)

So the most important message that comes from exercises in which aims, or checklists of areas of experience etc., are used as criteria to judge the curriculum is that they provide a valuable opportunity for teachers to explore issues they have not hitherto tackled[166].

Evidence and discussion of the use of aims and objectives for curriculum *planning*, the other element which HMI and DES publications have identified, is well worked and here we will only draw selectively upon the literature[167]. A major criticism of an 'aims and objectives' approach is that insufficient attention is paid to where the aims and objectives come from - a similar problem to that revealed by the schools, in the HMI-LEA exercise, which paid little attention to the basis of the 'eight areas of experience'. MacDonald-Ross (1973), in one of the most complete critiques of behavioural objectives as a basis for curriculum planning, singles out their origination as his first criticism. He considers three types of responses to the question of where objectives come from: there are those who avoid the issue[168]; there are the 'hardliners' who say that objectives are derived from an analysis of behaviour; and there are the 'softliners' who say that objectives come from a consideration of 'society', the 'learner' and 'subject-matter', but who have no rules for their derivation. MacDonald-Ross argues that the hardliners' case is unsupportable when applied to education (e.g. you cannot analyse the performance of a master economist to get economic objectives). The softliners' position, which resembles that of the HMI and DES[169], is quite defensible, but as an approach it provides very little guidance about how to derive objectives or how to proceed from them to design a curriculum[170].

Not only is the use of aims and objectives found wanting as a *prescription* for planning, but Walker (1975) argues that it does not *describe* what actually takes place when people plan. In his study of a curriculum project, he found that planning started from what he called a *platform* of ideas, 'a shared system of beliefs and working principles' (p. 108), and that 'aims' did not dominate the contents of such platforms. This therefore casts doubt on 'aims' as a starting point for review, as well as a guide to planning. From the evidence of curriculum reviews, we have shown that much needs to be elaborated and explored when starting from either statements of aims or checklists of 'areas of experience'. Schwab (1973) argued that this was essential in the case of aims, in order to make explicit the richness of the values embedded within them.

The treatment of values poses another problem, identified in Chapter 3. The HMI-LEA exercise strives for consensus. The instruments used by Cheshire, for example, ask for a consensus rating of a subject's contribution to the eight areas. This is likely to play down the importance of value issues[171], and the resulting conflict[172]. Lewy (1977) raises the problem of consensus in the context of summarising judgements made by 'experts' (e.g. teachers). He describes an important technique for considering the value judgements of a group of people: the Delphi technique. Although this was developed to help groups achieve consensus it does so in a way that attempts to preserve divergent views. It avoids spurious consensus by asking individuals to give in writing a list of, say, aims for a school. The responses are then tabulated and a summary circulated. Each individual then rates the aims according to personal priorities; these are again summarised and circulated showing the group rating as well as that of each individual. Individuals are then invited to reconsider their ratings. Where individuals' ratings diverge from the group consensus they are invited to give reasons. The method has been used to discover views about the aims that a University School of Education should have (Cyphert and Gant, 1973). In this case it was reported that the technique could be used to mould opinion, although it did allow minority views to be represented and hence created awareness. Cyphert and Gant selected a diverse group, and, because 'questionnaires' were used, they were able to select one that was geographically dispersed. Rasp (1974) also reports a study that used this technique to arrive at the relative importance of certain goals (see also Hunkins,

1980, pp. 172-6 and Brooks, 1979).

The Nominal Group Technique is a similar approach, although the people who are consulted meet together to carry out the process. This involves, first, members of the group individually listing, say, aims (without consultation). A master list displaying these is then compiled and any clarifications are made to the group. Individuals rank these (not necessarily all) and a master list showing total 'voting' is then displayed. It is possible to go into a second round of voting. Hegarty (1977) reports that the Delphi and Nominal Group techniques are equally effective; the Delphi technique involves more administration but saves participants' time.

However, we must be cautious about what can be expected from any review technique if teachers are considering their curriculum under a number of outside pressures. These pressures may make any fundamental reappraisal by the school impractical and, in a period of retrenchment, unlikely[173]. This is not to deny that pupils will benefit if their teachers explore the underlying issues of the curriculum, but this benefit may come from the increased awareness experienced by teachers, as for example, in the Cheshire exercise, and hence from teacher education and development[174]. If this is indeed the nature of curriculum review then the question to be answered is: are the methods advocated by the DES and HMI adequate? We have implied so far that they are not, although we recognise the importance of the review exercises conducted so far. This inadequacy stems not only from the procedure adopted, as we have argued above, but also from the 'starting points' or types of analyses employed. In Chapter 3 we have already made this point with regard to *The School Curriculum* (DES, 1981b) in comparing it with, for example, the Munn Report (SED, 1977a). The documents issued by the DES and HMI encouraging schools to review their curriculum also invite schools to consider more than one kind of analysis as working tools of curriculum planning (DES, 1981b, p. 6). This invitation is offered as if these types of analyses are all of equal merit: something we questioned in Chapter 3. Even if a consensus view of the curriculum can be achieved, as the Munn Report (SED, 1977a) argued, it cannot be done at the level of each school unless those involved recognise the underlying values and assumptions that they and others hold. Starting with a list of eight areas will not encourage such a recognition.

One element in any school's consideration of underlying curriculum issues must be the achievement of some familiarity with contrasting conceptions of the curriculum, such as are offered in curriculum studies courses[175], although we recognise that this may remain a concern of the few[176]. For the staff of a school, in general, it is still feasible to adopt ways of working which will maximise the concern for these basic issues. A modest beginning for this would be a consideration of Mode III school-based examinations. Although, as we have already noted (Chapter 6), this is a minority activity (and perhaps threatened with extinction), it offers an opportunity for teachers to be involved in curricular thinking, at least at the subject department level (Torrance, 1982). However, leaving details of this aside, we now turn to a consideration of more general ways of tackling basic issues.

Deliberation and negotiation

As we have suggested earlier, deliberation is regarded as the approach required to explore the underlying curriculum issues in a way that leads to practical action. Moreover, it promises a means to action that none of the approaches to curriculum review so far considered seem able to do. Such deliberation can be an ordered activity, and Walker's (1975) analysis of the deliberations of a curriculum project provides a useful insight into the process. Walker analysed transcripts of the discussion of the project team and identified three tiers. Here we will focus on the second and third tiers. Deliberative moves are at the second tier, and are of six kinds:

1. statements of problems - identifying problems;
2. proposals of courses of action - what the project group might do;
3. arguments for ⎤
4. arguments against ⎦ particular problems or proposals;
5. instances - neutrally offered illustrations of abstractions;
6. clarifications - modifying the above moves.

The three of most interest are problems, proposals and arguments. It was the nature of the arguments that Walker chose to explore and in particular what sources of *data* were employed (the third tier). Again he identified several categories, which can be considered in pairs:

1. *Observational* or *judgemental* - Is the item of data cited an actual observation; or, is it a judgement based on experience, conventional wisdom, or speculation?
2. *External* or *internal* - If this item of data is observational, does it come from within the project, its members, or its meetings; or, do the data come from the world outside the project?

3. *First-hand* or *reported* - Was this item of observational data gathered by a member of the project; or, was it reported by someone outside the project or in a book or other outside source?
4. *Purposefully* or *incidently obtained* - Was this item of observational data actively sought by one or more project members; or, was it obtained fortuitously?

(Walker, 1975, pp. 113-4)[177]

Applying those categories to transcripts of discussions to determine the proportion of use of the different data sources he found:

that slightly more than half of the *arguments* were based on judgements rather than data; that about equal numbers of *arguments* judged observational were later judged to have arisen inside the project and outside it; that of the *arguments* based on actual observations, an overwhelming majority were observations made by members of the project; and that most of the observations were made incidentally rather than purposefully. (His emphases.)

(Walker, 1975, pp. 121-2)

Walker notes that whether or not these proportions are *desirable* is a matter of judgement. Obviously if discussion was about the problems pupils were having with a particular course, a lack of observational data, or data that were only collected incidentally, would be a cause for concern.

The lesson for teachers, who, as Chapter 5 indicated, rely heavily upon discussion, is that it can be orderly. In view of this it might be valuable to reflect on its nature. Reflection on, for example, the number of proposals for action considered, the number and strength of arguments for or against, the degree of judgement in these arguments, and the type of observations made, might aid teachers in improving their deliberations. Being self-conscious about this process may seem artificial but no more so that trying to perfect other evaluation techniques such as questionnaires. Sadly there is little documented experience in this area, but it might be helpful if a few discussions were recorded and analysed and if members of staff who were involved reflected upon the nature of the deliberation. Discussions could also be formalised to reflect Walker's second tier moves; this might ensure, for example, that an adequate number of proposals for action were considered[178].

Of course, all this assumes that groups of staff in a school are like curriculum project teams in the way they function. Weston (1979) argues that schools are not like curriculum projects and that *negotiation* is a better description of curriculum thinking. She proposes a simple three stage model of negotiation:

1. definition - definition and discussion of problems;
2. generation and shaping of proposals - e.g. production of written plans or materials;
3. consolidation - e.g. consideration of implications of proposals.

Each of these stages overlaps such that, for example, while problems are being discussed proposals will be shaped. However, proposals should not come before any consideration of problems.

The decision-making mode, and hence management problems of feasibility and concern for effects, are common features of discussions in schools. Unlike Walker's project, schools (usually) have a permanent existence, a direct responsibility for decisions, and experience a cycle of events. (The life of a project can be considered as linear.) Those involved in a staff discussion, for example heads of departments, rarely take a neutral role but represent interests - their departments[179]. In our opinion, Weston's investigation is important and worthy of study for the insights it gives into curriculum negotiations[180]. The purpose of characterising these negotiations is not simply to describe them, but to encourage their more purposeful use. One key element in Weston's idea of negotiation is appreciation[181], which resembles Walker's notion of deliberation: 'it is a process of reasoned argumentation in the light of all the available experience and information which the participants can bring to bear' (Weston, 1979, p. 195). Moreover, it 'is in itself an educative process leading to new understandings for those who take part' (p. 195-6). This then takes us back to our earlier contention that a central concern of curriculum review must be to increase the understanding of teachers[182]. Taking 'problems, argumentation and decisions on courses of action' as central concerns in a curriculum review contrasts sharply with curriculum design based on either the approach of the hardliners (whose prescriptions are difficult to substantiate), or the approach of the softliners (which results in a rather vague exercise not always connected with real curriculum problems[183]). We will return to the ideas of deliberation briefly at the end of this section[184].

The analysis of curriculum materials

Curriculum materials of whatever kind - single worksheets, textbooks, curriculum packages - are a manifestation of the intended curriculum. They encapsulate, implicitly or explicitly, many curriculum decisions even when these have not been consciously made. Despite the different ways in which materials are used, they remain, in the eyes of the pupils, as a statement of curriculum intentions. As such they are worthy of examination. At one level they are documentary evidence of intentions, but they also constitute an 'agenda' or stimulus for classroom action. They therefore occupy a position somewhere between inactive statements of purposes and classroom activity. An examination of curriculum materials can be viewed in three ways: as an intrinsic evaluation; as a first stage in an empirical evaluation; as a tool for deliberation. We will consider each of these below, concentrating upon the analysis of materials as intrinsic evaluation.

Chapter 7 has already outlined intrinsic evaluation; in the context of the analysis of materials this can be seen as an attempt to elucidate important characteristics, such as value issues. This immediately raises the question of what characteristics, in particular, should be attended to in the analysis, and whether they should be pre-determined. Ben-Peretz (1981) talks of 'frames of reference', which serve as a source of categories for the analysis, and distinguishes between internal and external frames. Internal frames of reference come from developers of the material, and may be their rationale for constructing it (e.g. a list of objectives). In this case the task can be either to check the consistency of the rationale and the materials, or to question the rationale. Where materials have been constructed in the school then the evaluators could also be developers. External frames of reference can be narrow or singular, for example sex or cultural bias, or they can be global. Global frames can be further subdivided into those which remain open-ended or those that are closed. An example of the latter is one that questions whether the materials conform to a model of curriculum development, e.g. do the materials have a list of objectives, do the learning activities directly relate to the objectives, are assessments of pupils included (Tyler and Klein, 1976)? Here the criteria for judgement are built into the scheme, although the criteria themselves may be controversial.

An example of an open-ended and global frame of reference (or scheme) was produced by Eraut, Goad, and Smith (1975). This was produced for use in analysing published curriculum materials but has been adapted for use with school-produced materials (OU, 1981a, Block 5). It considers four aspects of the materials: aims (implicit or explicit); curriculum strategy (e.g. learning activities, content, assessment); adequacy of the materials (e.g. suitability of language); practical feasibility of their use (e.g. durability, cost etc.). The analyst can choose to evaluate the materials considering any, or all, of the four aspects; in this sense they act like a checklist. Indeed the first task is to settle on some issues to consider in the evaluation; these can arise from using or inspecting the materials.

The scheme envisages several stages after the identification of issues (which can, at any stage, be added to or revised):

1. the collection of *evidence* relevant to the issues, for example, an analysis of the concepts employed or the types of task included (a documentary analysis); or evidence about how the materials are used in the classroom (this need not be collected by direct observation but can be recalled by the teacher).
2. the posing of *arguments* for and against various positions (for example the flow of concepts being taught), for each of the four aspects (aims, strategy, adequacy and feasibility) identified in the issues.
3. the formation of *judgements* on the basis of the arguments.

McCormick (OU, 1981a, Block 5) gives various examples of the analysis of school-produced and published curriculum materials as well as details of the appropriate schemes[185].

In contrast to many of the techniques of empirical data collection presented in this chapter, the methods of collecting evidence are quite different for the analysis of materials. Again several techniques can be identified:

1. goal analysis - listing the aims and objectives explicitly stated or inferred from, for example, the pupil activities and assessment[186];
2. content analysis - this covers a variety of activities, for example, listing concepts in order of presentation, constructing a concept diagram to show inter-relationships, analysing tasks to see what intellectual level they imply, locating instances of bias in the material[187];
3. textual analysis - this requires a close attention to the text and the nature of the arguments, examples and conclusions reached[188];
4. readability - this is a measure of the difficulty of the text and is so frequently used that it warrants a separate heading[189].

Although a large part of the evidence is derived from documentary analysis, it is equally important to consider how the materials are used. Teachers can usually recall, in considerable detail, how they use materials, and this is particularly useful when the materials cover a large period of teaching (e.g. a term), or are used many times - situations that would generate a mountain of direct observational evidence. This makes use of the great store of evidence and experience that teachers have and which we think should first be tapped before embarking upon elaborate empirical exercises. Indeed an analysis of materials may be seen as a first stage in an empirical study, providing the opportunity to stand back from their day-to-day use and consider new aspects. The main product of such an analysis would be a list of questions to be investigated empirically[190].

Deliberation revisited

It will not have escaped the reader's notice that there are similarities between the stages of materials analysis and the 'moves' of deliberation. Both focus upon a clarification of problems or issues, and both employ argumentation. The arguments draw upon evidence: in the case of materials analysis, from the materials and their use. They also draw upon the expertise of teachers, in a systematic way, and point to other sources of evidence and knowledge.

The scheme proposed by Eraut, Goad and Smith (1975) envisaged that the judgements involved in the evaluation of materials would be carried out in a separate decision-making phase. In this phase the arguments would be weighed and the feasibility and consequences of various courses of action would be considered. The resemblance with deliberation[191] offers the possibility of using the analysis of curriculum materials as a device on which to base the deliberation process. Naturally curriculum materials are not always at issue in curriculum discussions, but they may be a good starting point for teachers to develop and 'practice' deliberation. A group of teachers could not only consider the aims and strategies implicit in materials, but look at how they use them, therefore relating their underlying beliefs and values to classroom practice. If the revision or replacement of curriculum materials is the focus for discussion, then a direct link with action is evident.

Curriculum Context

Introduction

So far in this chapter we have considered techniques that can be used to evaluate different aspects of the curriculum: transactions, outcomes and intentions. These aspects cover the mainstream activity of teaching and learning within the school. But teaching and learning take place within a school context that includes a building, an organisation and a mini-society (or a collection of subgroups). The school, in turn, is a part of a larger society. Illuminative evaluators characterise this context by the term 'learning milieu' (Parlett and Hamilton, 1972), which encompasses physical and social factors. Sociologists on the other hand refer to the 'culture' (or subcultures) of the school, meaning the shared norms, common values, understandings and agreements that bind together those within in (Musgrove, 1973, p. 156). There are several reasons why evaluation should consider this context:

1. the broad definition of the curriculum that we have adopted alerts us to a wide range of aspects of school life;

2. even if a narrow view of the curriculum is taken with, say, a focus on outcomes, then there is evidence, however contentious (Rutter *et al*, 1979), that contextual features (e.g. staff involvement in decision-making) affect pupil outcomes (e.g. academic success);

3. more pragmatically, many of the evaluation checklists used in LEA schemes (and USA accreditation) cover a variety of aspects of schools and their surroundings.

A consideration of the checklists used in LEA evaluation schemes reveals that they focus on observed antecedent conditions[192], to use Stake's terminology (see Chapter 7). However, they do this because those who constructed the checklists thought that to improve the quality of education a consideration of, for example, the state of repair of school buildings, was important[193]. Because these kinds of checklists represent the collective thinking of a range of professionals, it is worthwhile examining the aspects of schools that they include in them. From a variety of checklists, we have selected items which (in our judgement[194]) relate to the context of learning. For each item we have indicated the checklists in which it is included.

Key to checklists:
1 ILEA (1977)
2 Jackson and Hayter (1978)
3 NSSE (1978)
4 Schools Council (1982)
5 NCA (1980a)
(The notes refer to qualifications on the categorisation of checklist items.)

Aspects covered	*Source*
School Environment[195]	
a. tidiness, displays, repairs and noise	1
b. facilities, resources and finance	5,3
School climate[196]	5
Staff a. structures and responsibilities	1,3,4
b. decision-making	1,2,4
c. development	1-5
d. planning (curriculum)[197]	5
Pupils a. school internal concerns: how they are welcomed; welfare and psychological services; absenteeism.	1,2
b. characteristics not related to school[198] e.g. ethnic origin.	3
Teacher-pupil relationships[199]	4
School and Community	
a. parental involvement in school, parent-staff links, community use of resources.	1-5
b. composition of local community.	3

This list can usefully be compared with one extracted from the research of Rutter *et al* (1979)[200], which, despite its shortcomings (see note 4, Chapter 6), is created not from a consensus view of professionals, but from previous research and statistical correlations on school processes.

1. Academic emphasis - homework setting and checks on this; teacher expectations; displays of pupil work; use of library; teacher group planning of courses.
2. Rewards and punishments - praise in assembly; sports prizes; displays of pupil work.
3. Pupil conditions - working conditions; tidy classrooms; pupils able to approach staff with personal problems.
4. Responsibilities and participation (of pupils) - school assembly

participation; collections for charity.

5. Stability of teaching and friendship groups - stability of peer group.

6. Staff organisation - group planning; check on staff work and punctuality; high morale and routine of people working harmoniously together; decision making at senior teacher level coupled with representation of teachers' views.

In addition they investigated (on the basis of previous research) the relationships between their outcome measures and 'physical and administrative features' and 'ecological influences'[201]. Of these only the 'ecological influences' significantly distinguished the schools in their sample; and in relation to this only the 'balance of intake' was significant. However, they established a correlation between the academic balance (i.e. the proportion of the various ability bands) in a school and academic outcomes, but considered only the *group effect* of, for example, a high proportion of able children (see note 201).

Our purpose in examining these items, from both checklists and the Rutter study, is to show the range of aspects of a school, other than the main activity of teaching and learning, that are worthy of evaluation. The resulting array is daunting and, particularly in the case of checklists, somewhat formless[202]. Here we are reminded of Parson's plea, which we referred to in Chapter 7, for evaluators to be more concerned with the role of theory. However, it would be wrong to assume that those drawing up checklists for evaluation take no heed of theory. For example, all of those mentioned above included reference to school-parent links. This was shown to be important in much early British research in the sociology of education. In addition, concern for decision-making stems from ideas about the nature of organisations and how they are managed. Most teachers are likely to possess a variety of concepts for thinking about the school as an organisation, for example: decision making; communications; bureaucracy; role; hierarchy; power; pupil subgroups. When it comes to evaluation of the curriculum context we feel it is important to be aware of the theory that underpins some of these concepts[203]. As Davies (1973) put it, in relation to organisational analysis of educational institutions: 'The specification of research problems does rest on the conceptual framework within which they are conceived ' (p. 253)[204]. This we feel applies equally to evaluation problems, for, however they arise, their investigation will rely on how they are conceived, which in turn relies upon some conceptual framework (however incomplete or implicit it may be). As we shall see, in relation to ethnographic research based upon symbolic interactionism, not all theories imply a rigid specification of the events and aspects of the school (e.g. decision-making; teacher roles) that are attended to.

Given the variety of theories and, in the opinion of Davies (1973), the lack of a widely accepted theory of organisations, any account of possible theories would be highly selective[205]. The theories we consider are concerned with the internal aspects of schools; the external curriculum context is less tractable but we will also consider it briefly later.

Theories of schools as organisations

We shall consider theories from two traditions, management and sociology, both of which are influential in organisational theory[206]. Management approaches to theories are considered prescriptive (Davies, 1973, p. 252) and focus on formal organisational structure and functions. One such approach deals with decision-making and leadership. Silverman (1970, p. 204) describes the rationality of decision-making systems as following three elements: an ordered set of preferences, procedures for revealing available courses of action, and an ability to choose between preferences. This, you may remember, was used to characterise the process of deliberation outlined in the section on the 'Intended Curriculum'. This of course ignores the fact that those who 'people' the organisation may bring motives and meanings other than those of the formal system. An example of this is the bargaining for subject department status, rather than curriculum planning, identified by Hurman (1978) (see Chapter 3). Cohen and Manion (1981, p. 361) identify what they call the *Model B* version of leadership and decision-making, which is based upon the human relations tradition in management. *Model B* stresses shared decision-making, and horizontal not vertical patterns of authority, democracy, participation, harmony and conflict resolution[207]. This kind of approach is used in Weston's (1979) analysis of problems of participation and consultation for the Heads of Department Committee (see 'Intended Curriculum').

A consideration of 'organisational climate' also has a tradition in management approaches. School climates can be characterised in terms of, for example, leadership, autonomy, job satisfaction (see Zak, 1981), or production emphasis (headteachers' close supervision of staff), consideration (headteachers' attempts to treat staff humanly), and staff morale (see Cohen & Manion, 1981). Here we are moving away from formal organisation to consider some of the social systems that exist within the school (informal systems). Treating a school as an 'open system' provides a framework for the consideration of such social systems (or subsystems) - some of which (e.g. staff cliques) may be informal. For instance, open systems can be regarded as having inputs, processes and outputs. A crude version of this framework is employed in John Gray's analysis of examination results ('Curriculum Outcomes'), where the effectiveness of the school's system is being measured. There are a variety of characteristics of systems[208], but for the moment we will only discuss Davies's (1973) 'three reminders' of neglected areas:

1. External relationships and boundary maintenance - this reminder draws attention to schools dealing with the various and conflicting pressures from outside, by either reconciling them, or by developing devices to insulate themselves against some of the pressures.
2. Formal and informal organisation - this reminder encourages us to view the relationship between these two as complex, and discourages us from assuming that the informal is a result of the formal organisation (we shall return to informal organisation when we consider sociological theories).
3. Output and self-maintenance - this reminds us that 'much of the activity that occurs within an organisation will be geared to repair and self-maintenance rather than to the production of an explicit, official output'[209] (Davies, 1973, p. 262).

Richardson's (1973) classic study employed systems theory as part of the theoretical underpinning for the investigation. However, she used the idea of a 'socio-technical system' (although she did not use the term), which stresses the inter-relationships of technology (e.g. subject and teaching method specialisms), the school's environment, the sentiments of participants (e.g. the purposes of the teachers and pupils) and the organisational form[210]. The crucial problem lies in describing the primary task of the school when the school is viewed as a conversion process i.e. where children are taken in (input), experience conversion processes of growth and learning (process), and leave as mature people (output) (Richardson, 1973, pp. 17-18). The argument is too complex to expand here but Davies (1981, 1973) argues that such an approach offers a possibility for relating the formal system (concerned with the task) to the informal (sentient[211]) system, as well as focusing upon the work being done in schools. Although the ideas contained in systems approaches seem far removed from the schools 'everybody works in or knows about', it must be remembered that some of the ideas do nevertheless exist in our thinking. For example, we differentiate the school's system according to ability groups, age groups, pastoral care and academic systems (or organisations), classrooms, in-school and out of school activities, and subject departments[212]. A systems approach attempts to give some order to these and provides a way of thinking about the individual parts (or subsystems), while bearing in mind the whole.

Management approaches to thinking about schools as organisations have led to methods of evaluation, although there is no straightforward connection between the theories outlined above and the evaluation approaches that follow[213]. First, several measures of organisational climate have been constructed. These cover such things as institutional control (e.g. the degree of supervision of children's movements and the extent and power of the school to limit and restrict pupil behaviour), and pupil and teacher perceptions of their own and each other's behaviour. They are based upon carefully constructed and validated questionnaire-type instruments (see Cohen, 1976, pp. 276-8). Secondly, role definition and analysis can be carried out. Shipman (1979, pp. 131-5), for example, suggests an approach that requires a careful description of the various roles that teachers take, as well as a regular review of them. Again questionnaire instruments exist, using Likert scales, to define roles or role expectations (Cohen, 1976, pp. 265-73). Thirdly, and related to Shipman's conception of a review of roles, is staff-appraisal. This refers to a review of staff, individually by a senior member(s) of staff. It would cover such things as teaching performance in the classroom (strengths and weaknesses), problems encountered in the department (or school, if a small primary school), in-service or other professional development needs, and career plans and prospects[214,215].

Interest in the informal systems within an organisation is also reflected in sociology, where the concept of pupil or teacher 'sub-culture' is employed. Musgrove (1973) also identified 'power' as a central concern of sociologists. The investigation of a school's sub-cultures is considered to be helpful to teachers who wish to 'understand and perhaps influence the motivation of [their] pupils' (Musgrove, 1973, p. 168). Sociologists' interest in 'power' leads them to look at such things as:

the structure of authority, the manner and basis of task allocation,
the influence of pressure groups inside and outside the school,
the nature of the head [teacher's] authority and the way it

differs from the authority of . . . [the deputies] , the cleavage and camps among pupils and staff which are based on age and seniority, formal stratification, subject allegiance, or simply physical isolation or proximity. (Musgrove, 1973, p. 162)

Lacey's study (Lacey, 1970, pp. 165-9) elaborated how status was ascribed to staff through seniority, and the effect on the formal and informal organisation of staff. The study of the informal systems of educational institutions was a major concern of Lambert and his colleagues (1973): in particular, pupils' informal social systems. They describe an informal system as 'the pattern of norms, values and relationships not prescribed structurally or normatively by the official goals of the organisation, but which may still have effects on these goals' (Lambert, Bullock and Millham, 1973, p. 298). Such systems can be functional or disruptive[216], but the structural variables of the organisation (e.g. streaming), they claim, do not necessarily determine the pupil society. They identified three features of informal systems which could be used to characterise them: degree of consensus within them; the strength of informal control; the pervasiveness of the informal system in the areas and activities controlled by its informal norms. Woods (OU, 1977, Unit 7-8, pp. 19-21) characterises such research as being concerned with 'experience' (e.g. how pupils and teachers negotiate their day, their relationships and the requirements made of them, and how this affects their lives and self-concepts) rather than 'process' (e.g. teaching methods). It is, therefore, concerned with the hidden curriculum. Woods identifies various aspects of the hidden curriculum which have been investigated: distortions of the manifest curriculum (e.g. some aspects of the curriculum which act as a form of social control); teacher and pupil strategies (e.g. pupils not engaged in learning, but getting by with minimum effort and unpleasantness); the 'unalterable framework of the system' (e.g. its tendency to alienate)[217]. There is a growing literature in this area including Woods (1979, 1980a, 1980b) and Willis (1977). See Hammersley (1980) for a comprehensive review.

The methodology sociologists adopt to investigate 'experience' is ethnography, because this approach tries to give a holistic 'picture of the way of life of an interacting human group' (OU, 1977, Unit 7-8, p. 12). It requires participant observation, including the appropriate techniques outlined in the section on 'Observation', for example, unstructured observation and interviews. (See Wilson (1977) for an outline of these techniques.) Although there is no pre-existent definition of what is going on in the school, and the theory to explain the particular meanings pupils and teachers attach to their behaviour is developed by induction (Chapter 7), ethnographers nevertheless employ overarching theories about such behaviour. Symbolic Interaction is one such theoretical approach. Case study research is often taken to be synonymous, but Woods (OU, 1977, Unit 7-8, p. 12) feels that this implies the study of a more particular aspect or theme in the life of teachers and pupils. Stenhouse (1978) also argued that case study research emphasises interviews, rather than observation.

By taking theories of schools as organisations from management and sociology[218], teachers are faced with a difficult task if they are to use them to inform their evaluations. We are not, of course, suggesting that teachers have to get to grips with all available theories before carrying out a study. However, some of these theories may offer useful ways of thinking about the context of the curriculum; as such they may be an advance on *ad hoc* categories. Precisely because these theories have often been developed by outside researchers, they may help teachers to distance themselves from their schools[219]. When James and Ebbutt (1981) were teachers they carried out investigations in their own schools, and later had this to say about the experience:

> It is often hard to pick out and reflect upon what is significant and what is merely 'noise'. One of the problems is learning how to reappraise what has been thought of as merely institutional 'noise' and hear it with 'new ears'. In a school with a public address system, DE had become so inured to its disembodied commanding edicts, that its messages went unremarked. Until, that is, the realisation dawned that the electronic voice carried illuminating evidence with respect to hidden curriculum. In the same school he had also accepted differential treatment of boys and girls unquestioningly; but the implications of this, that large parts of the school were in fact 'no go' areas for one sex or the other, was not appreciated. Even the assembly hall had a male half and a female half, a feature that was obvious, but which had actually gone un-noticed for ten years.   (p. 90)

External context

We have already drawn attention to the way that research on education has informed checklists for evaluation with regard to home-school links. In general, however, there seems to be much less obvious theoretical work to turn to for help in considering the external context of the curriculum. It is possible to detect a systems influence in the NSSE (1978) checklist, especially with regard to pupil and community characteristics as inputs, and the economic development of the community as a system environment to which the system process must adapt. However, that may merely be a rather grandiloquent way of saying that the school must make sure its objectives and methods suit the kind of children who come to it, and the kind of future they are likely to experience. Although such checklists require statistics to be collected about pupils, and the environment they will enter[220], no guidance is given concerning the use of this information. Davies (1981, p. 54) seems to imply that Marxist approaches, which consider education as social reproduction[221], have left school organisation as a 'black box' and hence fail to link social context to the school's internal operation[222].

An interest in urban schooling or multi-ethnic education emphasises the need for an examination of the surrounding community[223]: its physical, political, economic and cultural aspects. Although such an analysis, carried out by teachers, would clearly help their understanding of the task of the school, rarely are the links between the context and the internal operations of the school made clear. Curriculum review does of course require such an analysis if, for example, the curriculum is to be examined for its match with the needs, aspirations and conditions of the local community. NSSE (1978. p. 14) put it thus: 'the question should be "what is important to know about the young people and the community supporting this school in order to determine whether the school is meeting the needs of the community?".' Skilbeck's (OU, 1976, Unit 26) notion of school-based curriculum development also requires a situational analysis (i.e. an analysis of factors which constitute the situation). This includes an external component:

(i)   cultural and social changes and expectations including parental expectations, employer requirements, community assumptions and values, changing relationships (e.g. between adults and children), and ideology;

(ii) educational-system requirements and challenges, e.g. policy statements, examinations, local authority expectations or demands or pressures, curriculum projects, educational research [. . .]

(v)   flow of resources into the school. (OU, 1976, Unit 26, p. 96)

Writing for a course on education and the urban environment, Golby is forced to admit: 'The outlook for situational analysis is therefore cloudy. For those committed to it, it looks like a matter of excursions into educational experiment with the community' (OU, 1978, Block VI, Unit 14, p. 47). Need we say more!

Conclusion

For a school interested in investigating the internal curriculum context, there are a rich variety of theories available to help in conceptualising the evaluation problem. This is not so for the external context; in this area we are left with the *ad hoc* recommendations of various checklists. Putting the problems of information use to one side, schools will still be faced with problems of data collection and, if these are to be quantified, with statistical analysis. With a large community to find out about, sampling becomes a problem. Even in ethnographic approaches, where theoretical sampling is important, the resources needed to mount an ethnography of the local community are substantial[224]. Then there is the nation: indeed the whole of society! In this sphere schools must be left to use their commonsense about what is relevant: as Golby implied, 'you're on your own'.

Notes

1. The literature on observation has a variety of terms to describe each. Systematic observation is the commonly used term, but it is not legitimate to refer to unstructured observation as 'non-systematic'. Similarly the formal/non-formal division is inappropriate; which is why we prefer to use the terms structured/unstructured observation.
2. Hamilton and Delamont (1974) and Delamont (1976) consider the development of this in the USA in relation to unstructured observation and the state of British classroom research.
3. Simon and Boyer (1974) and Borich and Madden (1977) contain details of a large number of observational systems in use in the USA; and Rosenshine and Furst (1973), Brophy and Good (1974), and Dunkin and Biddle (1974) review research using such systems.
4. Boydell (1975) discusses the issue of how to carry out systematic (structured) observation in informal classrooms.
5. Bennett & McNamara (1979) give a selection of observation systems, most of which were carried out in primary schools. McIntyre (1980) gives a selection that is not confined to primary schools.
6. Comparative studies require experimental research procedures with rigorous requirements that are not always possible to meet within schools: for example; the need for sampling. The statistical manipulations for process-product studies are also a problem for schools without access to suitable computer programmes (e.g. for regression analysis).

7. Borich (1977) gives a slightly different set of definitions of sign, category and rating; however the definitions we give are the most common. In any case his definitions contain the same elements as ours (i.e. exclusiveness, exhaustiveness and level of inference).

8. This is used by Hook *et al* (1981) and Boehm & Weinberg (1977). Wragg and Kerry (1979) refer to this as a form of 'natural sampling' i.e. a record is made when there is a change of category, topic or speaker (Galton, 1978).

9. This term is used by Dunkerton & Guy (1981). Wragg & Kerry (1979) refer to it as a 'static sample' and Galton (1978) and Cooper (1974) call it a 'time sample'.

10. Cooper (1974) uses this term. Galton (1978) uses 'time unit' and Wragg & Kerry (1979) use 'unit sampling'.

11. The length of the intervals in 'instantaneous sampling' and 'interval recording' depend upon the nature of the decisions that have to be made by the observer. See the argument between Dunkerton & Guy (1981) and Eggleston & Galton (1981).

12. Galton (1979) notes that the over-representation of some curriculum areas may occur if pupils choose their own activities within a primary classroom.

13. McIntyre (1980, p. 15) says that two observers can develop implicit mutual understanding and become more reliable than the system itself. For a somewhat technical discussion of problems with measures of reliability see Harrop (1979).

14. For an analysis of sources of invalidity in structured observation see Borich (1977). He also gives a general account of the principles of structured observation, but draws only upon USA literature.

15. A point noted by Hook *et al* (1981, p. 53) when discussing validity and reliability in the context of teachers researching in their own classrooms.

16. Hook *et al* (1981, p. 55) suggest that triangulation can be used to check 'observations', but this is not likely to prove very practical; rather the 'inferences' drawn from the observations in general are more properly checked by triangulation.

17. The 'classic' text on constructing a structured observation schedule is Medley & Mitzel (1963).

18. A consideration of intentions and interpretations of teacher and pupil behaviour is the foundation of symbolic interactionism. See Delamont (1976) for an account of this approach.

19. This is not to imply that evaluation need not concern itself with theory: an issue we come to in the section on 'The Curriculum Context'. For a review of the theories developed by classroom ethnographers see Hammersley (1980). See Wilson (1977) for a review of the use of ethnographic technique.

20. Clift (OU, 1981a, Block 4), drawing upon Gronlund's earlier writings, also gives an account of anecdotal records as a device for recording pupil assessment.

21. Hammersley (1986a & b), Chanan & Delamont (1975), McAleese & Hamilton (1978), and Bennett & McNamara (1979) each contain the work of both traditions, although the latter book is biased in favour of structured observation. Stubbs & Delamont (1976) represent the side of the debate in favour of unstructured observation.

22. We have outlined what we take to be major criticisms and the reader is

recommended to consult McIntyre & MacLeod (1978) for a fuller discussion of all the criticisms.

23. McIntyre & MacLeod (1978) note that such criticisms of structured observation are sometimes based upon Flanders' Interaction Analysis Categories. As we have indicated, many more complex systems have been developed.

24. An issue we referred to when discussing field notes used in unstructured observation.

25. A stance we do not have much sympathy for, since we believe that teachers' and pupils' mutual understanding and private language are important.

26. Also, McIntyre (1980, p. 14) says that those constructing structured observation systems can only validate them by relating them to evidence about how the participants construe the relevant events.

27. See, however, Delamont (1981) for an 'internal' critique, particularly of the narrow range of reading by educational ethnographers of work in other countries, and other theoretical traditions.

28. McIntyre (1980, p. 3) also notes such denunciations of the positivistic approach, but says they are rarely argued and consist of either polemical attacks or contemptuous dismissals.

29. Smetherham (1978) sees it as a problem of commitment to the participant role, which occurs when the teacher is too busy deriving data as a researcher.

30. It is structured rather like an Open University text with many examples and exercises; indeed like the Open University, Deakin teaches at a distance.

31. Davis (1980), also an Australian author (but not connected with Deakin), writes specifically for teachers carrying out evaluation in their own schools. However, in our opinion his approach is overburdened with theories and models of evaluation; indeed he relegates a consideration of techniques to an appendix.

32. Smith & Geoffrey (1968) see this as a strength of the classroom teacher as a participant observer. It is also referred to in Hook (1981, p. 107). Hamilton & Delamont (1974, p. 9) make a similar point.

33. Hamilton & Delamont (1974, p. 7) talk of the 'prolonged presence' of an observer in a classroom.

34. This lack of access to pupils' perceptions etc. can be overcome by interviewing them. Better still, those working in the Ford Teaching Project (1975) found that a multiple interview was useful because pupils were more forthright and honest to an outsider than to their teacher. Jeffcoate (1981) also found his role as an outside interviewer useful in evaluating the sensitive area of multicultural education.

35. A conflict noted in Hook (1981, p. 59) and Harris, Bell & Carter (1981, p. 212. 1/6). The latter authors and Stenhouse (1975, p. 155), quoting from a PhD study by David Hamilton, recognise that this conflict will vary with the kind of classroom organisation. The quotation from Hamilton indicates that any adult observer is likely to be taken as a teacher and hence subject to the same conflict. Stenhouse concludes that 'open' classrooms with their more fluid teacher role are therefore more likely to encourage the development of the observer role.

36. However, teachers in the Ford Teaching Project (1975) did regard the lack of visual cues as a disadvantage.

37. Adelman & Walker (1975) note that the conventions of television programme making often get in the way of observational recording. This is a
problem experienced at The Open University in making programmes on
classroom life. See for example the three programmes associated with
E364 (OU, 1981a). In a two-camera set-up it is, of course, possible to
record using a split-screen technique thus avoiding selection through
cutting (used by Adams & Biddle, 1970).

38. It can of course be used purely as a stimulus for thinking, rather than as a
source of data which demand analysis. In the context of a research study,
Adams & Biddle (1970) estimated 20-25 hours coding time for every hour
of recording!

39. The difficulties for teachers in moving the equipment about was the main
reason for Bassey & Hatch (1979) abandoning the use of video in favour of
audio-recording.

40. Denton & Sexton (1978) list the advantages of photography in terms of its
availability, ease of operation, technical reliability, versatility (e.g. close-up
work and use without a flash), durability of data, appeal in reports and
capacity to provide a validity check.

41. They also deal with stop-frame photography which is a true compromise
between movie films and audio-recording. However this is a sophisticated
research tool and therefore beyond the resources of most schools. Technical
details of this approach are in Adelman & Walker (1971/2).

42. The general approach to such analysis, which is characteristic of that in
ethnography, is covered later in the section. The crucial feature is the
development of hypotheses and testing these against the data, for example,
by searching for negative cases.

43. Complete transcription is difficult because some elements of speech are
difficult to represent. In fact Anderson (1979) gives advice on conventions
to be adopted to help improve this representation.

44. Members of the Ford Teaching Project (1975) suggested transcribing the
relevant data, based on a clear idea of what evidence is required. In contrast
to Anderson (1979), the project team did not regard the audio-recording
as the main source of data, but as a basis for reconstructing the lesson.

45. Naturally, these writers (e.g. Stubbs, 1981, and Atkinson, 1981) are
concerned with the language of the classroom. Stubbs (1981) talks of the
unprincipled selection of data from transcripts that ignores linguistic
organisation. However he gives few details about how to attend to it.
Hammersley (1980, p. 56), in comparing the approaches of classroom
ethnographers with sociolinguists and ethnomethodologists, sees nothing
intrinsically wrong with selections that are illustrative (effectively what the
Ford Teaching Project team recommended), provided the criteria of choice
are clear.

46. Anderson (1979) provides a sequence for such an analysis using a series of
levels which bear similarity to 'A System for Analysing Instructional
Discourse' (Brown & Armstrong, 1978). OU (1981a, Case Study 4) gives
two case studies of teachers analysing their lessons using transcripts. Both
work mainly at the detailed technical level.

47. From the ethnographic research tradition Becker & Gear (1960) provide a
classic account. OU (1981a, Block 3) contains a characterisation of a
teacher's self-evaluation according to the various stages of such a research
tradition.

48. This is a technique used by David Jenkins in an evaluation of a curriculum project (Shipman, 1974, Chapter 6). He uses nine 'guiding metaphors' to describe how the project was perceived by the teachers in the trial schools, for example: 'The exchange of gifts: the project as reciprocal obligation'; 'Free sample: the project as commercialism' (p. 99).

49. As noted at the beginning of the chapter observation outside the class-room is usually accomplished through indirect methods, for example by interviews, and often results in case studies (see 'The curriculum context').

50. This technique is recommended to schools in 'The Practical Curriculum' (Schools Council, 1981, pp. 43-4).

51. The period occurred just before the school Spring Fayre and this led to 'abnormal' activities in some lessons.

52. Advocates of unstructured approaches include: Stenhouse (1975), Elliott (1978) and the Ford Teaching Project (1975). Examples of teachers employing structured observation can be found in OU (1981a, Case Study 4). Ainley and Lazonby (1981) combined an unstructured teachers' account of his lesson with a structured observation by a researcher.

53. Power (1977) criticises ethnographic researchers who are 'restricted to methodological individualism and case studies of single situations [and hence who] are doomed to practical irrelevance.' (p. 22).

54. Anderson (1979) advocates the analysis of lesson transcripts as a method for explicating teacher classroom knowledge and advises teachers to avoid analysing transcripts quantitatively in the first instance. If they do so they may lose the context of the interaction, miss the point of a lesson sequence, and in any case have insufficient transcripts from which to generalise.

55. For example a case study of a teacher's self-evaluation, involving only one lesson (OU, 1981a, Case Study 4), resulted in 18,000 words being written, with only fifteen minutes of audio-recording having been transcribed!

56. They also say that, over a long period of time, the children changed the role of the outsider. From being a non-participant observer the outsider became a participant observer - which created problems for recording behaviour on the schedule. They note that using another teacher, in the school, as observer would speed up the process of becoming involved in classroom activities.

57. For example Smith (1981) makes this point in discussing interviews and questionnaires as part of the 'survey' approach.

58. Becker & Geer (1957), from this kind of tradition, also argue for observation, but participant observation, in preference to interviewing. Their position, however, should not be polarised as becomes clear in their dialogue with Trow (see Trow, 1957, and Becker and Geer, 1958).

59. There is, for example, more recognition of the need to triangulate methods. See the references in Note 58.

60. We originally contemplated including discussions of sociometry and personal constructs. Although sociometry is recommended for teachers as a research tool (e.g. Hook, 1981, and Gronlund, 1981) and eliciting personal constructs has obvious applications in evaluation (e.g. for investigating pupil and teacher perceptions of each other - see Nash, 1976), no published evidence of their use in evaluation exists to guide teachers. For those interested in these techniques the following offer explanations and advice: sociometry - Cohen (1976) Hook (1981) and Gronlund (1981): personal

constructs - Hall (1980) provides a basic account and Bannister & Mair (1968) and Fransella & Bannister (1977) are more advanced. The original construct theory is contained in Kelly (1955).

61. Stenhouse (McCormick *et al* 1982, p. 267) makes this point, noting that Master's theses are a major source of experience.

62. We are aware, that in trying to cover the full range of interviews in the discussion which follows, we at times misrepresent some. We have sacrificed some of the integrity of the approaches for the sake of economy and have tried to add qualifications where necessary without, we hope, becoming pedantic. Powney & Watts (1987) give a detailed account of interviewing specifically for educational researchers.

63. Patton (1980) calls this an 'interview guide approach', although it does not necessarily focus on a specific event.

64. Patton (1980) gives a slightly different version: the standardised open-ended interview. The questions are standardised; the replies open.

65. There is some difficulty in sorting out the labels here. Some ethnographers are inclined not to see this kind of approach as an interview, but as integral to participant observation (e.g. Becker & Gear, 1957, Hammersley in OU, 1979, Block 4). However, they may still describe these interviews as 'informal, unstructured, non-directive' (OU, 1979, Block 4, p. 149). Spradley (1979) distinguishes the ethnographic interviews of informants (i.e. those who help the ethnographer to understand the culture) from participant observation. In the former the informant and the ethnographer both know they are going somewhere and the ethnographer controls the situation to varying degrees. In distinguishing case study research, conducted by outsiders, from ethnography, Stenhouse (1978) tends to talk only of the observation element of ethnography, neglecting to discuss the interviewing of informants.

66. It is possible to test hypotheses in an unstructured interview, an approach adopted by Piaget (1929) in his 'clinical method'.

67. Smith (1981) and Hook (1981) give examples of interview guides.

68. There are a variety of texts on this subject but we have limited our references to standard ones from the social science literature. See also Bynner in OU (1979, Block 4) for an introductory account of survey interviewing, and Spradley (1979) on the ethnographic interview. Oppenheim (1966), like Smith (1981), the reference we use, also combines a discussion of interviewing and questionnaires, giving some guidance to the literature.

69. Patton (1980), from the qualitative tradition, and Smith (1981), from the quantitative tradition, both give detailed examples of the do's and don'ts of question wording.

70. This is debatable in other than a structured or semi-structured interview. The analysis of these two types of interviews is often unconcerned with the flow of ideas which could make the lack of singularity quite acceptable.

71. Smith (1981, p. 163) also says that clarity is improved if, when asking about past behaviour, a specific time is mentioned. This is better than asking for a generalisation. Thus 'How many times have you skipped school in the last month?' is preferable to 'How many times a month do you skip school?'.

72. For example the question in Note 71 would be a leading one if it was a first question on the subject. However, it would signal to a pupil that the

interviewer would not be surprised to find out that the pupil truanted.

73.   A particular form of this is the quintamensional design used in questionnaires and semi-structured interviews to elicit responses about, for example: (1) the respondents' awareness of an attitude, then (2) their general attitudes, followed by (3) their possession of the specific attitude, then (4) reasons for holding this attitude, and finally (5) the intensity of feeling (Smith, 1981, p. 161). Hook (1981, pp. 144-5) talks of 'funnel questions' as a way of progressively narrowing the focus of the enquiry. With regard to the ethnographic interview, Spradley (1979), although not recommending such a tight structure, suggests a development in the questions.

74.   Patton (1980) advises against lumping all the factual questions (e.g. age; occupation) in one place and suggests spacing them throughout the interview.

75.   It is interesting to note that there is little empirical evidence for suggesting which characteristics contribute to good or bad interviewing (Smith, 1981, p. 167).

76.   Smith (1981) gives a similar list in the context of structured interviews as part of a survey.

77.   In this context Stenhouse's (1982, p. 265) suggestion that the interviewer should sit side by side with the interviewee, rather than face to face, is interesting. This may make the interview less like an interrogation.

78.   Riecken (1956) discussed the dilemma for participant observers studying an apocalyptic group. Revealing themselves would mean that they could not gain entrée to the group, but passing as members would create pressures to reinforce the convictions of the group. This reinforcement would constitute a form of observer bias. This is also the situation where, in Spradley's (1979) terms, the informant cannot be interviewed. As we shall argue in Chapter 9 evaluations make covert investigation difficult to justify ethically.

79.   Simons (1977) recommends that questions should be deflected. Smith (1981, pp. 177-8) gives instances of how control is lost. Here we are not, of course, discussing the conversations that take place as a natural part of participant observation.

80.   James and Ebbutt (1981, p. 88) note that pupils often assume the teacher has the right to ask questions; in consequence they are concerned to give 'correct' answers.

81.   A point not often made, but noted by Wragg (undated).

82.   Becker (1958) gives a three stage analysis for participant observation research. Others say little more than that it depends upon the purpose (e.g. Hook, 1981).

83.   While in hospital as a patient Roth (1974) sent summaries of his field notes to colleagues outside to help him conduct a study of 'life' as a patient, and to help in the interpretation of observations. The position of the teacher is analogous - except that Roth had to pass his notes out secretly in case anyone in the hospital saw them!

84.   From another field there is the classic work of Piaget (1929) using clinical method. The introductory chapter of this, 'Problems and Methods', is useful for advice on interviewing children.

85.   Simons (1977, p. 113) talks of the problem, for an outside researcher, of maintaining a balance between being on the side of the teachers or on the

side of pupils. It is doubtful whether teachers, interviewing their own pupils, are able to switch sides at all!

86. Simons (1977, pp. 111-6) gives some very important advice for outside researchers, most of which is equally useful to teachers, and upon which we have drawn.

87. This will relate to the role the teacher adopts and also the normal classroom atmosphere. As with direct observation, the role change is easier when the normal classroom atmosphere is informal (Simons, 1977, p. 114).

88. Dalton (1964) conducted research in factories in which he worked and only carried out formal interviews with senior managers to obtain the 'official line', or to catch any slips of the tongue! (We are indebted to Martin Hammersley for bringing this, and other papers from non-educational settings, to our notice.)

89. These points on group interviews with staff are made by Simons (1980a).

90. Smith (1981, pp. 182-4), in detailing the disadvantages of survey methods, discusses these kinds of biases. Boyd & Westfall (1970) discuss interviewer bias in the survey approach, and Dean & Whyte (1958) discuss informant (respondent) bias from the ethnographic research perspective (of equal significance to survey interviewing).

91. Becker (1958) suggests this approach for dealing with suspect individual accounts and group interviews. He also gives a list of questions for testing the validity of respondent's accounts.

92. These techniques are covered by attitude measurement which we will consider in the next section on 'Curriculum Outcomes'. Oppenheim (1966) for example considers them in the same text.

93. Fraser (1981) argues for the use of the Individualised Classroom Environment Questionnaire for evaluation purposes, particularly for comparing the discrepancies between pupils' and teacher's perceptions of certain aspects of the classroom environment. However, he was only able to trace one study using such environmental measures and that at higher education level.

94. Moser and Kalton (1971, Chapter 13) consider general principles of question wording in social research surveys, and review the relevant literature. Bynner (OU, 1979, Block 4) gives an introductory account and some useful illustrations of survey questionnaires. Oppenheim (1966) is a standard text which gives advice on design, wording and response types.

95. Youngman (undated) and Hook (1981) give details and examples of these response formats, as well as advice on wording of questions.

96. The Ford Teaching Project (1975, Unit 2, Team Based Action Research) gives an example of the construction, piloting, revision and analysis of a questionnaire. The analysis included the successive cross tabulation of one question with several other questions.

97. These can be further subdivided (see Webb et al, 1966, and Bouchard, 1976). However these subdivisions do not seem appropriate to the school setting and they give little extra insight into possible uses.

98. Miller (1978) gives an extensive list of measures but many of them are more properly categories for direct observation e.g. number of situations in which teachers are smiling (telling jokes etc.).

99. Shipman (1979) gives a list of such indicators including: number of windows repaired per term; number of chairs smashed or desks defaced.

100. Bouchard (1976) emphasises this point in the inventory compiled from

various research studies, which gives the measures and the variables that are indicated by them.

101. Webb *et al* (1966) give a careful consideration to these issues in their discussion of all the types of unobtrusive measures, although their examples are not drawn from educational situations.

102. Holsti (1968, p. 598) briefly reviews the arguments.

103. Obviously if the categories can be defined clearly in advance, a pre-specified response format should be used; unless of course it is difficult to word them, or the categorisation refers to linguistic elements (e.g. vocabulary) or latent meanings (e.g. sex bias).

104. This could of course be judged in the interview itself but this depends upon the skill of the interviewer in terms of his/her 'clinical method', and upon the complexity of the pupil's thinking. For example, Perry (1970) tried to identify students' stage of development in their views of knowledge (e.g. absolute or relativistic views) from interview transcripts. He identified certain characteristic statements and trained judges to classify each student's thinking (i.e. a whole transcript) according to one of several categories. (This is an example of a qualitative use of content analysis.)

105. But see Cairns (1982) for an example of the content analysis of curriculum materials.

106. Deale (1975), who has written the best text for secondary school teachers in the UK, gives evaluation as one of his introductory examples on uses of assessment (p. 15). He also includes the evaluation of curriculum materials as a purpose (p. 20). However he only deals directly with these in three pages at the end of the book (p. 160-2), and then only four lines are devoted specifically to the assessment of a group. (Otherwise the book concentrates on the assessment of an individual.) Similarly Satterly (1981), in a more recent British book, cites evaluation as the main purpose of assessment (p. 6) but does not address it in the consideration of techniques. Allowing for the different use of the terms evaluation and assessment in the USA, Gronlund (1981) for example, talks of the use of assessment for the improvement of learning and instruction (pp. 8-9) but only refers to summative evaluation in pages 497-8.

107. Macintosh & Hale (1976) give five purposes: diagnosis, evaluation, guidance, grading, selection and prediction.

108. Considering individuals is, in the terms we have been using in this book, a central concern for assessment rather than evaluation. Shipman (1983) disagrees with this distinction, and we discuss it further, but indirectly, when we consider 'ipsative comparison'. See also the discussion of records of achievement in Chapter 4.

109. Lewy (1977) and Eggleston (1974) are among the few writers who directly address the problems of using assessment information for curriculum evaluation, although Lewy does this within the context of a curriculum project or central curriculum agency, rather than a school.

110. Satterly (1981), for example, describes criterion-referenced tests in relation to mastery learning and the objections to them that he considers are largely objections to mastery learning. Hambleton *et al* (1978) suggest that 'domain-referencing' is the correct term, but that it is not worth trying to make a change in terminology since confusion would arise.

111. Writers such as Eggleston (1974), assume that norm-referencing is not suitable for evaluation, and it is commonly thought that teachers do not want the kinds of comparisons involved in norm-referencing. However, Shipman (1979) argues that teachers do want, for example, to compare their pupils with respect to, say, national norms. Data emerging from the University of London Institute of Education study of LEA and school use of tests confirm this.

112. Like Shipman (1979) we use the distinction of internally and externally-referenced assessment. However we shall not be concerned with what he calls the 'running assessment programme' as part of our internally-referenced category. We have already argued that is concerned with the organisation of learning.

113. We use the term 'assessment procedure' to cover all kinds, from formal tests to classroom exercises that are assessed. The USA literature uses 'test' to cover the whole range of assessment, but we feel that the connotations of this word are unhelpful.

114. But see, Harlen, Darwin & Murphy (1977), for Britain, and Goodwin & Driscoll (1980), for the USA.

115. An 'objective' test is one with items which have unambiguous answers e.g. yes or no. It is the marking which is objective, not the test.

116. Ebel (1972) has a similar hierarchy starting at 'understanding of terminology' and ending with, 'ability to make an evaluative judgement'.

117. We will consider non-cognitive objectives later, but not those in the psycho-motor domain, although the latter are especially appropriate for younger children (see, for example, Goodwin & Driscoll, 1980). In the subsection on qualitative approaches we also mention an alternative typology which relates to pupil learning interactions.

118. It could be argued that in Britain, at secondary level at least, the public examination 'industry' has been responsible for a good deal of innovation in methods of assessment. Macintosh (1974) discusses a range of such innovations.

119. Even mathematics problems that allow a 'free response' suffer from low reliability (Ingenkamp, 1977).

120. The Open University uses it as part of its assessment at undergraduate level.

121. Miller (Deale, 1975; OU, 1982a, Block 4) developed a system for assessing group discussion which also helped the evaluation of this new element in the curriculum.

122. This has much in common with Harlen, Darwin & Murphy (1977) although they covered both the affective and cognitive domains.

123. The fact that teachers may not have time to construct assessment procedures carefully in order to assess individual pupils should, however, be a cause for concern.

124. Rowntree (1977, p. 185) implies that there are no such things as norm-referenced or criterion-referenced tests because the important distinction is the way that scores on tests are interpreted, not how the tests are designed. We would disagree with this interpretation, as do Hambleton *et al* (1978), but see Christie & Forrest (1981, p. 56).

125. See Choppin (1981) for a brief discussion of this view of measurement, and Christie & Forrest (1981, pp. 48-52) for a review of current thinking.

Notice also that most such discussions assume that the assessment procedure is a 'test' and that 'objective' test items are used with right and wrong answers. We follow this.

126. Classical test theory assumes that each item score is an estimate of the pupil's 'true score' (the score free from error) on the trait being measured.

127. Nuttall & Willmott (1972, pp. 19-20) show the mathematical justification for this, based on classical test theory.

128. Only limited information would be obtained by saying that a pupil has 'above average' mathematics ability for pupils in class 1B in school X - although that is what many school reports say.

129. A normal distribution is a theoretical distribution, with known mathematical properties, which approximately describes the distribution of physical properties, e.g. height and mental measurements, in the population.

130. The acceptable limits are usually: facility index, between 30 and 70 per cent; discrimination index, greater than +0.3. (The latter is a measure of correlation; negative figures indicate a negative correlation.)

131. Hambleton *et al* (1978) report that doubt is even cast upon behavioural objectives; these are more usually criticised for being too specific!

132. In this situation Rowntree's (1977) position that there are no differences between norm- and criterion-referenced tests has some justification - see Note 124. However domain (criterion)-referenced tests are more specific and have more items for each objective.

133. Sumner & Robertson (1977) review what is available in Britain.

134. Gower (Nixon, 1981) did manage some test construction but admitted that it took a lot of time. Although in the introduction to the description of his experiences he talks of using the tests to evaluate an approach to a topic, he appears to have constructed the tests as part of an approach to mastery learning.

135. We would like to acknowledge Desmond Nuttall's help with some of the ideas in this section, but as is usual we accept responsibility for any faults that may exist.

136. For multiple choice questions the distractors can be analysed to see what errors are being made. Distractors are the alternative, plausible, but incorrect answers offered. They should ideally be chosen so that pupils who make certain kinds of errors will select them; hence not only is a measurement of error given, but the reason can be hypothesised.

137. One cannot, however, be sanguine about what can be achieved by using outcome measures. Harlen (1973, p. 31), for example, developed elaborate outcome measures to help in evaluating a curriculum project's materials. She had this to say about the results: 'Satisfying though these overall test results were, they had little consequence for rewriting'. She did, however, say they gave guidance on which parts of the material were weak, although the 'reasons' required information from other sources.

138. For example, it might be assumed that the children from the lower social classes (e.g. according to the Registrar General's scale) would perform equally well in all classes. If their performance differs across classes, some further investigation could be instituted. Clearly this is not without its problems because its implications for the teaching of individual teachers could be sensitive, especially if the subgroups considered were also categorised on the basis of ethnic origin.

139. Usually percentiles give a measure of rank order and standard scores give a measure of difference from mean score. Percentiles cannot be added or computed in anyway, whereas z-scores can.

140. Assuming that there are no special steps being carried out to ensure that they are comparable.

141. Deale (1975, pp. 133-9) gives two techniques for this; one involving 'mapping scores' and another involving the combining of rank orders.

142. Deale (1975, p. 130) also places some faith in the stability of the class group and therefore the assumption that the performance of the group as a whole should be roughly similar in all subjects. However, as pointed out earlier, it is only sensible to compare subgroups within a class because all subjects are given the same mean by the standardising process (or are reduced to the same rank orders, in the case of percentiles) i.e. no subject differences exist at the group level.

143. This is because assumptions about the normal distribution of ability are more likely to be valid for a year group; only one in 400 class groups would fit this assumption (Ingenkamp, 1977, p. 28).

144. In the USA standard texts on assessment, such as TenBrink (1974), contain much the same information but without the details of particular tests. Gronlund (1981) contains this latter information. In relation to early childhood, Goodwin & Driscoll (1980) give a very detailed account of a sample of achievement tests. Nuttall (OU, 1981a) analyses a particular test battery ('Richmond Tests of Basic Skills') illustrating the kind of questions that should be asked of tests.

145. The London University Institute of Education research study of LEA and school testing reveals that many LEAs are using tests that were standardised over ten years ago. Even where recent norms exist, the LEA testing programme would provide a bigger sample size than that used by the test developers.

146. In an English county O'Donnell (1981) could only find a few schools, out of several hundred, who even mentioned curriculum evaluation as a reason for testing.

147. The test developers do not claim that their subscores represent unique abilities, although it would not have been an unreasonable assumption, and hence the test does not appear to have construct validity.

148. A combined total score can be found by assuming certain equivalence on each of the two grade scales. Below are some possibilities suggested by Shipman (1979, p. 85) and John Gray (OU, 1982, p. 12).

'O' level GCE	A	B	C	D	E	(or D	E)	U	
CSE			1	2	3		4	5	U
Total score	8	7	6	5	4		3	2	1	(Shipman)
Total score	7	6	5	4	3		2	1	0	(Gray)

(Plewis *et al* (1981, p. 41) give other possibilities.)
Shipman also suggests a positive and negative total score which is useful for teachers who are concerned to minimise failure (p. 86).

149. Alternatively they may all be restricted to a single intake band with the result that there are few other pupils in the band with whom they can be compared.

150. Nor indeed are we qualified to assess its standing in cognitive psychology.

151. This has, as far as we know, received little attention for evaluative purposes.

Codd (1981) gives a very general description of its use. Dahlgren & Marton (1978) give an example of using interviews to look at student knowledge structures in higher education, although certainly Marton has moved into a phenomenological approach. There is in fact a growing research interest in student learning in the post-school sector but there has been little application in the evaluation world. At a more practical level, James (1979) has used interviews to examine pupils' 'social understanding' in the evaluation of a social studies course, but as with Dahlgren and Marton, she did not use the clinical interview technique.

152. Oppenheim (1966, p. 105) defines an attitude as 'a tendency to act or react in a certain manner when confronted with certain stimuli'. If it does not have an enduring quality it would be impossible to measure it with any reliability.

153. Oppenheim (1966) and Thomas (undated) describe these in some detail and Lewis (1974) gives a more general account of them.

154. Wood & Napthali (1975) also recommended the behavioural representation of such assessments, which, in the non-cognitive area, they categorised into motivational and affective aspects. (There exists quite a variety of categories in this area - see also Brown, S., 1979).

155. This is suggested by Shipman (1979, p. 119). The categories are: apprenticeship to skilled employment; employment leading to recognised professional qualifications; clerical employment; other employment - with or without planned training.

156. One school with which we are familiar contacted all local employers to see if it could secure jobs for its school leavers.

157. To establish common views on individual progress would perhaps be a contradiction in terms; in any case, it would be extremely difficult. As we noted earlier (Note 108) not everyone shares this view.

158. Shipman (1979 & 1983) is one of the few authors who has addressed this from the point of view of a school, but then only in the most general terms.

159. Weston (1979, p. 225) notes that curriculum discussion is important to broaden teachers' outlook on curriculum issues and as a valuable form of in-service training.

160. Schools were given a 'Supplementary to Curriculum 11-16' which elaborated each of the eight areas in a few lines.

161. The second instrument (S2) was not reproduced in the report (Cheshire Education Committee, 1981) and so we are unable to comment on its format.

162. The lists of objectives produced by subject departments were used similarly, as the extract on 'concept objectives' indicates.

163. The North West Educational Management Centre study (1981) characterised this by saying that the analysis of subjects helps departments to articulate and justify intentions as well as reminding them of intentions lost in content.

164. The importance of increasing awareness of their colleagues' work was also an important aim for teachers involved in a school initiated curriculum review in which a team made up of members from a variety of faculties reviewed the work of a particular faculty (OU, 1982, Case Study 2).

165. It is a measure of the extent to which this model dominated the outcomes

that Wrigley (1981), a teacher involved in the exercise, only hoped that the review would yield something worthwhile in that it would protect the curriculum base in the current, stringent financial climate.

166. A similar conclusion is drawn by O'Hare (1981) from a survey of Lancashire schools involved in discussing curriculum guidelines.

167. In Chapter 3 we noted Lawton's (1980) reservation about the model of planning being perpetuated by the HMI, but the evidence from the review exercises does not show that it is being taken up in this way, i.e. planning based on aims and objectives is not a dominant activity.

168. In effect this is what the schools in the HMI-LEA review did when they accepted the eight areas without question.

169. In part because they do not insist that objectives should be behavioural, i.e. specified in terms of pupil outcome behaviours.

170. MacDonald-Ross (1973) also considers a number of other issues, including the use of behavioural objectives in designing instructional programmes. However, as an approach this fares not better in the scrutiny he employs. There are other more philosophical critiques which say that planning by objectives is based upon a misconception about the nature of planning (see Sockett in OU, 1976, Units 16-18).

171. Chapter 3 presented Reid's view that approaches involving aims and objectives, as a first step, try to adopt procedural solutions that are inappropriate for curriculum problems.

172. There is a difference of opinion over whether or not opposing ideological views can be reconciled. In Chapter 3 we gave Darling's (1978) view that doubted it, but Lawton (1973, p. 30) claims that a balanced curriculum can be derived from competing views. Many writers who take the consensus view have not attempted to analyse the conflicting stances for their incompatibilities; they have simply assumed that they can be reconciled. Whitty (1981) has argued that the consensus approach taken by Lawton obscures the nature of the curriculum issues he seeks to address.

173. Here we have to express some scepticism about the role of the teacher portrayed in Skilbeck's vision of school-based curriculum development (OU, 1976, Units 24-26, pp. 90-102), although, at the time it was first written (1975), the climate of the late 1970s and 1980s could not perhaps have been foreseen. The small study by Taylor, P. *et al* (1974) in the early 1970s showed grounds for pessimism.

174. Weston (1979, p. 259) saw this as important even in the limited context of innovation across subject boundaries within a science department. Reynolds and Skilbeck (1976) saw participation in curriculum planning as a means of clarifying a teacher's own value position.

175. This is the stance taken by Horton when he explores four curriculum models: liberal, dual, community and learner-chosen (OU, 1983b, Unit 7). These, he admits, should be treated as orientations, a greater awareness of which should expand the available options in curriculum planning. This of course opens up the whole area of curriculum studies literature, to which we could not possibly do justice, and therefore have not addressed.

176. We would hope that senior staff see it as an important part of their responsibilities to become familiar with some of the literature in this area.

177. Walker also considered what the subjects of the data were (i.e. internal -

e.g. staff members, curriculum materials; external - e.g. students, schools, society), but these are context specific and would be different if the discussions were conducted by teachers in a school. However, the internal - external division is useful.

178. Hegarty (1977) suggests a nominal group technique which could be considered as a suitable formalisation procedure. It is intended to prevent the tendency to jump to solutions before elaborating the problem. A group meets and each member individually lists problems relating to an issue. These are pooled on a flip chart and the group votes on the five most important. Discussion further clarifies the pooled list, with the voting figures shown and a second vote is taken. The ten most important problems are then selected for practical consideration.

179. It may be that a primary school, with a small number of staff who form a cohesive group, could resemble the curriculum project group more closely than the large secondary school that Weston studied.

180. Although the report of the research is long, almost 300 pages, there are identifiable sections where she discusses the main principles: Negotiation and the curriculum, pp. 40-4; Chapter 11, pp. 189-98; Characterising the work of the committee, pp. 217-226; Reflections, pp. 257-60; Chapter 16, pp. 264-71.

181. This is a term she takes from Vickers (1965).

182. We realise we may be accused of assuming a link between professional development and change, an issue explored in Chapter 2 that we have tried to keep open. Nevertheless we feel it is possible to argue that if teachers are unaware of the issues underlying the curriculum choices they make, then they will not be able to make these choices wisely. Also this educative function could be seen as a first stage. In any case, we have argued that curriculum problems and decisions regarding their solution must be central, thus a concern for the mechanisms of deliberation and negotiation can only help.

183. A caricature, of course!

183. Although we have discussed two techniques (the Delphi and nominal group techniques), we are aware of being selective in our discussion of the evaluation of curriculum intentions. In particular we have ignored techniques associated with timetabling. For example, Zarraga & Bates (1980) describe a computer feasibility study of various ways of implementing a particular curriculum philosophy. This is based upon Davies's (1969) ideas, and does not address fundamental curriculum issues; rather it is the 'final link in the curriculum planning chain' (Zarraga & Bates, 1980, p. 115). In contrast Wilcox & Eustace (1980) argue that their notation for describing the curriculum allows review to take place. The notation generates indices from which ability grouping and curriculum differentiation and emphasis can be described. The curriculum can then be reviewed against criteria concerning such things as 'balance' and the 'common core'. They recognise that this has limitations, for example, the notation is not concerned with what lies beneath the subject label.

185. Examples of analysis of published curriculum materials can also be obtained from Dr. Michael Eraut, Education Area, University of Sussex. Lewy (1977) gives two examples of schemes. One is for social studies and considers: pictorial sources, key terms and concepts, adequacy of data, accuracy

of facts, ethnic bias, levels and types of thinking, values and conflict, the way different abilities are catered for. The other resembles Tyler & Klein's (1976) framework. Hull & Adams (1981, p. 94-6) present detailed questions for science materials, exploring the way the style of the material relates to the aims and content of the course, the use of materials, and their suitability for pupils.

186. Fraser (1977) presents an approach to such an analysis which involves categorising aims and working out indices of frequency, although not within the context of analysing curriculum materials.

187. See the discussion earlier in the chapter on content analysis ('The Observed Curriculum').

188. This is an extensive area covering the analysis of rhetoric and other presentational devices. Anderson (1981) applies some of these ideas to the analysis of curriculum proposals, in particular those issued by various curriculum projects. For those interested in following up the general literature in this area see OU (1974a).

189. This has an extensive literature and useful references include: OU (1974b, Units 1-4); Gilliland (1972); Klare (1978); Moyle (1978); Harrison (1980).

190. This approach has been used in an evaluation of an Open University course (P970 'Governing Schools') in which the curriculum designers' intentions are explicit because they carry the main 'learning messages'. See Somekh (1980) and OU (1981, Block 5, Appendix 4) for evaluations which combine analysis of curriculum materials and classroom observation methods.

191. It does not appear that Eraut, Goad and Smith (1975) were influenced at all by Walker's work; they arrived at their formulation independently. It must also be recognised that we have laid stress on certain aspects of the analysis of materials which emphasise the similarities with deliberation.

192. See Clift's (OU, 1982, Block 2, Part 1, p. 47) classification of the questions etc. in 'Keeping the School Under Review' (ILEA, 1977).

193. Rutter *et al* (1979) found that this did not distinguish schools' outcome measures!

194. It may be that we make what appear to be arbitrary decisions in both these regards, but our purpose is only to illustrate the range of aspects covered.

195. In contrast to those under 'school climate', the aspects here are physical.

196. Many questions or items in the checklist are likely to contribute to 'climate', for example 'rewards and punishments' (ILEA, 1977), but only NCA (1980a) refers explicitly to this.

197. ILEA (1977) includes this under 'departmental self-assessment'.

198. ILEA (1977) includes an indication of 'free lunches', which could be taken as an indicator of social class.

199. NCA (1980a) indicates these indirectly through school climate. ILEA (1977) implies relationships under 'Pupil' aspects.

200. On the basis of what was found to be significantly (in statistical terms) correlated with outcome measures - behaviour, delinquency, academic attainment and attendance. The list is presented under their headings, not those drawn from checklists.

201. 'Physical and administrative features' included age of buildings, number of sites and internal organisation (pastoral and academic). Ecological in-

fluences refer to aspects external to the school: catchment area, balance of intake and parental choice. Both of these sets were also investigated to see whether they related to an overall school process measure, which, in the case of ecological features, discounted any direct effect of these variables on individuals. In other words, although intake ability affects individual outcomes, Rutter and his colleagues, in this part of the study, were concerned only with a group effect of, for example, a high proportion of low ability children in a school.

202. The controversy over the Rutter study (Note 4 Chapter 6) means that the form established through their six areas of internal school processes must be treated with some caution.

203. A point one of us has made elsewhere (James and Ebbutt, 1981, p. 92). It could, of course, be argued that when considering the evaluation of teaching and learning (curriculum intentions, transactions and outcomes) attention to theory is equally important. However, we have delayed the discussion of this until Chapter 11.

204. Following similar thinking, Lambert, Bullock & Millham (1973, p. 312), state that organisational analysis is useful because 'objective findings are more likely to result from a valid theoretical framework than from value-free research workers'. Unfortunately they do not elaborate the point.

205. For a review of the literature on schools as organisations see Brian Davies (1981). We feel obliged, however, to warn readers unfamiliar with the literature of sociology and systems analysis that this article is hard going! For summaries of organisational theory in general see Pugh, Hickson & Hinnings (1971), and Silverman (1970).

206. Brian Davies (1981, pp. 51-4) identifies three strands, the first stemming from educational administration, and the second and third from sociology ('single institutional study' and 'streaming'). He acknowledges that all three overlap and this appears to be true of many theories of organisations; for this reason we often adopt the word 'approach' rather than 'theory'.

207. Cohen & Manion (1981) also describe a Professional Model which recognises collegial organisations with decisions being made at the appropriate level so that, for example, teacher autonomy in the classroom is not affected. This still, however, leaves the problem of the legal authority of the headteacher.

208. For example, they maintain steady states and they are self-regulating.

209. Davies goes on to argue that there is so little agreement on the goals of schools that it is impossible to distinguish the two.

210. This description of socio-technical systems, with additions, is taken from Silverman (1970, p. 109) and not from Richardson's account. Although there are similarities Richardson draws explicitly on a range of theories.

211. The sentient system or group, a concept used by Richardson (1973, e.g. pp. 22-3), is the group from which individuals within an organisation draw their emotional strength to do their 'job'. A person may belong to more than one sentient group, which are not necessarily related to the task, and can exist outside the school boundary. Richardson gives the example of a teacher who is a member of a subject association.

212. These are taken from Richardson (1973, pp. 21-2).

213. Not surprisingly the socio-technical systems approach has not given rise to methods of evaluation!

214. This kind of review was employed in, for example: Sir Frank Markham School (see Chapter 5) and Ernulf Community School (James, 1982, pp. 47-8).

215. Other measures exist for decision-making, hierarchies, and control - see Cohen (1976) pp. 284-7, 295-8 and 299-303, respectively. Most of the methods for evaluation, stemming from the management tradition, are prescriptive. So, for example, a favourable school climate, or a more sensible decision-making strategy will be defined.

216. Lambert *et al* (1973) describe four ways of relating the informal to the formal system: supportive of the formal, manipulative of it, passive towards it, and rejecting it.

217. It may be worth distinguishing the idea of the informal system from that of the hidden curriculum. The latter is the learning and experience which result from both the formal and informal systems. For example, the formal system may require pupils to stand when a teacher enters a classroom; the informal 'gang' (system) may require compliance to its norms. Both leave impressions and, for example, affect the self-concept of the pupil. In addition the hidden curriculum usually refers to the pupils' curriculum, although, as Hargreaves (undated) notes, the teachers' hidden curriculum is at least as important. Hargreaves gives a very accessible account of the literature on which he prefers to call the 'paracurriculum'.

218. And we are quite aware of how selective we have been on this account.

219. The idea that some familiarity with extant theories may help teachers to 'render the familiar strange' will be developed in Chapter 9.

220. NSSE (1978) lists the following data to be collected for the study body: ethnic composition, scholastic aptitude, interests, talents, handicaps, perceptions of educational needs and intentions, and occupational needs and opportunities. ILEA (1977) suggests that secondary schools should collect details of leavers' jobs and further education. The latter may of course be considered purely as outcome measures.

221. Social reproduction and correspondence theorists maintain that education is a form of social control designed to reproduce and legitimate the existing social order. Bowles and Gintis (1976), perhaps the best known theorists of this genre, posit a one-to-one correspondence between schooling and work that ensures the maintenance of the social relations of production in capitalist society. A similar kind of analysis also informs a study by Willis (1977).

222. See however Hammersley's (1980) review of classroom ethnography which attempts to show that links do exist between models of the classroom and macro issues.

223. This is not to suggest that only these areas of inquiry call for such an analysis; they are simply examples where effort has been concentrated.

224. James and Ebbutt (1981, p. 83) note that in one of their studies 'early thoughts in terms of an explanation [of why girls are 'turned off' by physical science] would have involved writing a sociology of the entire locality'.

9   Issues

Introduction

The review of specific techniques (Chapter 8) was organised partly on
the basis of substantive aspects of the curriculum that may be evaluated
(e.g. context, intentions, outcomes), and partly on the basis of distinctions among techniques. In relation to the latter, a major distinction
was drawn between research techniques (either quantitative or
qualitative) that contribute to empirical evaluation, and deliberative
techniques that contribute to intrinsic evaluation. By now it should be
obvious that whatever techniques, or combination of techniques, are
employed in a specific evaluation, and whatever its substantive focus, a
number of practical, ethical and organisational problems arise that
demand attention.

In this chapter, therefore, the discussion centres on the practical,
rather than theoretical, problems faced by those wishing to implement
evaluation procedures. In particular we consider the difficulties that
may be encountered by 'insiders', notably teachers. For this reason the
problems of outsiders (e.g. test constructors and inspectors) are not
examined in any detail although this does not deny either their role in
evaluation, or the practical issues associated with it.

Throughout this book we have also been concerned to distinguish
'curriculum evaluation in schools' from 'programme evaluation', although we have acknowledged certain links and the derivation of a
number of important ideas. As the two labels imply, a chief distinction
between the two kinds of evaluative activity concerns differences in the
systems to which they relate. Unlike programme evaluation which is
concerned with a 'temporary system' (e.g. a project), curriculum
evaluation in schools involves a 'permanent system' (i.e. a school)[1].
Inevitably, therefore, the latter is constrained by existing structures,
relationships, and procedures in a way that programme evaluation rarely
is. For instance evaluation in schools (1) involves non-professional
evaluators, who (2) have a vested interest in, or commitment to, the

system or practices they are concerned to evaluate, and who (3) have an existing and continuing role in relation to others within that system, be it the total institution, a department or classroom. Consequently, many of the issues that arise are concerned with organisation, including the management of time, and in-service education and training designed to encourage the acquisition of evaluative skills. Equally important, however, are questions concerning ethics and issues of role ambiguity. In the following discussion we will deal with the role issue first.

Roles

Unlike most professional evaluators, or people engaged in conventional educational research, teacher-evaluators are 'true participants' in the processes they are interested in evaluating[2]. In some measure this observation also applies to others who might be involved in conducting in-school evaluation: governors, advisers, parents and pupils, for instance. As with teachers, each of these groups has an existing role in relation to the social system of the school, so none can claim to be solely an observer.

The literature on participant-observation, and related areas of field research, is extensive (see, for example, Webb *et al*, 1966; McCall and Simmons, 1969; Schatzman and Strauss, 1973; and Burgess, 1982), and many of the problems likely to be encountered by participant-evaluators are discussed there. For this reason, a number of strategies designed to overcome the most obvious difficulties may be extrapolated from this same literature. Perhaps this is best illustrated by an example. One of the most frequently cited dangers of social-anthropological research is the danger of 'going native'; in other words, researchers are prone to become so involved in the processes which they are observing that the research task becomes impossible. In relation to teacher-conducted research or evaluation some degree of involvement must, of course, be assumed, so the question is not 'How can going native be prevented?', but 'How can teachers detach themselves sufficiently to criticise what they have hitherto taken-for-granted?' Since schools provide teachers with employment and therefore compel a degree of loyalty and commitment, this detachment needs to be emotional as well as intellectual. In sociological jargon the task is articulated as a need to 'make the familiar strange'.

As we mentioned briefly in Chapter 8, Delamont (1981) proposes four strategies for making the familiar seem novel. She advises those who study classrooms to:

1. study unusual, bizarre or 'different' classrooms;
2. study schools in other cultures;
3. study non-educational settings that have a bearing on life in schools e.g. hospitals, factories, street-corner societies, prisons!
4. make the familiar problematic by self-conscious strategies, such as focusing on a taken-for-granted feature of the setting e.g. gender differences.

Clearly, some of these strategies are beyond the scope of many in-school evaluators because it is unlikely that they will have the opportunity to spend time in schools, classrooms or cultures markedly different from their own. Neither are they likely to be able to spend a lot of time reading the sociological literature of hospitals, prisons and street-corner societies before embarking on the evaluative task that confronts them. Realistically, Delamont's fourth option appears to offer the best hope for the insider, and indeed there have been cases where Delamont's suggested focus on gender differences has been employed in teacher self-evaluation (see Ebbutt, 1976, and James and Ebbutt, 1981[3]).

Delamont's other strategies for rendering the familiar strange do, however, suggest a methodological role for external reference groups. For example, educational advisers and inspectors, professional researchers and 'visitors' from other cultures or spheres of life could be invited to share their experience of different classrooms, schools, cultures or settings, in order to raise teachers' awareness of taken-for-granted assumptions, or to introduce theoretical constructs relevant to the area of study. On the one hand they would be assuming the role of 'consultants'; on the other they would be acting as 'critical friends'. (It will be recalled that the role of outsiders in insider evaluation was discussed towards the end of Chapter 5.)

One particularly important function that the 'critical friend' could fulfil would involve the validation of studies conducted by 'true' participants. An example is furnished by the Ford Teaching Project (Elliott, 1976), which aimed to foster teachers' self-monitoring ability. In order to assist teachers in recognising performance gaps, and such like, the central project team established a role for itself in 'triangulating' the perceptions of teachers, pupils and themselves, as observers (see also Chapter 7)[4]. This version of triangulation involved the full-time researchers in a considerable amount of data-gathering, which itself can provide a further role for outsiders in making the familiar strange.

The suggestion is that the perceptions of 'true' participants are likely to be reinforced because they simply cannot get at a certain kind of information. In the context of schools, it is sometimes the case that outsiders will be given access to information that pupils hesitate to tell teachers for fear of sanctions.

The last point is a useful reminder that although we have talked of teachers as participants in the processes they seek to evaluate, they are not of course 'true' participants in every sense. They are excluded from pupil sub-cultures and they may be kept deliberately ignorant (by pupils) of certain interactions within their own classrooms. Even other adults may be unable to elicit certain pupil perspectives. If this kind of information gap is a particular problem then one potential solution is to involve children as data-gatherers. In Chapter 8 we referred briefly to Pollard's (1982b) strategy for involving middle school children in data collection[5] . He describes this approach fully in the following passage.

I began to identify children whom I judged to be amenable to participation in the study, who reflected the range of types of friendship group existing, and who were fairly popular within those groups. In this I was assisted by sociometric data when it became available. In September 1977 these children were invited to form a dinner-time interviewing team to help me, as I put it, 'find out what all the children think about school'. This group very quickly coined the name 'The Moorside Investigation Department' (MID) for themselves and generated a sense of self-importance. Over the next year the membership of MID changed gradually but I always attempted to balance it by having members of a range of groups. Normally about six children were involved at any one time and the total number of children involved during the year was thirteen. This small group were very interested. In particular they seemed to enjoy being 'investigators' which fitted into a theme of the child culture then existing; they enjoyed using the recording equipment which they did not normally have access to; they enjoyed being in the role of interviewer and questioning other children and they seemed to enjoy the fact that they were working *with* an adult. Of course my intention in setting up a *child* interviewing team was to break through the anticipated reticence of children towards me as a teacher. I firstly spent a lot of time with the MID members discussing the types of things I was interested in and establishing the idea of immunity to teacher-prosecution and of confidentiality. We then

began a procedure of inviting groups of children - in twos, threes
or fours to give confidence - to be interviewed by a MID member
in a building which was unused at dinner-times. Sometimes the
interviewers would interview their own friends, sometimes they
would interview children whom they did not know well. Initially,
I did not try to control this but left it very much to the children.
Interviews were recorded onto cassettes which I analysed each
evening.   (Pollard, 1982b, pp. 12-13)

Most of the preceding discussion has focused on the *difficulties* of
the participant role of insider evaluators. It is as well to remember,
therefore, that there are a number of things in its favour. First, unlike
the outsider, the in-school evaluator has no difficulty in gaining entry
to the setting under study. Whilst teachers may not be privy to all in-
school interactions, they already have access to the school, both physi-
cally and phenomenologically. This has obvious advantages, not the
least of which is an accumulation of 'tacit knowledge' (Polanyi, 1958)
acquired through direct experience and participation in social processes[6].
For example, in the context of evaluation an awareness of what it is
like to teach endows teachers with a kind of understanding that outsiders may not be able to achieve vicariously i.e. without going through
the process themselves. It is crucial, however, to ensure that 'tacit
knowledge' is used to enhance, rather than prejudice, an evaluation.
(This is the issue of bias discussed in Chapter 7.)

A second potential advantage of the participant role in evaluation is
associated with motivation. In most cases insiders have a clear interest
in contributing something to the system that provides them with a
living, and to which they have a professional responsibility. Thus their
examination of practice is unlikely to be merely destructive; if shortcomings are revealed a natural response would be to seek remedies[7].

Thirdly, sustained contact with the school, its personnel and its
processes enables participant evaluators to take advantage of spontaneous events and situations because they are 'on the spot'. Like many of
the issues raised in this section, the issue of opportunistic research as an
investigative strategy has been discussed in the social science literature.
For instance, Reimer (1977) proposes various strategies of opportunistic
research that exploit the researcher's unique biography, life experiences,
and situational familiarity[8]. In support of the general concept, he
adumbrates a number of advantages, most of which we have considered
already since they are characteristic of much 'true' participant observation. Similarly the most obvious disadvantages of opportunistic research

apply equally to insider investigations. In particular Reimer points to the dangers of over-involvement, the difficulty of replication, the expense of the enterprise, in terms of time and effort, and the problems of selective perception and data-saturation (mentioned also by Roth, 1974). Interestingly, Reimer does not raise any of the ethical issues associated with opportunistic research, which by its nature may remain 'covert' unless there is a deliberate effort to 'go public'.

The question of whether research should be covert or overt is another familiar issue in the literature of participant-observation, and opinion surrounding it seems to be divided[9]. Homan (1980), for example, justified his secrecy in studying a Pentecostal group by arguing that open entry would have caused more disruption. In a critical rejoinder Bulmer (1980) argues that covert research of this kind is indefensible since it constitutes a betrayal of trust and an invasion of personal privacy. Nevertheless Bulmer does not eschew covert methods altogether; he merely counsels caution. In contrast, some researchers (e.g. Whyte, 1955, and Polsky, 1969) argue that research activities should always be public. If they are not, researchers are in danger of finding themselves in situations which force them to act in ways that they may later regret. Whyte and Polsky were both involved in the study of deviance but their warnings have relevance to other fields, including educational evaluation[10].

Ethics in Evaluation

The debate about covert versus overt techniques illustrates the pervasiveness of ethical issues in all forms of social and educational research, and especially in evaluation. In relation to the latter, the central issue concerns the need to decide whether, in any given situation, priority ought to be given to the public's 'right to know' over and against the individual's 'right to privacy'[11]. (The 'public' here refers to any group with a legitimate interest in what happens in schools, which are, after all, public institutions.) It would, however, be misleading to suggest that decisions of this nature are always a result of moral reasoning. Such a decision is likely to be as much 'culture-bound' as it is a rational choice of the greater good. The USA, for example, has a rather longer history of allowing prompt public scrutiny of official decisions, than has Britain. (Whereas the USA has Freedom of Information Acts, Britain still has 'D' notices and a 30 year embargo on public access to Cabinet proceedings.) Things change, of course, and in relation to school evaluation, the implementation of the 1980 Education Act in England and Wales, which required schools to reveal both their pupils' examination results and their own curricular arrangements, brought practice in the UK somewhat closer to that of the USA.

Historical and cultural traditions aside, the issue that confronts curriculum evaluators in schools is still one of the most fundamental and universal of moral dilemmas. In practical terms it usually involves deciding how to fulfil a responsibility to those private individuals from whom information has been sought, with a similar responsibility to provide 'an information service to the community' (MacDonald, 1977a). To imagine that an evaluation can be conducted in a way that avoids hurting either individuals or groups is probably unrealistic. And this is likely to be true whether or not the evaluation is explicitly judgemental (see Chapter 7). Simply making certain kinds of information public is almost guaranteed to show some individuals in an unfavourable light, so those engaged in evaluation need to be convinced that potential gain outweighs present suffering. According to Becker (1970a) a major problem in the publication of field studies is: 'Since one cannot achieve consensus with all factions simultaneously, the problem is not to avoid harming people but rather to decide which people to harm' (p.111). To a large extent Becker's caution applies to evaluation especially if, as Stenhouse (1982) maintained, evaluation 'always involves case study, and [. . .] it is characteristic of evaluation as opposed to research that the case in point - be it policy, programme, institution or individual - be identified (not anonymised)' (p. 263). (The ethical issues specifically associated with reporting are taken up again in Chapter 10.)

Even evaluators who assume a 'democratic' stance (see MacDonald, 1977a, and Chapter 7) and who aspire to act as 'brokers' in exchanges of information between groups, must be aware that certain kinds of information will disadvantage some individuals (usually the least powerful). Becker (1970b) uses the notion of a 'hierarchy of credibility' to elucidate a common experience:

> In any system of ranked groups, participants take it as given that members of the highest group have the right to define the way things really are. In any organisation, no matter what the rest of the organisation chart shows, the arrows indicating the flow of information point up, thus demonstrating (at least formally) that those at the top have access to a more complete picture of what is going on than anyone else [. . .] Thus, credibility and the right to be heard are differentially distributed through the ranks of the system. (pp. 126-7)

Since schools are organisations too, any evaluation which does not intend merely to reinforce the dominant hegemony (as many 'bureaucratic' evaluations seem to do) needs to be conducted with a good deal of sensitivity and discretion. According to Stenhouse (1982): 'Studies which open the process in a particular school to scrutiny do not merely put personal relations at risk: they shift the balance of power' (p. 267)[12],[13].

If this is so, as we believe it is, then among the critical issues that evaluators need to address are a number identified by MacDonald and Walker (1977) in connection with educational case study. (Their reference to the 'researcher' can equally well apply to an evaluator.) Thus:

> To whose needs and interests does the research respond?
> Who owns the data (the researcher, the subject, the sponsor)?
> Who has access to the data? (Who is excluded or denied?)
> What is the status of the researcher's interpretation of events, *vis-a-vis* the interpretations made by others? (Who decides who tells the truth?)
> What obligations does the researcher owe to his subjects, his sponsors, his fellow professionals, others?
> Who is the research for?
>
> (p. 185).

In his description of 'democratic' evaluation (referred to in Chapter 5), MacDonald (1977a) identified 'confidentiality', 'negotiation' and 'accessibility' as its key concepts. It follows then that these should be the principles that guide the evaluator's responses to the questions set out in the previous paragraph. Indeed, Simons (1979) attempts to translate these principles into procedures for the conduct of school self-evaluation by teachers. We do not have space here to reproduce all of Simons' suggestions but an example may suffice to illustrate how procedures can be derived from ethical principles.

Confidentiality/Control
1. Conversations are confidential to the individual person; knowledge within the school is subject to release by them.
2. The evaluator will not report anything or examine documents relevant to a particular person without his/her consent.
3. Interviews, discussions, staff meetings, committee meetings, written statements are all potential data for the evaluation.

But individuals have the right to restrict parts of the exchange or to correct or improve their statements.

4. Contributors to the evaluation have control over to whom it is released.
5. Reports should aspire to be issue not person-oriented.
6. Pseudonyms or role designation should be used in reporting if attributing quotations to people. While this does not offer anonymity it depersonalises issues that may be critical to discuss and which, if contentious, might become 'too personal'.
7. Clearance need not be sought for information summarising findings or reporting general perspectives on issues which involve no specific details about persons or groups.
8. Where details are included which do identify the person or source clearance is necessary. (Simons, 1979, p. 15)[14]

Similar sets of procedures can be found elsewhere in the evaluation literature and these too can form a basis for curriculum evaluation in schools. Kemmis and Robottom (1981), for instance, offer a detailed list of procedures relating to an extended list of 'democratic' principles, including: independence, disinterest, negotiated access, negotiation of boundaries, negotiation of accounts, negotiation of release, publication rights, confidentiality, accountability, and agreement to the principles of procedure themselves!

Since there are still comparatively few accounts of in-school evaluations it is hardly surprising that descriptions of ethical procedures in practice are difficult to find. Some evidence is provided by a number of case studies drawn on by the Open University (1982, Block 2, Part 2). These include a departmental self-study in which ethical procedures were adapted from Simons (1979); a primary school self-evaluation in which the teachers' centre warden, who acted as facilitator, insisted on confidentiality, the negotiation of whole school commitment, and the maintenance of neutrality in his own involvement; and an account of the operation of curriculum review groups at Stantonbury Campus, where the headteacher gave control of the evaluative process to teachers who were free to negotiate their own conditions and procedures[15].

It is significant perhaps that most procedures for ensuring the protection of participants in school evaluation, seem to pay particular attention to safeguarding the privacy of teachers. One assumes that the same consideration is extended to pupils, although problems of negotiating access, clearance and release of data from very young children has, to our knowledge, never been adequately addressed - at least in the UK[16].

However, in discussing the ethical dimensions of conducting research in her own tutorial group of eleven and twelve year olds, Sadler (1980) recognises the problems associated with gathering information from children who never questioned her *right* to record what went on in her classroom. Parents, too, accepted her authority *as a classteacher* and although one mother expressed the feeling that she had a 'bloody nerve' to administer attitude surveys, none took any action to prevent her from doing so. Clearly here, as elsewhere, it is within the power of the teacher to use authority to disguise accountability, unless some deliberate effort is made to raise pupils' and parents' awareness of their right to withhold certain kinds of personal information, if this is their wish.

Several other ethical issues are worthy of mention here although we do not have the space to discuss them fully. First, although we have been careful to exclude the evaluation of teacher competence from our consideration of curriculum evaluation in schools, it needs to be acknowledged that the 'portrayal of persons' is a potentially fruitful source of evaluation data. For instance, in a given context there may be strong evidence to suggest that the success, or otherwise, of a particular programme depends on the individual qualities of a change agent. Therefore these personal characteristics demand to be understood. Now, while no-one is likely to take exception to a biographical study that reflects glory on a particular individual; if it proves less than flattering then the implications of making it public need to be considered carefully. This issue is particularly important in that, as MacDonald (1977b) points out, there are always social consequences for the subjects of evaluation portrayals.

MacDonald's (1977b) paper is an interesting discussion of this issue; the more so because he admits some unease whilst generally defending the importance of this kind of data. On the one hand he believes that a focus on personalities and their influence on events is justified in that the personal dimension is never ignored by the decision-maker if information about it is available; on the other hand he realises that portrayals created in this spirit (i.e. to inform decision-making about educational programmes) may not always be received in the same way. Once more the need to protect those without the power to protect themselves becomes an issue. (McAllister (1984), a barrister, gives a useful account of the implications of the English Law of Defamation and Privilege for the work of the evaluator.)

Another moral dilemma, which in-school evaluators are likely to encounter, concerns the use of information that the evaluation was not expected to reveal. 'Off the record' information about unprofessional conduct or illegal activity might fall into this category. For example, the children in Pollard's (1982b) study told him about 'nicking' sweets and the theft of a five pound note from a local shop. He interpreted this as a test of the credibility of his promises of confidentiality. In the event he chose to do nothing about it, although he felt uneasy about seeming to condone the activity. In many ways the dilemma for the evaluator is little different from that experienced by the priest in the confessional or the journalist, and like these two the best course of action is probably to do nothing to betray any confidence that has been established. However, unlike the journalist, if not the priest, the urge to intervene is almost second nature to the teacher, and to resist it seems tantamount to a dereliction of duty. Indeed, if pupils test the credibility of the teacher's 'evaluator role' in this way, and (s)he does not act, then the 'teacher role' might be undermined at a later date. Once more the roles of teacher and evaluator appear to pull in opposite directions.

The Acquisition of Skills

If the above discussion of ethical issues suggests that in-school evaluators need some of the skills of the moral philosopher, then this cannot be denied. Moreover, the review of specific techniques in Chapter 8 implies that they need to acquire various skills associated with deliberation and research. And all this is over and above those skills needed to perform their existing professional duties! The task seems daunting although some consolation is offered by the fact that many of these problems are faced by most tyro researchers.

One constructive way to view the task is to recognise that teachers, and others who work within the education system, already have skills which can serve as the basis for developing further expertise. For instance, teachers customarily employ the forms of problem-solving that Becher *et al* (1981) describe as 'spotting' and 'scanning'[17], and it is a small step to make these activities more self-conscious, systematic and accurate. Like the skills of observation, those of deliberation could be acquired by building on existing practice, since most school staffs have some experience of discussion of curricular issues (a point made in Chapter 8).

This incremental approach to the acquisition of evaluative skills receives support from MacDonald (1978) who suggests that 'the road to educational critique' may pass through several stages (from informal to formal) and take several years to travel. He proposes three phases in the development of a rigorous approach to school evaluation: *a descriptive phase*, which involves the collection of routine information; *an anecdotal phase* which represents a move to teachers' accounts of their own performance and the collection of critical incidents; and *the phase of formal educational critique*, which entails formalised procedures of research and deliberation. In some respect these phases are reflected in Walker's (1975) account of the deliberative process in a curriculum project (see also Chapter 8).

Much of the evidence available to us suggests that teachers do indeed lack confidence in implementing formal research techniques. For example, teachers at Wakeland Junior School, Stantonbury Campus, and an Oxfordshire Primary School (reported in OU, 1982, Block 2, Parts 1 and 2 and Case Studies 1 and 2) seemed to 'fight shy' of direct observation, preferring to dwell on prolonged discussions of the intended curriculum. The group at Melbourn School (Farnell, 1981, quoted in Chapter 5) was also unprepared for the kind of classroom action-research methods proposed by its consultants. However, a lack of research skills may not be the only cause of anxiety. Turning the full beam of the searchlight on to curriculum practice carries with it an element of threat because it has the potential to reveal some things that teachers and schools would rather not know. If teachers are aware of this, they may be tempted not to get involved. Nevertheless, there are a number of examples of schools that have managed to overcome most of the obvious disincentives. For instance, the curriculum review at Sir Frank Markham School (see Chapter 5) demonstrates that teachers are quite capable of achieving a considerable level of sophistication in the use of research methods, in a very short time, and without any obvious external support.

If we accept that the acquisition of evaluative skills is within the grasp of teachers, but that the process needs to be incremental, then proposals for a staged approach, like MacDonald's, are appropriate. A first stage might be for teachers to view themselves as sources of data, since they carry with them the accumulated baggage of practical experience. However, in drawing on this experience they need to be encouraged to be more self-conscious (and self-critical) in giving accounts of their practice. In Chapter 8 we outlined Walker's (1975) notion of deliberative 'moves' and his discussion of the nature of argument. We noted there that his suggestions for the treatment of observational versus judgemental data, internal versus external data, and first-hand versus reported data, could assist teachers in evaluating the status of their routine discussions of curriculum matters.

Once a greater degree of self-reflection is achieved in this context, then we might expect teachers to realise that in some circumstances there will be a need for more data of an observational, external and first-hand kind. Thus it would be a quite natural second step to collect, analyse and interpret data using various observational research techniques, and thence to 'theorise' about specific situations. Eventually, teacher evaluators should have sufficient confidence to take account of formal theory and assess its potential to illuminate the social processes they discover in their own schools[18]. In Hoyle's (1980) terms the teacher-evaluator would then have become an 'extended professional' (see Chapter 2).

The suggestion that the development of formal research methods might constitute a fairly late stage in the acquisition of skills is not intended to imply that research is necessarily 'higher order' than deliberation. On the contrary, even when research data have been fully analysed, the act of judgement and the development of proposals for future action requires further deliberation. Thus, as Walker (1975) points out in his critique of classical models for curriculum design, deliberation does not precede research and development but is inseparable from it.

Issues of Time

This optimism about teachers' capacity to develop evaluative skills is all very well, one may argue, but when are people who already have full-time jobs going to find the time to engage in something that is rarely regarded as having the same priority as lesson preparation or pupil assessment? Formal curriculum evaluation is surely a long way from being perceived as crucial to effective practice; indeed it is still a marginal activity.

Whatever the prevailing professional attitudes, the constraints imposed simply by lack of time are sufficient to constitute a serious obstacle. Thus, with respect to data collection and analysis, there is a tendency to rely almost wholly on incidental or indirect observation (Pollard, 1982b, Walker, 1975), or to collect large amounts of data but postpone analysis, sometimes indefinitely (see examples in Nixon, 1981). Worse still, good intentions may be undermined by a failure even to get started on any practical activity. By way of consolation it should once more be noted that these difficulties are not confined to teacher-researchers and evaluators - university corridors are littered with research kites that never quite got off the ground!

The effects of time constraints on deliberations can be equally damaging and lead to what Weston (1979) has described as 'pseudo-deliberation' or 'deliberation under constraint' (p. 218). In situations such as these the pressure to reach a decision as soon as possible makes it difficult for a group to commit itself to the arduous deliberative process. Thus, although members are allowed their say, their views rarely influence the outcome since this may already have been decided by the headteacher or the senior management team.

Clearly issues of time are formidable. However, they are not insuperable. Almond (1982), for instance, proposes a strategy for maximising the use of time that is available to teachers after they have completed their routine tasks. Noticing that curriculum development activity can be sustained for a period but will then tail off, he asked teachers to plot the peaks and troughs of their routine commitments throughout the school year. On this basis he established that each school has a rhythm which prevents additional commitments being taken on at some periods, but which allows extra work at others. For instance, secondary teachers seemed to have more energy in the middle of the Autumn term and towards the end of the Spring term, than in the illness-prone months of January, February and March, and at the busy or disrupted end of the school year. Moreover, during the periods when extra work was feasible, it seemed advantageous to set some goal that was achievable within a 'containable' period of four to six weeks. Over a period of years it would then be possible to build this circumscribed task into a cycle of curriculum development. For the purposes of curriculum evaluation, it should be possible to take account of these notions of school rhythm, 'containable' or 'bounded' time, and developmental cycle, in an effort to plan evaluative activity. Moreover, the formalisation of the process by means of a 'time contract' (Elliott, 1981a) might not only ensure that tasks are completed, but lend them status and eventually encourage the acceptance of evaluation as a routine part of professional practice in schools.

Organisation and Management

Many of the issues raised in the preceding sections have implications for school management and organisation. For example, the argument for an incremental approach to the development of skills generates a need for an organisational structure that will support it. This may take the form of provision for school-based or school-focused INSET courses and conferences, or opportunities for research, deliberation and collaboration among teachers, or between teachers and outsiders. With respect to issues of time, some need to build research time and meeting schedules into the school's timetable will almost inevitably arise, since this is likely to be the only way to ensure that evaluative tasks are given sufficient priority and much needed status[19]. Further-more, if evaluation is to become routine, some attention needs to be paid to incentive systems (Sieber, 1982). In other words, the risks associated with evaluation need to be offset by some prospect of advan-tage, not only to pupils, but to the institution and the individuals who have given time and energy. In the case of the institution, a system of accreditation (see Chapter 6) might serve this purpose, whereas the individual might seek some form of career advancement.

At various points we have suggested that, in contrast to outsider evaluations, staff discussion may constitute a major (if not *the* major) part of evaluations conducted mainly by teachers. Yet, as Moon (1980) points out, the collaborative dimension of teachers' work has been much neglected in curriculum research, although it features in the literature on leadership and management in schools. Despite a different orientation, some of this literature has considerable relevance to evalua-tive practice, particularly issues relating to committee structures and working groups. Richardson (1973) and John (1980), for instance, dis-cuss the relative merits of formal and informal, permanent and temp-orary consultative systems (e.g. *ad hoc* committees, permanent study groups, standing committees and senior management teams). Both agree that whatever meeting structure is adopted participants need to know that ideas generated in discussion have a good chance of being translated into action. At Nailsea School (where Denys John was the Head) Richardson (1973) interpreted the substitution of a standing committee for three temporary working groups, and the evolution of the continuous staff conference, as expressions of a need to give staff meetings a genuine policy-making function. In the case of the staff conference the old-style whole staff discussion based on a pre-meeting manifesto of the head's ideas was replaced by a statement of problems to be examined, a schedule of dates by which particular decisions had to be made, meetings in which the first hour was devoted to inter-departmental small group discussion followed by a plenary session, and a post-meeting summary based on the verbal contributions of all staff. There is no suggestion that the head delegated all responsibility for decision-making, but he obviously attempted to construct a system which encouraged all teachers to become personally and professionally involved in the formulation of policy.

In contrast, the failure of the heads of department committee at West Mercia High School (Weston, 1979) to shape proposals for the restructuring of the third year, was undoubtedly related to the fact that although the committee had the *form* of a decision-making body, the *substance* was known to lie with the head and his senior colleagues. According to Weston: 'for deliberation to be educative it has also to be responsible; only with a strong degree of commitment will it be possible for individuals and groups to make the fundamental adjustment of out-look which will make possible a shift from what Stenhouse (1975) calls "individual autonomy" (what I do in my classroom or department) to a shared responsibility' (p. 226).

In summary, then, it seems that given the crucial importance of leadership and management a participatory style of evaluation in schools almost inevitably requires a participatory or 'open' management style (a point made in OU, 1982, Block 6, pp 19-20). In the context of curriculum review (see Chapter 3), which by definition involves the whole school, this may be particularly important. Indeed, the joint study of Curriculum 11 to 16 by HMI and five LEAs (DES, 1981a) identified participation in decision-making as an important general principle in facilitating the process of change[20].

Notes

1. Walker (1975) uses the term 'temporary system' to describe the kind of structure that is set up to develop new curricula, but which remains independent of existing structures. Weston (1979) contrasts this milieu for curriculum deliberation with the organisational constraints imposed by the permanent system of the school.

2. The literature on roles in participant observation is vast. However, it is probably worth noting that Schwartz and Schwartz (1955) argued that the role of the participant observer could be placed on a continuum ranging from 'passive' participant-observation on the one hand to 'active' participant-observation on the other. Gold (1958) further elaborated four master roles: the complete observer, the observer-as-participant, the participant-as-observer, and the complete participant. It is a matter of argument whether any researcher can claim to be a complete or passive observer, since the act of observation almost invariably has some effect on the processes being observed. (This is the issue of reactivity discussed in Chapter 7.)

3. See also the quotations from this at the end of Chapter 8.

4. The collaborative approach adopted by the Ford Teaching Project has been developed further in the Schools Council's Teacher-Pupil Interaction and the Quality of Learning (TIQL) Project, also directed by Elliott. Both projects represent attempts to test the potential of Stenhouse's hypothesis concerning the 'teacher-as-researcher' (see Chapter 2).

5. In many respects this is simply an adaptation of the classic ethnographic strategy of identifying 'key informants' (see Chapter 8).

6. Polanyi's thesis is that 'we know more than we can say'. Thus skills such as bicycling and glass-blowing must be learned by 'doing' rather than having the process explained to us.

7. On the other hand, teachers may rationalise problems or regard both causes and solutions as existing outside their immediate situations (e.g. with headteachers or the LEA) and therefore beyond their control.

8. According to Reimer (1977), one variety of opportunistic research takes advantage of unique circumstances and timely events, such as a stay in hospital (see also Roth, 1974); another exploits familiar social situations such as bus-riding or pub-visiting; and the third takes advantage of special areas of expertise such as experience as a jazz-musician, or burglar!

9. Roth (1962) maintains that the distinction between covert and overt research cannot be fully sustained since it is neither possible to tell the 'researched' everything, nor to contact all those in a public setting who may be affected by the research activity.

10. There has been much criticism of the lack of communication between groups working in related fields of social and educational research. For example, Delamont (1981) makes a sustained attack on the failure of the sociology of schools and classrooms to have impact on the sociology of education, and the failure of British Studies to be taken note of in the USA. Similarly, researchers in the tradition of curriculum studies have tended to ignore much of the work of researchers in sociological traditions, although we are inclined to think that the oversight has been greater on the part of sociologists. Pollard (1982b) for instance, makes no reference whatsoever to curriculum studies literature on the 'teacher-as-researcher'. Inevitably the effect of this lack of communication is the creation of a number of reinvented, and sometimes redundant, wheels.

11. A full discussion of the issues surrounding privacy and ethics in social science is contained in Barnes (1977, 1979). A more specific discussion of the politics and ethics of evaluation is found in Adelman (1984).

12. Interestingly, the problems of studying one's own institution, as opposed to one's own classroom, are not well documented. As Stenhouse (1982) observed, a number of excellent accounts do exist now, but they are mostly in the form of masters' theses. See, however, James and Ebbutt (1981).

13. Biott (1981) notes that: 'In the quest for procedural neutrality one tends to relish evidence of divergence. There may be a tendency, however, to become what Elliott (1977) called the "underdog's advocate". Smetherham (1978) also noted this tendency in his work and Wolcott (1977) recognised how he "tried to resist the anthropological tendency to identify single-mindedly with the underdogs, the oppressed or the colonised".' (p. 50).

14. Researchers in a tradition of 'pure' research would probably object that procedures such as these would inevitably result in some data-loss or distortion. In response, evaluators working for school improvement would undoubtedly argue that teachers who feel threatened or are divested of control over the evaluation process are likely to be hostile to suggestions for change (see also the discussion of research versus evaluation in Chapter 7). Significantly, in a review of twenty three studies Perloff and Perloff (1980) note that evaluation researchers appeared to adhere to stringent ethical practices whilst 'pure' researchers often used dubious ethical

practices because they wanted to get at 'truth' regardless of its positive or negative value.

15.   Other examples of ways in which protection for participants has been built into the evaluative process by means of an internal contract, come mainly from the tertiary sector (see, for example Alexander, 1978b, Adelman, 1979, Biott, 1981).

16.   In the USA it is standard practice to seek parental permission to gather information from pupils.

17.   'Spotting' is equivalent to trouble-spotting by an alert observer, whereas 'scanning' involves a constant monitoring of situations in an effort to anticipate potential problems. 'Monitoring' also involves systematic data collection.

18.   This should go some way towards meeting Delamont's (1981) criticism that researchers working in one area of social and educational research, rarely take note of work in another.

19.   The operation of the curriculum review groups at Stantonbury (OU, 1982, Case Study 2) suffered because it was not given a 'time slot' in the school's busy calendar of staff meetings. Consequently it was perceived as having low priority and little status.

20.   By way of qualification, it should be noted that empirical evidence of the contribution of participatory decision-making to change is ambiguous and sometimes contradictory. Sieber (1981) maintains that the reason for this is the complexity of participation as a source of incentives and disincentives (more of which in Chapter 11). On the one hand it offers performance-related and interpersonal rewards; on the other hand it can create the disincentives of conflict, overload, and risk of failure.

Part Four

Using Evaluation

10   Reporting Evaluation

Introduction

As we argued in Chapter 6, the nature of the reporting process is important in determining whether an evaluation is *primarily* for contractual accountability or improving education. In this chapter we look at what form and procedure of reporting is most appropriate to each of these two purposes. We do not feel obliged to question the need to give some kind of report, because arguments usually reduce to questions concerning *form*[1].

A key to the form of any report is the concept of audience. This should take account of the division into insiders and outsiders (to the school), but also consider the audience group and its accountability relationship to the teachers in the school[2]. The parents are the most obvious group to receive a report; not only is this a matter of their rights[3] (contractual accountability) but teachers have a sense of moral accountability. However, it has to be noted that the latter is usually expressed through the reporting of children's learning (East Sussex Accountability Project, 1979) and hence concerns the usual connotation of 'school reports' (e.g. see Clift, Wilson and Weiner, 1981). A second audience is constituted by governors, who have a legal responsibility to represent the community (contractual accountability). However Chapter 6 also argued for a role which would involve them in change and the improvement of the school (as did the Taylor Report: DES, 1977c). The Education Committee of a local authority does not have this direct involvement in improvement and is therefore likely to be a similar audience to governors, when the latter are acting in their contractual accountability role. The final group are the professionals, both inside the school and within the local authority[4]. Clearly both school and LEA staff are interested in the improvement of education, but, as Chapter 5 illustrated, schools can operate a kind of 'legal-formal' accountability which resembles contractual accountability. Moreover, LEA staff have an obvious contractual accountability relationship with the staff of schools.

Bearing in mind the different relationships these groups have with schools, Becher, Eraut and Knight (1981, p. 91) suggested three forms of reporting:

1. at the lowest level, reports to parents concerning evaluation *procedures* and who has access to the resulting information;
2. at the next level, regular reports to governors and advisers which are brief summaries of the evaluation containing a note of any action taken;
3. at the highest level, regular full evaluation reports which are available on request to governors and advisers (the school obviously has access to these).

In drawing up these suggestions Becher, Eraut and Knight were aware of MacDonald's (1978) concern to protect schools in the early stages of their evaluative efforts, and his recommendations that self-reports only be made available to outsiders once a school has developed the necessary skills. (Chapter 5 gives this as one of the features of the 'process approach'.) As we pointed out in earlier chapters, time has overtaken MacDonald's suggestions and legislation now requires information to be made available to parents. However, apart from the requirement to publish public examination results, the information required is mostly uncontentious description (as in a prospectus) - not an evaluation as such. Indeed, evidence presented by Becher, Eraut and Knight (1981, pp. 41-5) and Green (1975 pp. 3-6) shows that parents have a low level of expectation and are satisfied with descriptive information (in addition to direct contact with the school). ILEA (1981), for example, adopts a straight forward annual report to parents[5], and, as we noted earlier, the only 'evaluative evidence' is the examination results[6]. Given this treatment of parents, we will focus our concerns in this chapter on *external* reporting to governors and LEA professional staff, and *internal* reporting (which could involve LEA professional staff).

External Reporting

In addition to an annual report to parents, ILEA also has a scheme for reporting to governors (contractual accountability). This has two elements: an annual review, and a quinquennial review. The annual review need not be considered at a single meeting but should include (for secondary schools): the annual report to parents; a curriculum analysis and details of academic organisation (e.g. departmental organisation and examination policy); additional statistics such as 11-plus transfer entrants, suspensions, expulsions, attendance, court appearances and pupil mobility; information on the 'education offer' (e.g. fourth and sixth year arrangements); a review of some departments each year; information on finance and staff (ILEA, 1981, p. 3-4). The quinquennial review requires an intensive examination by school staff which will be commented upon by the ILEA inspectorate. This review will include: a consideration of the five year trends in the annual reports (mainly the quantitative indicators); an assessment of the work of departments, pastoral work and school organisation, by those responsible and monitored by senior staff; the headteacher's assessment of progress in relation to the school's aims and objectives (ILEA, 1981, p.4)[7].

The experience of pilot annual reports to governors showed that they found the range of information helpful. The school staff also felt it a good opportunity to bring together usually disparate material. Problems for staff included, not surprisingly, the strain caused by the time and effort required to produce a report. The governors also found it difficult to cope with the sheer volume of material. In fact much of the information was already available, but not in one document. Interestingly, the experience of these pilots suggested that it would be better to present the information in a number of smaller papers, to aid assimilation, provided repetition was avoided.

This kind of reporting is not practicable within the kind of context argued for in Chapter 6, and illustrated in the Huntingdale Technical School example, because it is primarily intented to fulfil contractual accountability (at least in the case of ILEA). However, there are examples of a form of reporting that allows a different kind of relationship. The visit by a member of the Oxfordshire Education Committee to a school in the four-yearly reporting scheme is one [8].

Three issues relevant to reporting arise from the above procedures for governors. First is that of confidentiality, which we have already dealt with in Chapter 6. Here, however, it is worth noting the kind of control that the Taylor Report envisaged governors would have over publication of a school's review report: they could specify any items that were to be withheld (DES, 1977c, p. 61). Secondly there is a problem concerning the credibility of reports (MacDonald, 1978). In the case of ILEA's quinquennial reviews, this is alleviated by having an inspector's comment. Nevertheless, as we have already argued, credibility is not just a matter of the methodological soundness or veracity of the reports. It depends in part upon the predisposition and trust of the reader. A useful lesson, derived from the literature on educational and other social programme evaluation, concerns the realisation that evaluation and the way it is reported are political acts (e.g. Wolf, 1979). Thus views on the validation of reports by proof and justification are not totally appropriate (e.g. Becker, 1958). In relation to the reporting of case study, Wilson (1979) says that such studies never demonstrate the effectiveness of education programmes so unequivocally as to convince those who doubt[9]. The information is rarely powerful enough to change attitudes. In addition to readers' predispositions to the school being evaluated, they also have predispositions towards certain kinds of data. So, for example, they may have a naive confidence in the rigour of any study which uses quantitative measures and a suspicion of qualitative data - irrespective of the thoroughness with which an evaluation is conducted.

This brings us to our third issue, which concerns intelligibility. This we will further sub-divide in relation to two questions: do the readers understand the report? can they act upon or make use of it? The ubiquity of quantitative measures suggests that understanding of, for example, assessment scores is widespread. However, as we have shown in Chapters 4 and 8 ('Curriculum Outcomes'), the bases and implications of these scores are unlikely to be appreciated, particularly by lay-people. Claims are also often made for the accessibility of case studies and ethnographies to lay people (e.g. Walker, 1981, Spradley, 1979), but this is open to question. Evidence relating to the second aspect of intelligibility is similarly inconclusive. Chapter 4, for example, argued that test programme results appeared to be of little use to decision-makers. The fact is that we know very little about how reports help and can only rely upon them 'informing and educating'. (This issue is taken up again in Chapter 11.)

Turning to LEA professional staff who are involved in processes of reporting to governors and Education Committees, the issues are slightly different. Of course, they also have an overload problem in trying to process the endless stream of reports (cf. Chapter 6); in fact the Taylor Report (DES, 1977c, p. 61) suggested that LEAs should consider establishing an 'analysis or research function'. As professionals, LEA staff will have different information requirements from those of governors: they can comprehend educational issues and problems in a specialised language; and, because they are involved directly or indirectly with schools, they will look for constructive self-criticism as a basis for providing help[10]. In so far as they are involved with schools and their improvement, their views on reporting must in some ways parallel those of teachers. The fact that they still 'carry into school' their contractual accountability relationship does not alter this. In any case, as we have seen in Chapter 5, a legal-formal accountability relationship can exist between professionals within the school.

One group we did not consider in our introduction is the Press. Although not strictly an audience, the Press has a powerful influence on all audiences. The controversy over the examination results of Highbury Grove and Islington Green, noted in Chapter 4, arose partly because of the different interpretations national newspapers put on the results, and partly because of the amount of information to which they were given access. The position is likely to be worse for local newspapers with low resources; their reporting of any evaluation report could cause serious problems. Clift (OU, 1982, Block 2, Part 1, p. 39) recounts the experience of a report considered by Salford Education Committee, one small element of which was an analysis of the role of deputy heads in primary schools. In one school it was the deputy head's job to ring the bell, a fact that provided a basis for a local newspaper's lampooning of schools[11].

Internal Reporting

Reporting is firstly a procedure or process, but it also has to do with the production of a report (written or audio-visual), particularly if a regular reporting procedure exists for evaluation[12]. In institutions of higher education, where procedures are generally more formal, evaluation procedures are also likely to be formalised (see Alexander, 1978b, p. 97-8). In a school, however, consideration will need to be given to procedures for ensuring, where appropriate, that reports are *confidential*. This may be achieved in a similar way to confidentiality of data collection (considered in Chapter 9) although the situation is sometimes more acute for reporting than for data collection because teachers, and others, are often willing to give away their rights in relation to the latter. Seeing themselves portrayed in a report, however, may make them more aware of these rights[13]. The form of the report, either a case study or a quantitative study, and the size of the school will effect the acuteness of such problems. As Barnes (1979) argues in more general terms, it is necessary to balance the short-term interests of the LEA (governors and Education Committee) to 'know', with the need for teachers to be protected in the long-term interests of informed criticism.

If a regular reporting procedure exists then *strategic* issues arise: how frequent and extensive should the report be? what routine data collection activities can be used?[14] Frequent extensive reports are a source of strain on staff, therefore some form of rotating or rolling review is preferable since it will spread the strain over, say, different departments of the school at different times. However, since this will not lessen the strain on the individuals involved in the department, it more often relieves 'collective strain' and the load on senior staff, such as deputy heads, who may have a co-ordinating role. This benefit must, of course, be balanced against the loss of a thorough evaluation of the school as a whole.

The use of routine data (recommended by MacDonald, 1978, and the Taylor Report, DES, 1977c) requires, for quantitative measures, that good records be kept. For example, assessment information must be recorded in a standard format, and, where comparisons are to be made, this must be based upon standard assessment or marking procedures. If records are compiled at class level then a procedure for aggregating the data is necessary for analysis purposes. This problem is eased if computer storage facilities are available, as is increasingly becoming the case. Where assessment data are primarily used for assessing individuals, it is important that the assumptions used to produce or process such data should be compatible with use for curriculum evaluation (see Chapter 8, 'Curriculum Outcomes')[15]. Collecting routine data on the chance that they might be of use has its dangers; it may breed disenchantment and lead to a ritualistic and inaccurate collection by teachers, if there are no signs that the data are actually being used. A crass example of this would be the collection of structured observational data which, if done routinely, may become mechanical and ignore important contextual aspects[16]. For qualitative data the possibilities of routine collection seem remote and it may be more sensible to do something similar to Becher, Eraut and Knight's (1981) suggestion for parents i.e. report the procedures, and any action taken. This gives an inevitable bias to routine data collection, which will have to be counteracted in non-routine evaluation.

Any consideration of reporting as a procedure must also take account of how the report will be *produced*. How will the confidentiality be protected? Who will participate in producing the report? The protection of confidentiality, even in a large secondary school, is very difficult. In the example of Huntingdale Technical School (Chapter 6) this was achieved by avoiding criticism of individuals, and focusing instead upon the corporate body. However, this may result in a bland report[17]. Ernulf Community School used a system of teacher self-assessments such that discussions between teachers and their head of department were confidential to that head of department. The heads of departments then wrote several reports, on the departments (not just the teachers), which were passed to the deputy heads for collation. They, in turn, reported to the head, again keeping details of the heads of departments' reports confidential. Finally, the head wrote a whole school report (reported in James, 1982). Nuttall (1981) suggests a system of reciprocity e.g. if a head evaluates the staff, the staff evaluate the head[18]. Ultimately, however, the balance of power is in the hands of senior staff so it is not a symmetrical arrangement. Other ways of protecting confidentiality rely upon techniques for writing the report, for example, the use of pseudonyms (Barnes, 1979), or even the use of fiction as a means of disguise (Walker, 1981). Neither of these will be entirely effective in a school however, because individuals will always be recognised[19]. Finally a right of reply could be afforded to individuals in the departments which are scrutinised (cf. the appeal against non-accreditation mentioned in Chapter 6), although Harlen and Elliott (1982) warn against stretching out the negotiating process.

This approach, involving the subjects of the evaluation in writing a report (if they are not intimately involved in the evaluation process - see the Sir Frank Markham study described in Chapter 5), is one element of *participation*. In addition to being a matter of rights, it has practical benefits with regard to workload. Certain individuals (headteachers, deputy heads etc.) often carry the major load for compiling or writing reports. Even if others are involved, co-ordination is required so that, where relevant, a 'wholeness' is obtained. The workload can, however, be spread by having small scale interim reports. These are important in their own right since they are a source of useful feedback, and help ease the final analysis. Circulation and discussion of the report is also part of the reporting process, although its form will depend partly upon the way confidentiality has been secured, and partly upon the way the school organises its routine communications and discussion. We are therefore unable to explore the possibilities here (see Note 12). Instead we turn to the report itself.

The form of a report is largely dictated by the nature of the evaluation itself[20], but within this constraint there is room for a consideration of presentation. Naturally report writing requires skill - most of the advice available relates to written reports. However, there are a number of pointers which are helpful and need to be stated. For instance, it is important to keep the audience always in mind; to write clearly using straight-forward language; and to use illustrations, photographs and diagrams wherever possible or necessary (e.g. pie-charts, bar-charts, and line graphs)[21]. Above all such advice stresses brevity. A consciousness of this requirement is particularly important for narrative accounts produced in case studies. Wilson (1979) recounts the complaints that teachers make about the length of case studies, and their lack of time to read them. Apparently this occurs in spite of what advocates say about the naturalism of this approach for communicating with teachers (e.g. Stenhouse, 1978; Walker, 1981).

Stenhouse (1982) suggested three forms of reports - narrative, vignette and analytic - all of which are possible only if the data is qualitative. Of the narrative mode Stenhouse had this to say:

> Narrative, as a form of presentation has two great strengths: it is simple and direct to read and it is subtle. Its simplicity and directness is partly due to its being within a convention of representing the natural world that is thoroughly established and that most readers meet in the nursery, but it is also partly because, as compared with analysis, the narrative form constrains the author from presenting his own logic in the teeth of resistance from the story. He does not drag the reader on to the territory of his own mind, but rather goes out to meet him. The subtlety of narrative lies in its capacity to convey ambiguity concerning cause and effect. In telling a story the author does not need to ascribe clearly causes and effects. Rather he may select from the record an array of information which invites the reader to speculate about causes and effects by providing him with a basis for alternative interpretations.   (Stenhouse, 1982, p. 268).

The vignette, in contrast, is a sketch which is inevitably interpretative, but could provide a useful way of extracting from, and condensing, case studies to make them easier to read (Wilson, 1979). Analytic reports, as might be expected, are based upon an explicit debate drawing upon the evidence. This approach can of course be adopted, and usually is, when quantitative data are collected in the evaluation. Oral reporting (or some other audio-visual technique) gives a complete alternative to these written presentations, and it has been used in many instances (see Chapters 4 and 6). Wilson (1979) talks of the possibility of debriefing, or using written case studies in a workshop session. Indeed it would be possible for an evaluation report to form the basis of a school's in-service day[22].

Exploring the form of the report is not just about fitting the report to the data, as the quotation from Stenhouse makes clear. Obviously the form of the evaluation is important, and indeed constraining to some extent, but it is the way that the report affects changes in teachers which is the main criterion for its construction. Stenhouse's concern for ambiguity is one such guiding principle which we are encouraged to use. There is, however, very little research on the impact of reports on teachers although we will examine some contrasting stances[23].

In arguing for the reporting of single cases (drawing on experience in medicine), Stenhouse (1982) claimed that such cases improve teachers' judgements and help them treat experience more reflectively and analytically[24]. (As we noted above ambiguity is a device used to encourage speculation.) In this respect single case reporting contrasts with analytic reporting and therefore with reports drawing primarily upon quantitative data, which are necessarily analytic. Stenhouse's view is in part related to his view of the role of theory, which we return to in the final chapter.

Becker (1958) takes a more traditional research approach, which Stenhouse (1982) is at pains to distance himself from. Like all researchers, of both the positivistic and interpretative traditions, Becker is concerned with proof and justification. He thus implicitly sees man as a rational being who weighs up evidence and arguments in making inference about social events (which include curriculum exercises). Wilson (1979), however, casts doubt on both Becker's and Stenhouse's stances. We have already noted his reservations about the power of information from an evaluation to change minds, and the practical difficulties associated with the length of reports, both of which reduce the potency of Becker's and Stenhouse's arguments. In addition Wilson makes three other points which further undermine their arguments. First, the role that teachers have as practitioners does not allow them the freedom to consider the whole variety of measures that might be taken in response to reading the report; such are the constraints on them[25]. Secondly, the reaction of teachers to the report will depend upon their particular experience, style and expertise. A study may show them a range of options for action, but individual teachers know their own limitations and some approaches may be beyond them, although they appear attractive. Thirdly, the logic of the case study approach in dealing with everyday life is based upon a simple psychological theory of learning. It therefore depends upon the degree of correspondence between the teacher's situation and that described in the report. For a report originating within a particular school this approach might indeed be reasonable because of shared experience and the ease with which any one teacher can 'fill in the gaps' between an account of, say, another teacher's classroom and her own.

Lest it be thought that the arguments considered so far relate only to the reporting of interpretative research or evaluation, we turn to a stance taken by Galton and Simon (1980, pp. 200-4). In considering the implications of their large scale (nomothetic) research, using structured observation methods and pupil outcome measures, they also put forward some ideas about how teachers improve. They contrast their position with Stenhouse's (1975) teacher-as-researcher stance (see Chapters 2 and 5) and argue that the findings of their research about successful teaching styles may draw teachers' attention to particular features of these styles. The teacher can thus focus upon relevant aspects of her own teaching with dramatic results[26]. Furthermore, this relates to Wilson's second point, and offers a way of encouraging teachers to explore their limits. Although these ideas may be encouraging, in the end we are forced to admit that they are simply hypotheses, all with some logic and persuasiveness, but as yet possessing no empirical base.

Finally, what of pupils as an audience? Our account, and indeed that of others, has not considered them at all. If teachers argue that researchers and outside evalutors ignore their needs and concerns when investigating them, pupils can make the same complaint when teachers evaluate the schools and classrooms in which they spend 25 hours a week. We raised this as an issue in relation to data collection (see Chapters 8 and 9), but pointed out that little is said about the situation. The position with respect to evaluation reports is even worse[27].

Despite all this, differences in views about how reports are received and used should not be viewed pessimistically, but taken as an important point for development. Producing a report is not simply a technical exercise that requires data, arguments and presentation to be correct - though this is important. Reports should aim for change and development; in this respect different people may need different approaches to which those producing a report should be sensitive. Moreover, how a report is formulated and used in the process of change requires some view of how evaluation fits into this process. This is the subject of our final chapter.

Notes

1. Three reasons for reporting have been given, however: to educate and inform; to stimulate action; to permit validation of the evaluation (OU, 1982, Block 6, p. 22). In the case of teachers evaluating their own class-rooms, with no other audience, then the last of these is the justification for producing a report - a form of reflexivity. James and Ebbutt (1981, p. 84) see a report as establishing the 'confidence to continue'.

2. Although much of what is said in this chapter has a general import, clearly discussions of particular accountability relationships are context-specific. We have chosen to deal with England and Wales.

3. Nor just in the interest of improving learning through mobilising the home, nor for enlightened self-interest by obtaining public confidence through school-parent communication (East Sussex Accountability Project, 1979, p. 42).

4. We see no sense in drawing the bounds any wider than the LEA, given their current legal responsibilities.

5. There is now quite a lot of advice and examples available. Taylor, F. (1980) draws upon an 'earlier' study, Community Education Working Party (1981), and gives detailed guidance on planning a prospectus; Green (1975) helps to a lesser extent; Gibson (1980) gives examples; and Gibson (Elliott *et al*, 1981) analyses the requirements of parent-teacher communication.

6. ILEA (1981) contains an appendix giving guidance to its schools on how to present the results. See also Shipman (1979).

7. The quinquennial reports are still only required in pilot schools. Oxford-shire has a similar scheme i.e. a four-yearly report (c.f. Chapter 6).

8. Elliott (Elliott *et al*, 1981, Chapter 12) reports a case where informal meetings of governors were held in addition to formal ones. These informal meetings, which were open to all staff, allowed a more fruitful discussion of educational issues between staff and governors. It will require a more thorough implementation of the Taylor Report's recommendations on partnership (DES, 1977c) if governors are to be involved in the improvement of education.

9. Although Wilson was specifically discussing case study reports, he thought that his argument applied to other forms.

10. We realise we are here disagreeing with many programme evaluators who advocate illuminative approaches (e.g. Parlett & Hamilton, 1972). In our opinion they have provided little evidence to support their claim that a report can address multiple audiences, and, as we have argued, predispositions may be more important than 'readability'.

11. In giving advice to programme evaluators on relationships with the press, Morris and Fitz-Gibbon (1978) suggest that not only should an evaluator write press releases for them, but also train them to interpret the data!

12. We will, however, not be able to consider all the organisational features of schools this may involve (Chapter 9), nor indeed every kind of evaluation. Therefore we confine our attention to general issues.

13. Barnes (1979) recounts a rather extreme example of a published ethnography of a Vietnam village which was used by the USA armed forces as

briefing material in the Vietnamese War. The villagers gave away their rights with no thought for, or control over, the consequences. In fact, in the act of publication the researcher also relinquished control over the use of the research.

14. We realise this blurs the distinction between data collection, analysis and report writing, but any attempt to separate them rigidly would be artificial.

15. For example, Clift, Wilson & Weiner (1981) recommend the recording of 'z'-scores for assessments; this makes certain comparisons impossible.

16. This may be a danger inherent in such information irrespective of whether or not it is used.

17. This did not occur at Huntingdale, but in another case study (OU, 1982, Case Study 1) it did. To be fair, however, this report was for the Education Committee, as part of the Oxfordshire four-yearly reporting scheme.

18. Nuttall was actually discussing the reciprocity between a school and the LEA officers, but the analogy is still appropriate.

19. Fictional accounts focus on people and, as Walker (1981) admits, this makes personal relations more vulnerable - a point noted in Chapter 9 in relation to the role of the teacher-as-researcher (Stenhouse, 1982). However, reports relating especially to pupils have been anonymised by teachers working their own schools (James and Ebbutt, 1981, p. 85). Notice here we talk of 'writing the report'; audio-visual presentations make such disguises impossible.

20. See for example four contrasting reports given in Sjorgren *et al* (1974).

21. Morris and Fitz-Gibbon (1978) writing for programme evaluators, provide useful general advice. Cooper (1974) and Hook (1981) provide advice on the use of diagrams etc. to present data. OU (1982, Block 6) gives a general account of this advice. Cooper (1974) and Taylor, F. (1980) also give advice on printing and reprographics. From the ethnographic tradition, Spradley (1979) gives some very useful guidance on writing an ethnography. This involves a consideration of the level of generality of statements used: from universal ones like 'all societies create separate identities for the sexes', to specific incidents that occur in the situation being researched.

22. Solihull local authority's evaluation scheme provides the agenda for a staff conference - see Chapter 6.

23. Nor indeed on decision makers. As Chapter 4 showed advocates of testing, for example, use crude theories of change for both decision-makers and teachers.

24. Walker (1981) takes a similar stance when arguing for the use of fictional accounts.

25. Wilson (1979) argues that 'interveners' like LEA advisers may feel free to consider this variety, but that the report, if written in a narrative style, will deal too much with particulars when they require generalisations.

26. They argue this on the basis of an analogy, used by Stenhouse (1975), of teachers as actors: if a rehearsal performance is going badly it would destroy an actor to have a video replay (or transcript) dissected bit-by-bit by the director. Much more productive would be to focus on one or two aspects of the performance; and subsequent improvement of these will, so the argument goes, lift the whole performance. They also point out that experience with micro-teaching techniques supports this view.

27. But see James (1979) reported in OU (1982, Block 2, Part 2). No doubt there are other such cases but they have not come to our notice.

11 Learning from Evaluation

Introduction

It is reasonable to expect the last chapter of a book to present a set of conclusions or a final summary of what has gone before. Our intention, however, is to do almost the opposite: to end with a discussion of issues and questions that is necessarily speculative and open-ended. The reason is simple. Although earlier chapters included debates on a number of issues we intentionally gave the impression that most of the arguments are resolvable if would-be school evaluators are prepared to reflect on purposes and make informed choices regarding appropriate strategies and techniques. Indeed the point of writing this book was to increase awareness of the options available. However, it takes little imagination to realise that all this begs a crucial question. It implies that we understand how people *learn* from the activity of evaluation. After all, it is only in the act of learning that the value of evaluation can be assured. The problem is that we still know relatively little about the way people, especially adults, learn and change. Thus the question that we first raised in Chapter 2 emerges again and we have to reconsider how evaluation might be expected to contribute to educational improvement and professional growth.

For this reason, then, the present chapter makes no attempt to tell the reader what to do when the evaluation is over. In any case, Patton (1978, p. 21) suggests that the potential of a particular study to influence practice has, by that time, already been determined. Instead we want to address what is, in essence, a prior question and consider how learning *might* take place throughout the evaluative process. (The emphasis is important since we have no conclusive evidence at present - only hypotheses.) In doing this our intention is both to break the linear pattern imposed by the written word, and to stress that curriculum evaluation in schools is best conceptualised, not as a phased *event*, but as a cyclical (or spiral) *process*.

In his seminal paper on the methodology of evaluation, Scriven

(1967) drew a now familiar distinction between *formative* and *summative* evaluation. He defined the role of formative evaluation as concerned with identifying and remedying problems during the developmental stages of a programme. Summative evaluation, on the other hand, is concerned with assessing the worth of a programme in its final form. Clearly, Scriven's main involvement was with the evaluation of specific programmes or projects (temporary systems) which required decisions concerning their continuance. In contrast, curriculum evaluation in schools is concerned with a 'permanent system', so the principal role for evaluation is almost invariably formative. Again this reiterates the point that learning needs to take place *during*, not after, evaluation.

The Countenance of Learning

Before we go further, we should perhaps examine the meanings that we attach to learning. Throughout this book we have assumed, as others have done, that curriculum evaluation in schools is intended to contribute to an understanding of educational aims, processes and outcomes, and to stimulate change, if change is needed. More specifically it seeks to provide various kinds of information needed by different groups of decision-makers, among whom classroom teachers, parents, governors, administrators and policy makers may be numbered (see the definitions of evaluation in Chapter 7). The usual assumption is that the impact on decision-making will be visible in some form of behavioural change: a change in school policy or classroom practice, for instance. Alkin, Daillak and White (1979, p. 230) propose an alternative view, however, and suggest that in some cases there will be no real decision to be made. Instead information may be required to substantiate prior decisions or actions, or established a climate of opinion or alter attitudes. Similarly, Patton (1978) avoids narrowly constructing information use as equivalent to behavioural change. In the context of his work as a professional evaluator of US federal programmes (the field of policy studies) he reported that, 'information capable of reducing uncertainty was meaningful, important and in scarce supply' (p. 290).

If this wider definition of what constitutes information use is accepted then a number of difficulties arise in establishing whether learning has taken place. First, it requires an interpretative rather than positivistic social science (see Chapter 7) since the *meanings* that people ascribe to their experience of evaluation are likely to be as important as the visible changes that take place as a result of it. Secondly, since changes in attitude or climate tend to be gradual and cumulative (Alkin *et al*, 1979, p. 225), it is also likely to be difficult to isolate the influence of a single evaluation immediately after it has taken place.

Professional programme evaluators have long been aware of these problems since evaluations are themselves evaluated, if only informally. Like programme developers, evaluators need to feel that their efforts are justified. Understandably then, many evaluators have been disturbed to discover that some, if not most, of the evaluation reports they have been commissioned to write have been ignored (Patton, 1978; Alkin *et al*, 1979; O'Connor, 1980; Baron, Miller, Whitfield and Yates, 1981). According to Abt (1976) more than one thousand evaluation studies are produced for US federal agencies each year, yet less than an estimated one per cent reach the potential pay-off of policy application. MacDonald and Norris (1978) believe there is no cause for greater optimism in the UK. They also claim that: 'Evaluation studies are not used, at least in ways which are recognisably consonant with the model of rational decision-making within which they are typically conceived and carried out' (p. 6).

If indeed this is the general case in policy and programme evaluation, there is reason to suspect that it might also apply to in-school evaluation unless some attempt is made to understand why the efforts of evaluators are so widely ignored[1]. To this end much recent work has been directed towards the discovery of factors which influence 'knowledge utilisation' (to use a rather ugly phrase currently popular in the USA). Of course, interest in this particular issue is not exclusive to evaluation research; it is the central concern of all those involved with educational innovation (see, for example, Lehming and Kane, 1981), and those who experience the failure of research to inform practice. Indeed, it is no more and no less than a variant of the perennial problem of the relation between theory and practice.

What is interesting therefore is that, both in the context of programme evaluation and in the context of in-school evaluation, there seems to be a growing consensus that one important requirement is to establish the precise nature of the information needs and interests of those who are expected to learn or change. Thereafter the kinds of information collected must be relevant to those needs and the methods of collection must be likewise appropriate. (This accounts for the emphasis on purposes in this book.) Before any of this can be accomplished however there is a prior task: a need to identify those who are to be considered the 'users' in specific evaluation contexts[2]. According to Patton (1978), evaluation can only hope to influence policy or practice if two fundamental considerations are acted upon:

> First, relevant decision-makers and information users must be
> identified and organised - real, visible, specific, and caring human
> beings, not ephemeral, general, and abstract 'audiences', organisa-
> tions, or agencies. Second, evaluators must work actively, react-
> ively, and adaptively with these identified decision-makers and
> information users to make all other decisions about the evaluation
> - decisions about focus, design, methods, analysis, interpretation,
> and dissemination.   (Patton, 1978, p. 284)

On this basis Patton goes on to develop a conception of an evaluation
task-force, which brings decision-makers, information users and evaluators together into a collaborative work group whose role is to facilitate
the negotiation, adaptation, selection and matching of evaluative
strategies to information needs. Underlying such a notion is another
important principle regarding the conditions that need to be established
if change is to take place. Put simply, this emphasises the need for those
who are expected to learn *to participate actively* in the evaluative
process.

At school-level, the concept of an evaluation task-force has considerable relevance particularly in contexts where evaluation is conducted,
in whole or part, by outsiders, but where insiders are expected to act
on the findings (see Chapters 4 and 6). Although not described as such,
the Planning and Review Board (PARB) at Huntingdale Technical
School (Chapter 6) took on precisely this kind of role. Perhaps this
accounts for its apparent success, and particularly the success of the
final seminar where outsiders and insiders together discussed the policy
implications of the review exercise.

In the context of school-level evaluations by insiders the division
between evaluators and decision-makers is, of course, less clear cut. In
many cases the same people will assume both roles. (In teacher self-
evaluation this is often so.) Nevertheless, the task-force concept reinforces the point, made in Chapter 9, that a *participatory* style of
evaluation has the best hope of fostering a genuine interest in remedial
action or professional learning[3].

The Personal Factor

Patton's (1978) contention that evaluation should not focus merely on
the postulated needs of a generalised 'audience', but on the specific

concerns of individual caring human beings comes from a conviction that the utilisation of information is essentially a personal process (see also House, 1977; Tofte, 1981). Whilst interviewing US federal decision-makers and evaluators about various factors that had been said (in the literature) to influence utilisation, Patton and his colleagues were surprised to discover that something they had not anticipated was consistently quoted as crucially important. This they called the 'personal factor' and defined as: 'the presence of an identifiable individual or group of people who personally cared about the evaluation and the information it generated' (Patton, 1978, p. 64). Although other factors, such as political considerations, were also important, the weight of evidence eventually led Patton to conclude that the power of evaluation lies ultimately *in the mobilisation of individual energies for action* (Patton, 1978, p. 290. His emphasis).

If there is strength in Patton's argument then, in relation to in-school evaluation, it lends support to the argument that professional development - and curriculum improvement - is related to the personal growth of teachers (see the discussion in Chapter 2). In addition it casts doubt on some of the assumptions underlying 'strategies for change' which imply that change is something that someone does to someone else (see Bennis, Benne and Chin, 1969, and Chapter 2). The effect is to shift the focus of interest, from those who seek to change others, to those individuals who undergo change themselves.

A similar concern is evident in the work of Sieber (1981) who explicitly criticises strategy theorists for seeking a global language for formulating policies to promote change, whilst ignoring the molecular terminology of individual and institutional incentives and disincentives for action[4]. In his view, schools are complex social psychological worlds in which change will not be implemented unless incentives, such as performance-related, material, interpersonal and career rewards, outweigh corresponding disincentives: that is, 'unless imputed benefits exceed imputed costs' (Sieber, 1981, p. 119)[5]. Much of Sieber's analysis focuses on the individual, however, he also argues that *incentive systems* exist at the level of the institution. Thus:

> The array of incentives/disincentives, their distribution and methods of allocation, and the motivational modes that determine the value loadings of incentives/disincentives may be regarded as the incentive system of the school. These systems range from being highly coherent and resistant to change to being quite disorderly and dynamic, and even internally contradictory. (Sieber, 1981, p. 121)

Presumably the 'creative school' (see Hoyle, 1975, and Chapter 2), if it exists, could be defined in terms of a particular kind of incentive system.

Clearly the preceding discussion reaches into the realms of innovation theory. In our view, this is entirely appropriate if evaluation in schools is to be regarded as a strategy for educational improvement and professional development (Simons, 1981; Bolam, 1982b), which are forms of innovation. Moreover, such a discussion helps to clarify what questions are most important in considering the ways in which evaluation might promote change. According to Patton (1978), who reiterates Alkin (1975), one crucial question is: 'Evaluation: who needs it? who cares?'[6] The implication of this is that evaluation will only stimulate change if (1) it arises from 'real' questions that certain individuals, or groups of individuals, have concerning an aspect of policy or practice that affects them personally, and (2) if these individuals and groups are actively involved in the whole evaluative process. Similar assumptions underlie a number of approaches in action-research: the theme of our next section.

Evaluation as Action Research

Action research is a sufficiently important concept to command a literature of its own. Its introduction here, therefore, is not designed to provide a 'Cook's Tour' but to illustrate how the process of research, deliberation, decision-making and action can be *built into* evaluation. The suggestion is that if evaluation is conceptualised as action research then implementation of change becomes an integral part of the process, rather than a sequel to it.

It is usually acknowledged that the concept of action research was first articulated by Kurt Lewin (1946, 1947), a social psychologist, who employed it as the basis of a number of community projects in the USA after the Second World War. What is distinctive about the approach is its concern to promote improvement in practice and improvement in understanding *simultaneously*. According to Rapoport (1970): 'Action research aims to contribute *both* to the practical concerns of people in an immediately problematic situation and to the goals of social science by joint collaboration within a mutually acceptable ethical framework' (p. 499).

Although this definition is useful, it is not entirely satisfactory when applied to educational contexts. As Stenhouse (1979b) pointed out

Rapoport's formulation still implies two audiences: an audience of teachers for practical ideas, and an audience of social scientists for theoretical ideas. In Stenhouse's view such a dichotomy is unacceptable however well the two groups 'collaborate'. Instead he proposed that action research should contribute, not only to practice, but to 'a theory of education and teaching which is accessible to other teachers' (Stenhouse, 1979b, p. 4). The fact that early formulations of action research were not interpreted in this way might account for the relative neglect of the method in educational settings at a time (the 1950s and 1960s) when it was influential in social work and industry (Kemmis, 1981). On the other hand it might simply have been that the imperative for educational action was not as great as it then appeared in other social and economic areas. Whatever the facts of the case, educational action research has enjoyed a considerable revival in the latter half of the 1970s and the 1980s. In the UK this is largely attributable to the work of Lawrence Stenhouse, John Elliott, and those they have worked with on a number of action research projects: the Race Project (a 'spin-off' from the Humanities Curriculum Project), the Ford Teaching Project and The Teacher-Pupil Interaction and the Quality of Learning Project (TIQL)[7]. In Australia the development of educational action research theory and methodology is proceeding under the leadership of Stephen Kemmis at Deakin University.

According to Kemmis *et al* (1981), Lewin's model for action research is applicable in educational contexts because it represents a generalisable proposal for 'the way groups of people can organise the conditions under which they can learn from their own experience' (p.2). The key feature of the model is a *spiral of steps* which involves planning, action and evaluation of action. Kemmis *et al* (1981) describe the process in the following way:

> In practice, the process begins with a *general idea* that some kind of improvement or change is desirable. In deciding just where to begin in making improvements, one decides on a *field of action* . . where the battle (not the whole war) should be fought. It is a decision on where it is possible to have an impact. The general idea prompts a *"reconnaissance"* of the circumstances of the field, and fact-finding about them. Having decided on the field and made a preliminary reconnaissance, the action researcher decides on a *general plan* of action. Breaking the general plan down into achievable steps, the action researcher settles on the *first action step*. Before taking this first step the action researcher

becomes more circumspect, and devises a way of *monitoring* the effects of the first action step. When it is possible to maintain fact-finding by monitoring the action, the first step is taken. As the step is implemented, new data starts coming in and the effect of the action can be described and *evaluated*. The general plan is then revised in the light of the new information about the field of action and the second action step can be planned along with appropriate monitoring procedures. The second action step is then implemented, monitored and evaluated; and the spiral of action, monitoring, evaluation and replanning continues.   (p. 2)

The process outlined here has a number of attractions. Although it involves considerable systematisation, it builds on a naturalistic approach to decision-making. Unlike some evaluation procedures, which seem to assume that decisions will be delayed until all available evidence has been collected and processed, action research recognises that where change is desired the imperative for action may be so great that decisions have to be made almost immediately. The important point is that in action research the *implementation* of action is monitored carefully (for unintended as well as intended effects) then modified if the need arises.

The sequence of planning, action and monitoring is usually taken to refer to decisions relating to a system, programme or institution, but it is equally appropriate if decisions relate to a single individual. Harlen (1978), for instance, presents a model for decision-making which is designed to promote consideration of how decisions might be made in order to match the curriculum to the needs of individual pupils. According to this model teacher decisions are informed, not only by consideration of goals and external constraints, but by feedback concerning the pupil's interaction with the learning environment that the teacher has decided to create, feedback obtained directly from the pupil by interview and observation, and feedback from the constant monitoring of intended and unintended outcomes. Although she does not call it such, and although some of the details differ, Harlen's feedback model of decision-making shares much in common with the concept of an action research spiral. The major difference is that Harlen's is essentially a linear model (i.e. teacher considers goals and constraints, then makes decisions about a learning environment with which pupils interact and from which outcomes arise) with a *feedback loop*. Although there is no room here to examine in detail the logic of action research, one suspects that the difference between this feedback model and the action research spiral may be little more than semantic.

However, amongst some educationists the concept of an action research spiral is clearly finding favour and being promoted. In Australia it has been presented as a simple guide for teachers and school administrators (Kemmis *et al*, 1981), and with one or two conceptual modifications it has been adopted as the basis of the Teacher-Pupil Interaction and the Quality of Learning Project (TIQL) directed by Elliott in the UK. However it is difficult, on the basis of project publications (Elliott and Ebbutt, 1986b), to evaluate the extent to which the procedure has been institutionalised in schools, or assess its viability as a strategy for *institutional* change. Evidence of teachers adopting a research approach to their own teaching continues to grow (Ford Teaching Project, 1975; Nixon, 1981; Classroom Action Research Network Bulletins, Nos. 1 to 5; Acland, 1984; Baker, 1984; Elliott and Ebbutt, 1986b.), but the degree to which action research is effective in influencing *institutional policy and practice* remains uncertain. It is argued that action research has applications beyond the study of classrooms (Elliott, 1981a), but this presupposes the elimination of certain structural constraints - the issue we turn to next.

Collaboration and Emancipation

When writing about the Ford Teaching Project, Elliott (1976, 1980b) observed that teachers sometimes find that they are not free to change in ways they may have assumed they were. In other words, their 'field of action' may be very limited. For instance, they may discover that the implementation of what they regard as a desirable change, even in their own classrooms, requires a different distribution of resources, timetabling, pupil grouping, or other forms or organisation. All of these conditions would require change in other parts of the social system to which they belong[8]. If action research in schools is to be effective, therefore, it needs to embrace a procedure for promoting change at the level of the whole school. The TIQL project has attempted to confront this issue directly and in its first working paper Elliott (1981a) suggested that where there is a need for change, which is beyond the power of an individual, then 'the research team in the school should move into a period of negotiation with the relevant persons, committees etc. who control what needs changing ... While these "external" negotiations are going on the spiral of action research should focus on them directly, and away from classroom action' (p. 25). Clearly this proposal is quite radical; in certain situations it might even be regarded as subversive since it implies a form of collaborative political action that may involve the 'indians' in some sort of confrontation with the 'chiefs'.

Despite the obvious political difficulties, the collaborative element in action research was regarded as essential by Lewin and remains undiminished in the work of his successors. Moreover, Kemmis (1981) and Elliott (1982) believe that since action research has an emancipatory potential, it can be conceptualised as an appropriate expression of modern critical social science[9]. This means that the action research process is regarded as having the potential to help identify 'systematically distorted' practices and understandings, and to explain the mechanisms that 'cause' them (Elliott, 1982). Put simply, it offers possibilities for *consciousness-raising* - the stage that precedes action. Of course, it is unlikely that any collaborative group of teachers will be able to achieve enlightenment entirely by its own efforts; the point about distorted understanding is that the individual or group does not realise that it is distorted[10]. For this reason much of the work of people like Kemmis and Elliott is directed towards exploring the role of the external consultant, or facilitator, in action research (see, for instance, Brown, Henry, Henry and McTaggart, 1982). One problem that this raises is the possibility that action research will be allowed to fall back into the old academic imperialism that it first reacted against. The authority of the academic or other prestigious outsider is sometimes hard for teachers, and others, to resist and they might all too easily concede that (s)he automatically has greater access to the 'truth'. The dependency that this can create on the part of teachers is, of course, the very antithesis of autonomy or emancipation. Alternatively traditional prejudices concerning the usefulness of research (or lack of it) may cause some teachers to reject, out of hand, the outsider's perspective. Thus the ideal that practical deliberation can itself be freed from distortion engendered by role and status differences within a collaborative group remains to be tested. As yet the discussion of emancipatory action research tends to be at a theoretical level and we have little evidence of its successful implentation in schools.

Structures for Learning

Whatever the merits of action research, the arguments presented in this chapter suggest that participation and collaboration are indeed centrally important if evaluation is to bring about learning and change. Since these two aspects concern the nature and quality of relationships within the social systems of schools, we find that we need to reiterate some of the ideas concerning organisation and management that we discussed in Chapter 9. Assuming that curriculum evaluation requires a supportive organisational structure if it is to lead to improvement, we need to ask again: what kind of organisational structure? On this matter Elliott (1982) is uncompromising:

> Those policy-makers who are concerned that the organisational structures of schools should support deliberative self-evaluation and decision-making by individual teachers, will need to facilitate procedures by which the staff as a whole can collectively examine the relationship between organisational structures and their activities as individuals. If they resist supporting this 'bottom-up' approach to educational change, then one can be excused for concluding that the real intent behind the policy is one of 'top down' technical control. (p.31)

What Elliott implies is that if schools are expected to evaluate their practice, and if teachers, either individually or collectively, are expected to act on the results, then policy-makers at national, local or school level need to create structures for learning and grassroots change without imposing any too rigid definition of the kind of change that is expected. Obviously there is risk attached to leaving the situation so open-ended, and few administrators are happy with such ambiguity. Nevertheless, it is difficult to resist the conclusion that if policy and practice in education is to be opened up through evaluation procedures then this must happen at *all* levels in the system[11]. However if a system, whether it be a single school or local authority, succeeds in becoming more 'open' much of the groundwork for negotiated change is already accomplished.

Apart from the likely need for a particular organisational climate, there are a number of specific structures that can be created to foster effective use of evaluation procedures. At Stantonbury Campus, for instance, the creation of a staff development programme was designed to do just this (see OU, 1982, Case Study 2). Although one member of the senior staff was instrumental in setting up the programme, and arranging the input of resources (in terms of time, money and personnel), he allowed teams of more junior staff to determine the shape and direction of most of its activities. Sometimes this led to criticisms of lack of leadership, but he steadfastly adhered to his conviction that only collaborative group effort in a supportive environment will issue in constructive change.

At local authority level the creation of a similar structure might also be effective. This could take the form of a co-ordinated programme of school-focused INSET (as operates in Devon in association with the University of Exeter), or the development of a local network of self-evaluating schools[12]. There are already signs that some schools and local authorities are beginning to develop infrastructures of this kind. However, whether approaches to collaborative curriculum evaluation and action in schools involve only teachers, or teachers and outsiders, further progress is only likely if greater efforts are made to understand the way in which people, especially teachers, work and learn together in co-operative groups. As Moon (1980) pointed out this question ought to be a priority on the curriculum research and development agenda for the 1980s. Although our knowledge of any such initiatives is limited, we do know that in 1985 the Economic and Social Research Council (ESRC) funded one project very much along these lines. This was concerned with Primary School Staff Relationships and was directed by Jenny Nias at the Cambridge Institute of Education.

To sum up, the arguments advanced in this chapter suggest that the results of an evaluation are more likely to lead to educational improvement if all those whose practice is implicated (especially teachers) are actively involved in identifying evaluation needs, deciding general strategies, collecting and processing relevant information, proposing policy options and deciding and implementing action. In other words, *participation* in the *process* of evaluation seems particularly important. This implies, of course, that evaluation by 'outsiders' is likely to be ineffective in terms of change within schools unless the interest and co-operation of 'insiders' is fully mobilised. However, a collaborative approach to evaluation also raises questions to which we have no conclusive answers. For instance, we have no firm evidence of ways in which disparate groups of individuals can work together in a collaborative exercise without allowing power relations to distort their efforts. Neither are we yet clear about the role of theory in illuminating practice, nor of the kinds of organisational structures that are most likely to support individuals in 'learning together'. These are lines of enquiry that demand further investigation. In the meanwhile, our best hopes for curriculum evaluation in schools rests on a certain amount of faith in the effectiveness of collaboration and participation to promote learning - and indeed a belief in the importance of the democratic community[13].

Notes

1. Following Worth (1977), MacDonald and Norris (1978) remain sceptical of the rational possibilities for the use of evaluation reports. Attracted by the notion that policy formation is a process of conflict management and consensus building, they also subscribe to a political model of research/ evaluation. Whilst not denying a commitment to rationality they acknowledge that an evaluator who seeks influence 'has to learn the rules of the bargaining game and work within them' (p. 7). For an example of this see Simons (1980b; 1987).

2. This idea was important in the evaluation of the National Development Programme in Computer Assisted Learning (UNCAL) (MacDonald, 1973).

3. The idea that those who conduct evaluations should engage in continuous and serious dialogue with information users is strongly supported by both Stake (1975) and House (1977). Arguing that evaluations are fundamentally acts of persuasion House (1977) maintains that:

   > Persuasion is directly related to action. Even though evaluation is less certain than scientific information addressed to a universal audience, persuasion is effective in promoting action because it focuses on a particular audience and musters information with which this audience is concerned. (p. 6)

   House graphically illustrates his argument by claiming that at the time of writing he cannot be persuaded to remove himself from Los Angeles - sitting on top of the San Andreas fault. Whilst he is well aware of the scientific predictions regarding an imminent major earthquake, no one has been able to tell him how this general prediction would affect him personally. Therefore he stays.

4. This kind of emphasis is also reflected in Fullan (1972) and Doyle and Ponder (1976).

5. Sieber (1981, p. 123) proposes a taxonomy of incentives (positive and negative) and disincentives (positive and negative) for knowledge utilisation. Positive incentives may be performance-related (e.g. freedom to control tasks and conditions, goal achievement), material, authoritative, affiliative, or concerned with the physical environment, career advancement or novelty (i.e. providing new experience). Negative incentives for knowledge utilisation arise from threatened deprivation of rewards if action is not taken; positive disincentives are associated with prospective rewards for non-utilisation of knowledge; and negative disincentives arise from threatened deprivation of rewards if knowledge is utilised. This analysis may be compared with Nias's (1981) analysis of teacher job satisfaction. On the basis of a critique of Herzberg's (1966) two-factor hypothesis, she distinguishes 'satisfiers', 'negative satisfiers' and 'dissatisfiers'.

6. It is interesting that of all the examples of in-school evaluations that we have described, the one that most clearly resulted in change (i.e. Sir Frank Markham School's curriculum review) was also the activity where the interest and leadership of an individual was most easily identified.

7. The SSRC project on the Problems and Effects of Teaching about Race Relations was directed by Stenhouse; the other two were directed by John Elliott.

8. Once more Hoyle's (1975) dilemma of innovation is reiterated i.e. that innovation requires organisational change, but that organisational change is itself an innovation.

9.   Critical theory was introduced briefly in Chapters 1 and 7. According to Habermas (1972), one of its foremost proponents, all knowledge is constituted by interests. Critical theory is distinctive in that it acknowledges a specifically 'emancipatory' interest.

10.   Again this is the issue of rendering the familiar strange (see Chapter 9).

11.   One chief adviser known to us approached the schools in his authority with the idea of self-evaluation by first proposing to conduct a self-evaluation of his own department.

12.   David Alexander, an LEA adviser/inspector in Bedfordshire, is interested in developing a network such as this in his own authority. Each year a two day conference brings together teachers who are interested in starting evaluation, and those who have work in progress.

13.   Stenhouse (1975) closed his book on curriculum research and development with the sentence: 'Communications is less effective than community in the utilisation of knowledge' (p. 223).

Bibliography

ABEL, D.A. and CONNER, L.A. (1978) 'Educational Malpractice: one jurisdiction's response.' in HOOKER, C.P. (ed) *The Courts and Education: the seventy seventh yearbook of the National Society for the Study of Education* Part 1. Chicago, University of Chicago Press.

ABT, C (1976) *Supply, Demands, Motives and Constraints of the Evaluation Producing Community.* Paper given at the Annual Meeting of the American Educational Research Association (AERA), April.

ACKLAND, R. (1984) *Investigating talk in Cumbrian classrooms.* York, Longman for Schools Council.

ADAMS, R.S. and BIDDLE, B.J. (1970) *Realities of Teaching: Explorations with Video Tape,* New York, Holt, Rinehart and Winston.

ADELMAN, C. (1979) *Some Dilemmas of Institutional Evaluation and their Relationship to Preconditions and Procedures.* Paper presented at AERA Annual Conference, April.

ADELMAN, C. (ed) (1981) *Uttering, Muttering: Collecting, using and reporting talk for social and educational research.* London, Grant McIntyre.

ADELMAN, C. (ed) (1984) *The Politics and Ethics of Evaluation.* London, Croom Helm.

ADELMAN, C. and ALEXANDER, R. (1982) *The Self Evaluating Institution,* London, Methuen.

ADELMAN, C. and WALKER, R. (1971/2) 'Stop-frame cinematography with synchronised sound: a technique for recording in school classrooms'. *Journal of the Society of Motion Picture and Television Engineers. 83* (3).

ADELMAN, C. and WALKER, R. (1975) *A Guide to Classroom Observation.* London, Methuen.

ADVISORY CENTRE FOR EDUCATION (1979) *School Governors: partnership in practice.* The ACE guide to current arrangements for school government in the local education authorities of England and Wales, including a summary of the Taylor Report. Prepared by Joan Sallis, ACE.

AINLEY, D. and LAZONBY, J.N. (1981) 'Observation as a means of evaluation of science courses for less able children - a case study'. *School Science Review, 62* (221) pp 631-40.

ALEXANDER, R. (1978a) 'An internal evaluation: appraisal and speculations' in COLLIER, G. *Evaluating the new B.Ed.,* Guildford, Society for Research into Higher Education.

ALEXANDER, R. (1978b) 'Didsbury College Evaluation Committee' in OPEN UNIVERSITY (1982) (*see below*), Case Study 3. *The CNAA.*

ALKIN, M. (1975) 'Evaluation: Who needs it? Who cares?' *Studies in Educational Evaluation 1* (3) Winter, pp 201-212.

ALKIN, M.C., DAILLAK, R. and WHITE, P. (1979) *Using Evaluations: does evaluation make a difference?* Beverly Hills, Sage Publications.

ALMOND, L. (1982) 'Containable Time' in OPEN UNIVERSITY (1982) (*see below*), Block 2, Part 2, Appendix.

ANDERSON, D.C. (1979) *Evaluation by Classroom Experience: strategies for professional development.* Driffield, Nafferton.

ANDERSON, D.C. (1981) *Evaluating Curriculum Proposals: a critical guide.* London, Croom Helm.

ANDERSON, S.B., BALL, S., MURPHY, R.T. (eds) (1975) *Encyclopedia of Educational Evaluation.* San Francisco, Jossey-Bass.

ARGYRIS, C. and SCHON, D. (1974) *Theory in Practice: increasing professional effectiveness.* San Francisco, Jossey-Bass.

ARMSTRONG, M. (1981) *Closely Observed Children.* London, Writers and Readers.

ASHTON, P.M. and DAVIES, F.R. (1975) 'Two analyses of teachers' discussion of aims in primary education' in TAYLOR, P.H. *Aims, Influence and Change in the Primary School Curriculum.* Windsor, NFER.

ASHTON, P., KNEEN, P. and DAVIES, F. (1976) *Aims into Practice in the Primary School: a guide for teachers.* London, Hodder and Stoughton.

ASHTON, P., KNEEN, P., DAVIES, P. and HOLLEY, B.J. (1975) *The Aims of Primary Education: a study of teachers' opinions*, London, Macmillan Education.

ATKIN, J.M. (1978) 'Institutional Self-Evaluation versus National Professional Accreditation, or Back to the Normal School?' *Educational Researcher, 7* (10) November.

ATKIN, J.M. (1979) 'Education Accountability in the United States', *Educational Analysis, 1* (1) pp 5-21.

ATKIN, J.M. (1980) *The Government in the Classroom.* The Ninth Sir John Adams Lecture delivered at the University of London Institute of Education, 6 March.

ATKINSON, P. (1981) 'Inspecting Classroom Talk' in ADELMAN (ed) (1981).

BAKER, K. (1980) 'Planning School Policies for INSET: the SITE Project', in HOYLE, E. and MEGARRY, J. (eds) (1980).

BAKER, P. (1984) *Practical Self-evaluation for Teachers.* York, Longman for Schools Council.

BANNISTER, D. and MAIR, J.M.M. (1968) *The Evaluation of Personal Constructs*, London, Academic Press.

BARNES, J.A. (1977) *The Ethics of Inquiry in Social Science*, Oxford University Press.

BARNES, J.A. (1979) *Who should know what?* Harmondsworth, Penguin.

BARON, S., MILLER, H., WHITFIELD, R. and YATES, O. (1981) 'On the Social Organisation of Evaluation: a case study' in SMETHERHAM, D. (ed) (1981).

BASSEY, M. and HATCH, N. (1979) 'A seven-category interaction analysis for infant teachers to use themselves'. *Educational Research 21* (2) February, pp 131-7.

BECHER, A. (1978) 'Ends, Means and Policies' in BECHER, A. and MACLURE, S. (eds) (1978b).

BECHER, A. (1979) 'Self-accounting, Evaluation and Accountability', in STENHOUSE, L. (ed) *Accountability and Educational Analysis.*

BECHER, T., ERAUT, M., BARTON, J., CANNING, T., KNIGHT, J. (1979) *Accountability in the middle years of schooling.* Final report to SSRC, Part 1, Falmer, University of Sussex.

BECHER, T., ERAUT, M., and KNIGHT, J. (1981) *Policies for Educational Accountability.* London, Heinemann Educational.

BECHER, T. and MACLURE, S. (1978a) *The Politics of Curriculum Change.* London, Hutchinson.

BECHER, A. and MACLURE, S. (eds) (1978b) *Accountability in Education,* Windsor, NFER Publishing Co.

BECKER, H.S. (1958) 'Problems of inference and proof in participant observation', *American Sociological Review, 23* pp 652-60. (Reprinted in BECKER, H. (1970a) *Sociological Work,* Transaction Books, and McCORMICK, R. *et al* (1982).)

BECKER, H. (1970a) 'Problems in the Publication of Field Studies' in *Sociological Works.* New Brunswick, Transaction Books.

BECKER, H. (1970b) 'Whose Side are We On?' in *Sociological Work.* New Brunswick, Transaction Books. (First published in *Social Problems, 14* Winter 1967, pp 239-47.)

BECKER, H.S. and GEER, B. (1957) 'Participant observation and interviewing: a comparison' *Human Organization 16*(3) pp 28-32, reprinted in McCALL and SIMMONS (eds) (1969).

BECKER, H.S. and GEER, B. (1958) 'Participant observation and interviewing: a rejoinder'. *Human Organization, 17* (2) pp 39-40, reprinted in McCALL and SIMMONS (eds) (1969).

BECKER, H.S. and GEER, B. (1960) 'Participant observation: the analysis of qualitative data', in ADAMS, R.N. and PREISS, J.C. (eds) *Human Organization Research,* Homewood, Illinois, Dorsey Press.

BENNETT, N. (1978) 'Surveyed from a shaky base' *TES*, 3 November.

BENNETT, N. and McNAMARA, D. (eds) (1979) *Focus on Teaching: Readings in the observation and conceptualisation of teaching.* London, Longman.

BENNIS, W.G., BENNE, K.D. and CHIN, R. (1969) *The Planning of Change*, 2nd edn, New York, Holt, Rinehart and Winston.

BEN-PERETZ, M. (1981) 'Curriculum Analysis as a Tool of Evaluation' in LEWY, A. and NEVO, D. (eds) (1981).

BIOTT, C. (1981) 'Evaluator, Researcher, Participant: role boundaries in a long term study of innovation' in SMETHERHAM, D. (ed) (1981).

BLACK, H.D. and DOCKRELL, W.B. (1980) 'Assessment in the affective domain: do we, can we, should we?' *British Educational Research Journal 6* (2) pp 197-208.

BLACKIE, J.E.H. (1970) *Inspecting the Inspectorate*, London, Routledge and Kegan Paul.

BLOCK, J. (ed) (1971) *Mastery Learning: theory and practice*, New York, Holt, Rinehart and Winston.

BLOOM, B.S. (ed) (1956) *Taxonomy of Educational Objectives: the Classification of Educational Goals, Handbook I: Cognitive Domain* London, Longman.

BLOOM, B.S., HASTINGS, J.T., MADAUS, E.F. (1971) *Handbook on Formative and Summative Evaluation of Student Learning*. New York, McGraw-Hill.

BLOOR, M. (1978) 'On the Analysis of Observational Data: a discussion of the worth and uses of inductive techniques and respondent validation'. *Sociology 12* (3) pp 545-552.

BOBBITT, F. (1918) *The Curriculum*, Boston, Houghton Mifflin.

BOBBITT, F. (1924) *How to Make a Curriculum*, Boston, Houghton Mifflin.

BOEHM, A.E. and WEINBERG, R.A. (1977) *The Classroom Observer: a guide for developing observation skills*, Teachers College Press.

BOLAM, R. (1975) 'The Management of educational change: towards a conceptual framework' in HARRIS, A., LAWN, M. and PRESCOTT W. (eds) *Curriculum Innovation*, London, Croom Helm in association with the Open University Press.

BOLAM, R. (1980) 'In-service education and training' in HOYLE, E. and MEGARRY, J. (eds) (1980).

BOLAM, R. (1981) *In-service Education and Training of Teachers and Educational Change*, Paris, OECD.

BOLAM, R. (1982a) *Recent Research on the Dissemination and Implementation of Educational Innovations* University of Bristol (mimeograph). (Paper prepared for the National Conference on Research and Development in Health Education with Special Reference to Youth. Southampton University, Sept.)

BOLAM, R. (1982b) *Strategies for School Improvement*, Paris, OECD (mimeograph).

BOLAM, R., SMITH, E. and CANTER, H. (1978) *Local Education Authority Advisers and the Mechanisms of Innovation*, Windsor, NFER.

BORICH, G.D. (1977) 'Sources of invalidity in measuring classroom behaviour'. *Instructional Science 6*, pp 283-318.

BORICH, G.D. and MADDEN, S.K. (1977) *Evaluating Classroom Instruction: A Source Book of Instruments* Reading, Massachusetts, Addison-Wesley.

BOUCHARD, T.J. Jr. (1976) 'Unobstrusive Measures: an Inventory of Uses'. *Sociology Methods and Research, 4* (3) pp 267-300.

BOWLES, S. and GINTIS, H. (1976) *Schooling in Capitalist America: educational reform and the contradictions of economic life*. London, Routledge and Kegan Paul.

BOYD, H.W. and WESTFALL, R. (1970) 'Interviewer bias once more revisited'. *Journal of Marketing Research, 7*, pp 249-53, reprinted in BYNNER, J. and STRIBLEY, K.M. (eds) (1978).

BOYDELL, D. (1975) 'Systematic Observation in Informal Classrooms', in CHANAN, G. and DELAMONT, S. (eds) (1975).

BRANDT, R. (1978) 'Conflicting Views on Competency Testing in Florida' *Educational Leadership*, November.

BRIDGES, D. (1979) 'Some reasons why curriculum planning should not be "left to the experts",' *Journal of Philosophy of Education, 13*, pp 159-164.

BRIGHOUSE, T. (1982) *Development of Evaluation in Oxfordshire.* Paper presented at National Conference of Association for the study of the Curriculum, Oxford, April.

BROOKS, K.V. (1979) 'Delphi Technique: expanding applications' *North Central Association Quarterly 53* (3) pp 377-85.

BROPHY, J.E. and GOOD, T.L. (1974) *Teacher-Student Relationships: Causes and consequences.* New York, Holt, Rinehart and Winston.

BROUDY, H.S., SMITH, B. and BURNETT, J.R. (1964) *Democracy and Excellence in American Secondary Education.* Chicago, Rand McNally.

BROWN, G. and ARMSTRONG, A. (1978) 'SAID: A System for Analysing Instructional Discourse' in McALEESE, R. and HAMILTON, D. (eds) (1978).

BROWN, L., HENRY, C., HENRY, J., McTAGGART, R. (1982) 'Action Research: Notes on the National Seminar' (at Deakin University, Australia), *CARN Bulletin No 5.* Cambridge Institute of Education.

BROWN, M. (1979) 'Looking at Nursery and Infant Schools'. *Journal of NAIEA, 10*, Spring pp 9-11.

BROWN, R. (ed) (1973) *Knowledge, Education and Cultural Change*, London, Tavistock.

BROWN, S. (1979) 'Attitude assessment' in SCOTTISH EDUCATION DEPARTMENT (1979) pp 15-29.

BROWN, S., McINTYRE, D. and IMPEY, R. (1979) 'The Evaluation of School Science Departments', *Studies in Educational Evaluation, 5* pp 175-186.

BROWNE, S. (1979) 'The Accountability of the HM Inspectorate (England)', in LELLO, J. (ed) (1979) pp 35-44.

BRUNER, J. (1960) *The Process of Education*, Cambridge, USA, Harvard University Press.

BULMER, M. (1980) 'Comment on the ethics of covert methods' *British Journal of Sociology 31* (1) pp 59-65.

BURGESS, R.G. (ed) (1982) *Field Research: a sourcebook and field manual*, London, George Allen and Unwin.

BURSTALL, C. and KAY, B. (1978) *Assessment - the American experience* London, DES.

BYNNER, J. (1980) 'Experimental Research Strategy, and Evaluation Research Designs' *British Educational Research Journal, 6* (1).

BYNNER, J. and STRIBLEY, K.M. (eds) (1978) *Social Research: Principles and Procedures.* London, Longman in association with the Open University Press.

CAIRNS, M.A. (1982) *Content Analysis of Three Junior Mathematics Schemes* Centre for Educational Research and Development, University of Lancaster.

CALLAGHAN, J. (1976) 'Towards a national debate'. Reprinted in *Education, 22*, pp 332-333.

CALIFORNIA STATE DEPT. OF EDUCATION (1977) *California Curriculum Frameworks: a handbook for production, implementation and evaluation activities*, Sacramento.

CAMBRIDGE ACCOUNTABILITY PROJECT (1981) *Case Studies in School Accountability* (Three volumes), Cambridge Institute of Education, mimeograph.

CAMBRIDGE INSTITUTE OF EDUCATION (1985) *New Perspectives on the Mathematics Curriculum: an independent appraisal of the outcomes of APU mathematics testing 1978-82.* London, HMSO.

CAMPBELL, D. and STANLEY, J. (1966) *Experimental and Quasi-experimental Designs for Research.* Chicago, Rand-McNally.

CHANAN, G. (1977) 'The Curricular Transaction' in KING, E.J. (ed) *Reorganizing Edcuation* London, Sage.

CHANAN, G. and DELAMONT, S. (eds) (1975) *Frontiers of Classroom research* Windsor, NFER.

CHAPMAN, J.L. and CZERNIEWSKA, P. (eds) (1978) *Reading: from process to practice*, London, Routledge and Kegan Paul.

CHESHIRE EDUCATION COMMITTEE (1981) *Curriculum 11-16: Cheshire Reappraisal Group*, CEC.

CHOPPIN, B. (1981) 'Educational measurement and the item bank model', in LACEY, C. and LAWTON, D. (eds) (1981).

CHRISTIE, T. and FORREST, G.M. (1981) *Defining Public Examination Standards*, Basingstoke, Macmillan.

CLARKE, M. (1979) 'A Core-curriculum for the Primary School', *Forum, 21* (2) Spring.

CLIFT, P. (1982) 'LEA Schemes for School Self-evaluation: a critique.' *Educational Research, 25* (1) November

CLIFT, P., ABEL, B. and SIMPSON, G. (1982) *Case Study 5: Great Barr School.* Milton Keynes, Open University Press.

CLIFT, P., CYSTER, R., RUSSELL, J. and SEXTON, B. (1978) 'The Use of Kelly's Repertory Grids to Conceptualise Classroom Life', in McALEESE, R. and HAMILTON, D. (1978).

CLIFT, P., NUTTALL, D.L. and McCORMICK, R. (eds) (1987) *Studies in School Self-Evaluation.* London, Falmer Press.

CLIFT, P.S., WILSON, E.L., WEINER, G.G. (1981) *Record Keeping in Primary Schools*, London, Macmillan.

CODD, J.A. (1981) 'The Clinical Interview: an holistic approach to the evaluation of learning' *Journal of Curriculum Studies, 13* (2) pp 145-50.

COHEN, D. and HARRISON, M. (1979) 'Curriculum decision-making in Australian Education: what decisions are made within schools'. *Journal of Curriculum Studies, 11* (3) pp 257-62.

COHEN, D.H. and STERN, V. (1978) 'Observing and Recording the Behaviour of Young Children' *Teachers College Press* (2nd edition).

COHEN, L. (1976) *Educational Research in Classrooms and Schools.* London, Harper Row.

COHEN, L. and MANION, L. (1981) 'Perspectives on Classrooms and

Schools'. London, Holt, Rinehart and Winston.

COLEMAN, J.S., CAMPBELL, E.Q., HOBSON, C.J., McPARTLAND, J., MOOD, A.M., WINFIELD, F., YORK, R.L. (1966) *Equality of Educational Opportunity*, Washington D.C., US Government Printing Office.

COMMITTEE OF COUNCIL ON EDUCATION (1845) *Instructions for the Inspectors of Schools* MINUTES, 1844, Vol 1, pp 24-35. London, Board of Education.

COMMUNITY EDUCATION WORKING PARTY (1981) *Written Communication between home and school* Nottingham, Publications Unit, University of Nottingham.

COOPER, J.O. (1974) *Measurment and Analysis of Behavioral Techniques* Columbus, Ohio, Merrill.

COMPTROLLER GENERAL OF THE UNITED STATES (1976) *The National Assessment of Educational Progress: its results need to be more useful* Washington, D.C., General Accounting Office, July.

COUNCIL FOR NATIONAL ACADEMIC AWARDS (1979) *Developments in Partnership in Validation* London, CNAA.

COWEN, J. (1981) 'Curriculum Issues 1970-1990: contents, policies and practices in the USA'. *Compare, 11* (1) 1981.

CRADDOCK, J. (1979) 'Looking at schools in Hillingdon' *Journal of NAIEA, 10* Spring, pp 8-9.

CRONBACH, L.J. (1963) 'Course improvement through evaluation'. *Teachers College Record, 64*, pp 672-83.

CYPHERT, F.R. and GANT, W.L. (1973) 'The Delphi technique' in HOUSE, E.R. (1973).

DAHLGREN, L.O. and MARTON, F. (1978) 'Students' conceptions of subject matter: an aspect of learning and teaching in higher education' *Studies in Higher Education, 3* (1) pp 25-35.

DALTON, M. (1964) 'Preconceptions and methods in "Men who Manage".' in HAMMOND, P.E. (1964) *Sociologists at Work: Essays on the Craft of Social Research*. New York, Basic Books.

DARLING, J. (1978) 'Philosophy of education and the Munn Report' *Scottish Educational Review, 10* (2) November pp 25-36.

DAVIES, Brian (1973) 'On the contribution of organisational analysis to the study of educational institutions' in BROWN, R. (ed) (1973) pp 249-95.

DAVIES Brian (1981) 'Schools as organisations and the organisation of schooling' *Educational Analysis, 3 (1) pp 47-67.*

DAVIES, Bronwyn (1980) 'An analysis of primary school children's accounts of classroom interaction'. *British Journal of Sociology of Education, 1* (3) pp 257-80.

DAVIES, T.I. (1969) *School Organisation* Oxford, Pergamon.

DAVIS, E. (1981) *Teachers as Curriculum Evaluators* London, Allen and Unwin.

DEALE, R.N. (1975) *Assessment and Testing in the Secondary School* London, Evans/Methuen.

DEAN, J. (1982) 'Evaluation and advisers' in McCORMICK, R. *et al* (eds) (1982).

DEAN, J.P. and WHYTE, W.F. (1958) 'How do you know if the informant is telling the truth?' *Human Organisation, 17* (34-8) reprinted in BYNNER, J and STRIBLEY, K.M. (1978).

DELAMONT, S. (1976) *Interaction in the Classroom* London, Methuen.

DELAMONT, S. (1981) 'All too familiar? A decade of classroom research'. *Educational Analysis, 3* (1) pp 69-83.

DELVES, A.R. and WATTS, J. (1979) 'A year of evaluation'. *Forum, 22* (1) pp 25, 27-29.

DENTON, J.J. and SEXTON, M.J. (1978) 'Photography: an unconventional technique for the formative evaluation of a curriculum' *Educational Technology, 18* (11) November pp 26-9.

DEPARTMENT OF EDUCATION AND SCIENCE (DES) (1968) *Report from the Select Committee on Education and Science in Session 1967-68. Part I Her Majesty's Inspectorate (England and Wales): Observations by the Department of Education and Science on the Recommendations in Part 1* (Cmnd 3860) London, HMSO.

DES (1971) *HMI today and tommorrow* London, HMSO (First published in 1970, and revised in 1971).

DES (1977a) *Curriculum 11 - 16* (Working papers by HMI) London, HMSO.

DES (1977b) *Education in Schools: a consultative document* (Cmnd. 6869), London, HMSO. The Green Paper.

DES (1977c) *A New Partnership for Our Schools* London, HMSO. The Taylor Report.

DES (1978a) *Primary Education in England* London, HMSO.

DES (1978b) *Special Educational Needs* London, HMSO. The Warnock Report.

DES (1979a) *Aspects of Secondary Education in England: a survey by HM Inspectors of Schools* London, HMSO.

DES (1979b) *Local Authority Arrangements for the School Curriculum* London, HMSO.

DES (1980a) *A Framework for the School Curriculum* London, HMSO.

DES (1980b) *A view of the Curriculum* London, HMSO.

DES (1981a) *Curriculum 11-16: a review of progress* A joint study by HMI and five LEAs. London, HMSO.

DES (1981b) *The School Curriculum* London, HMSO.

DES (1983a) *Curriculum 11-16. Towards a statement of entitlement. Curricular reappraisal in action.* London, HMSO.

DES (1983b) *Teaching Quality.* Cmnd 8836, London, HMSO.

DES (1983c) *HM Inspectors Today: Standards in education.* London, HMSO.

DES (1984a) *Report by Her Majesty's Inspectors on the Effects of Local Authority Expenditure Policies on the Education Provision in England - 1983.* London, HMSO.

DES (1984b) *Education Observed. A review of the first six months of published reports by HM Inspectors.* London, HMSO.

DES (1984c) *Education Observed 2: a review of reports by HM Inspectors on primary schools and 11-16 and 12-16 comprehensive schools.* London, HMSO.

DES (1984d) *Records of Achievement: a statement of policy.* London, HMSO.

DES (1985a) *Better Schools.* London, HMSO.

DES (1985b) *The Development of Higher Education into the 1990s.* London, HMSO, May.

DES (1985c) *Quality in Schools: evaluation and appraisal.* London, HMSO.

DES (1985d) *The Curriculum from 5 to 16.* London, HMSO.

DES (1985e) *Science 5-16; a statement of policy.* London, HMSO.

DES (1985f) *Education Observed 3. Good teachers.* London, HMSO.

DES (1986) *Reporting Inspections: HMI methods and procedures - maintained schools.* London, HMSO.

DEWEY, J. (1916) *Democracy and Education*, New York, Macmillan Publishing Co.

DORSET COUNTY COUNCIL (1980) *Looking at Schools*, Dorset County Council

DOYLE, W. and PONDER, C.A. (1976) *The Practicality Ethic in Teacher Decision-Making* Denton, Texas, North Texas State University, mimeograph.

DRIVER, R. (1982) 'Children's learning in science', *Educational Analysis,* Vol. 4, No. 2, pp 69-79.

DRIVER, R. (1983) *The Pupil as Scientist.* Milton Keynes, Open University Press.

DUNKERTON, J. and GUY, J.J. (1981) 'The science teaching observation schedule: is it quantitative?' *European Journal of Science Education 3* (3) pp 313-6.

DUNKIN, M.J. and BIDDLE, B.J. (1974) *The Study of Teaching*, New York, Holt, Rinehart and Winston.

EASLEY, J.A. and ZWOYER, R.E. (undated) *Teaching by Listening - toward a new day in math classes*, Illinois, University of Illinois mimeograph.

EAST SUSSEX ACCOUNTABILITY PROJECT (1979) *Accountability in the Middle Years of Schooling: An Analysis of Policy Options* Brighton, University of Sussex, mimeograph. (pp 42-54 reprinted in McCORMICK, R. *et al* 1982, pp 307-18.)

EBBUTT, D. (1976) 'Some aspects of mixed ability science teaching with 2P' *Cambridge Journal of Education 6* (1), Lent Term.

EBBUTT, D. (1981) 'The role and tasks of school governors' in ELLIOTT, J. *et al* (1981).

EBBUTT, D. and WEST R. (1984) *A General Framework for the Evaluation of the Products of Local Working Groups.* London, Secondary Science Curriculum Review.

EBEL, R. (1972) *Essentials of Educational Measurement*, Englewood Cliffs, Prentice-Hall.

EDMONDS, E.L. (1962) *The School Inspector* London, Routledge and Kegan Paul.

EDUCATION, SCIENCE AND ARTS COMMITTEE (1981) 'House of Commons Second Report from ES&A Committee session 1981-82' *The Secondary School Curriculum and Examination: with special reference to the 14-16 year old age group*, Vol 1 Report. London HMSO.

EDUCATIONAL TESTING SERVICE (1973) *State Educational Assessment Programs* Princeton, ETS (revision).

EGGLESTON, J.F. (1974) 'Measuring attainment for curriculum evaluation' in MACINTOSH, H. (ed) (1974).

EGGLESTON, J.J. and GALTON, M.J. (1981) 'Reply to the article by J. Dunkerton and J.J. Guy' *European Journal of Science Education, 3* (3), pp 317-9.

EGGLESTON, J., GALTON, M.J., JONES, M.E. (1975) 'A Conceptual Map for Interaction Studies' in CHANAN, G. and DELMONT, S. (1975).

EISNER, E.W. (1969) 'Instructional and Expressive Objectives: their formulation and use in curriculum'. in POPHAM, J.W. (ed) *AERA Monograph on Curriculum Evaluation: Instructional Objectives* Chicago, Rand McNally, pp 1-18.

EISNER, E.W. (1979) *The Educational Imagination: on the design and evaluation of school programs.* New York, Macmillan Publishing Co. Inc.

EISNER, E. (1980) 'Some Observations on Qualitative Processes in Educational Evaluation' Paper presented at Homerton College, Cambridge, UK, 13 February.

ELLIOTT, G. (1981) *Self-evaluation and the Teacher, Part 4: a report on current practice, 1981*, London, Schools Council.

ELLIOTT, J. (1976) *Developing Hypotheses about Classrooms from Teachers' Practical Constructs*, Grand Forks, University of North Dakota Press (also in OU. 1976, Unit 28).

ELLIOTT, J. (1977) 'Conceptualising Relationships between Research/ Evaluation Procedures in In-Service Teacher Education' *British Journal of In-Service Education 4* (1 & 2) pp 102-115.

ELLIOTT, J. (1978) 'Classroom accountability and the self-monitoring teacher ' in HARLEN, W. (1978).

ELLIOTT, J. (1979) *Curriculum evaluation and the Classroom*, Paper prepared for DES Regional Course on 'Curriculum and Administration', Cambridge Institute of Education, mimeograph.

ELLIOTT, J. (1980a) *SSRC Cambridge Accountability Project: a summary report*, Cambridge Institute of Education, mimeograph.

ELLIOTT, J. (1980b) 'Implications of classroom research for professional development' in HOYLE, E. and MEGARRY, J. (eds) (1980).

ELLIOTT, J. (1981a) *Action-Research: a framework for self-evaluation in schools* Schools Council Programme 2: 'Teacher-Pupil Interaction and the Quality of Learning' Project. Working Paper No. 1. Cambridge Institute of Education, mimeograph.

ELLIOTT, J. (1981b) 'Educational Accountability and the Evaluation of Teaching' in LEWY, A. and NEVO, D. (eds) (1981).

ELLIOTT, J. (1981c) 'Teachers perspectives on school accountability' in ELLIOTT, J. *et al* (1981).

ELLIOTT, J. (1982) 'Self-evaluation, Professional Development, and Accountability' Cambridge Institute of Education. mimeograph.

(Paper presented at the Association for the Study of the Curriculum Conference on Curriculum Evaluation and Development at Oxford. 6-8 April 1982.)

ELLIOTT, J., BRIDGES, D., EBBUTT, D., GIBSON, R., and NIAS, J. (1981) *School Accountability* London. Grant McIntyre.

ELLIOTT, J. and EBBUTT, D. (1986a) 'How do Her Majesty's Inspectors Judge Educational Quality?' *Curriculum*, Vol. 7, No. 3, pp 130-40.

ELLIOTT, J. and EBBUTT, D. (eds) (1986b) *Case Studies in Teaching for Understanding*. Cambridge, Cambridge Institute of Education.

ELLIOTT, J. and WALKER, R. (1973) 'Teachers as evaluators' *The New Era*, Dec.

ERAUT, M. (1977) 'Strategies for Promoting Teacher development' *British Journal of In-Service Education*, 4 (1 and 2) Winter.

ERAUT, M. (1978) *Accountability at School Level: some options and implications*. Brighton, University of Sussex. mimeograph. Also in BECHER, A. and MACLURE, J. (eds) (1978b).

ERAUT, M., GOAD, L. and SMITH, G. (1975) *The Analysis of Curriculum Materials*. Brighton, University of Sussex, Education Area, Occasional Paper 2.

FAIRBROTHER, R.W. (ed) (1980) *Assessment and the Curriculum* Chelsea College, University of London.

FARNELL, D. (1981) *The Melbourn Project* Melbourn Village College, mimeograph. (Copy lodged at Cambridge Institute of Education.)

FISHER, R.A. (1953) *The Design of Experiments* New York, Hafner.

FLANDERS, N.A. (1970) *Analysing Teaching Behaviour* Reading, Massachusetts, Addison-Wesley Publishing Co.

FORBES, R.H. (1982) 'Testing in the USA' *Educational Analysis*, 4 (3).

FORD TEACHING PROJECT (1975) A series of booklets organised in four units: *Unit 1: Patterns of teaching; Unit 2: Research Methods; Unit 3. Hypotheses; Unit 4: Teacher case studies*. Cambridge, Institute of Education. (First published by CARE, University of East Anglia.) Most of the references in this book are to *Unit 2: Research Methods: Ways of doing research in one's own classroom*.

FOSTER, P. (1965) *Education and Social Change in Ghana* Chicago, The University of Chicago Press.

FRANSELLA, F. and BANNISTER, P. (1977) *A Manual for Repertory Grid Technique*, London, Academic Press.

FRASER, B.J. (1977) 'Evaluating the intrinsic worth of curricular goals: a discussion and an example' *Journal of Curriculum Studies* 9 (2) November, pp 125-132.

FRASER, B.J. (1981) 'Using environmental assessments to make better classrooms' *Journal of Curriculum Studies*, 13 (2), pp 131-44.

FULLAN, M. (1972) 'Overview of the Innovative Process and the User' *Interchange*, 3 (2-3).

GAGNE, R.M. (1970) *The Conditions of Learning* New York, Holt, Rinehart and Winston (2nd edition).

GALTON, M.J. (1978) *British Mirrors: A Collection of Classroom Observation Systems* University of Leicester, School of Education.

GALTON, M. (1979) 'Systematic - classroom observation: British research' *Educational Research, 21* (2), February, pp 109-115.

GALTON, M. (undated) 'Accountability and the teacher: some moves and counter moves' in RICHARDS, C. (ed) (undated).

GALTON, M. and SIMON, B. (eds) (1980) *Progress and Performance in the Primary Classroom* London, Routledge and Kegan Paul.

GARLAND, R. (1981) 'Developing policies for the whole curriculum' *School Organisation, 1* (1) pp 67-74.

GEORGE, A. *The Training of Volunteer Decision-Makers/Mediators through Distance Learning* PhD thesis, The Open University.

GERLACH, V.S. and SULLIVAN, H.J. (1969) 'Objectives, evaluation, and improved learner achievement' in POPHAM, W.J. (ed) (1969) *Instructional Objectives* Chicago, Rand McNally.

GIBSON, R. (1980) *Parent-Teacher Communication: one school and its practice* Cambridge, Institute of Education, mimeograph.

GIBSON. R. (1981) 'Curriculum criticism: misconceived theory, ill-advised practice' *Cambridge Journal of Education, 11* (3) Michaelmas Term.

GILLILAND, J. (1972) 'The assessment of readability - an overview' in MELNICK, A. and MERRITT, J. (eds) *The Reading Curriculum*, London, University of London Press.

GIPPS, C. (1982) 'A Critique of the APU' *Educational Analysis 4* (3).

GIPPS, C. (1987) 'The APU: from Trojan Horse to Angel of Light'. *Curriculum*, Vol. 8, pp 13-18.

GIPPS, C. and GOLDSTEIN, H. (1983) *Monitoring Children: An Evaluation of the Assessment of Performance Unit* London, Heinemann Educational.

GIPPS, C., STEADMAN, S., BLACKSONE, T. and STIERER, B. (1983) *Testing Children: standardised testing in local education authorities and schools.* London, Heinemann.

GLASAR, B. and STRAUSS, A. (1967) *The Discovery of Grounded Theory* Chicago, Aldine.

GOLD, R. (1958) 'Roles in sociology field observation' *Social Forces, 36* (3) pp 217-223.

GOLDSTEIN, H. (1979a) 'Consequences of using the Rasch model for educational assessment' *British Educational Research Journal, 5* (2) pp 211-220.

GOLDSTEIN, H. (1979b) 'The Mystification of Assessment' *Forum, 22* (1) Autumn, pp 14-16.

GOLDSTEIN, H. (1981a) 'Dimensionality, bias, independence and measured scale problems in latent trait test score models' *British Journal of Mathematical and Statistical Psychology, 33* pp 234-46.

GOLDSTEIN, H. (1981b) 'Limitations of the Rasch model for educational assessment' in LACEY, C. and LAWTON, D. (eds) (1981).

GOLDSTEIN, H. and BLINKHORN, S. (1977) 'Monitoring Educational Standards - an inappropriate model' *Bulletin of British Psychological Society, 30* pp 309-311.

GOOD, T.L. and BROPHY, J.E. (1978) *Looking in Classrooms* Harper Row (2nd Edition).

GOODING, C.T. (1980) 'An American looks at teacher views of the APU'. *Forum 23* (1) September.

GOODWIN, W.L. and DRISCOLL, L.A. (1980) *Handbook for Measurement and Evaluation in Early Childhood Education* San Francisco, Jossey-Bass.

GRAY, J. (1981) 'Towards Effective Schools: problems and progress in British research' *British Educational Research Journal, 7* (1) pp 59-69.

GRAY, J. (1982) 'Publish and Be Damned? The problem of comparing exam results in two inner London schools' *Educational Analysis, 4* (3) pp 47-56.

GRAY, J. and HANNON, V. (1986) 'HMI's Interpretations of Schools' Examination Results'. *Journal of Education Policy*, Vol. 1, No. 1, pp 23-33.

GRAY, J., McPHERSON, A.F. and RAFFE, D. (1982) *Reconstructions of Secondary Education*, London, Routledge and Kegan Paul.

GRAY, L. (1981) 'Self-Evaluation Procedures in Primary Schools' *School Organisation, 1* (3) pp 211-18.

GREEN, L. (1975) *School Reports and Other Information for Parents* Billericay, Essex, Home and School Council.

GREENBAUM, W., GARET, M.S. and SOLOMON, E.R. (1977) *Measuring Educational Progress* New York, McGraw Hill Inc.

GRETTON, J. and JACKSON, M. (1976) *William Tyndale: Collapse of a school - or a system?* London, George Allen and Unwin.

GRONLUND, N.E. (1981) *Measurement and Evaluation in Teaching* London, Collier Macmillan, 4th edn.

HABERMAS, J. (1972) *Knowledge and Human Interests* London, Heinemann (published in US by Beacon Press).

HABERMAS, J. (1974) 'Problems of Legitimation in Late Capitalism' in CONNERTON, P. (ed) *Critical Sociology*, Harmondsworth, Penguin Books.

HABERMAS, J. (1975) *Legitimation Crisis* Boston, Beacon Press. (Published in London by Heinemann in 1976.)

HABERMAS, J. (1979) *Communication and the Evolution of Society* Boston, Beacon Press (T. McCarthy, Translator)

HALL, E. (1980) *Using Personal Constructs* (Rediguide 9) Maidenhead, TRC Rediguides Ltd.

HALPIN, D. (1980) 'Exploring the Secret Garden' *Curriculum 1* (2) Autumn Term, pp 32-45.

HALSEY, A.H. (1979) *Accountability of government and public services*. Paper presented at SSRC Seminar on Aspects of Accountability, 11 September.

HAMBLETON, R.K. *et al* (1978) 'Criterion-referenced testing and measurement: a review of technical issues and developments'. *Review of Educational Research, 48* (1) Winter.

HAMILTON, D. (1976) *Curriculum Evaluation* London, Open Books.

HAMILTON, D. and DELAMONT, S. (1974) 'Classroom research: a cautionary tale' *Research in Education, 11*.

HAMILTON, D., JENKINS, D., KING, C., MACDONALD, B., PAR-LETT, M. (eds) (1977) *Beyond the Numbers Game,* Basingstoke and London, Macmillan Education.

HAMMERSLEY, M. (1980) 'Classroom Ethnography' *Educational Analysis, 2* (2) pp. 47-74.

HAMMERSLEY, M. (ed) (1986a) *Case Studies in Classroom Research.* Milton Keynes, Open University Press.

HAMMERSLEY, M. (ed) (1986b) *Controversies in Classroom Research.* Milton Keynes, Open University Press.

HAMMERSLEY, M. and ATKINSON, P. (1983) *Ethnography: principles in practice.* London, Tavistock Publications.

HARGREAVES, D. (undated) 'Power and the paracurriculum' in RICHARDS, C. (ed) (undated).

HARLAND, J. (1985) *TVEI: a model for curriculum change.* Paper presented at the BERA conference, August.

HARLEN, W. (1973) 'Science 5-13 project' in SCHOOLS COUNCIL (1973).

HARLEN, W. (1978) *Evaluation and the Teacher's Role* Schools Council Research Studies, London, Macmillan Education. (Her own chapter in this is 'Evaluation and Individual Pupils'.)

HARLEN, W., DARWIN, A. and MURPHY, M. (1977) *Match and Mismatch: Raising Questions* Edinburgh, Oliver and Boyd.

HARLEN, W., DARWIN, A. and MURPHY, M. (1978) *Finding Answers: guide to diagnosis and development* Edinburgh, Oliver and Boyd.

HARLEN, W. and ELLIOTT, J. 'A checklist for planning, or reviewing an evaluation' in McCORMICK, R. *et al* (eds) (1982).

HARLING, P. (1981) 'The primary school curriculum co-ordinator: a self-evaluation schedule' *School Organisation, 1* (3) pp 219-21.

HARRIS, N.D.C., BELL, C.D., and CARTER, J.E.H. (1981) *Signposts for Evaluating: a resource pack* London, Council for Educational Technology with Schools Council.

HARRISON, C. (1980) *Readability in the Classroom* Cambridge, Cambridge University Press.

HARROP, L.A. (1979) 'Unreliability of Classroom Observation' *Educational Research, 21* (3) June, pp 207-211.

HAVELOCK, R. (1973) *Planning for Innovation through Dissemination and Utilisation of Knowledge* Michigan, Center for Research on Utilisation of Scientific Knowledge.

HEGARTY, E.H. (1977) 'The problem identification phase of curriculum deliberation' *Journal of Curriculum Studies, 9* (1) pp 31-41.

HENDERSON, E. (1979) 'The concept of school-focused in-service education and training' *British Journal of Teacher Education, 5* (1).

HERZBERG, F. (1966) 'Motivation - hygiene theory' in PUGH, D. (ed) *Organisation Theory,* Harmondsworth, Penguin.

HIERONYMUS, A.N., LINDQUIST, E.F. and FRANCE, N. (1974) *Richmond Tests of Basic Skills.* Sunbury-on-Thames, Nelson.

HIGHAM, J. (1979) 'How to evaluate a History Department: a questionnaire approach' *Education, 24* June pp 14-16.

HILSUM, S. and CANE, B. (1979) 'The teacher's day' in BENNETT, N. and McNAMARA, D. (1979).

HIRST, P. (1965) 'Liberal education and the nature of knowledge' in ARCHAMBAULT, R. (ed) *Philosophical Analysis and Education* London, Routledge and Kegan Paul.

HIRST, P.H. (1974) *Knowledge and the Curriculum* London, Routledge and Kegan Paul.

HOGAN, R. and SCHROEDER, D. (1981) 'Seven Biases in Psychology' *Psychology Today 15* (7) July.

HOLSTI, O.R. (1968) 'Content analysis' in LINDZEY, G. and ARONSON, E. (eds) *The Handbook of Social Psychology*, vol 2: *Research Methods.* Reading, Mass., Addison-Wesley (2nd edition).

HOLSTI, O. (1969) *Content Analysis for the Social Sciences and Humanities* Reading, Mass., Addison-Wesley.

HOLT, M. (1981) *Evaluating the Evaluators*, London, Hodder and Stoughton.

HOMAN, R. (1980) 'The ethics of covert methods' in *British Journal of Sociology 31*, (1) pp 46-59.

HOOK, C. (1981) *Studying classrooms* Deakin University Open Campus Program. School of Education (Victoria 3217).

HOPKINS, R. (1982) 'Inspecting the inspectors again' *TES*, 8 January, p 4.

HOUSE, E.R. (1973) *School Evaluation: The politics and process* Berkeley, McCutchan.

HOUSE, E. (1977) *The Logic of Evaluative Argument*, CSE Monograph Series in Evaluation No. 7, Los Angeles, Center for the Study of Evaluation. University of California.

HOUSE, E. (1978) 'An American View of British Accountability' in BECHER, A. and MACLURE, S. (eds) (1978).

HOUSE, E. (1981) 'Three Perspectives on Innovation' in LEHMING, R. and KANE, M. (1981).

HOUSTON, W.R. *et al* (1978) *Assessing School/College/Community Needs*, Omaha, Center for Urban Education: University of Nebraska.

HOYLE, E. (1975) 'The creativity of the school in Britain' in HARRIS, A., LAWN, M. and PRESCOTT, W. (eds) *Curriculum Innovation*, London. Croom Helm in association with the Open University Press.

HOYLE, E. (1980) 'Professionalisation and deprofessionalisation in education' in HOYLE, E. and MEGARRY, J. (eds) (1980).

HOYLE, E. and MEGARRY, J. (eds) (1980) *World Yearbook of Education 1980: professional development of teachers* London, Kogan Page.

HOWELLS, J.G. (1980) *In-school Evaluation: an appraisal of the introduction of an accountability scheme in Oxfordshire Secondary Schools.* Unpublished M.Sc. thesis Dept. of Educational Studies, University of Oxford.

HULL, R. and ADAMS, H. (1981) *Decisions in the Science Department: organisation and curriculum* Hatfield, Assoc. for Science Education/Schools Council.

HUNKINS, F.P. (1980) *Curriculum Development: Program Improvement* Columbus, Charles E. Merrill.

HURMAN, A. (1978) *A Charter for Choice: a study of options schemes* Windsor, NFER.

HURWITZ, R.F. (1979) 'The reliability and validity of descriptive-analytic systems for studying classroom behaviour' in BENNETT, N. and McNAMARA, D. (1979).

INGENKAMP, K. (1977) *Educational Assessment* Windsor, NFER.

INGVARSON, L. (1979) 'Teacher-Initiated and School-Based: classroom-based developmental research projects' in *British Journal of In-service Education, 5* (3) pp 18-23.

INNER LONDON EDUCATION AUTHORITY (ILEA) (1976) *William Tyndale Junior and Infants Schools Public Inquiry* London, ILEA (The Auld Report).

INNER LONDON EDUCATION AUTHORITY (ILEA) (1977) *Keeping the School Under Review* London, ILEA.

INNER LONDON EDUCATION AUTHORITY (ILEA) (1981) *Information to Parents and Governors - secondary schools* (Item 13, ILEA, 1173). London, Education Committee - Schools Sub-committee, ILEA.

INTERNATIONAL SCHOOL IMPROVEMENT PROJECT (ISIP) (1983) *School Based Review for School Improvement: a preliminary state of the art.* Paris, OECD/CERT (Report prepared by David Hopkins).

IWANICKI, E.F. (1978) 'Review of Greenbaum *et al* (1977)' *Journal of Educational Measurement, 15* (2) pp 135-7.

JACKSON, R. and HAYTER, J. (1978) 'The Evaluation of the School as a whole' in HARLEN, W. (1978).

JACKSON, S. (1974) *A Teacher's Guide to tests and testing* London, Longman, 3rd edition.

JAMES, M.E. (1979) *Talking about Life: a study of teaching and learning sociology and social studies.* London, Unpublished MA Dissertation, University of London Institute of Education.

JAMES, M. (1982) *A First Review and Register of School and College Initiated Self-evaluation Activities in the United Kingdom* Milton Keynes, Educational Evaluation and Accountability Research Group. The Open University, mimeograph.

JAMES, M. and EBBUTT, D. (1981) 'Problems and Potential' in NIXON, J. (ed) (1981).

JEFFCOATE, R. (1981) 'Evaluating the Multicultural Curriculum: students' perspectives' *Journal of Curriculum Studies, 13* (1) pp 1-15.

JENCKS, C.S., SMITH, M., ACLAND, H., BANE, M.J., COHEN, D., GINTIS, H., HEYNS, B., MICHELSON, S. (1972) *Inequality: a reassessment of the effects of family and schooling in America* New York. Basic Books.

JOHN, D. (1980) *Leadership in Schools,* London, Heinemann Educational.

JOHNSON, M. *et al* (1975) *An Evaluation of the NAEP* Washington DC, Center for Education Statistics.

JONES, A. (1980) 'An in-school approach to in-service training' *Curriculum 1* (1) pp 6-7.

JONES, R. (1982) 'Devon's very modern model for curriculum staffing.' *Education 5,* March, pp 172-3.

KALLENBERGER, N. (1981) 'Values and curriculum decision-making: teachers' perceptions of an ideal curriculum' *Journal of Curriculum Studies, 13* (4) Oct-Dec, pp 363-6.

KAY, B.W. (1975) 'Monitoring pupils' performance', *Trends in Education, 2*, pp 11-18.

KEAST, D. (1980) 'Primary curriculum planning: responsibility or right?' *Forum 22* (3) Summer, pp 87-8.

KELLY, A.V. (1987) 'The Assessment of Performance Unit and the School Curriculum'. *Curriculum,* Vol. 8, No. 1, pp 19-28.

KELLY, G.A. (1955) *The Psychology of Personal Constructs* Vols 1 & 2, New York, Norton.

KELLY, P. 'Nuffield A Level Biological Science Project' in SCHOOLS COUNCIL (1973).

KEMMIS, S. (1981a) 'Research Approaches and Methods: Action Research' in ANDERSON, D.S. and BLAKERS, C. (eds) *Transition from School*, Australian National University Press.

KEMMIS, S. *et al* (1981b) *The Action Research Planner* Geelong, Victoria. Deakin University Press, Open Campus Program.

KEMMIS, S., ATKIN, R., WRIGHT, E. (1977) *How Do Students Learn?* Norwich, Centre for Applied Research in Education, University of East Anglia.

KEMMIS, S. and ROBOTTOM, I. (1981) 'Principles of Procedure in Curriculum Evaluation' in *Journal of Curriculum Studies, 13* (2), pp 151-155.

KIBBLEWHITE, D. (1981) 'Test reliability: a practical approach for the teacher' *Educational Studies, 7* (3), pp 205-13.

KIRK, G. (1978) 'Philosophy of Education and the Munn Report: a rejoinder' *Scottish Educational Review, 10* (2), pp 33-6.

KIRST, M.W. and WALKER, D.F. (1971) 'An analysis of curriculum policy-making', *Review of Educational Research, 41* (5) December, pp 479-509.

KLARE, G.R. (1978) 'Assessing Readability' in CHAPMAN, J. and CZERNIEWSKA, P. (eds) (1978).

KOGAN, M. (1978) 'The impact and policy implications of monitoring procedures' in BECHER, A. and MACLURE, S. (eds) (1978b).

KOHLBERG, L. (1964) 'Development of moral character and ideology' in HOFFMAN, M.L. (ed) *Review of Child Development Research* Vol. 1. Russell Sage.

KRIPPENDORFF, K. (1981) *Content Analysis: an introduction to its methodology*, Beverly Hills, Sage.

KUHN, T. (1962, 1970) *The Structure of Scientific Revolutions*, Chicago, University of Chicago Press, 2nd edition, enlarged 1970.

LACEY, C. (1970) *Hightown Grammar: the School as a social system* Manchester, Manchester University Press.

LACEY, C. (1977) *The Socialisation of Teachers* London, Methuen.

LACEY, C. and LAWTON, D. (eds) (1981) *Issues in Evaluation and Accountability* London, Methuen.

LAMBERT, R., BULLOCK, R. and MILLHAM, S. (1973) 'The informal social system: an example of the limitations of organisational analysis' in BROWN, R. (ed) (1973).

LAWN, M. and BARTON, L. (eds) (1981) *Rethinking Curriculum Studies* London, Croom Helm.

LAWTON, D. (1973) *Social Change, Educational Theory and Curriculum Planning* London, University of London Press.

LAWTON, D. (1980) *The Politics of the Curriculum* London, Routledge and Kegan Paul.

LAWTON, D. and GORDON, P. (1987) *HMI.* London, RKP.

LEHMING, R. and KANE, M. (1981) *Improving Schools: using what we know*, Beverly Hills, Sage Publications.

LELLO, J. (ed) (1979) *Accountability in Education* London, Ward Lock.

LEWIN, K. (1946) 'Action research and minority problems' *Journal of Social Issues, 2*, pp 34-46.

LEWIS, D.G. (1974) *Assessment in Education*, London, University of London Press.

LEWY, A. (ed) (1977) *Handbook of Curriculum Evaluation* Paris, International Institute for Educational Planning, UNESCO.

LEWY, A. and NEVO, D. (eds) (1981) *Evaluation Roles in Education* London, Gordon and Breach.

LORTIE, D. (1975) *School teacher: A sociological study* University of Chicago Press.

McALEESE, R. and HAMILTON, D. (1978) *Understanding Classroom Life* Slough, NFER.

McALLISTER, A. (1984) 'Guidelines II' in ADELMAN, C. (ed) (1984)

McCALL, G.J.C. and SIMMONS, J.L. (eds) (1969) *Issues in Participant Observation: a text and reader* Reading, Massachusetts, Addison-Wesley.

McCORMICK, R. (1981) *'Externally-audited self-evaluation'.* Paper presented at the Annual Conference of BERA, Crewe, 1-3 Sept.

McCORMICK, R. *et al* (eds) (1982) *Calling Education to Account*, London, Heinemann Educational in association with the Open University Press.

McCORMICK, R. (1987) *Assessing Technology* (E887/897 Module 4 Units 3 and 4). Milton Keynes, Open University Press.

McINTYRE, A. (1981) *After Virtue: a study in moral theory.* London, Duckworth.

McINTYRE, D.I. (1980) 'Systematic observation of classroom activities' *Educational Analysis, 2* (2) pp 3-30.

McINTYRE. D. and MACLEOD, G. (1978) 'The characteristics and uses of systematic classroom observation' in McALEESE, R. and HAMILTON, D. (1978).

McCLEAN, L. (1982) 'Educational Assessment in the Canadian Provinces' *Educational Analysis 4* (3).

MACDONALD, B. (1973) *Educational evaluation of the National Development Programme in Computer Assisted Learning* Proposal prepared for consideration of the Programme Committee of the National Programme.

MACDONALD, B. (1977a) 'A political classification of evaluation studies' in HAMILTON, D. *et al* (eds) (1977).

MACDONALD, B. (1977b) 'The Portrayal of Persons as Evaluation Data' in NORRIS, N. (ed) *SAFARI: Papers Two: Theory and Practice* CARE, University of East Anglia.

MACDONALD, B. (1978) 'Accountability, standards and the process of schooling' in BECHER, A. and MACLURE, S. (eds) (1978b).

MACDONALD, B. and NORRIS, N. (1978) *Looking up for a Change: political horizons in policy evaluations*, Norwich, C.A.R.E. University of East Anglia.

MACDONALD, B. and WALKER, R. (1976) *Changing the Curriculum* London, Open Books.

MACDONALD, B. and WALKER, R. (1977) 'Case-study and the social philosophy of educational research' in HAMILTON, D. *et al* (eds) (1977).

MACINTOSII, II.G. (ed) (1974) *Techniques and Problems of Assessment* London, Edward Arnold.

MACINTOSH, H.G. and HALE, D.E. (1976) *Assessment and the Secondary School Teacher* London, Routledge and Kegan Paul.

MACDONALD-ROSS, M. (1973) 'Behavioural Objectives: a critical review' *Instructional Science, 2*, pp 1-52.

McMAHON, A., BOLAM, R., ABBOTT, R. and HOLLY, P. (1984a) *Guidelines for Review and Internal Development in Schools: primary school handbook.* York, Longman.

McMAHON, A., BOLAM, R., ABBOTT, R. and HOLLY, P. (1984b) *Guidelines for Review and Internal Development in Schools: secondary school handbook.* York, Longman.

MARLAND, M. (1981) *The New Fourth-Year Curriculum* London, North Westminster Community School. (Unpublished discussion document.)

MEDLEY, D. and MITZEL, M. (1963) 'The scientific study of teacher behaviour' in BELLACK, A (ed) *Theory and Research in Teaching* Columbia, Teachers' College.

MILLAR, R. and DRIVER, R. (1987) 'Beyond Processes'. *Studies in Science Education* Vol. 14, Driffield, Studies in Education Limited.

MILLER, W.C. (1978) 'Unobtrusive measures can help in assessing growth' *Educational Leadership*, Jan. pp 264-9.

MILLS, C. (1980) 'Primary teachers as curriculum developers: some perceptions, problems and implications' *British Journal of Inservice Education 6* (3) Summer, pp 144-7.

MOON, B. (1980) *Curriculum Research: Agenda for the Eighties* Paper prepared for the SSRC Seminar University of Birmingham, 7-9 Jan. 1981.

MORRIS, L.L. and FITZ-GIBBON, C.T. (1978) *How to Present an Evaluation Report*, Beverly Hills, Sage Publications.

MOSER, C.A. and KALTON, G. (1971) *Survey Methods in Social Investigations* London, Heinemann.

MOYLE, D. (1978) 'Readability: the use of cloze procedure' in CHAPMAN, J. and CZERNIEWSKA, P. (eds) (1978).

MUNCEY, J. and WILLIAMS, H. (1981) 'Daily evaluation in the classroom' *Special Education: Forward Trends, 8* (3) September.

MURPHY, J.T. and COHEN, D.K. (1974) 'Accountability in Education - the Michigan Experience' *The Public Interest* No. 36, Summer.

MUSGRAVE, P. (1968) *Society and Education in England since 1800* London, Methuen. (Reprinted 1976.)

MUSGRAVE, P.W. (1979) *Society and the Curriculum in Australia* Sydney, George Allen and Unwin.

MUSGROVE, F. (1973) 'Research on the sociology of the school and of teaching' in TAYLOR, W. (ed) *Research Perspectives in Education* London, Routledge and Kegan Paul.

NASH, R. (1976) *Teacher Expectation and Pupil Learning* London, Routledge and Kegan Paul.

NATIONAL STUDY OF SCHOOL EVALUATION (NSSE) (1975) *Secondary School Evaluative Criteria: narrative edition.* Arlington, USA, NSSE.

NATIONAL STUDY OF SCHOOL EVALUATION (NSSE) (1978) *Evaluative Criteria* (5th Edition) Arlington, USA, NSSE.

NIAS, J. (1981) 'Teacher Satisfaction and Dissatisfaction: Herzberg's "two-factor" hypothesis revisited' *British Journal of Sociology of Education, 2* (3).

NISBET, J. (1978) 'Procedures for Assessment' in BECHER, A. and MACLURE, S. (eds) (1978b).

NISBET, J. (1979) *Accountability in Education.* Paper given to SSRC Seminar on Aspects of Accountability, 6 November.

NIXON, J. (ed) (1981) *A Teachers' Guide to Action Research: evaluation, enquiry and development in the classroom* London, Grant McIntyre.

NORMAN, R. (1982) *Faringdon School. Oxfordshire LEA.* Paper presented to Association for the Study of the Curriculum, National Conference, April.

NORTH CENTRAL ASSOCIATION (NCA) (1980a) *Policies and Standards for the Approval of Elementary Schools 1980-81,* Boulder, Colorado, NCA Commission on Schools.

NORTH CENTRAL ASSOCIATION (NCA) (1980b) *Policies amd Standards for the Approval of Secondary Schools 1980-81.* Boulder, Colorado, NCA Commission on Schools.

NORTH WEST EDUCATIONAL MANAGEMENT CENTRE (1981) *A study of the process of curriculum re-appraisal in a group of secondary schools in one local education authority* Warrington, NWEMC.

NUTTALL, D.L. (1979) 'A rash attempt to measure standards' *Education,* 21 Sept. pp ii-iii (supplement).

NUTTALL, D.L. (1980) 'Did the secondary schools get a fair trial?' *Education,* 11 Jan. pp 40-1.

NUTTALL, D.L. (1981) *School Self-evaluation: accountability with a human face?* London, Schools Council.

NUTTALL, D.L. (1982a) 'Problems in the measurement of change' *Educational Analysis, 4* (3)

NUTTALL, D.L. (1982b) 'Prospects for a common system of examining at 16+' *Forum, 24* (3) Summer, pp 60-2.

NUTTALL, D., BACKHOUSE, J. and WILLMOTT, A. (1974) *Comparability of Standards between Subjects* London, Evans/Methuen Educational. (Schools Council Examinations Bulletin, 29).

NUTTALL, D.L. and WILLMOTT, A.S. (1972) *British Examinations: techniques of analysis* Slough, NFER.

O'CONNOR (1980) ' "Chocolate Cream Soldiers": evaluating an experiment in non-sectarian education in Northern Ireland' *Journal of Curriculum Studies 12* (3) pp 263-270.

O'DONNELL, D.H. (1981) 'Assessment within schools: a study in one county' *Educational Research, 24* (1) November.

O'HARE, E. (1981) *The impact of primary school curriculum review in Lancashire schools* Centre for Educational Research and Development, University of Lancaster, unpublished mimeograph.

OLSON, M.N. (1970) 'Classroom variables that predict school system quality' *Research Bulletin 11* (1) Nov. New York, Teachers College, Columbia University.

O'NEIL, M.J. (1981) 'Nominal Group Technique: an evaluation data collection process' *Evaluation Newsletter 5* (2) September.

OPEN UNIVERSITY (1974a) *Bibliography for Textual Communication* Monograph No. 3, Institute of Educational Technology, Milton Keynes, The Open University.

OPEN UNIVERSITY (1974b) PE261 *Reading Development* Milton Keynes, The Open University Press.

OPEN UNIVERSITY (1976) E203 *Curriculum Design and Development,* Milton Keynes, The Open University Press.

OPEN UNIVERSITY (1977) E202 *Schooling and Society* Milton Keynes, The Open University Press.

OPEN UNIVERSITY (1978) E361 *Education and the Urban Environment* Milton Keynes, The Open University Press.

OPEN UNIVERSITY (1979) DE304 *Research Methods in Education and the Social Sciences* Milton Keynes, The Open University Press.

OPEN UNIVERSITY (1981a) E364 *Curriculum Evaluation and Assessment in Educational Institutions,* Blocks 3, 4 and 5. Milton Keynes, The Open University Press.

OPEN UNIVERSITY (1981b) P234 *Curriculum in Action: an approach to evaluation.* Milton Keynes, The Open University Press.

OPEN UNIVERSITY (1981c) E353 *Society, Education and the State,* Block 6 Unit 14 *The Politics of the Teaching Profession,* Milton Keynes, The Open University Press.

OPEN UNIVERSITY (1982) E364 *Curriculum Evaluation and Assessment in Educational Institutions.* Blocks 1, 2 and 6. Milton Keynes, The Open University Press.

OPEN UNIVERSITY (1983a) E364 *Curriculum Evaluation and Assessment in Educational Institutions* Block 2, Part 3 *Inspections* Milton Keynes, The Open University Press.

OPEN UNIVERSITY (1983b) E204 *Purpose and Planning in the Curriculum* Milton Keynes, The Open University Press.

OPPENHEIM, A.N. (1966) *Questionnaire Design and Attitude Measurement* London, Heinemann.

ORGANISATION FOR ECONOMIC CO-OPERATION AND DEVELOPMENT (OECD) (1978) *Creativity of the School: conclusions of a programme of enquiry*, Paris, Centre for Educational Research and Innovation (CERI), OECD Publications.

OSBORNE, R., BELL, B. and GILBERT, J. (1983) 'Science Teaching and children's View of the World'. *European Journal of Science Education.* Vol. 5. No. 1, pp. 1-14.

PARLETT, M. (1974) 'The New Evaluation' *Trends in Education, 34* pp 13-18. Reprinted in McCORMICK, R. *et al* (eds) (1982).

PARLETT, M. and HAMILTON, D. (1972) *Evaluation as Illumination: a new approach to the study of innovatory programmes.* Occasional Paper 9, Centre for Research in the Educational Sciences, University of Edinburgh. Reprinted in HAMILTON *et al* (eds) (1977).

PARSONS, C. (1976) 'The New Evaluation: a cautionary note'. *Journal of Curriculum Studies 8* (2) pp 125-38.

PATTON, M.Q. (1978) *Utilisation-focused evaluation*, Beverly Hills, Sage Publications.

PATTON, M.Q. (1980) *Qualitative Evaluation Methods*, Beverly Hills, Sage Publications.

PEARCE, J. (1979) 'Advisers and Inspectors' in LELLO, J. (ed) (1979) pp 71-9.

PEARCE, J. (1982) 'Local Authority Monitoring of Schools: a study of its arithmetic' in McCORMICK, R. *et al* (eds) (1982).

PERLOFF, E. and PERLOFF, J. (1980) 'Ethics in Practice' in *New Directions for Program Evaluation* No. 7 *Values, Ethics and Standards in Evaluation* San Francisco, Jossey-Bass Inc.

PERRY, W. (1970) *Forms of Intellectual and Ethical Development: A Scheme*, New York, Holt, Rinehart and Winston.

PETERS, R.S. (ed) (1967) *The Concept of Education* London, Routledge and Kegan Paul.

PIAGET, J. (1929) *The Child's Conception of the World* translated by Joan and Andrew Tomlinson. London, Routledge and Kegan Paul.

PILLINER, A.E.G. (1979) 'Norm-referenced and criterion-referenced tests - an evaluation' in SCOTTISH EDUCATION DEPT. (1979) pp 33-52.

PINAR, W. and GRUMET, M. (1981) 'Theory and Practice and the Reconceptualisation of Curriculum Studies' in LAWN, M. and BARTON, L. (eds) (1981).

PINCOFFS, E.L. (1975) 'Educational Accountability' *Studies in Philosophy and Education 8* (2).

PLEWIS, I *et al* (1981) *Publishing School Examination Results: a discussion*, Bedford Way Papers 5, London, University of London, Institute of Education.

POAD, J. (1981) *The Evaluation of Schools: An analysis of some of the issues involved in the process adopted by Oxfordshire County Council, Education Committee, illustrated by its application in the self-evaluation of one secondary school*, Warwick, Unpublished M.Ed. thesis, University of Warwick.

POLANYI, M. (1958) *Personal Knowledge* London, Routledge and Kegan Paul.
POLLARD, A. (1982a) 'A Model of Coping Strategies' *British Journal of Sociology of Education 3* (1) March, pp 19-37.
POLLARD, A. (1982b) *Opportunities and Difficulties of a Teacher-Ethnographer* Dept. of Education, Oxford Polytechnic. (Paper prepared for the Ethnography of Educational Settings Workshop Two, Whitelands College, London, July 1982.)
POLSKY, N. (1969) *Hustlers, Beats and Others* Harmondsworth, Penguin.
POPE, M. and GILBERT, J. (1983) 'Personal Experience and the Construction of Knowledge in Science'. *Science Education,* Vol. 67, No. 67, No. 2, pp 173-203.
POPHAM, J. (1967) *Educational Criterion Measures* Inglewood, California. Southwest Regional Laboratory for Educational Research and Development.
POPPER, K. (1963) *Conjectures and Refutations: the Growth of Scientific Knowledge* London, Routledge and Kegan Paul.
POPPER, K. (1972) *Objective Knowledge: an evolutionary approach* Oxford University Press.
POWER, C. (1977) 'A Critical Review of Science Classroom Interaction Studies' *Studies in Science Education 4*, pp 1-30.
POWNEY, J. and WATTS, M. (1987) *Interviewing in Educational Research.* London, Routledge and Kegan Paul.
PRAISE (1987 forthcoming) *Interim Report to the Records of Achievement National Steering Committee.* London, DES.
PRING, R. (1976) *Knowledge and Schooling* London, Open Books.
PRING, R. (1981) 'Monitoring performance: reflections on the Assessment of Performance Unit' in LACEY, C. and LAWTON, D. (eds) (1981) pp. 156-71.
PROVUS, M. et al (1974) *An Evaluation of the NAEP by the Site Team established by the NCES* Washington D.C., Evaluation Research Center, National Center for Education Statistics, June.
PUGH, D.S., HICKSON, D.J. and HINNINGS, C.R. (1971) *Writers on Organisations* Harmondsworth, Penguin.
RAPOPORT, R. (1970) 'Three Dilemmas in Action Research: with special reference to the Tavistock experience' *Human Relations 23* (6) pp 499-513.
RASP, A.F. (1974) 'Delphi: a strategy for decision implementation' *Educational Planning, 1* pp 42-7.
RAWLS, J. (1971) *A Theory of Justice.* Cambridge, Mass., Belknap Press.
REGAN, D.E. (1977) *Local Government and Education* Hemel Hempstead, Allen and Unwin.
REID, W.A. (1978) *Thinking about the curriculum: the nature and treatment of curriculum problems* London, Routledge and Kegan Paul.
REIMER, J. (1977) 'Varieties of Opportunistic Research' *Urban Life 5* (4) January pp 467-477.

REYNOLDS, D., SULLIVAN, M. and MURGATROYD, S. (1987) *The Comprehensive Experiment*. Basingstoke, Falmer Press.

REYNOLDS, J. and SKILBECK, M. (1976) *Culture and the Classroom* London, Open Books.

RICH, J. (1968) *Interviewing Children and Adolescents* New York, St. Martin's.

RICHARDS, C. (undated) *Power and the Curriculum*, Driffield, Nafferton Books.

RICHARDSON, E. (1973) *The Teacher, the School and the Task of Management* London, Heinemann.

RIECKEN, H.W. (1956) 'The Unidentified Interviewer' *American Journal of Sociology, 62*, pp 210-2. (reprinted in McCALL and SIMMONS, 1969.)

RIGBY, D. (1982) ' "The School Curriculum" and "The Practical Curriculum" ' *Curriculum*, 3 (1) Spring pp 11-16.

RISEBOROUGH, G.S. (1981) 'Teacher Careers and Comprehensive Schooling: an empirical study' *Sociology 15* (3) August pp 352-80.

ROBERTSON, I. (1980) *Language across the curriculum: four case studies* (Schools Council Working Paper 67), London, Methuen Educational.

RODGER, I. and RICHARDSON, J. (1985) *Self-evaluation for Primary Schools*. London, Hodder and Stoughton.

ROSENSHINE, B.V. and FURST, N. (1973) 'The Use of direct observation to study teaching' in TRAVERS, R.M.V. (ed) *Second Handbook of Research on Teaching*, Chicago, Rand McNally.

ROTH, J.A. (1962) 'Comments on "secret observation" ' *Social Problems 9* (3) pp 283-284.

ROTH, J.A. (1974) 'Turning adversity to account' *Urban Life and Culture, 3* (3) Oct. pp 347-61.

ROWNTREE, D. (1977) *Assessing Students: How shall we know them?* London, Harper and Row.

RUTTER, M., MAUGHAN, B., MORTIMORE, P., OUSTON, J. with SMITH, A. (1979) *Fifteen Thousand Hours: secondary schools and their effects on children* London, Open Books.

SADLER, D.R. (1985) 'The Origins and Functions of Evaluative Criteria' *Educational Theory*, Vol. 35, No. 3, pp 285-297.

SADLER P. (1980) 'Personal Decisions in Classroom Research Ethics' *C.A.R.N. Bulletin No 4*, Cambridge Institute of Education.

SAISI, R. (1976) 'Factors perceived to aid or impede the process of self-study' *North Central Association Quarterly 50* Spring pp 374-8.

SALLIS, J. (1979) 'Beyond the Market Place: a parent's view' in LELLO, J. (ed) (1979) pp 110-16.

SALTER, B. and TAPPER, T. (1981) *Education, Politics and the State: the theory and practice of educational change* London, Grant McIntyre.

SATTERLY, D. (1981) *Assessment in Schools*, Oxford, Basil Blackwell.

SCHATZMAN, L. and STRAUSS, A.L. (1973) *Field Research: strategies for a natural sociology* Englewood Cliffs, New Jersey, Prentice-Hall.

SCHON, D. (1971) *Beyond the Stable State* London, Temple Smith.

SCHOOLS COUNCIL (1973) *Evaluation in Curriculum Development: Twelve Case Studies* Basingstoke, Macmillan.

SCHOOLS COUNCIL (1975a) *The Curriculum in the Middle Years* (Schools Council Working Paper 55) London, Evans/Methuen.

SCHOOLS COUNCIL (1975b) *The Whole Curriculum 13-16* (Schools Council Working Paper 53), London, Evans/Methuen Educational.

SCHOOLS COUNCIL (1979) *Standards in Public Examinations: problems and possibilities* (Comparability in Examinations, Occasional Paper 1) London, Schools Council.

SCHOOLS COUNCIL (1981) *The Practical Curriculum: a report from the Schools Council* (Schools Council Working Paper 70), London. Methuen Educational.

SCHOOLS COUNCIL (1982) *Guidelines for Review and Institutional Development in Schools (GRIDS)* Booklet 1 *Getting Started*. Booklet 2 *The Initial Review Priorities*. A Schools Council Programme 1 Activity. University of Bristol, School Education. (Drafts)

SCHWAB, J.J. (1973) 'The practical 3: translation into curriculum *School Review, 81* pp 501-22.

SCHWARTZ, M.S. and SCHWARTZ, C.G. (1955) 'Problems in participant-observation' *American Journal of Sociology 60* (4) pp 343-353.

SCOTTISH EDUCATION DEPARTMENT (1977a) *The structure of the Curriculum in the third and fourth years of the Scottish Secondary School* (The Munn Report) SED, Edinburgh, HMSO.

SCOTTISH EDUCATION DEPARTMENT (1977b) *Assessment for All: Report of the Committee to Review Assessment in the third and fourth years of secondary education in Scotland* (The Dunning Report) SED, Edinburgh, HMSO.

SCOTTISH EDUCATION DEPARTMENT (1979) *Issues in Educational Assessment* SED, London, HMSO.

SCRIVEN, M. (1967) *The Methodology of Evaluation* AERA Monograph Series on Curriculum Evaluation. No. 1. Chicago, Rand McNally pp 39-89.

SCRIVEN, M. (1971) 'Goal-free evaluation, Part I' 11-71, NIE, 2A and 'Goal-free evaluation, Part II' 11-71 NIE 2B. Reproduced in HAMILTON, D. *et al* (eds) (1977).

SELECT COMMITTEE ON EDUCATION AND SCIENCE (1968a) *Report from the Select Committee on Education and Science. Session 1967-68, Part I, Her Majesty's Inspectorate (England and Wales)*, London, HMSO.

SELECT COMMITTEE ON EDUCATION AND SCIENCE (1968b) *Report from Select Committee on Education and Science. Session 1967-8, Part II, Her Majesty's Inspectorate (Scotland)* London, HMSO.

SHIPMAN, M. (1974) with BOLAM, D. and JENKINS, D. *Inside a Curriculum Project: a case-study in the process of curriculum change* London, Methuen.

SHIPMAN, M. (1979) *In-school Evaluation*, London, Heinemann.

SHIPMAN, M.D. (1980) 'Evaluation in the organisation of learning' *Journal of NAIEA, 8* Spring pp 8-10.

SHIPMAN, M. (1983) *Assessment in Primary and Middle Schools.* London, Croom Helm.
SHUTZ, A. (1953) 'Common-sense and Scientific Interpretation of Human Action' *Philosophy and Phenomenological Research 14.*
SIEBER, S. (1981) 'Knowledge Utilisation in Public Education: incentives and disincentives' in LEHMING, R. and KANE, M. (1981)
SILVERMAN, D. (1970) *The Theory of Organisations* London, Heinemann.
SIMON, A. and BOYER, E.G. (eds) (1974) *Mirrors for Behaviour III: an Anthology of Classroom Observation Instruments* Philadephia, Research for Better Schools, Inc.
SIMON, J. (1979) 'What and Who is the APU?' *Forum, 22* (1) Autumn pp 7-11.
SIMONS, H. (1977) 'Conversation Piece: the practice of interviewing in case study research' in NORRIS (1977) pp 110-135; ADELMAN (1981) and McCORMICK *et al* (1982) (latter only has edited version).
SIMONS, H. (1979) 'Suggestions for a school self-evaluation based on democratic principles' *Classroom Action Research Network, Bulletin No. 3* Cambridge, Cambridge Institute of Education.
SIMONS, H. (1980a) *Evaluation Methods in Use: a summary of views expressed by teachers after attempting evaluation in their schools* London University Institute of Education (unpublished draft).
SIMONS, H. (1980b) *Negotiating conditions for Independent Evaluations.* Paper presented at the British Educational Research Associations Annual Conference, Cardiff, September 1980.
SIMONS, H. (1981) 'Process Evaluation in Schools' in LACEY, C. and LAWTON, D. (eds) (1981).
SIMONS, H. (1987) *Getting to know Schools in a Democracy: the politics and process of evaluation.* Lewes, Falmer Press.
SIR FRANK MARKHAM SCHOOL (1981) *Entry Year Curriculum Evaluation:* Stage 1 *An analysis of content and teaching methods;* Stage 2 *'Shadow' Study;* Stage 3 *Discussion document* Milton Keynes, SFMS, mimeograph.
SIZER, J. (1979) 'Performance indicators for institutions of higher education under conditions of financial stringency, contraction and changing needs' in McCORMICK, R. *et al* (1982).
SJOGREN, Q.D. *et al* (1974) *Four Evaluation Examples: anthropological, economic, narrative and portrayal* AERA, Monograph Series in Curriculum Evaluation No. 7, Chicago, Rand McNally.
SKILBECK, M. (1975) *School-based Curriculum Development and Teacher Education* Mimeograph, private circulation (reprinted in OU, 1976, Unit 26, pp 90-102).
SKILBECK, M. (1981) 'Curriculum Issues in Australia, 1970-1990: contexts, policies and practices' *Compare, 11* (1), pp 59-76.
SMETHERHAM, D. (1978) 'Insider Research' *British Educational Research Journal 4* (2) pp 111-127.
SMETHERHAM, D. (ed) (1981) *Practising Evaluation* Driffield, Nafferton Books.

SMITH, H.W. (1981) *Strategies of Social Research* Englewood Cliffs, New Jersey, Prentice-Hall (2nd edition).
SMITH, L.M. and GEOFFREY, W. (1968) *The Complexities of an Urban Classroom* New York, Holt, Rinehart and Winston
SOCIETY FOR RESEARCH IN HIGHER EDUCATION (1981) *Higher Education at the Crossroads* Proceedings of 1980 Conference, SRHE.
SOCKETT, H. (ed) (1980) *Accountability in the English Educational System* London, Hodder and Stoughton.
SOLIHULL, LEA (1979) *Evaluating the school - a guide for secondary schools in the Metropolitan Borough of Solihull*, Solihull, LEA.
SOMEKH, B. (1980) 'An examination of pupils' use of reading material in a classroom situation' *Classroom Action Research Network Bulletin No. 4* Summer.
SPRADLEY, J.P. (1979) *The Ethnographic Interview* New York, Holt, Rinehart and Winston.
STAKE, R. (1967) 'The Countenance of educational evaluation' *Teachers College Record 68* (7) April.
STAKE, R. (1972) *Analysis and Portrayal* Paper originally written for the AERA. Annual Meeting presentation 1972. Revised at the Institute of Education, University of Goteborg, 1975.
STAKE, R.E. (1975) *Program Evaluation, particularly Responsive Evaluation* Occasional Paper 5. Kalamazoo. The Evaluation Center, Western Michigan University. Also in DOCKRELL, W.B. and HAMILTON, D. (eds) *Rethinking Educational Research* Kent, England, Hodder and Stoughton, 1979.
START, K. and WELLS, B. (1972) *The Trend of Reading Standards* Slough, NFER Publishing Co. Ltd.
STEADMAN, S.D., PARSONS, C. and SALTER, B.G. (1980) *Impact and Take-up Project: a second interim report on the Schools Council* 2nd edition, London, Schools Council.
STENHOUSE (1975) *An Introduction to Curriculum Research and Development* London, Heinemann.
STENHOUSE, L. (1978) 'Case Study and Case Records: towards a contemporary history of education'. *British Educational Research Journal, 4* (2) pp 21-39.
STENHOUSE, L. (1979a) 'The Problem of Standards in Illuminative Research' *Scottish Education Review, 11* (1) May.
STENHOUSE, L. (1979b) *What is action-research?* Norwich C.A.R.E. University of East Anglia (mimeograph).
STENHOUSE, L. (1982) 'The Conduct, Analysis and Reporting of Case Study in Educational Research and Evaluation' in McCORMICK, R. et al (1982).
STENHOUSE, L. (undated) *Accountability in Florida Schools* C.A.R.E, University of East Anglia mimeograph.
STONES, E.(1979) 'The World of APU' *Forum, 22* (1) Autumn, pp12-13.
STUBBS, M. (1981) 'Scratching the surface: linguistic data in educational research' in ADELMAN, C. (ed) (1981).
STUBBS, M. and DELAMONT, S. (1976) *Explorations in Classroom Observation* London, Wiley.

STUFFLEBEAM, D.L., FOLEY, W.J., GEPHART, W.J., GUBA EGAR, G., HAMMOND, R.I., MERRIMAN, H.O., PROVUS, M.M. (1971) *Educational Evaluation and Decision-Making.* Itasca, Illinois: F.E. Peacock for Phi Delta Kappon National Study Committee on Evaluation.

SUFFOLK EDUCATION DEPARTMENT (1985) *Those Having Torches . . . . Teacher Appraisal: a study.* Ipswich, SED.

SUMNER, R. and ROBERTSON, T.S. (1977) *Criterion-Referenced Tests* Windsor, NFER.

TABA, H. (1962) *Curriculum Development: theory and practice* New York, Harcourt Brace and World.

TALL, G. (1981) 'The possible dangers of applying the Rasch model to school examinations and standardised tests', in LACEY, C. and LAWTON, D. (eds) (1981).

TAYLOR, D. (1976) 'Eeny, Meeny, Miney, Meaux: Alternative Evaluation Models' *North Central Association Quarterly 50* (4) Spring 1976.

TAYLOR, F. (1980) *School Prospectus Planning Kit* London Advisory Centre for Education.

TAYLOR, P.F. *et al* (1974) *Purpose, Power and Constraint in the Primary School Curriculum,* London, Macmillan Education.

TAYLOR, W. (1978) 'Values and Accountability' in BECHER, A. and MACLURE, S. (eds) (1978b).

TAYLOR, W. (1980) 'Professional development or personal development?' in HOYLE, E. and MEGARRY, J. (eds) (1980).

TEACHERS AS EVALUATORS PROJECT (1978) *Bibliography* Canberra Curriculum Development Centre.

TEACHERS AS EVALUATORS PROJECT (1979) *Bibliography: Part II* Canberra, CDC.

TEACHERS AS EVALUATORS PROJECT (1980a) *Bibliography: Part III* Canberra CDC.

TEACHERS AS EVALUATORS PROJECT (1980b) *Discussion Paper 2: Curriculum evaluation in the 1980s: A review of current school level Evaluation Initiatives* Canberra, Curriculum Development Centre.

TENBRINK, T.D. (1974) *Evaluation: A practical guide for teachers* New York, McGraw-Hill.

THOMAS, K.C. (undated) *Attitude Assessment* Rediguide 7, YOUNGMAN, M.B. (ed) Maidenhead, TRC-Rediguides.

THOMAS, W.I. (1928) *The Child in America* Knopf.

THORNTON, G. (1986) *APU Language Testing 1979-83. An independent appraisal of the findings.* London, DES.

TIZARD, *et al* (1980) *Fifteen Thousand Hours: a discussion* London, University of London Institute of Education.

TOFTE, T. (1981) 'Factors Affecting Evaluation Utilisation' *North Central Association Quarterly 55* (4) pp 400-407.

TORRANCE, H. (1982) *School-based Examining in England: a focus for school-based curriculum development and accountability* Norwich Centre for Applied Research in Education; University of East Anglia; mimeograph.

TROW, M. (1957) 'Comment on "Participant observation and interviewing: a comparison" ' *Human Organisation, 16* (3) pp 33-5 (in McCALL and SIMMONS, 1969).

TURNER, G. and CLIFT, P. (1985) *A First Review and Register of School and College based Teacher Appraisal Schemes.* Milton Keynes, The Open University, School of Education.

TYLER, L.L., KLEIN, M.F. and ASSOCIATES (1976) *Evaluating and choosing curriculum and instructional materials,* Los Angeles, Educational Resource Associates.

TYLER, R. (1949) *Basic Principles of Curriculum and Instruction* Chicago, University of Chicago Press.

VAN TIL, W. (1976) 'What should be taught and learned through secondary education? in VAN TIL (ed) *Issues in Secondary Education,* 75th Yearbook of NSSE. National Society for the Study of Education, Chicago, Illinois.

VENNING, P. (1979) 'Threequarters of staff back common core and caning' *TES,* 23 Nov., p. 9.

VICKERS, Sir G. (1965) *The Art of Judgement* London, Chapman and Hall.

WALKER, D.F. (1975) 'Curriculum Development in an Art Project' in REID, W.A. and WALKER, D.F. (eds) *Case Studies in Curriculum Change* London, Routledge and Kegan Paul.

WALKER, R. (1979) *Classroom Practice: The Observations of LEA Advisers, Headteachers and Others,* London, Final Report to SSRC.

WALKER, R. (1981) 'On the Uses of fiction in educational research - (and I don't mean Cyril Burt)' in SMETHERHAM, D. (ed) (1981) pp 147-65.

WALKER, R. (1985) *Doing Research: a handbook for teachers.* London, Methuen.

WALLACE, G. (1980) 'The constraints of architecture on aims and organisation in five middle schools' in HARGREAVES, A. and TICKLE, L. (eds) *Middle Schools: Origins, Ideology and Practice* London, Harper Row.

WATTS, D.M. and ZYLBERSTEJN, A. (1981) 'A Survey of Some Children's Existing Ideas about Force'. *Physics Education,* Vol. 16, pp 360-5.

WEBB, E.J., CAMPBELL, D.T., SCHWARTZ, R.D., SECHREST, L. (1966) *Unobtrusive Measures: Non-reactive Research in the Social Sciences* Chicago, Rand McNally.

WATSON, J.K.P. (1979) 'Curriculum development: some comparative perspectives' *Compare, 9* (1) April, pp 17-31.

WESTON, P.B. (1977) *Framework for the Curriculum* Slough, NFER.

WESTON, P.B. (1979) *Negotiating the Curriculum: study in Secondary Schooling* Windsor, NFER Publishing Co. Ltd.

WHITE, J. et al (1981) *No Minister: a critique of the DES paper 'The School Curriculum',* London, University of London Institute of Education.

WHITE, J. (1982a) *The Aims of Education Restated* London, Routledge and Kegan Paul.

WHITE J. (1982b) 'Three perspectives on a national curriculum' *Forum, 24* (3) pp 71-3.

WHITTY, G. (1981) 'Curriculum studies: a critique of some recent British orthodoxies' in LAWN, M. and BARTON, L. (eds) (1981).

WHYTE, W. (1955) *Street Corner Society* 2nd edn. Chicago, University of Chicago Press.

WICKSTEED, D. and HILL, M. (1979) 'Is this you? A survey of primary teachers' attitudes to issues raised by the Great Debate' *Education 3-13, 7* (1) pp 32-6.

WILCOX, B. (1986) 'Contexts and Issues' in DOCKRELL, B. *et al Appraising Appraisal: a critical examination of proposals for the appraisal of teachers.* Kendal, British Educational Research Association.

WILCOX, B. and EUSTACE, P.J. (1980) *Tooling up for Curriculum Review* Windsor, NFER Publishing Co.

WILLIS, G. (ed) (1978) *Qualitative Evaluation: Concepts and Cases in Curriculum Criticism* McCutchan Publishing Corporation.

WILLIS, P (1977) *Learning to Labour* Farnborough, Hants, Saxon House.

WILSON, S. (1977) 'The use of ethnographic techniques in educational research' *Review of Educational Research, 47* (1) pp 245-65.

WILSON, S. (1979) 'Explorations of the usefulness of case study evaluations' *Evaluation Quarterly, 3* (3) August, pp 446-59.

WIRTZ, W. and LAPOINTE, A. (1982) *Measuring the Quality of Education: a report on assessing educational progress* Washington, Wirtz and Lapointe.

WITHERS, G. (1982) 'Australian examination systems: a review of recent change and development' *Educational Analysis, 4* (3) (forthcoming).

WOLCOTT, H. (1977) *Teachers v. Technocrats*, Centre for Policy and Management Studies.

WOLF, R.M. (1979) *Evaluation in Education: foundations of competency, assessment and program review* New York, Praeger.

WOOD, R. and GIPPS, C (1982) 'An enquiry into the use of test results for accountability purposes' in McCORMICK, R. *et al* (eds) (1982).

WOOD, R. and NAPTHALI, W.A. (1975) 'Assessment in the Classroom: what do teachers look for?' *Educational Studies* 1 (3) pp 151-61.

WOODS, P. (1979) *The Divided School* London, Routledge and Kegan Paul.

WOODS, P. (1980a) *Teacher Strategies* London, Croom Helm.

WOODS, P. (1980b) *Pupil Strategies* London, Croom Helm.

WORTH, W. (1977) *Perspectives on Policy Formation: an administrator's view* Paper presented to the National Conference on Educational Research and Policy Formation, Calgary, September.

WRAGG, E.C. (undated) *Conducting and Analysing Interviews* Rediguide 11, YOUNGMAN, M.B. (ed) Nottingham, Nottingham University School of Education.

WRAGG, E.C. and KERRY, T.L. (1979) *Classroom Interaction Research* Rediguide 14, edited by YOUNGMAN, M.B. Nottingham, School of Education, Nottingham University.

WRIGLEY, R.N. (1981) 'Curriculum evaluation' *School Organisation, 1* (1) pp 39-45.
YOUNGMAN, M.B. (undated) *Designing and Analysing Questionnaires* Rediguide 12. Nottingham, University of Nottingham School of Education.
ZAGGAGA, M.N. and BATES, S. (1980) 'Computer timetabling and curriculum planning' *Educational Research, 22* (2) pp 107-20.
ZAK, I (1981) 'School's organisational climate' in LEWY, A. and NEVO, D. (eds) (1981).

Index